REGIMENTAL RECORDS
OF THE
ROYAL WELCH FUSILIERS

H.M. KING GEORGE V, COLONEL-IN-CHIEF OF THE ROYAL WELCH FUSILIERS.
From a photograph by Messrs. Downey.

Frontispiece

REGIMENTAL RECORDS

OF THE

ROYAL WELCH FUSILIERS

(LATE THE 23RD FOOT)

COMPILED BY

A. D. L. CARY, O.B.E., & STOUPPE McCANCE
LIBRARIAN, R.U.S.I.   CAPTAIN (LATE R.A.S.C.)

WITH ILLUSTRATIONS BY
GERALD C. HUDSON
CAPTAIN (LATE DURHAM L.I.)

VOL. I
1689—1815

The Naval & Military Press Ltd

❖

Reproduced by kind permission of the Regimental Trustees

Published by
The Naval & Military Press Ltd
Unit 10, Ridgewood Industrial Park,
Uckfield, East Sussex,
TN22 5QE England
Tel: +44 (0) 1825 749494
Fax: +44 (0) 1825 765701
www.naval-military-press.com

© The Naval & Military Press Ltd 2005

In reprinting in facsimile from the original, any imperfections are inevitably reproduced and the quality may fall short of modern type and cartographic standards.

Printed and bound by Antony Rowe Ltd, Eastbourne

PREFACE.

From the raising of the Royal Welch Fusiliers on the 16th March 1689 to the Armistice in 1918 the story of a great regiment has been one long series of splendid deeds, which in every quarter of the globe have conduced to the building up and defending of the British Empire. The pity of it is that those deeds, performed by officers, non-commissioned officers, and men alike, for the most part, must ever remain in obscurity for the want of diaries and memoirs—those precious scraps of paper which, where they exist, give us a glimmering of the past. It is true that there is such a one, and and a most interesting one, from an officer of the 23rd after Dettingen, which only makes us wish for more. What a breath of air from the seventeenth century it would be to read how Colonel Toby Purcell lived, and moved, and had his being; and of the conversation and views of the officers when the Duke of Marlborough suddenly marched on the Danube!

The compilers, Mr. A. D. L. Cary, O.B.E., and Captain Stouppe McCance, admirably assisted by Major G. F. Barttelot, Captain Gerald Hudson, and those gentlemen whose names are given in the Introduction, have surmounted the difficulty so far as is possible, and by accuracy of treatment and attention to detail have given at any rate a reliable record of the deeds of the regiment.

The narrative is relieved from all dullness by a vigorous account of the campaigns in which the 23rd has taken part, and wherever it has been possible to illustrate by incident, such as the fording of the river at the siege of Athlone by the three Danes condemned to death, the story has been graphically told.

In reading of the battle of the Boyne, the attack on the heights of Schellenberg, and the advance of Row's Brigade at Blenheim, one not only feels that it is good history but the narrative thrills.

A touch of the human comes in too, for, judging by the Royal Welch of to-day and all that one knows of the 23rd of the past, one can imagine

PREFACE

what the talk of the mess-room of a regiment equally great in sport as in war must have been when Prince Ferdinand's order was issued: " It is forbid on pain of death to all and everyone to go a sporting."

To sum up: this, the first part of the Regimental History, is good reading, and I recommend its ably written pages to all who love the past and the present and are certain of an equally great future for the grand old 23rd.

FRANCIS LLOYD,
Lieutenant-General.
Colonel, Royal Welch Fusiliers.

CARLTON CLUB, LONDON.
  31st *December* 1920.

INTRODUCTION.

THE compilers of this historical record have been considerably handicapped in their task by the almost entire absence of letters, diaries, or journals of officers who served with the regiment during the period of its existence treated of in this volume. This loss is greatly to be deplored, as documents of that nature go a long way towards depicting the life and conditions of a regiment, both in the piping times of peace and also on the battlefield, in which case only records of the nature indicated faithfully depict its prowess and powers of endurance.

As regards the structure of the book, it is compiled in the form of a running narrative chronologically arranged, with a calendar of events for the convenience of any reader who desires to look up dates.

The thanks of the compilers are due in particular to Colonel Sir Arthur Leetham, C.M.G., Secretary of the Royal United Service Institution, for the benefit of his valuable advice which has been sought from time to time in the preparation of the narrative; to Brigadier-General Sir Robert Colleton, Bart., C.B., and Major G. F. Barttelot (members of the Regimental Records Committee), for the suggestions they were kind enough to make when revising the proofs; to Colonel Willoughby Verner (late of the Rifle Brigade), for presenting the map illustrating the movements of the opposing forces during the progress of the battle of the Boyne, which has been prepared from a sketch of the ground taken by the late Field-Marshal Viscount Wolseley and the donor; to Colonel Gerald Boyle (late of the Rifle Brigade), for permission to make transcripts from his voluminous notes respecting the history of several famous British regiments, which have been most useful to the compilers; to Colonel Harold Wylly, C.B., the author of the History of the 15th Hussars and other military works, for indicating sources of information which have been tapped with most satisfactory results; to Lieutenant-Colonel Sir H. C. W. Verney, Bart., D.S.O., for kindly affording facilities for the perusal of the correspondence of Lieutenant-General Sir Harry Calvert, Bart., while Adjutant-General to the Forces, 1799–1820; to Captain Henry McCance (late The Royal Scots), for most kindly perusing the proofs. The help afforded by Mr. Wilfred Baldry, the Deputy Librarian of the War Office, and by Mr. W. E. Govier, the principal library attendant, has also been much appreciated.

CHRONOLOGICAL SUMMARY.

As far as possible "Old Style" has been adopted in this Summary and in the text.

1689.	Mar. 16.	Henry, Lord Herbert of Cherbury, authorised to raise the Twenty-third, and appointed colonel of the regiment.
	April 10.	Charles Herbert, his cousin, appointed colonel in his place.
	Aug. 30.	Disembarked at Bangor, co. Down.
	,, 31.	Reviewed at Belfast by the Duke of Schomberg.
	Sept. 7.	Encamped near Dundalk.
	Winter.	Quarters at Rathfriland and Ballinahinch, co. Down.
1690.	June 14.	Arrival of King William at Carrickfergus.
	,, 27.	The Army concentrated at Dundalk.
	July 1.	Battle of the Boyne.
	,, 2.	Regiment ordered to Drogheda, which surrendered next day.
	,, 27.	Three companies remained at Drogheda, ten proceeded to Dublin.
	Aug. 9.	Siege of Limerick.
	,, 31.	,, ,, ,, raised.
	Sept. and Oct.	Sieges of Cork and Kinsale.
	Dec.	Three companies at Longford, 3 at Castleforbes, 3 at Drogheda, 2 at Foxhill, 2 at Dromin.
1691.	June 6.	Under General Douglass, joined Ginckle's army at Ballymore.
	,, 8.	Ballymore captured.
	,, 30.	Athlone captured.
	July 12.	Battle of Aughrim; death of Colonel Charles Herbert.
	,, 13.	Lieutenant-Colonel Toby Purcell promoted to the colonelcy in his place.
	,, 26.	Galway captured; the regiment remains as garrison.
	Nov. 23.	Marched from Galway for Cork.
	Dec. 25.	Embarked at Cork; landed at Barnstaple on 27th.
1692.	Jan. 12.	Arrived at Portsmouth.
	April 19.	Colonel Toby Purcell resigned the colonelcy on account of ill-health.
	,, 20.	Sir John Morgan was appointed to the colonelcy in his place.
	July.	Encamped on Portsdown Hill.
	,, 25.	Embarked; proceeded to the Downs.
	Aug. 21.	Left the Downs.
	,, 23.	Disembarked at Ostend.
	Oct.	Returned to England.

CHRONOLOGICAL SUMMARY

1693.	Jan.	Colonel Sir John Morgan, Bart., died early in this month.
	Feb. 28.	Lieutenant-Colonel Richard Ingoldsby was promoted from the 18th Royal Irish Regiment to the colonelcy in his place.
	June.	Served on twelve men-of-war as marines.
	Dec. 28.	Reviewed in Hyde Park.
1694.	Jan.	Embarked for Holland, landing at Ostend.
	Sept. 27.	Surrender of Huy.
	Winter.	Quartered at Bruges.
1695.	June 8.	Attack on Fort Knocque.
	,, 21.	Siege of Namur.
	July 24.	Surrender of town of Namur.
	,, 25.	Proceeded to the relief of Brussels, returning to Namur.
	Aug. 26.	Surrender of the Castle of Namur.
	Winter.	In quarters at Bruges.
1696.	May.	Left Bruges.
	May 29.	Reviewed by King William at Bellem.
	Winter.	In quarters at Bruges.
1697.	May 28.	Surrender of Ath.
	Sept. 11.	Peace of Ryswick.
	Dec. 16.	Landed at Gravesend, proceeding to Bristol, Gloucester, etc.
1698.	Feb. 8.	Marched to Bristol and embarked for Waterford and Clonmel.
	Mar. 17.	Left Clonmel for Limerick.
	July 28.	One company reduced.
	Aug. 1.	Reviewed by the Lords Justices of Ireland, and marched to Drogheda.
1699.	Aug. 2.	Arrived in Dublin.
1700.	,, 15.	Proceeded to Londonderry and Coleraine.
1701.	June 6.	Arrived at Carrickfergus, and embarked on June 7.
	July 2.	Disembarked at Helvoetsluys.
	August.	Augmented with two companies.
	Sept. 21.	Reviewed at Breda Heath by King William.
	Winter.	In garrison at Worcum and Heusden.
1702.	Mar. 10.	Proceeded to Rosendahl.
	Oct. 23.	Capture of the citadel of Liège.
	Winter.	In quarters in Holland at Breda.
	Dec. 15.	Regiment "formed into a regiment of Fusiliers, and will be called the Welsh Regiment of Fusiliers."
1703.	April 8.	Left Breda.
	Aug. 25.	Capture of Huy.
	Winter.	In quarters in Breda, Dutch Brabant.
1704.	May 9.	Proceeded to Germany.
	June 21.	Battle of Schellenberg.
	Aug. 2.	Battle of Blenheim.
	Nov. 24.	Surrender of Landau.
	Winter.	In garrison at Ruremonde.

CHRONOLOGICAL SUMMARY

1705. April 1. Lieutenant-General Richard Ingoldsby was appointed colonel of the 18th Regiment, Royal Irish, Lieutenant-Colonel Joseph Sabine, of the 23rd Regiment, being appointed colonel in his place.
    May 3. Reviewed by Duke of Marlborough.
    July 17. Forced French lines at Helix and Neerhespen.
    Nov. Marched into Holland for the winter.
1706. May 10. Marched to camp at Borchleon.
    ,, 12. Battle of Ramillies.
    July 8. Surrender of Ostend.
    Nov. Marched to Ghent for winter quarters.
1707. May. With the army at Anderlecht.
    June 26. In camp at Meldart, near Louvain.
    Winter. In quarters at Ghent.
1708. May 11. Marched from Ghent to rendezvous near Brussels.
    June 30. Battle of Oudenarde.
    Aug. 13. Siege of Lille.
    Sept. 30. Surrender of the town of Lille.
    Nov. 28. Surrender of the citadel of Lille.
1709. June 26. Siege of Tournay.
    Aug. 31. Battle of Malplaquet.
    Sept. 28. Surrender of Mons.
    Winter. Quarters at Ghent.
1710. April. Siege of Douay.
    June 15. Surrender of Douay.
    Winter. Quarters at Courtray.
1711. July 25. Passage of the French lines at Arleux.
    ,, 27. Siege of Bouchain.
    Sept. 2. Surrender of Bouchain.
1712. June 22. Surrender of Quesnoy.
    July. Marched to Ghent.
1713. April 11. Treaty of Utrecht.
    ,, 23. First time styled officially as "The Royal Regiment of Welsh Fusiliers."
    June 24. Placed on the Irish Establishment.
    July 1. Reduced to ten companies of forty-one N.C.O.s and men.
    Aug. 22. Landed at Kinsale and moved to Cork.
1714. ,, 16. Arrived in Dublin.
    Nov. 9. Styled "Prince of Wales's Own Royal Regiment of Welsh Fusiliers."
1715. August. Moved to Athlone.
    Sept. Returned to Dublin.
    Oct. 9. Arrived at Parkgate, Chester; proceeded to Hereford.
1716. January. Moved to Birmingham, Wolverhampton, etc.
1717. May 9. Moved to Dunstable, St. Albans, etc.
    June. Moved to Chatham, Tilbury, etc.
1718. Nov. Embarked for Ireland.

CHRONOLOGICAL SUMMARY

1718.	Dec. 2.	Landed at Waterford.
		Reduced from twelve to ten companies.
1719.	May 2.	Left Ireland; landed at Bristol and stationed there.
1720.	April 5.	Moved to Manchester, etc.
1721.	Feb. 10.	Moved to Hereford, Ludlow, etc.
	Sept. 9.	Moved to Chester.
1722.	Jan. 15.	Moved to Manchester.
	Feb. 20.	Moved to Berwick, thence to Perth.
1723.	April.	Moved to Inverness.
1724.	April.	Moved to Fort William.
1725.		Remained at Fort William.
1727.	April.	Two additional companies added, making twelve companies.
	June.	Marched to Berwick and Sunderland.
1728.	March.	Proceeded to London.
	May 18.	Reviewed by King George II on Hounslow Heath; proceeded to Shrewsbury, etc.
	June.	Proceeded to Manchester.
1729.		Stationed at Chester, Shrewsbury, etc.
	Nov.	Two companies were reduced, making ten companies.
1730.	June.	Moved to Birmingham.
	Oct.	Four companies moved to Portsmouth.
1731.	July.	Remaining six companies moved to Portsmouth.
1732.	Jan.	Moved to Manchester, Warrington, etc.
	April.	Six companies to Newcastle, four to Durham.
	June.	Moved to Berwick.
1735.	Aug.	Stationed in Edinburgh.
1736.	Sept. 7.	"Porteous Riots" in Edinburgh.
1737.	July.	Proceeded to Berwick.
1738.	May.	Moved to York, etc.
	July.	Moved to Dover, Canterbury, Battle, etc.
1739.	July.	Moved to Kew, etc.
	Aug. 31.	Reviewed by King George II at Kew, and proceeded to Winchester, Southampton, etc.
	Oct. 24.	Death of General Joseph Sabine at Gibraltar.
	Nov. 23.	Lieutenant-Colonel Newsham Peers appointed to the colonelcy.
1740.	June.	Proceeded to camp at Newbury.
	Sept.	Moved to Marlborough, Devizes, etc.
1741.	Summer.	Encamped at Lexden Heath, near Colchester.
1742.	April 28.	Reviewed by King George II on Kew Green.
	May.	Embarked at Deptford for Ostend.
1743.	Feb. 10.	Assembled at Maestricht.
	June 16.	Battle of Dettingen.
	,, ,,	Colonel Newsham Peers died of wounds received at Dettingen.
	July 28.	Major-General John Huske appointed colonel of the 23rd in his place.
1744.	Sept.	Two additional companies added.

CHRONOLOGICAL SUMMARY

1745.	April 30.	Battle of Fontenoy.
	July 9.	Taken prisoners at Ghent.
	Oct.	Landed at Harwich.
	Dec.	Moved to London and then Chatham, etc.
1746.	Jan. 13.	Moved to Guildford and Godalming.
	April 17.	Moved to Reading, Newbury, etc.
	June.	Five companies to Exeter.
	Aug. 5.	One company in attendance on H.R.H. Princess Caroline at Bath.
	Sept.	Moved to Portsmouth and embarked on transports.
	Oct.	Disembarked at Gravesend, and moved to Reading and Newbury.
1747.	Jan. 12.	Moved to London.
	,, 17.	Reviewed by King George II in the Green Park, London, and proceeded to Greenwich, etc.
	,, 28.	Embarked at Gravesend; landed at Wilhelmstadt.
	June 21.	Battle of Lauffeld or Val.
1748.	Oct. 7.	Treaty of Aix-la-Chapelle.
	Nov. 8.	Two additional companies disbanded.
	Dec.	Disembarked at Leith.
1750.	May.	Moved to Banff, Elgin, etc.
	June.	Moved to Inverness.
1751.	Sept.	Moved to Glasgow.
1752.	Sept.	Moved to Carlisle.
	Oct.	Moved to Reading.
	Nov.	Moved to Dover, Canterbury, Maidstone, etc.
1753.	April.	Five companies to Exeter.
	Aug. 22.	Five companies to Bristol.
1754.	March.	Moved to Plymouth.
	April.	Embarked for Minorca.
1756.	April 27.	Siege of Minorca.
	June 29.	Capitulation of Minorca.
	July 12.	Proceeded to Gibraltar.
	Aug. 25.	A second battalion of ten companies formed at Leicester.
	Nov.	First battalion landed at Southampton, proceeding to Leicester.
1757.	May 23.	Both battalions moved to Newbury and then Chatham.
	Sept.	Both battalions reduced to nine companies each.
	,,	Both battalions proceeded to Dover.
1758.	May 1.	Both battalions moved to the Isle of Wight.
	June 1.	Both battalions embarked for St. Malo.
	,, 25.	Second battalion was regimented as the 68th Regiment.
	July 1.	Disembarked at St. Helens.
	,,	Re-embarked for Germany.
	Aug. 2.	Landed at Hartsum.
	Nov. 13.	Cantoned at Münster.
1759.	Aug. 1.	Battle of Minden.
	Winter.	Cantoned in Osnaburg.

CHRONOLOGICAL SUMMARY

1760.	July 31.	Battle of Warburg.
	Oct. 16.	Action at Campen.
	Winter.	Cantoned in Hesse.
1761.	Jan. 16.	Death of General John Huske. Lieutenant-General the Hon. George Boscawen appointed colonel in his place.
	July 16.	Battle of Kirch Dünckern or Fellinghausen.
	Winter.	Cantoned in Osnaburg.
1762.	June 24.	Action at Wilhelmstahl.
	Nov. 3.	Peace of Fontainebleau.
	Winter.	Quartered at Belem, etc.
1763.	Feb.	Marched to Williamstadt, and embarked for Harwich.
	March.	Proceeded to Windsor and Exeter.
1764.	April 7.	Proceeded to Plymouth.
1765.	June.	Marched to Exeter.
	July.	Marched to Rochester and Chatham.
1766.	March.	Proceeded to Cirencester.
	April.	Proceeded to Berwick.
1767.	April.	Proceeded to Edinburgh, Dundee, and Aberdeen.
1768.	July.	Five companies at Glasgow, four companies at Perth.
1769.	June.	Eight companies at Fort George, one company at Aberdeen.
1770.	Aug.	Five companies at Fort William, four at Fort Augustus.
	Oct.	Proceeded to Berwick.
	Dec. 25.	A light company added.
1771.	Jan.	Proceeded to Manchester.
	June.	Proceeded to Chatham.
	Aug. 10.	Reviewed by King George III at Blackheath.
1772.	,, ,,	Reviewed by King George III at Wimbledon.
	Sept.	Proceeded to Plymouth.
1773.	April 15.	Embarked for America.
	June 14.	Disembarked at New York.
1774.	July 27.	Embarked for Boston; disembarked Aug. 7.
1775.	April 19.	Action at Lexington.
	May 3.	Death of Lieutenant-General the Hon. George Boscawen in London.
	,, 11.	Major-General the Hon. Sir William Howe (afterwards Viscount Howe) appointed to succeed him.
	June 17.	Battle of Bunker's Hill.
	Aug. 31.	Two additional companies added.
1776.	March.	Evacuation of Boston; sailed for Halifax, N.S.
	June 11.	Left Halifax.
	July 3.	Landed on Staten Island.
	Aug. 27.	Action on Long Island.
	Nov. 16.	Reduction of Fort Washington.
1777.	April 25.	Embarked for Norwalk Bay.
	,, 26.	Action at Ridgefield.
	Sept. 11.	Action at Brandywine.

CHRONOLOGICAL SUMMARY

1777.	Winter.	At Philadelphia.
1778.	June 18.	Evacuation of Philadelphia.
	,, 28.	Action at Monmouth Court-house.
	Aug.	Regiment serves as marines.
	Dec.	Two additional companies authorised to be raised for regiments in N. America.
1779.	May 27.	Capture of Fort Lafayette.
	July 3.	Expedition to Newhaven.
	,, 11.	Expedition to Norwalk.
	Dec. 26.	Expedition to South Carolina.
1780.	April 1.	Siege of Charleston.
	May 11.	Surrender of Charleston.
	Aug. 16.	Action at Camden.
	Sept.	Action at Polk's Mill.
1781.	March.	Action at Wetzell Mill.
	,, 15.	Action at Guildford Court-house.
	Sept. 28.	Yorktown invested by the Americans.
	Oct. 19.	Capitulation of Yorktown.
	Nov. 15.	Reached Winchester, Virginia.
1782.	Jan. 12.	Left Winchester for Lancaster, Pennsylvania.
	Dec.	Evacuation of Charleston; detachment at Galveston sailed for New York.
1783.	Jan. 7.	Detachment lands and rejoins headquarters.
	May.	Return of the prisoners of war.
	Dec. 5.	Sailed for England.
1784.	Jan. 17.	Disembarked at Portsmouth.
	March 16.	Proceeded to Doncaster.
1786.	Jan.	Proceeded to Tynemouth and Sunderland.
	April 21.	Lieutenant-General the Hon. Sir William Howe, K.B., was transferred to the colonelcy of the 19th Light Dragoons; succeeded by Major-General Richard Grenville.
1787.	May.	Proceeded to Berwick.
	Sept.	Proceeded to Chatham.
1788.	,,	Proceeded to Windsor and Slough.
1789.	June.	Encamped in Windsor Forest.
	Oct. 6.	Marched to Portsmouth.
1790.	April 3.	Embarked at Spithead.
	,, 12.	Disembarked at Cork.
1791.	Jan.	Proceeded to Waterford and Wexford.
1792.	Aug.	Proceeded to Armagh.
1793.	Nov. 13.	Flank companies embarked at Cork.
1794.	Jan. 6.	,, ,, arrived at Barbadoes.
	Feb. 3.	,, ,, sailed for Martinique.
	Mar. 8.	Battalion companies embarked at Cork for St. Domingo.
	,, 23.	Flank companies at surrender of Martinique.

1—*b*

CHRONOLOGICAL SUMMARY

1794.	April	1.	Flank companies arrived at St. Lucia.
	,,	2.	,, ,, at capture of Morne Fortuné.
	,,	11.	,, ,, landed in Guadeloupe.
	,,	12.	,, ,, at capture of Fort La Fleur d'Épée.
	May	6.	Battalion companies arrived at Martinique.
	,,	19.	,, ,, arrived at St. Domingo.
	June	8.	Flank companies rejoin battalion companies.
	Dec.	5.	Defence of Fort Bizothon.
	,,	25.	,, ,, Fort Tiburon.
1796.	Feb.	22.	Part of regiment embarked at Port-au-Prince.
	April	27.	Landed at Portsmouth; proceeded to Kidderminster.
	Sept.	9.	Remainder of regiment landed at Deptford.
	Oct.	29.	Proceeded to Chatham.
1797.	April.		Proceeded to Chelmsford.
	Sept.		Proceeded to Deal.
1798.	Jan.		Proceeded to Norwich.
	April.		Proceeded to Canterbury.
	May	15.	Embarked at Ramsgate for Ostend.
	,,	19.	Flank companies landed.
	,,	20.	,, ,, made prisoners of war.
	June.		Stationed at Guernsey.
1799.	Feb.		Stationed at Southampton.
	June.		Flank companies returned from having been prisoners of war.
	Aug.	9.	Embarked at Ramsgate for the Helder.
	,,	27.	Action on the sandhills.
	Oct.	2.	Battle of Alkmaar.
	,,	29.	Embarked for Yarmouth.
	Nov.	10.	Three companies lost by shipwreck.
	,,	23.	Stationed at Battle.
1800.	June.		Moved to Plymouth.
	July	1.	Embarked for Island of Houat.
	,,	19.	Embarked for Ferrol.
	,,	26.	Attack on Ferrol.
	,,	27.	Embarked for Vigo.
	Sept.	19.	Arrived at Gibraltar.
	Oct.		On board ships in Mediterranean.
	Nov.	24.	Disembarked at Malta.
	Dec.	20.	Embarked for Marmorice Bay.
1801.	Mar.	8.	Action on landing at Aboukir Bay.
	,,	21.	Battle of Alexandria.
	Oct.		Embarked for Malta.
	Dec.	12.	Embarked for Gibraltar.
1803.	June	21.	Embarked for Portsmouth.
	Oct.		Proceeded to Freshwater, Isle of Wight.
1804.	May.		Proceeded to Eastbourne.

CHRONOLOGICAL SUMMARY

1804.	Dec. 25.	A second battalion added to the regiment.
1805.	Oct. 29.	First battalion embarked at Ramsgate for Germany.
	Nov. 17.	,, ,, landed at Cuxhaven.
	Winter.	,, ,, stationed at Bremen.
	Feb. 1.	Second battalion stationed at Wrexham.
	Nov.	,, ,, ,, at Chester.
1806.	Feb. 15.	First battalion proceeded to Cuxhaven and embarked for Harwich.
	June.	,, ,, stationed at Colchester.
1807.	July 25.	First battalion embarked at Harwich for Copenhagen.
	Aug. 16.	,, ,, disembarked at Vedbeck.
	Oct. 18.	,, ,, embarked for Yarmouth.
	Nov. 23.	Second battalion proceeded to Portsmouth and embarked for Cork.
1808.	Jan.	First battalion proceeded to Portsmouth and embarked for Nova Scotia.
	April 16.	First battalion stationed at Halifax, Annapolis.
	Dec. 6.	,, ,, sailed for Barbadoes.
	Jan.	Second battalion stationed at Loughrea.
	June.	,, ,, ,, at the Curragh.
	Sept. 9.	,, ,, proceeded to Cork and embarked for Spain.
	Oct. 29.	,, ,, landed at Corunna.
1809.	Jan. 30.	First battalion landed at Martinique.
	Feb. 1.	,, ,, in action at Morne Bruneau.
	,, 2.	,, ,, ,, ,, at the Heights of Sourier.
	,, 24.	,, ,, at surrender of Fort Bourbon.
	Mar. 9.	,, ,, embarked for Nova Scotia.
	Jan. 16.	Second battalion: battle of Corunna.
	,, 18.	,, ,, embarked for Portsmouth and Horsham.
	June 28.	,, ,, five companies proceeded to Portsmouth.
	July 30.	,, ,, ,, ,, landed on Walcheren.
	Oct. 6.	,, ,, ,, ,, marched to Flushing.
	Nov.	,, ,, ,, ,, rejoined battalion at Horsham.
1810.	Nov. 10.	First battalion embarked at Halifax for Portugal.
	Dec. 12.	,, ,, disembarked at Lisbon.
	Feb.	Second battalion proceeded to Portsmouth and Guernsey.
1811.	Mar. 12.	First battalion: skirmish at Redinha.
	May 16.	,, ,, battle of Albuhera.
	Sept. 27.	,, ,, action at Aldea da Ponte.
	Aug.	Second battalion moved to Haverford West, Carmarthen, Milford, etc.
1812.	April 6.	First battalion: capture of Badajoz.
	July. 22.	,, ,, battle of Salamanca.
	,, ,,	Second battalion remained at Haverford West, etc.
1813.	June 21.	First battalion: battle of Vittoria.
	July 28—Aug. 3.	First battalion: battles of the Pyrenees.
	Aug. 31.	First battalion: assault of San Sebastian.

CHRONOLOGICAL SUMMARY

1813. Nov. 10. First battalion: battle of the Nivelle.
      April. Second battalion moved to Honiton.
      Aug.   ,,   ,,   moved to Berry Head.
1814. Feb. 27. First battalion: battle of Orthes.
      April 10. ,,   ,,   battle of Toulouse.
      June 14. ,,   ,,   embarked at Pauillac for Plymouth.
      July 16. ,,   ,,   arrived at Gosport.
      Feb. Second battalion moved to Winchester.
      July.   ,,   ,,   ,,   ,, Gosport.
      Oct. 24. ,,   ,,   disbanded.
1815. Mar. 23. Embarked at Gosport.
      ,, 30. Landed at Ostend.
      April 25. Stationed at Grammont.
      June 18. Battle of Waterloo.
      ,, 24. Capture of Cambray.
      Autumn and winter. Stationed outside Paris.

BADGES AND BATTLE HONOURS.

The Regimental Colour bears the following badges and battle honours:

BADGES.

The device of the Prince of Wales, namely, Three feathers issuing out of the Prince's coronet, with the motto "Ich Dien" in the centre. The "Red Dragon" in the lower dexter corner, the "Rising Sun" in the upper sinister corner, these two being the badges of Edward the Black Prince.

The "White Horse" of Hanover upon a mount, with the motto "Nec aspera terrent" underneath in the lower sinister corner; this being the badge of King George II, was conferred by him as a mark of royal favour after the battle of Dettingen.

BATTLE HONOURS.

The word "NAMUR 1695," as a mark of the gallant services of the regiment at the capture of that town and castle.

The words "BLENHEIM," "RAMILLIES," "OUDENARDE," and "MALPLAQUET," in commemoration of the distinguished services of the regiment at those battles, fought in 1704, 1706, 1708, and 1709 respectively.

The word "DETTINGEN," for the steadiness and intrepidity displayed in the action at that place on the 27th of June 1743.

The word "MINDEN," in commemoration of the gallantry displayed in the battle fought at Minden on the 1st of August 1759.

The word "EGYPT," with the "SPHINX," in commemoration of its services in the expulsion of the French army from Egypt in the year 1801.

The word "CORUNNA," as a testimony of the gallant services of the second battalion on the 16th of January 1809.

The word "MARTINIQUE 1809," as a testimony of the distinguished conduct of the first battalion in the capture of the island of Martinique on the 24th of February 1809.

The words "ALBUHERA," "BADAJOZ," "SALAMANCA," "VITTORIA," "PYRENEES," "NIVELLE," "ORTHES," "TOULOUSE," and "PENINSULA," in commemoration of the services of the first battalion during the Peninsula War from 1810 to 1814.

The word "WATERLOO," as a lasting testimony of the distinguished services of the regiment at the memorable Battle of Waterloo on the 18th of June 1815.

The words "ALMA," "INKERMAN," and "SEVASTOPOL," for its devotion and gallant conduct during the Crimean War, 1854-6.

The word "LUCKNOW," for the distinguished part the first battalion took in the Relief of the Residency in 1857.

The word "ASHANTEE 1873-4," in commemoration of the services of the second battalion in the Ashantee War, 1873-4.

The word "BURMA 1885-87," as a recognition of the services of the first battalion during the Burmese War of 1885-7.

The words "RELIEF OF LADYSMITH" and "SOUTH AFRICA 1899-1902," as a mark of the gallant conduct of the first battalion in the South African War; and

The word "PEKIN 1900," to commemorate the services of the second battalion in the operations for the relief of that city.

LIST OF ILLUSTRATIONS.

COLOURED PLATES.

	After page
PRIVATE, 1689	190
THE COLOURS, 1742 AND 1807	190
GRENADIER, 1753	190
DRESS, ETC., 1766–1836	190
OFFICER AND PRIVATE, 1791	190
OFFICER, 1800	190
OFFICER AND SERGEANT, 1808	190
OFFICER AND SERGEANT-MAJOR, 1814	190

BLACK AND WHITE PLATES.

H.M. KING GEORGE V, COLONEL-IN-CHIEF OF THE ROYAL WELCH FUSILIERS	*Frontispiece*

	FACING PAGE
HENRY, FOURTH LORD HERBERT OF CHERBURY	2
MAP OF THE BATTLE OF THE BOYNE	12
MAJOR-GENERAL SABINE	68
ARMS, ETC., 1689–1815	124
MAJOR-GENERAL THE HON. SIR WM. HOWE, K.B.	154
THE KEYS OF CORUNNA	227
COLONEL SIR HENRY WALTON ELLIS, K.C.B.	284

REGIMENTAL RECORDS OF THE ROYAL WELCH FUSILIERS

1689.

IN order to account for the raising of the Marching Regiment of foot to which the number "23" was assigned, it will be necessary to review briefly the state of Ireland at the time of its being called into existence.

When James II ascended the throne, that country was outwardly calm, and had this sovereign possessed the attributes of a statesman, all would probably have been well; but hardly had he been seated on the throne before he appointed the notorious Richard Talbot, known to posterity as the Earl of Tyrconnel, Commander of the Army in Ireland. One of the first acts of this evil genius of James was to disband the Militia, which stood for law and order, mainly on the score of religion. Early in 1687 Tyrconnel was advanced to the post of Lord Deputy of Ireland. He soon took advantage of his position to increase the army to no less than 100,000 men. In 1688 the Revolution had taken place in England. Tyrconnel, realising that a blow must speedily be struck on behalf of the Stuarts, let loose his army, and by force of overwhelming numbers speedily overran the three southern provinces, and achieved his object, which was to break the power of the colonists, who were the supporters of the Revolution.

Being driven from their homes, they fled to Ulster. Some found their way to Enniskillen, while the major portion of the fugitives pushed on at all hazards to Londonderry.

This condition of affairs brought home vividly to the English Government the absolute necessity for reconquering Ireland, which could not be undertaken by the force available, owing to several regiments having been already sent to Flanders to aid the States-General.

An augmentation of the army having been decided upon, an estimate was laid before Parliament of the cost and strength of the force that was considered necessary for the reduction of Ireland. It consisted of six regiments of horse, two of dragoons, and twenty-five regiments of infantry. Sixteen of the latter were to be newly raised. This estimate was voted by the House of Commons on the 21st of March 1689, but four days prior to this King William III authorised Henry, fourth Baron Herbert of Cherbury, to raise a regiment of infantry, one of the sixteen regiments referred to. This Lord Herbert was a zealous supporter of the Revolution of 1688, and for his steady adherence to the House of Orange was rewarded by the King by being made a head or "proprietary" Colonel, which was a considerable source of income down to a comparatively modern period.

The "Letter of Service" authorising the raising of the regiment does not exist.

In the War Office Miscellany Books at the Public Record Office there is a copy of a letter addressed to the Duke of Norfolk, dated the 16th of March 1689. From the footnote at the end of the document it will be seen that a similar "Letter of Service" was addressed to Lord Herbert of Chirbury (*sic*).

"For raising the Duke of Norfolk's Regt:
"These are to authorize you by beat of drum or otherwise to raise voluntiers for a Regiment of Foot under your command wch is to consist of 8 companys of sixty private soldiers: three sergeants, three corporals, and two drummers in each company, and as you shall raise the said voluntiers and non-commission officers of each company, you are to give notice thereof to our Commissionary General when and where you shall have twenty five soldiers, that he or his deputys may muster them accordingly: and from such muster those soldiers with all the commission officers of such company are to command, and be in our pay and from thence forth as you shall, from time to time, entertain any more soldiers fitt for service and shall produce them to muster, they are to be respectively mustered thereupon untill you shall have sixty soldiers besides officers in each company. And when the whole number of non-commission officers and soldiers shall be fully or near compleated in each company, then they are to be sent under the command of a commission officer to Reading and Norwich appointed for the rendezvous of the said regiment: where they are also to be mustered and to remain untill further order. Provided always that the respective company be fully compleated within one month from the date herof. In which case and not otherwise there shall be

HENRY, FOURTH LORD HERBERT OF CHERBURY.
From a portrait at Powis Castle. Block supplied by "Country Life."

allowed for the raising of every private soldier, twenty shillings as levy-money, over and above the pay due unto them: And all Magistrates, Justices of the Peace, constables, and other our officers, whom it may concern, are required to be assisting in providing quarters and otherwise, as there shall be occasion: and the officers are to be carefull that the soldiers behave themselves civilly, and duly pay their landlords: and you are also to appoint such person, or persons, as you shall think fitt to receive arms for the said soldiers and non-commission officers out of the stores of our Ordnance. Given at the Court at Whitehall the 16th day of March 1688/9 in the first year of Our reign

"by H M command
[Signature omitted].

"A like order dated 16 March 1688/9 for the raising of the Lord Herbert of Chirbury's Regiment of Foot, and quartering them at Ludlow."

Like letters and dates to: Colonel Erle, at Dorchester and Sherburn; Earl of Drogheda, at Brecknock and Abergavenny; Lord Lovelace, at Oxford; Earl of Roscommon, at Salisbury, Wilton, and Amesbury; Sir Thomas Grove, at Doncaster.

The order for arming the 23rd, addressed "To the Duke ffrederick, Marechal de Schomberg, Master General of Our Ordnance," is dated the 16th day of March 1688/9.

For some unexplained reason—probably ill-health—Lord Herbert's tenure of command was exceedingly brief—from the 17th of March to the 9th of April only. He was succeeded by his cousin Colonel Charles Herbert.

The recruiting of the regiment appears to have been attended with success, but if it was brought in a few months "into a state of fitness for military duty," as is stated by Mr. Richard Cannon in his *Historical Record of the 23rd Foot*, it must have rapidly deteriorated, as is evidenced by the report of the condition of the regiment in the autumn of 1689, which will be referred to in its proper place.

The General selected to command the expeditionary force, which was mainly concentrated in Cheshire, was the aged Marshal Frederic, Duc de Schomberg, who, though a German by birth, had entered the French army and had risen to high command. He was well versed in the art of war, having learned in the school of Condé and Turenne. Although in his eighty-second year he was still hale, very active, and a first-rate horseman. Courteous and affable to both his equals and inferiors, but at the same time a strict disciplinarian, he was well qualified to attempt the task of improving as rapidly as possible the efficiency of his untried army. Count Solmes was his second-in-command.

On the 20th of July he reached Chester, where he was received by the mayor and aldermen " in their scarlets," with the accompaniment of the ringing of bells and other demonstrations. Great must have been his misgivings when he inspected his troops, many of whom were raw recruits, badly clothed and indifferently armed. To crown all there was no transport train, and hardly any artillery to speak of. Working with prodigious energy—considering his time of life—to make good these deficiencies, in twenty-two days (12th of August) he embarked with about 10,000 men, of whom very few were cavalry, and part of his artillery. Lack of transport ships prevented the embarkation of more than this number.

On the afternoon of the following day the transports—ninety in number—anchored in the Bay of Carrickfergus (Belfast Lough), the troops being permitted to land at Groomsport, near Bangor, Co. Down, without encountering the slightest opposition.

Schomberg's first move was to invest the fortress of Carrickfergus, which was surrendered in a few days with the loss of about 150 on both sides, the garrison being permitted to retire to Newry. He then marched to Belfast, where he established his headquarters.

While these events were taking place the remainder of the expeditionary force, in which the 23rd Regiment was included, embarked at Highlake (Hoylake), near Chester, and reached the shores of Ireland on the 30th of August, the 23rd being quartered temporarily " at Holiwood, Bangor, and places adjacent." On the following day Schomberg reviewed his army at Belfast preparatory to his march to Dundalk, the 23rd being one of the eighteen regiments of foot mustered there. In cavalry and artillery he was very weak, as compared with the Jacobite forces, but he calculated that the bogs and mountainous country which he would have to traverse on his line of march would nullify any advantage the enemy was likely to gain thereby. He contented himself, therefore, with taking his lightest field-pieces, sending the rest of his artillery by sea to Carlingford. Orders were issued to the Inniskilling Horse and the 5th and 6th Inniskilling Dragoons to meet him en route.

During the short time the regiment lay in the vicinity of Belfast it nearly lost the services of Colonel Herbert. While rashly flourishing a loaded pistol, the weapon went off, fortunately inflicting nothing more than a superficial head wound.

On the 2nd of September Schomberg put his army in motion, and made for Newry. On his approach the Duke of Berwick, who commanded the Irish Army on behalf of King James, caused both Newry and Carlingford to be burnt, and retired on Drogheda, breaking up the main roads as far as possible. On Schomberg intimating to him " that if for the future he found in his marching any more French tricks plaid he would not give quarter to man, woman or child," he ceased to fire the towns on his line of retreat.

Loughbrickland was reached on the 4th, where the army " encamped in two lines as from the beginning of the march." Newry was reached on the 6th of September.

After a well-earned rest Schomberg's army pushed on to Dundalk. Then it was that their troubles began in earnest. Incessant rain, broken roads, the country devastated, and the want of baggage waggons necessitating the carrying of both cannon and supplies, told heavily upon his troops.

On the 7th of September he reached Dundalk, and pitched his camp a little to the north-west of the town. The position was not an ideal one, as the ground was spongy, but it had the advantage of being protected in front by a river, an arm of the sea made the left flank secure, while the right flank was rendered practically unassailable by a series of entrenchments. The rear was well guarded by the mountains and bogs, and the entrance to the town entrenched. Here he was joined by the 2nd, 9th, and 11th regiments of foot.

The 23rd formed part of the 2nd Brigade along with Stuart's, Wharton's, Kingston's, and Gower's Regiments.

King James and Tyrconnel with about 40,000 men advanced from Drogheda within three miles of Schomberg's camp, hoping to draw him to an engagement, but the cautious old warrior declined the unequal contest. The Jacobite army then retired to a position between Ardee and Drogheda.

Schomberg's troubles grew apace. As the rain continued to descend in torrents, he issued an order that the troops were to erect huts in place of their tents. The foreign element in the army, which consisted of experienced soldiers, obeyed the order with alacrity, but the inexperienced English soldiers failed to grasp the urgent necessity for doing so. Being prone to laziness at the time and having a bad example set them by their officers, they deferred taking steps to procure dry timber for the walls and straw for thatching purposes until they were unprocurable. Being for the most part insufficiently clothed, they suffered terribly from exposure, coupled with insufficient food and most defective sanitation, the latter of which could easily have been remedied had they not been too lazy to work. It is on record that out of a total of 14,000 men who occupied the camp, over 6,000 perished through hardship and disease, and many hundreds were disabled for life. The continental regiments, being wise in their generation and adopting all possible precautions, lost very few men.

The Jacobite army, although better clothed and fed, was, owing to climatic and other conditions, in an equally sorry plight, its casualties amounting to about 15,000 out of a total of 40,000 men.

King James, abandoning all hope of enticing his opponent to a general engagement, retired into winter quarters along the Boyne, and in the vicinity of Dublin. His example was quickly followed by Schomberg.

On the 1st of October 1689 an abstract of musters taken at the camp at Dundalk shows that the condition of Colonel Herbert's regiment was: 12 captains, 1 dead; 14 lieutenants; 10 ensigns, 2 sick; 34 sergeants; 33 corporals; 25 drummers; 587 private men, 128 sick, 6 absent.

On the 18th of the same month a further muster was taken, of which the following is a copy. A comparison between the two musters shows the mortality due to the prevalence of diseases which might have been prevented.

HERBERT'S.

—	—	Lt.	Ensigns.	Sergeants.	Drummers.	Fitt.	Sick.	Dead.
1. Grenadier Capt. Robt. Thomas		1	1	3	1 1 S	26	28	5
2. Colonel Charles Herbert		1	1	2 1 S	1 1 S	20	20	4
3. Sir Francis Edwards		1 S	1	1 2 S	2	24	10	1
4. — Richard	S	1 S	1 S	1 2 S	2	20	20	4
5. Walter Winn	S	1	1 S	2 1 S	2	17	20	3
6. — Wingfield	S	1	1	1 2 S	2 S	28	15	2
7. — Wogan		1 S	1	2 1 S	1 1 S	17	20	4
8. John Jones	S	1 S	1	3	1 1 S	39	17	3
9. Timothy Waring		1 S	1	1 2 S	2	22	27	0
10. Hugh Hookes	1		1 S	3 S	2 S	20	14	1
11. — Tayler		1 S	1	2 1 S	1 1 S	29	16	4
12. — Mainwaring		1 S	1	1 2 S	1 1 S	28	13	2
13. — Price	1		1	3	2 S	29	11	3
Totals	4	6 7 S	10 3 S	22 17 S	14 12 S	319	231	36

S = sick.

A still later return, as under, shows the appalling increase in the mortality in the regiment.

Captains.	Lieutenants.	Ensigns.	Effectives.	Sick.	Dead.
Col. C. Herbert	Gorden	Mann	14	16	30
Lt.-Col. Sir F. Edwards	Whitemore	Dickens	13	13	34
Major Richards	Cheap	Parey	18	11	31
Capt. Mainwaring	Disney	Howill	18	11	31
,, T. Waring	Powell	Griffith	9	15	36
,, Jn. Jones	Knot	Floyde	14	—	46
,, Price	Price	Farrel	12	7	41
,, Thomas	Ormy & Cook		14	10	36
,, Hookes	Lloyd	Whitely	8	10	42
,, Tayler	Stedman	Jones	8	5	47
,, James Jones	Devereux	Frazer	8	5	47
,, Francis Purefoy	Mumford	Major	60	—	—
,, Joseph Sabine	Hamilton	Sabine	60	—	—
			256	103	421

On the 28th of October the troops were mustered at Dundalk, and the inspecting General, in his Confidential Report and Inspection Return respecting their condition on that occasion, comments on the 23rd Regiment as follows: "Herbert's (23rd Foot), Colonel very assiduous, but too easy to the officers, who are the most negligent that can be imagined. Often he is the only officer present with the regiment, which he never quits: yet the regiment is in a bad condition: clothing good, but arms almost useless."

On the 3rd of November all the sick in camp were carried to the sea and transported by ship to Belfast; three days later orders were issued for the whole of the troops to march away. The 23rd was one of four regiments that were ordered to Newry, the others being Stuart's, Gower's, and Sankey's. Story, in his *Narrative*, gives the following harrowing account of the sufferings endured by the men on the march: "So little did the poor men value dying that some of them being in a stable overnight, the next day two were dead: and the rest entreating me to get a fire which I did: coming about two hours later, they had pulled in the two dead men to make seats of." He also states that the hills were covered with snow; a most unusual circumstance in Ireland. The remainder of the army were instructed to proceed to Armagh and Antrim.

The English army made good its retreat to the north, and went into winter quarters, such small loss as it sustained while effecting its retirement being due solely to disease. While it was in winter quarters its frontier was Lough Erne, with a series of garrisoned posts extending thence to both Newry and Belfast. The 23rd was quartered during the winter of 1689/90 at Rathvillan (Rathfryland) and Ballinahinch, Co. Down.

Schomberg fixed his headquarters at Lisburn, Co. Down, and devoted himself whole-heartedly during the winter to restoring health and vigour to his disheartened troops. Nor was he less attentive to the discipline of both officers and men, which left much to be desired.

Few incidents occurred during the winter beyond the almost successful attempt of a small Jacobite force under Captain Christopher Plunkett to seize Newry, and so penetrate within the English lines.

A description of this incident, extracted from Luttrell's *Historical Relation*, is as follows: "The Irish, in a good body, came about 2 in the morning to beat up the English'es quarters at the Newry, entering the town at both ends: but our men, under the command of Major Toby Purcell, behaved themselves very bravely, and drove them out: they kill'd 15 of the Irish, one a lieutenant colonel, and lost captain Whitwood and captain Mills, and 6 common soldiers." This detachment must have been composed of men of Sir Henry Ingoldsby's Regiment, as Story, in his *Narrative*, under date 24th November, remarks as follows: "There was then in the garrison most of what was left of Colonel Ingoldsby's Regiment which were not many above 60, and not 40 of those able to present a musket."

The following return of the pay of the regiment at this period is interesting:

STAFF.

	Per diem. £ s. d.	Per annum. £ s. d.
Colonel as Colonel	0 12 0	219 0 0
Lieutenant-Colonel as Lieutenant-Colonel	0 7 0	127 15 0
Major as Major	0 5 0	91 15 0
Chaplain	0 6 8	121 13 4
Adjutant	0 4 0	73 0 0
Quarter-Master	0 4 0	73 0 0
Chirurgeon	0 4 0	} 118 12 6
,, Mate	0 2 6	

THE COLONEL'S COMPANY.

	Per diem. £ s. d.	Per annum. £ s. d.
Colonel as Captain	0 8 0	146 0 0
Lieutenant	0 4 0	73 0 0
Ensign	0 3 0	54 15 0
3 Sergeants at 18d. each	0 4 6	82 2 6
3 Corporals at 12d. each	0 3 0	54 15 0
3 Drums at 8d. each	0 2 0	36 10 0
60 Private soldiers at 8d.	2 0 0	730 0 0
The pay of 11 companies more at the same rates and numbers	35 9 6	12,948 7 6

ONE COMPANY OF GRENADIERS BELONGING TO THE REGIMENT.

	Per diem. £ s. d.	Per annum. £ s. d.
Captain	0 8 0	146 0 0
2 Lieutenants at 4s. each	0 8 0	146 0 0
3 Sergeants at 18d. each	0 4 6	82 2 6
3 Corporals at 1s. each	0 3 0	54 15 0
2 Drums at 1s. each	0 2 0	36 10 0
60 Grenadiers at 8d. each	2 0 0	730 0 0
Total for the Regiment	£44 4 8	£16,145 3 4

1690.

Another incident was the defeat early in February of the Jacobite Commander near Cavan, with the result that the town was captured, and the consequent destruction of a large quantity of the enemy's stores and powder which had been accumulated therein.

In March Schomberg received a reinforcement of 6,104 Danes, who landed at Carrickfergus under the Duke of Würtemburg. A contemporary writer describes these troops as "being proper men, very well clothed and armed."

In April Schomberg opened the campaign by investing the fort of Charlemont situated near Moy. It was a very strong place, and was surrounded by a river called the Black Water and an impassable bog. After a close investment the Governor, an aged officer named Teague O'Regan, surrendered on the 14th of May on honourable terms. A considerable quantity of arms and ammunition was found in the fort. Killishandra, near Belturbet, was captured on the 6th of April by a detachment of 700 men under Colonel Wolseley.

While these operations were taking place Schomberg received a considerable number of recruits from England together with several new regiments, both English and foreigners. On the 4th of June King William set out from Kensington Palace for Ireland, accompanied by a small staff, and embarking at Highlake near Chester, arrived at Carrickfergus on the 14th, where he was met by Marshal Schomberg. Both proceeded to Belfast without delay. There the King remained for three days and then proceeded to Lisburn, where the headquarters of the army was located. He devoted himself heart and soul during this brief period to the inspection of regiments, the formation of brigades, etc., intimating "that he did not come to let the grass grow under his feet." On the 27th King William's army concentrated on Dundalk. In approaching this town the King was careful to avoid the old encampment for fear of raising sad recollections in the minds of his soldiers. Here he was joined by General Douglass with 10,000 men, who had marched from Armagh, bringing his total strength to over 36,000. Towards this total Colonel Herbert's regiment contributed 600 men.

King James had concentrated his forces between Ardee and Dundalk, but upon the advance of King William he deemed it prudent to retreat, first to a place named Drumlane, and thence to the right bank of the River Boyne between Duleek and Old Bridge, where he formed in line of battle on the 29th of June.

On the 28th King William encamped at Ardee, and at daybreak on the 30th his army, marching in three columns, reached the banks of the Boyne and found themselves facing King James's troops. William rode forward to observe the enemy's strength and position, and whilst resting on some slightly rising ground near the Ford at Old Bridge was observed by some Irish officers, who quickly brought up " two pieces of six Pound Ball " concealed in the centre of a body of about forty horsemen. The gunners then proceeded to open fire. The first shot fired between the rival armies killed a trooper and two horses. The second struck the bank of the river, ricochetted, and " passed so close to His Majesty that it took away a piece of his coat, waistcoat and shirt, raised the skin on the blade of his right shoulder and drew a little blood, but a plaister being put on, His Majesty continued on Horseback without the least concern till 4 in the afternoon when he dined." It was quite a lucky shot that grazed the King's shoulder, as the enemy gunners that same afternoon fired about 400 shots with the result that four men were killed and about ten horses. During the afternoon William's batteries came up and opened fire on the Irish battery and quickly silenced it. They then bombarded the part of the Irish camp that was in view, and obliged the enemy to strike their tents and seek cover behind the hill.

It has been stated on good authority that King James ordered the bulk of his artillery to be withdrawn to Duleek after nightfall—at any rate there seems to be no doubt but that little use was made of it on the morrow when the eventful battle took place.

A council of war was held at 9 p.m. on the night of the 30th of June, when Marshal Schomberg strongly urged that not a moment should be lost in detaching part of the army to the right to effect the passage of the Boyne, either at Slane Bridge, if still intact, or failing that, at the ford of Rossnaree, which was about two miles farther downstream. He pointed out that if this operation was successful, it would secure the pass at Duleek and effectually cut off the enemy's communication with Dublin.

Although several of the general officers present supported Marshal Schomberg's proposal, the King decided that no action should be taken that night. After deliberating for some time, the following plan was adopted. With the object of turning both flanks of the Jacobite army, Lieutenant-General Douglass, in command of the right wing of the infantry, supported by the greater part of the horse under Count Meinhardt Schomberg (a son of Marshal Schomberg), were to march early the following morning towards Slane and endeavour to turn the left flank of the enemy. The Marshal in the centre, at the head of a large body of infantry, consisting mainly of foreigners, was to pass at the fords near Old Bridge fronting the enemy's main position. The left wing, led by the King, was to pass at a ford between the enemy's camp and Drogheda.

As both armies were dressed much alike, the necessity for distinguishing friend from foe was imperative. In consequence King William's troops were directed to wear green sprays in their hats. Those of King James wore pieces of white paper in their hats to bring them into line with their French allies, who wore white cockades.

The following morning, the 1st of July, Count Meinhardt Schomberg and General Douglass started off in the direction of Slane. They had with them the whole of the cavalry of the right wing and part of that of the left, five six-pounders, and the 2nd, 4th, 13th, 23rd, and Erle's Regiments of Foot, in all some seven or eight thousand men. While on the march they learned that the bridge at Slane had been broken down, which caused them to alter their plan and attempt the crossing of the river at the fords at and above Rossnaree.

When they arrived at Rossnaree ford they found the passage disputed by Sir Neil O'Neil's regiment of Irish Dragoons. For the best part of an hour O'Neil offered a spirited resistance; but upon General Douglass bringing some guns to bear upon his men, they gave way and retreated upon their main body, the gallant O'Neil falling badly wounded in the thigh. The crossing was then effected with comparatively trifling loss.

Upon Count Meinhardt Schomberg making good his footing on the right bank of the river, he observed a reinforcement hurrying up to bar his further progress, whereupon he sent back a message to the King urging the necessity for assistance; but William had already forestalled his request by detaching two brigades of English infantry with orders to join him as speedily as possible, thus increasing his strength to about 10,000 men.

The French General Lauzun, fearing that the force opposed to General Douglass and Count Schomberg would be insufficient to bar their further progress, in which case the Irish army would be taken in rear, now hurried up with the whole of his French troops, approximately 5,000 strong, leaving the centre of James's army weakened to that extent. The latter, from his post of observation on Donore Hill, noticing the progress that had been made by Count Schomberg's troops, still further weakened his centre by withdrawing from it several regiments of infantry together with his reserve, and led them in person to the support of Lauzun.

When Douglass received the reinforcement sent him by the King, he advanced in two lines and bore down upon the enemy, who had taken up a position between Rossnaree and the Dublin road.

Some marshy ground as well as two double ditches with high banks separated the combatants and effectually prevented the Jacobite horse from charging their opponents. This Lauzun had hoped to be able to do.

While James and Lauzun were endeavouring to find a means of holding back Count Schomberg's vigorous advance, an aide-de-camp galloped up with the alarming news that King William's centre had succeeded in forcing the passages at Old Bridge, and had worsted the Irish army there.

Lauzun instantly perceived that the day was lost, and urged the immediate retirement upon Duleek with a view to securing the pass there—his line of retreat. He also advised James to take his own regiment of horse, together with some dragoons, and make the best of his way to Dublin. King James was little loath to act upon this advice, for apparently on this fateful day all his thoughts were concentrated more upon flight than upon a fight to the finish, as shown by the withdrawal of some of his artillery on the previous night.

Lauzun thereupon made off for Duleek, his rear being pressed upon by Count Schomberg's cavalry. Soon it began to be whispered among the Irish soldiers that they had suffered a severe reverse at Old Bridge, which told upon their *moral* and caused them to press unduly upon their comrades in front, the result being great confusion and, so far as the Irish were concerned, breaking of ranks, the French maintaining theirs unbroken. The English cavalry bore down upon the broken Irish troops and slew considerable numbers of them.

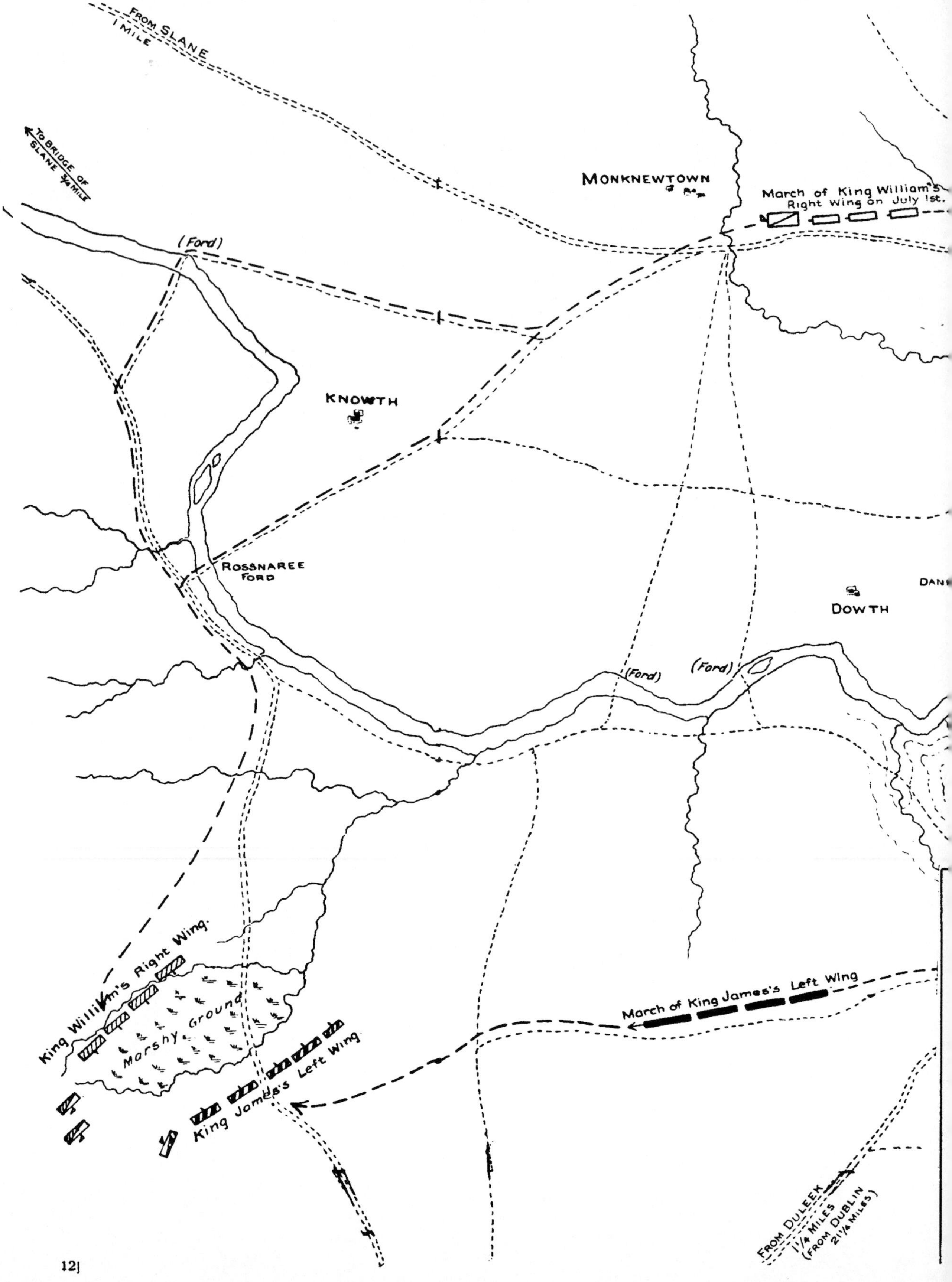
From Slane
1 Mile
To Bridge of Slane 3/4 Mile
Monknewtown
March of King William's Right Wing on July 1st.
(Ford)
Knowth
Rossnaree Ford
Dowth
(Ford)
(Ford)
King William's Right Wing
Marshy Ground
King James's Left Wing
March of King James's Left Wing
From Duleek 1 1/4 Miles
(From Dublin 21 1/4 Miles)

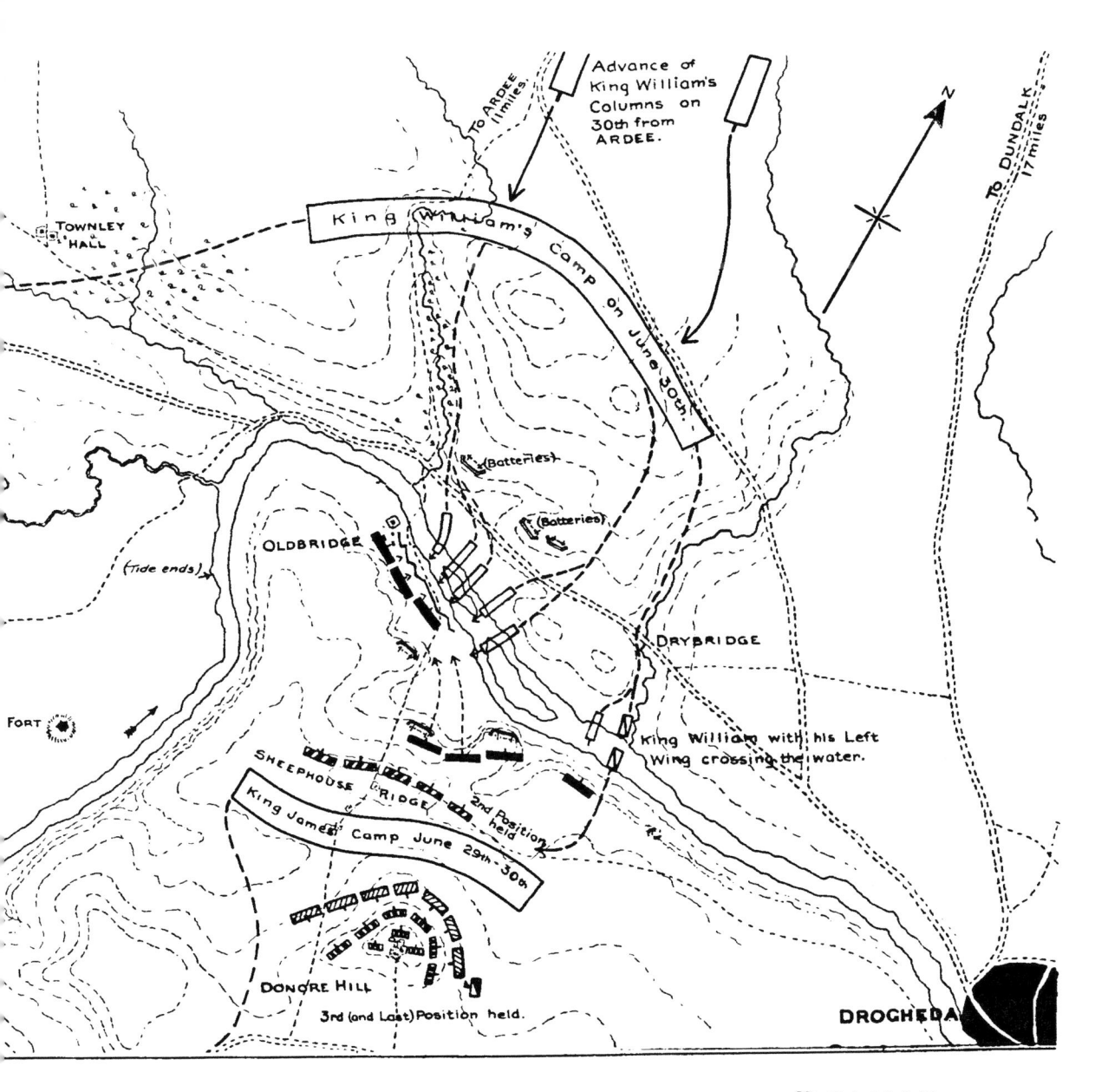

SKETCH MAP OF THE BATTLE OF THE BOYNE
JULY 1ST, 1689.

Compiled from a Sketch taken on the spot by JOHN BROWN, Major of Engineers, in August, 1795.
In August, 1895, I visited the battle-field with F.M. Viscount WOLSELEY, and subsequently made a Sketch of the ground. In the Map here given the dispositions, etc., are as shewn by Major BROWN.
The general nature of the ground across which the Attack was made is indicated by form lines.

Key to Dispositions of Troops.

	King William's Troops.	King James's Troops.
1st Position	▭	▬
2nd Position	▨	▨
3rd or Final Position	▭▭▭	▬▬▬

Scale of Miles

The fortunes of the centre, the main body, and left wing of King William's army must now be followed and narrated.

When William heard of the success that had attended Count Meinhardt Schomberg's and Douglass's turning movement, he issued orders for the advanced body of his centre, a motley throng consisting of the Dutch Blue Guards, Brandenburgers, Ulster troops, French Huguenots, certain English regiments, and the Danes, to cross by the fords at Old Bridge without delay. To oppose this mixed force Tyrconnel, the Irish commander at Old Bridge, had under him nine regiments of foot, including the Irish Guards, and a body of horse and dragoons, consisting of three and a half regiments—all Irish. King William, having given his orders, rode off to direct the movement of the left wing, his intention being to lead it in person.

In the centre, the Dutch Guards led the way, crossing the river ten abreast, followed by the Brandenburgers. No sooner had they effected a lodgment on the far bank than five battalions of the Irish infantry bore down upon them, but were speedily driven back. The Irish Horse now charged, only to meet with a similar fate. At this stage of the conflict the Dutch Guards were joined by the Ulster troops and part of the foreign corps.

In the meantime part of the enemy's cavalry swooped down upon the French Huguenots, who, owing to their being unsupported and not being armed with pikes to resist cavalry, had their ranks broken and their gallant leader, Caillemotte, was mortally wounded.

Marshal Schomberg saw the disorder into which the Huguenots had been thrown, and that the Dutch had received a check, also that the Danish Horse after crossing the river had been attacked by the Irish Horse, who charged home and drove them back to the opposite bank. He thereupon dashed into the river with a strong body of troops and, placing himself at the head of Caillemotte's leaderless Huguenots, quickly rallied them. In the meantime the Irish Horse, which had ridden through the Huguenots, encountered the Dutch Guards and part of the Ulster troops, with the result that they were driven back upon Caillemotte's regiment. In the confusion a few of the Irish Horse, being mistaken for friends, succeeded in wounding Marshal Schomberg in the head, and were carrying him off as a prisoner, when his own men, perceiving their mistake, fired at the Irishmen and in doing so unfortunately killed the Marshal. The firing then slackened, and it was at this critical moment that King William appeared upon the scene.

As already narrated, his Majesty, on giving the order for the centre to advance, rode off to head the left wing, which consisted of Dutch and Danish Horse, Colonel Wolseley's Horse, and a few dragoons.

William's plan, which was kept secret until the last moment, was to cross the Boyne by a ford a mile north of Donore, about a mile and a half above Drogheda, and to swoop down upon the right flank of the enemy.

As he emerged from the ravine below Dry Bridge at the head of the Inniskilling Horse, and was about to traverse a flat green meadow near the river bank, an unexpected difficulty presented itself. For the meadow proved to be a morass! The King's horse and those of many of the troopers were bogged, and had great difficulty in extricating themselves from their perilous position, which was rendered doubly so by the fact that they were being fired upon by a dragoon regiment under Lord Dungan, drawn up on the far bank to bar the passage.

As soon as the King and the leading files reached hard ground, the troopers in the rear closed up rapidly, having by good luck hit upon practicable spots in the swamp. Leaving some of his Danish troopers behind him to fire volleys from the bank, the King with the main body plunged into the river and crossed it. It is said that in some cases the horses had to swim. Thereupon the Irish Dragoon Regiment, which had been exposed to a galling fire from the opposite bank, and had suffered the loss of Lord Dungan, who was killed, and of several other officers killed or wounded, gave way and, galloping off towards Duleek, took no further part in the battle. The effect of this was to leave the right flank of the Jacobite army uncovered.

King William, meeting with little opposition, quickly traversed the ground between the Donore ford and the position near Old Bridge. As already stated, he arrived there just as the fire slackened, which gave him time to re-form his troops. Leading the cavalry in person, he now threw himself upon the uncovered flank of the enemy, and after a desperate struggle, which lasted for quite half an hour, the Irish infantry gave way along the line and, retreating with all speed in great disorder, streamed through the pass of Duleek, hotly pursued for some time by the English dragoons. The pursuit was continued relentlessly by Count Schomberg (who was maddened on learning of the death of his father the famous Marshal), and was not given over until he received positive orders from King William to cease the pursuit of the fleeing enemy and to fall back on Duleek. Thus ended the famous battle of the Boyne.

The loss in King William's army was about 400 men, whilst that of the Jacobite army exceeded 1,000, including Lords Dungan and Carlingford, Sir Neil O' Neil, and others of lesser note. The strength of King James's army appears to have been about 25,000 men, while that of King William's was nearer 35,000.

On the day following the battle the King directed Brigadier-General de la Melonière to proceed with five regiments (one being the 23rd) to Drogheda, where a vast quantity of stores was collected, and summon it to surrender. This was done, but the Governor stoutly refused to do so; however, on receiving an intimation from William that he would bring cannon to bear upon the town, he decided next day to capitulate. The garrison, consisting of three regiments and some odd companies, was allowed to march out without arms and proceed under safe-conduct to Athlone.

On the 3rd of July the army marched to Balbriggan. While there information was received that the enemy had evacuated Dublin. Thereupon the Duke of Ormonde was instructed to push forward with the Dutch Guards and a thousand cavalry with the object of taking possession of the city.

On the 4th the army halted at Swords, nine miles from Dublin, and was given a well-deserved rest. On the following day it reached Finglas, a suburb of Dublin, where it encamped. Next day the King rode into the city, issued a proclamation, and returned to Finglas.

On the 7th and 8th a general muster of the troops took place in the presence of the King. The 23rd did not appear on the muster, being still in garrison at Drogheda. He then decided to divide his army into two. Lieutenant-General Douglass was ordered to take five regiments of horse, ten of infantry, together with ten field-pieces and two mortars, and reduce Athlone, the capture of which was of great strategic importance. The remainder of the army, under the King's personal command, marched due south with the object of securing all places of military importance before branching off to the Shannon. On reaching Castledermot he dispatched a strong party of dragoons to secure Wexford, which had been deserted by the enemy.

On the 19th of July he arrived at Kilkenny, which had been seized on his behalf by the Duke of Ormonde. On the following day Count Schomberg was sent with a detachment to occupy Clonmel, which had also been evacuated by the enemy.

On reaching Carrick-on-Suir the following day he ordered Major-General Kirke to proceed with the 2nd and 12th Regiments together with a body of cavalry to Waterford and summon it to surrender. The place was garrisoned by two Irish regiments. On an investment being threatened, it capitulated. The garrison was allowed to march out with arms and baggage under safe-conduct to Mallow.

On the 28th of July the following order, which is preserved among the Additional MSS. in the British Museum, was addressed to—

"The Commander in Chief of Coll^{n.} Herbert's Regiment at Drogheda. Given at our camp near Kilcullen Bridge, this 28th day of July 1690 in the second year of our reigne.

"Our will and pleasure is that upon sight hereof you appoint three companyes of your Regiment to remayne in garrison in the Towne of Drogheda. And that you march to Dublin with the other ten companyes with all convenient speed, and there to remayne in Garrison till further order.

"By His Majesty's command."

On the same day the King resumed his march via Clonmel and Golden Bridge, adjoining Cashel, to a small place named Cahercoulish, about six miles from Limerick. Here he was joined by Lieutenant-General Douglass. That general officer, it will be remembered, had received orders to advance to Athlone and use every endeavour to capture it, owing to its strategic importance. The Governor, Colonel Grace, was a man of grit and resource. On Douglass summoning him to surrender, he returned a message to the effect that if it were necessary to eat his boots he would do so before he surrendered. Thereupon a bombardment was commenced with the ten field-pieces and two mortars brought from Dublin.

At the end of a week little or no progress had been made. The supply of powder ran perilously low, the enemy's fire combined with sickness had carried off between three and four hundred of Douglass's men, and to crown all, he learned that Sarsfield with a considerable force drawn from Limerick was marching to cut off his communication both with Dublin and King William.

After an investment of eight days he raised the siege, and marching by the left bank, set off to rejoin the King. On learning that the enemy had assembled in force at Banagher, where there was a bridge over the Shannon, to bar his progress, he made a wide detour by by-roads to Balliboy and from thence to Roscrea, when he received an urgent order from the King to rejoin him with all possible speed for fear of being cut off by Sarsfield. Had the latter succeeded in intercepting him, it is highly probable that his division would have suffered severely, as it was latterly in a state of semi-starvation.

On the 9th of August the English army assembled in force before Limerick. Nature, by means of the Shannon, had endowed this city with a somewhat formidable defence, but the fortifications, if a straggling uncemented wall without ramparts can be dignified by the term, were poor in the extreme. The garrison numbered about 15,000 men under the command of a capable French officer named Boisseleau, who had been Governor of Cork.

King William's summons to surrender having been rejected by Boisseleau, the bombardment of the city with field-guns only was commenced at once, in anticipation of the arrival of the siege artillery from Kilkenny, which was due to reach the King in a couple of days.

Two days later a deserter from the English army brought the news to the beleaguered city of the expected arrival of a convoy with the artillery train. The possibility of intercepting this convoy was eagerly debated. Sarsfield, who happened to be in the city at the moment, offered to make the attempt, and his offer was accepted by Boisseleau.

Riding off to the camp in Co. Clare some miles from Limerick, where the Irish cavalry lay under the command of the Duke of Berwick, he informed the latter of his project and requested to be furnished with 500 troopers to make the attempt. The Duke of Berwick acceded to his request.

At the head of his band Sarsfield crossed the Shannon, by swimming his horses, at Killaloe, some miles above Limerick, and swooped down upon the convoy when it had reached its last halting-place, Ballyneedy Castle—then in ruins—about seven miles from the King's camp. The hour chosen was 2 a.m., when the escort, drivers, and conductors of the train were sunk in sleep, not a sentry or a vedette having been posted outside the camp. The convoy consisted of eight 18-pounder guns and several waggons containing powder and ball. The powder was collected together and blown up. The force of the explosion burst two of the guns and rendered the other six unserviceable for the time being. Although hotly pursued, Sarsfield dexterously managed to elude his pursuers and succeeded in crossing the Shannon at Banagher. The moral effect of this disaster upon the besiegers was far greater than what was caused by the loss of war material.

The drooping spirits of the garrison perceptibly revived, Sarsfield was magnified into a hero, and all were now ready to fight to the death.

From the 12th to the 26th of August a series of minor assaults were made upon the city with a considerable degree of success. Trenches were advanced from time to time, and red-hot balls and bombs were rained in frequent discharges upon the besieged. One such ball fell upon a huge magazine of hay, causing a conflagration that was not extinguished for six hours. On the 27th orders were issued for an attack in force. Several untoward circumstances combined to render it unsuccessful. The King from a neighbouring hill viewed with great concern his gallant troops being driven back. The loss on this occasion was particularly heavy. No less than five hundred men lay dead upon the field, and the number of wounded amounted to several hundreds.

No appreciable gain had accrued to the besiegers during the siege, casualties had mounted up, disease was on the increase, and the ammunition all but spent.

Under these circumstances William called a council of war on the 29th, at which it was decided to raise the siege; this took place on the 31st of August.

The King hastened to return to England. He embarked at Duncannon Fort, and arrived at Kingweston, near Bristol, on the 6th of September.

The following items of expenditure, incurred whilst the regiment was stationed in county Down, are interesting as showing the prices of commodities, etc., at this period. They have been extracted from documents preserved in the Public Record Office, Dublin.

	£	s.	d.
Due by the Grenadiers of Coll. Herbert's Regiment for a mare they took from Andrew McIveen	1	0	0
,, ,, Ensign Dickens for 7 weeks diet and other things	2	13	6
,, ,, ,, ,, ,, ,, ,, washing	0	5	0
,, ,, Private Richard Phillips for a cow	0	15	0
,, ,, Captain Warren for 2 lambs	0	7	0
,, ,, Dr. Okely for a mutton	0	12	0
,, ,, Captain John Jones for candles for ye guard	0	7	6
,, ,, the Regiment for 2 muttons for sick men	0	4	0
,, ,, Lieutenant Price for pipe and tobacoe to Widow Morrell	0	2	0

	£	s.	d.
Due by Captain Thomas for 26 horses for bringing bread from Lisburn to Ballinahinsh	1	6	0
,, ,, Captain Thomas for carriage of municon to Newry to Andrew McCance	0	6	0
,, ,, Captain Gordon for a veall	0	6	0

The record of the cost of hospitality displayed by the regiment, when stationed at Ballinahinch in June 1690, towards the officers of Colonel John Coy's Regiment of Horse, is as follows:

	£	s.	d.
19 June, 1690. Captain Huke [Hooke] for meat and drink with the officers of Coll. Coy's Regiment	0	8	0
20 June, 1690. Due by Captain Richard Price with Coll. Coy's officers	0	8	0
Lieutenant Floyd [Lloyd] with Coll. Coy's officers and others	0	10	0

There also exists in the Dublin Record Office a book with the following title: "Colonel Charles Herbert's Charge of Country Debts in quarters." It contains a nominal list of all officers, non-commissioned officers, and men by companies, the creditor's name, and sums due.

The King on departing for England handed over the command of the army to Count Solmes. It marched by easy stages to Tipperary, where it arrived on the 7th of September. The same day General Douglass marched towards the north with several regiments of horse and foot, including the 23rd, which appears to have joined the army from Dublin some time in August.

On the 13th Major-Generals Lanier and Kirke set out with the English regiments of horse and foot for King's and Queen's Counties, where it was intended they should be quartered during the winter. On the following day Count Solmes started off with the Dutch and French troops for Kilkenny, which was to be their headquarters during the winter.

The King, on his return to London, conceived the idea that it would materially help the army in Ireland if the two southern ports, Cork and Kinsale, were wrested from the enemy. He therefore directed Lieutenant-General John Churchill, recently created Earl of Marlborough, to proceed to Ireland for that purpose. This is noteworthy as being Marlborough's first independent command.

On the 21st of September, in command of seven regiments of foot, two marine regiments, and a few independent companies of foot, he reached Passage, which is about six miles from Cork. On the following day the news of his arrival there reached the English camp, which was then at Cashel. Thereupon certain Danish regiments, under the command of the Duke of Würtemburg, together with detachments of the Dutch and French Huguenot troops, were ordered to join him with all speed. A further reinforcement, consisting of 1,200 horse and dragoons and two battalions of Danish troops, who were posted near the Blackwater, also reached Marlborough.

On the 24th Cork was invested, and by the 27th a practicable breach was made in the eastern portion of the city wall, which caused the enemy to beat a parley with the object of capitulating. The terms being agreed to by Marlborough, the garrison surrendered as prisoners of war.

The new fort of Kinsale was invested on the 5th of October, and trenches immediately opened. On the 12th and 13th several heavy pieces of ordnance were got into position. By this time the trenches were advanced to the counterscarp. After a heavy bombardment on the forenoon of the 15th, the Governor, Sir Edward Scott, who had already lost 300 men, decided to surrender on the following day. The garrison, consisting of about 1,100 men, was allowed to march out with arms and baggage under safe-conduct to Limerick.

At this juncture the Irish were deprived of the services of their French allies. The condition of affairs on the Continent of Europe was then such as to necessitate the recall of the aid in men which Louis XIV had afforded James. A French fleet arrived at Galway in October, and embarked all the French troops, who were inspected on their return to French soil, when it was manifest that their efficiency had been materially impaired. They were accompanied by the French General Lauzun.

In December 1690 the 23rd was quartered as follows : 3 companies at Longford, 2 at Foxhill, 3 at Castleforbes, 2 at Dromin, and 3 at Drogheda.

During the winter and well into the summer of 1691 armed bands of peasants with a sprinkling of soldiers, known as " Rapparees," roamed over a great part of the country at will, burning houses, plundering, murdering all those who they suspected were favourable to the cause of King William, and endeavouring at times to cut the communications of the English army. The county Wicklow in particular suffered from their lawlessness.

Many bands of these marauders were almost exterminated by parties of English soldiers sent out to waylay them. Lieutenant-Colonel Toby Purcell, of the 23rd, was most zealous in the performance of this harassing duty. In one week alone in March 1691 he accounted for sixty of them killed and thirty wounded. His activities were mostly confined to the county Longford. The "Rapparees" were eventually suppressed by the aid of the newly raised regiments of Militia.

The following is an extract from Story's *Impartial History* respecting Lieutenant-Colonel Toby Purcell's activity:

"The Rapparees at this time were very troublesome, nigh Fox Hall in the County of Longford till Lieut.-Colonel Toby Purcell at three several times kill'd about 100 of them: in the last of which they kill'd 52: and, returning towards quarters, they were waylaid by the greatest part of Sir Donald O'Neal's Dragoons: our party were 35 dragoons and 140 foot: one quartermaster Topham with 9 dragoons being in advance to view the enemy, seeing them in confusion at his appearing he charged their front: who running away made all the rest of the same humour."

1691.

From the 1st of January of this year the 23rd, which had hitherto been in the receipt of English pay, although serving in Ireland, was placed on the Irish Establishment with the corresponding rate of pay.

For the campaign of 1691 both armies had made all possible preparations, as it was obvious to each of them that the result would be decisive. Count Solmes having left Ireland to accompany his royal master to the Continent, where he was about to wage war against Louis XIV, the command of the army was conferred on Lieutenant-General de Ginckle.

What was in those days considered a formidable train of artillery, consisting of "39 pieces of cannon, 12 field-pieces and 6 mortars," was landed at Dublin about the 24th of May, and dispatched two days later to the rendezvous of the English troops at Mullingar. Ginckle and his staff had also reached Dublin in that month. They left that city on the 28th of May, arriving at Mullingar on the 31st idem. Lieutenant-General Douglass at the head of his troops had reached Ardagh from the north, and the Duke of Würtemburg had occupied Thurles.

The Irish on their side were equally active. Tyrconnel, who had left Ireland in October 1690 to consult with James at the French Court about the next year's campaign, and at the same time to invoke all possible assistance from Louis, returned to that country three months later with supplies of stores, arms, money, and promise of further succour in the shape of men later on. He set himself vigorously to the task of reorganising his troops, who, he discovered, were being badly fed and were worse clothed, and also of erecting fortifications at important points.

For a time all went well, but as a considerable amount of the money furnished by the French monarch had been expended on defences, the effect was felt by his army in due course when their rations were cut down to such an extent as to leave them in a constant state of hunger.

Such was the condition of affairs when the French General St. Ruth arrived at Limerick on the 20th of May, having been convoyed thither by a French squadron. He carried in his pocket a commission from James appointing him Commander-in-Chief of his army in Ireland. St. Ruth brought with him considerable supplies of food, clothing, and ammunition, which soon put the troops collected there, nearly 20,000 strong, in good fettle for the ordeal which all knew lay before them.

St. Ruth was slightly stronger in infantry than Ginckle, but the latter had a decided advantage in cavalry.

On the 6th of June Ginckle started the campaign by marching from Mullingar, his objective being Athlone, which, if once in his hands, would open the way to Connaught. On reaching a place called Rathcondra he encamped. Here he was joined by General Douglass, who had marched from the north with three regiments of horse and eight of foot, one of the latter being the 23rd Foot.

On the following day he arrived at Ballymore, about halfway between Mullingar and Athlone. Although it was hardly more than a village, it contained a recently erected fort on what was practically an island in a small lake adjoining the town. Ginckle resolved to take it. It was defended by Lieutenant-Colonel Miles Bourke, who had under him about 500 men, and two antiquated cannon, which were mounted on cart-wheels.

Bourke refused the terms offered him, whereupon Ginckle ordered up a few field-pieces to batter the fort. So effectually did the gunners do their work that by next day a considerable portion of the masonry had become dislodged. Seeing that it was hopeless to continue the struggle, Bourke surrendered at discretion, the garrison being sent as prisoners to Dublin. The damage to the fort was repaired as speedily as possible, and a garrison, consisting of four companies of General Douglass's regiment under the command of Lieutenant-Colonel Toby Purcell of the 23rd Foot, was left there.

At this crisis in the fortunes of the Irish army, when everything depended on unanimity, dissensions broke out between St. Ruth, backed up by several Irish officers of superior rank, and Tyrconnel. The latter, recognising that divided counsels would be fatal to the cause, in the most chivalrous manner resigned his appointment, and, mounting his horse, accompanied by his personal staff, rode off to Limerick.

The sole direction of affairs was now in the hands of St. Ruth, who, owing to his lack of local knowledge, together with the fact that he was utterly ignorant of the English language, had to depend largely on his Irish officers for guidance, with what baneful effect will be shown hereafter.

Ginckle continued his march until he arrived at Ballyburn Pass, where he was joined by the Duke of Würtemburg and Count Nassau with about 7,000 Danish and Dutch troops. This brought his total strength up to about 18,000 men. Resuming his march, he arrived in the neighbourhood of Athlone on the 18th of June.

Athlone stands on both banks of the Shannon. The part of the town which was situated on the Leinster shore of the river was known as English-town, while that on the Connaught bank was called Irishtown. A stone bridge connected the two towns. English-town was defended by walls of a kind which Irish-town did not possess, but the latter had the advantage of earthworks which had been thrown up to protect it, and an old castle which was obstinately defended.

Early in the morning of the 19th of June the enemy's scouts were driven in. Advantage was taken of this to plant a battery on the north-west of English-town. By the afternoon of the following day a large breach had been made in the walls. The grenadiers were ordered forward, supported by the 9th Foot. Other regiments followed in quick succession. A brief but sharp struggle took place, resulting in the retreat of the defenders, who made for the bridge, over which they retreated precipitately, so much so that in their wild rush many of them were crushed to death, while others were drowned by being forced over the side of the bridge.

The loss on the English side was trivial, amounting to about twenty killed and double that number wounded.

Entrenchments were immediately thrown up at the foot of the bridge to prevent the possibility of recapture, and batteries constructed to play upon the Connaught side of the town. The castle was defended by Colonel Nicholas Fitzgerald with a garrison of about 1,500 picked men.

On the 22nd one whole side of the castle was beaten down, which rendered it unserviceable to the besieged.

The same day there arrived at the camp a number of "tin boats" (pontoons), floats, etc., which were landed at Dublin on the 16th of the month. A great effort was now made to capture the stone bridge leading to Irish-town. Inch by inch the besiegers gained ground, until finally all the arches were in their hands except the last, which had been broken by the Irish. The captured arches were repaired as they were taken. Beams were then with great difficulty got into position over the broken arch and then planked. No sooner was this done than a detachment of the enemy with great intrepidity succeeded in destroying this temporary construction, all but two members of the party perishing in the daring feat. The next day a further attempt was made to bridge over the difficulty by means of fascines, but the intrepid defenders succeeded in burning the lot.

It then became evident to Ginckle's staff that it was only by a direct assault that Irish-town could be taken, but the General at first would not entertain the idea, believing that it was rash in the extreme and most unlikely to be attended by success.

Being pressed in particular by Major-General Talmash and the Duke of Würtemburg to effect an entrance into the town by means of a ford, which it was understood was in close proximity to the town, he reluctantly consented to call a council of war to discuss the project.

At the council a general assault was determined upon. It now became imperative to ascertain whether such a ford existed. How was this information of such vital importance to be obtained? The General solved the problem. It came to his recollection that three Danish soldiers had for some crime been sentenced to death. To them he offered free pardon and a gratuity if they were willing to attempt fording the river at the spot indicated. The offer was readily accepted, and the men, donning their armour, proceeded in broad daylight to cross the Shannon, keeping some distance from each other. Some of the men in the trenches were ordered to fire as if at them, but in reality over their heads, so as to make it appear that they were deserters. Not a shot was fired at them by the besieged until they were beyond the centre of the river and were returning, when, their object becoming manifest, a fusilade was started. The enemy's firing, however, was at random, as " the great and small shot prepared for the purpose " was rained upon them " with such fury " that they could not observe their target. One of the three returned unhurt and the other two were but slightly wounded.

The existence of the ford being no longer in doubt, Ginckle issued orders for a storming party, consisting of sixty grenadiers and eighty-three picked men from the service companies of every regiment—which included the 23rd—to be ready to advance at the toll of the church bell.

At ten minutes past six o'clock on the evening of the 30th of June the preconcerted signal rang out. Instantly the storming party, under the command of General Mackay, leaped from the trenches and dashed into the river. The sixty grenadiers, in armour twenty abreast, led the way, followed by the general body of the men, who, though up to their armpits in water, made such rapid progress that reinforcements could not reach the scene in time to stem the onward progress of the English. Of the three regiments that endeavoured to oppose the progress of General Mackay's advance, two of them had been but a few months in existence and could only be described as raw soldiers. The result of the bursting of the grenades with deadly effect among a number of partially trained men can be readily comprehended. Their *moral* was quickly destroyed.

Some of the storming party, on reaching the opposite shore, rushed to the end of the bridge, and assisted their comrades on the other side of it to lay beams and planks over the broken arch. Others helped in the laying of " tin boats " across the river. So rapidly was this service performed that very soon the troops were streaming over the extemporised bridge. In less than half an hour the town was theirs and the garrison in full retreat making for St. Ruth's camp, which had been pitched about two miles south of Athlone.

In this gallant action the English loss was only fifty killed and wounded. The enemy's casualties amounted to 200 prisoners and about 1,000 killed.

Six brass cannon and two mortars were taken from the enemy, but the supplies of powder, ball, and provisions found in the town were small. According to Story, "Fifty tons of gunpowder were expended, and 12,000 cannon balls, together with 600 bombs and several tons of stones, were fired by the besiegers during this siege, which lasted eleven days."

Ginckle remained at Athlone ten days, during which time he replenished his depleted stores, a great convoy of provisions and ammunition having reached him from Dublin, and placed the town in a good state of defence.

The fall of Athlone necessitated the retreat of the Irish army. Falling back slowly, it followed the course of the Shannon towards Limerick until it arrived at the town of Aughrim. The nature of the ground here appeared to St. Ruth to be so favourable whereon to risk a pitched battle that he lost no time in making the necessary dispositions. He drew up his army in two lines on rising ground behind an extensive morass, which could barely be traversed by foot, and was impassable by cavalry. A small ford on the right of the bog, and a narrow causeway on the left of it protected by the dismantled castle of Aughrim, were the only passages by which the wings of the Irish army could be threatened by cavalry.

The castle, although to all intents and purposes a ruin, was surrounded with walls and ditches which could be lined by men—a style of fighting at which the Irish were adepts.

Ginckle left Athlone on the 10th of July and marched as far as Kilcashel, about five miles from Athlone, where he encamped. On being informed when there that the enemy had retired from Ballinasloe, leaving the passage of the Suck open, he decided to march the following day towards Ballinasloe and encamp on a position to the left of that town adjacent to the river.

The next day, Sunday the 12th of July, at 6 a.m., the army was in motion crossing the Suck—the artillery and foot by a stone bridge, and the cavalry by two fords. By 11 a.m. all had crossed, except two regiments which had been left to guard the baggage at the camp.

On reaching the outskirts of Aughrim, Ginckle halted his army for a brief rest preparatory to attempting to dislodge the enemy.

The morning was foggy, but by noon it had cleared, disclosing the rival armies confronting each other.

The English General then drew up his army in two lines on a ridge close to the village of Urachree, his flanks being protected by cavalry. On the right of the first line Major-General Mackay's division, under the command of Brigadier-General Bellasis, was posted. It consisted of the following regiments: 2nd, 12th, 20th, 22nd, 23rd, Ffoulk's, and Lord George Hamilton's.

The engagement commenced by an artillery duel and an affair of outposts, or "outguards" as they were then styled, in which the enemy's were driven back.

Ginckle, from his post of observation having carefully studied his opponent's dispositions, resolved to force the passage on the right flank of the Irish army, and for this purpose ordered Sir Albert Conyngham's Dragoons to endeavour to hold it while the army advanced. The enemy being, however, in much greater strength than was anticipated, the dragoons were driven back. Thereupon Eppinger's Dutch Dragoons and Lord Portland's Horse were ordered to the assistance of Conyngham. After a stiff fight, which lasted nearly an hour, the Irish retired on their main body, leaving the pass in the possession of Ginckle. By this time the afternoon was so far advanced that it became a question whether the fight should be resumed or deferred until the following morning. The former course was adopted. At 5 p.m. the fight on the left of the English was resumed in deadly earnest. The Irish fought heroically, but were compelled to give ground gradually, which necessitated the sending of reinforcements to them from their left. Up to this point the English centre and right had not come into action, but were exposed to artillery fire.

On observing that the enemy was weakening his left, Ginckle gave orders for his centre to advance across the bog, and for his right wing at the same time to force the passage on the left of the enemy, adjoining the castle of Aughrim. Accordingly four battalions of foot, one of which was the 23rd, plunged into the bog directly in front of the enemy, and though up to their waist in mud and water and stoutly opposed, they advanced straight through it. So great was their ardour that on reaching firm ground they dislodged the enemy from a series of hedges on his main line. Their impetuosity was, however, their undoing. Advancing too far to receive support from either wing, the Irish Horse bore down upon them through gaps which had been specially cut in some of the ditches, with the result that they were mown down in large numbers, the remnant of the brigade being driven back into the bog. Colonel Herbert of the 23rd was unfortunately taken prisoner, and a few hours later barbarously murdered to prevent his being rescued.

While part of the brigade commanded by Major-General Bellasis was being severely handled, as already described, a further attack on the Irish main position was being developed more to the right. Three regiments of Stuart's brigade, one of Bellasis's brigade (Lord George Hamilton's), and the French Foot succeeded in crossing the bog without encountering the slightest opposition. When, however, they got within range of the foremost hedge they were met by a withering and altogether unexpected fire from behind it, which tore great gaps in their ranks. The men in the rear gallantly pressed on and drove the Irish out of ditches and hedges. Unfortunately in this operation the men of the different regiments got mixed up, causing considerable confusion and disorder, necessitating a general retirement.

The advantage gained by the enemy was but momentary. Instead of contenting themselves with reoccupying the ground protected by hedges, the Irish in their elation pursued the fugitives halfway through the morass. This tactical error was not lost upon Major-General Talmash, who determined to take full advantage of it. Coming up with a fresh body of men he rallied the fugitives, reformed the men in their respective regiments, and so vigorously attacked the Irish, now floundering in the bog, that before they could extricate themselves and reach their original position, three hundred were slain.

This success raised the spirit of Talmash's men to such an extent that not only did they reoccupy the lost ground, but were soon hotly engaged in driving the enemy slowly, but surely, up the incline.

While these events were happening in the centre, the English Horse on the right had been making desperate efforts to force the passage at Aughrim Castle. For some time the issue was in doubt, but eventually the pass was stormed, which enabled part of the horse under Ruvigny to flank that portion of the enemy which had driven back the English centre. At the same time the horse on the left were successfully overcoming all opposition offered by the enemy's right.

Now was the time for a master-mind to reorganise the wavering Irish, and possibly snatch a victory at the eleventh hour. Fate decreed otherwise. Just at this critical moment St. Ruth was killed by a cannon ball fired from the English army. Sarsfield, who would naturally have succeeded to the command, was some distance off in charge of the reserve, where he was ordered to remain until his services were required. This order he was most punctilious to obey, as a coolness had sprung up between him and St. Ruth some days before. When late in the evening he learned of the death of the latter, the time had gone for making an effort to retrieve the fallen fortunes of the army.

The left of the Irish, which had been worsted by Ruvigny's Horse, was the first to give way; the centre soon followed suit, owing to the pressure exercised upon it by Major-General Talmash. The last to give way was the right, which withstood a fierce onslaught of the Danes for quite half an hour, but on discovering that it was in great danger of being taken in the rear, it retreated with all speed. The horse fled in the direction of Loughrea, while the foot spread themselves over an extensive bog that lay behind their camp. The fleeing enemy were pursued for four miles, until night and a misty rain closed the pursuit. The number of those slain in the retreat far exceeded the fallen on the battlefield.

The last act in the drama was the taking of Aughrim Castle, when Colonel Walter Burke, the commander, twelve other officers, and forty men were taken prisoners. The rest of the garrison was put to the sword.

The English army present at the battle numbered about 17,000, including the foreign corps. Out of this total 673 of all ranks were killed and 1,017 wounded. The Irish army appears to have consisted of about 20,000 foot and 5,000 horse. Its casualties were 450 prisoners and between 5,000 and 7,000 killed.

The loss sustained by the 23rd was one officer, Lieutenant-Colonel Herbert, taken prisoner and inhumanly murdered, Captains Robert Thomas (Grenadiers), Timothy Waring, and Hugh Hookes, and thirty-two rank and file killed, one lieutenant and forty-five rank and file wounded.

The English captured nine pieces of cannon, twelve standards, thirty-two colours, and a kettle-drum, also all the enemy's baggage, tents, provisions, and ammunition. The standards and colours were forwarded to London as a present for Queen Mary.

The *London Gazette* containing an account of the battle concludes with the following eulogistic remark on the English troops: " The bravery and courage of our men on this occasion exceeded all the accounts that can be given, and the vigour and conduct of the general officers contributed extremely to this great and glorious victory."

Lieutenant-Colonel Tobias Purcell was promoted Colonel of the

23rd in succession to Colonel Charles Herbert. His commission is dated the 13th of July 1691.

The day following this memorable battle was employed by Ginckle in getting together all his baggage and stores. When this had been done, he left Aughrim, taking with him only his field-pieces, his heavy cannon being still at Athlone, and marched a short distance in the direction of Loughrea. He then halted for three days, and while there sent forward a detachment of 1,200 horse and dragoons under Brigadier Eppinger to seize Portumna and Banagher, where Irish garrisons were located to guard the passes of the Shannon. Both surrendered without delay, owing to the favourable terms offered them—permission to take their baggage and arms and retire to Limerick if they so desired.

On the 16th Ginckle reached Loughrea, and on the following day arrived at Athenry. From there he proceeded to Galway, taking care to leave behind a strong force to prevent the possibility of his communications by the Dublin road being cut off.

On arriving before Galway he summoned the Governor, Lord Henry Dillon, to surrender. On the latter stating that it was his intention to defend the place to the last, the investment commenced.

On the 19th Ginckle planted a battery against an almost completed fort concerning which a deserter had given him valuable information. He succeeded in taking it the same day. Other batteries were speedily raised against the town, which contained a garrison of about 2,500 men indifferently armed, while the artillery consisted of no more than six pieces of cannon. To make matters worse, Lord Henry Dillon discovered that an appreciable number of the townsmen were disaffected, being favourable to the English cause.

Under these circumstances he deemed it prudent to call for a parley, the result of which was that negotiations were entered into for the town's capitulation. Three hostages were exchanged as a preliminary to the pourparlers. One of those selected by the English commander was Colonel Tobias Purcell of the 23rd, the others being Lieutenant-Colonel Coote and the Marquess de Rhada.

Lord Henry Dillon evacuated Galway on the 26th of July, being permitted to march under safe-conduct with drums beating and colours flying to Limerick. He was also permitted to take his six pieces of cannon with him. Considerable quantities of food and ammunition were found in the town.

Three regiments of foot, one of them being the 23rd, were left to garrison Galway, under the command of Sir Henry Bellasis as Governor. For some weeks after the departure of the army the garrison were actively employed in the capture of the island and castle of Boffin.

On the 28th Ginckle began his march on Limerick, which he invested on the 25th of August. Although gallantly defended, the city was compelled to surrender on the 3rd of October.

An examination of the *Custom House Records* in Dublin for July 1691 discloses the fact that it was customary for regiments to brew their own beer, the licence to do so being obtained from the local excise officers. At this date in the "Gallway District" amounts ranging from 4s. 9d. to £2 11s. 4d. were debited to the following companies of "Colonel Purcell's Regiment, the Colonel's Co., also Captains Gordon, Purefoy, Bennett, Genestet, Cobett and Lee."

On the 9th of October a list of the forces which the King considered necessary for the next year was presented to Parliament. The 23rd is included therein with an establishment of 13 companies and 780 men.

On the 23rd of November the regiment marched from Galway, and embarked at Cork on Christmas Day 1691, landing at Barnstaple two days later. Thence the regiment marched to Chipping Norton and Witney. When there it received orders to march to Portsmouth.

1692.

The regiment reached Faringdon and Wantage on the 5th of January, Newbury on the 6th, Basingstoke on the 7th, Alton on the 9th, Petersfield on the 11th, and Portsmouth on the 12th.

The one great idea ever uppermost in the mind of King William III was how effectually to curb the overweening ambition of Louis XIV of France. When as a young man he had seen his beloved country overrun by the armies of that monarch and fearfully devastated, he resolved to be one day even with the detested oppressor.

As Stadtholder of the Netherlands he had succeeded in forming a combination of powerful European States against France.

When the fates decreed that he should be King of England, his satisfaction was great, as he believed that the weight of this country, which had hitherto been neutral, would now be thrown into the scale. His belief was not unfounded, as the English people had several cogent reasons for desiring to humble the French autocrat. These reasons were set forth in a declaration of war by the English Parliament in May 1689.

As the condition of affairs then prevailing both in Scotland and Ireland necessitated King William's presence at home, he selected the Prince of Waldeck—a General who had seen a considerable amount of active service, but who was notoriously unlucky—to take command of the Allied army in the Netherlands. A contingent of 8,000 troops under the command of the Earl of Marlborough was dispatched as soon as possible to the Continent.

The condition of Ireland prevented any appreciable augmentation of the contingent being made until a much later date in this protracted campaign. Although comparatively a mere handful, the reputation of the contingent for valour was maintained at a high level.

The suppression of the rebellion in Scotland in 1691 enabled the King to dispatch more troops to Flanders, but not to anything like the extent desired by him for his summer campaign in that country, owing to the great difficulty experienced in obtaining recruits.

The campaign of that year was barren of any decisive result. The Allies, although numerically superior to the French, were made up of several nationalities, with the inevitable result that there was a striking lack of cohesion which neutralised any possible advantage that might accrue from this superiority. William's anxiety to collect a large army in Flanders for the campaign in the summer of 1692 was so great that the country had been dangerously denuded of troops. When, therefore, the news of a probable invasion of the country by Louis reached the ears of the Government in April of that year, steps were immediately taken to place it in the best possible state of defence. The Queen, in the absence of the King in Holland, countermanded the embarkation of six regiments of foot, including the 23rd, which were under orders for Holland. All of them were hurried off to the south coast. Luckily for all concerned, the panic was short-lived.

On the 19th of May a combined English and Dutch fleet, under the command of Admiral Russell, signally defeated off Cape La Hogue the French fleet which was to convoy the transports containing the invaders.

Instead of alarums and excursions one now saw London illuminated, bonfires in the streets, and flags flying from steeples!

At the time when Queen Mary, owing to the absence of the King in Holland, countermanded the order for the embarkation of these six regiments, the command of the 23rd became vacant. Mr. Cannon, in his record of the regiment, states that the vacancy was caused by the decease of Colonel Purcell, which was not the case. Colonel Purcell resigned on account of ill-health. His life was prolonged for some years. He was succeeded in the colonelcy of the regiment by Sir John Morgan, Bart., on the 20th of April 1692.

The nation was so heartened by the naval victory off Cape La Hogue, that a scheme was devised for a descent in force upon the coast of France—preferably upon St. Malo. During the month of July great preparations were made for carrying out this project. Fourteen regiments of foot, one of which was the 23rd, were collected together and encamped on Portsdown Hill. All the preparations being completed by the 25th of July, the expedition, under the command of the Duke of Leinster (Count Meinhardt Schomberg that was), started from Portsmouth on the following day, the transports being convoyed by a squadron of men-of-war under Admiral Russell, who picked them up in Portland Roads.

An unfortunate incident occurred on board H.M.S. *Elizabeth*, on which ship the 23rd had embarked for duty as marines. As narrated by Luttrell, " Captain Willmot of the Elizabeth hath killed Ensign Royden of Colonel Ingoldsby's regiment on board in a duel." Willmot was charged with manslaughter and arrested by the Marshal of the Admiralty. Thereupon Sir John Trenchard, the Principal Secretary of State, wrote on the 19th of March 1693 to the two judges who were to try him at the Assizes, as follows :

" WHITEHALL, *March* 1693.

" To Mr. Justice Lowell or Mr. Justice Rookby.

" The King being informed that Captain Robert Willmot is to be tryed before you for the death and killing of Mathew Roydon, and it having been represented to his Majesty that Mr. Willmot had very great provocation from the deceased person, His Majesty commands me to signify his pleasure to you that in case Captain Willmot be convicted, the execution of the sentence be respited till you shall have given His Majesty an account of how the matter appeared upon the Tryal and that if the conviction be only for Man-slaughter the burning of the hand be also respited till His Majesty's pleasure be further known.

" I am your most humble servant,

" [*signed*] J. TRENCHARD."

Captain Willmot was acquitted. A petition was presented by Roydon's mother to the Treasury for arrears of pay due to her son whilst recruiting in May and June 1692, but it was not entertained, although supported by a certificate from Lieutenant-Colonel Montargyer.

Luttrell's statement that the duel took place " on board " is incorrect, as the Admiralty record is as follows : " For killing a land ensigne on shoare at Torrbay."

A general council of war was then held to discuss primarily the St. Malo project. The naval commanders, led by Russell, vehemently maintained that it would be little short of madness to bring the ships within range of the guns of St. Malo ; that the only hope of success lay in closely investing the town on the land side ; and that when it had been reduced to straits it would then be possible to attack the men-of-war that were known to be anchored in the harbour.

The military men, on their part, were unanimous in declaring that all the efforts of the land force would be neutralised without the hearty co-operation of the fleet. A descent upon either Brest or Rochefort was then discussed, but as the flag-officers were agreed that the summer was too advanced, nothing definite was decided.

When the report of the proceedings of the council of war was laid before the Queen, she dispatched several Lords of the Council to assist in the deliberations. No satisfactory result was arrived at. It was, therefore, decided to refer the matter to the King, who was then in Holland.

A portion of the fleet then proceeded to St. Helens, under Admiral Russell, while the remaining ships, under Admiral Sir Cloudisley Shovell, convoyed the transports to the Downs, where they arrived on the 8th of August. There they remained at anchor until orders from the King to proceed to Flanders reached them on the 20th. On the 29th passes were issued for Sir John Morgan, Bart., Captain James Jones, Captain Roger Whitley, and their seven servants to embark for Holland.

On the 21st the expedition sailed out of the Downs and reached Ostend on the 22nd of August. The following day the troops disembarked and marched to Marieburg, which is about four miles from Ostend. Here they were joined by a force of 10,000 men under Lieutenant-General Talmash.

The united force, under the command of the Duke of Leinster, then marched in the direction of Nieuport. On the way thither he detached some regiments to take Furnes and Dixmude. Both of these had, however, been abandoned by the French on the approach of the English troops. They were now put into a better state of defence. Towards the close of September King William decided that nothing more could be done that year. In consequence of this decision the army went into winter quarters, but the greater part of the English troops marched back to Ostend, where they re-embarked and returned to England.

On their way thither they encountered a heavy gale which scattered the transports. About twenty-five of them fetched Harwich on the 18th of October; the remainder safely reached the " Buoy of the Nore." One of these tempest-tossed battalions was the 23rd.

A muster taken in December 1692 shows that the following was the state of the regiment in that month: " Sir John Morgans 12 field officers and captains, 14 lieutenants, 12 ensigns, 39 sergeants, 39 corporals, 26 drummers, 573 private soldiers appeared, 61 sick, 20 on pass, prisoners nil, 69 servants, 62 required."

As the 23rd had spent a few weeks on the fringe of the theatre of war this year, a brief reference to the operations of the Confederate army will not be out of place.

The features of the campaign were the taking of the city and fortress of Namur in May, and the hard-fought battle of Steenkirk in July. Namur was an important fortress on the Meuse. All through the previous winter the French had been busily occupied in collecting a formidable siege-train for its investment. King William, on the other hand, had been negligent about putting it in a proper state of defence.

On learning that it had been invested, he marched from Anderlecht with all possible speed to raise the siege. To effect this it was necessary for him to cross the Mehayne (Main). Torrential rains had swollen the river to such an extent that the construction of bridges proved to be an exceedingly difficult task. This so impeded his progress that when by great efforts he had almost arrived upon the scene, he had the mortification to find that the fortress had capitulated.

To rehabilitate himself in the eyes of his Allies he laid his plans for surprising Marshal Luxemburg at Steenkirk, where he had taken up a strong position after the capture of Namur.

Although the latter was at first deceived as to William's real intention, his genius for war was so great that he quickly divined the King's object, and without a moment's delay made certain dispositions to counter it. Even then it is possible that the Allies would have won the day had not Count Solmes at a critical moment obstinately refused to send reinforcements, which, had they been promptly furnished, would in all probability have enabled the British contingent, which was in the thick of the fight, to carry the French camp.

Slowly but surely the Allies were pushed back, with the result that what promised in its conception to bring disaster to the enemy ended in the retreat of the Confederate army, which fortunately was carried out in an orderly manner.

1693.

In tne early part of the year Sir John Morgan, Bart., who was Colonel of the regiment, died, and was succeeded by Richard Ingoldsby, who was appointed on the 28th of February, having been transferred from the lieutenant-colonelcy of the 18th Regiment (Royal Irish).

During the whole of 1693 the 23rd remained at home. Quite a number of regiments (including the 23rd) were employed as marines from May to September. This service necessitated the partial rearming of, and provision of medical comforts for, the regiments so employed, as will be seen by the following warrants.

"WHITEHALL, 4*th May* 1693.

"Having directed our regiments of foot, whereof O T and Well Beloved Sir David Collyear Bart, Edw: Lloyd, Frederick Hamilton, Richard Ingoldsby, and Samll: Venner Esqrs are colonels to embark on board our Fleet, O W & Pleasure is that you immediately prepare chests of good and wholesom medecines as well internal as external for our said five regiments according to the proportions directed and provided by you for our regiments of foot in Flanders. Given this 4th May 93,

"To Isaac Teale, Apothecary General."

"Marie R.

"Whereas we have thought fitt to command ye Regiments of Foot commanded by our trusty and well-beloeved Collonel Sir David Collyer, Coll: Edward Lloyd, Coll: Richard Ingoldsby & Coll: Saml Venner to embark on our Fleet this summer, our will and pleasure therefore is That you cause the pikes of the said regiments to be exchanged for Snaphance Musquetts causing the said musquetts to be forthwith sent by land carriage to Portsmouth & there delivered to the respective Coll: or whom they shall appoint to receive them in lieu of these pikes, and their indents taken as is usuall causing the said pikes to be lodged apart in our Stores that they may be delivered againe to the said regiments, and the musquetts in good order and serviceable condicion received from them att the end of the expedicion and lodged in our Magazines for our future service, and for so doing—

"Whitehall 17th day of May 1693,
" By Her Matys command
" NOTTINGHAM.

"To Sir Henry Goodrick Knt."

The distribution of the 23rd on board ship was as follows:

On the *Restoration* the company of the Colonel.
On the *Elizabeth* the company of Lieutenant-Colonel Montargyer.
On the *Essex* the company of Major Sabine.
On the *Devonshire* the company of Captain John Jones.
On the *Northumberland* the company of Captain Jas. Jones.
On the *Edgar* the company of Captain Purefoy.
On the *Hope* the company of Captain Genestet.
On the *Mary* the company of Captain Bennett.
On the *Albemarle* the company of Captain Lee.
On the *London* the company of Captain Hamilton.
On the *Duke* the company of Captain Mumford.
On the *Grafton* the company of Captain Goubet.

Another interesting incident is recorded by Luttrell under date 28th of December 1693: "The regiments of colonel Ingoldsby, St. George Loyd, and Hamilton, shewed this day in Hide park, and are marching to embark at the Red House for Flanders."

1694.

In January four regiments of foot embarked for service on the Continent, one of which was the 23rd, and landed at Ostend, where they performed garrison duty until the middle of May.

From warrants covering the period February to May of this year that are preserved at the Public Record Office, it appears that regiments of foot were allowed sixty horses per battalion, and £200 was allowed for carriages per campaign.

King William, who had crossed from England on the 6th of May, issued orders from the Hague that the garrisons of Ostend, Bruges, and such troops as were quartered in the vicinity of Nieuport were to rendezvous at Bethlehem, close to Louvain. In consequence of this order the 23rd, which formed part of Major-General Ramsay's division, under the command of Brigadier-General Sir David Collier, set out for the general rendezvous. At Vilvorde it joined up with a portion of the army under Count Nassau and Sir Henry Bellasis, which was also making for Bethlehem.

On the 31st of May the King, who had fixed his headquarters at the Abbey of Bethlehem, reviewed the army, which amounted to about 82,000 men, about 7,000 men having been left to garrison Ghent, and expressed himself as well pleased with their efficiency and general appearance.

The question of precedence of regiments having reached an acute stage, the matter was brought to the notice of King William at Roosbeck by the Secretary-at-War. His Majesty referred the matter to a Board of General Officers, whose recommendations on the subject he reluctantly confirmed on the 10th of June. By this the 23rd was given twentieth place in the order of seniority.

From Vilvorde the army marched to Roosbeck and from there to Tirlemont. By this time the opposing armies had arrived within a day's march of each other. The King advanced in the hope of drawing Luxemburg on to a general engagement, but the Marshal declined to give him battle and retired behind the Mehayne (Main), where he could remain in comparative security.

Then followed a period of inactivity due in great measure to weather conditions, to be followed by another which is described by Lord Wolseley in his Life of the Duke of Marlborough as one of " marches and countermarches, of lines and entrenchments from behind which the two armies watched each other."

While this manœuvring was taking place it occurred to the King that it might be possible to cut off the French line of communication between the Scheldt and the Lys by crossing the former river at Pont d'Espierre. To effect his purpose he dispatched the Elector of Bavaria to secure that passage, while he with the remainder of the army followed a day's march in the rear. Unfortunately timely notice of this move reached Luxemburg, who immediately dispatched Marshal

Boufflers with a strong body of cavalry and infantry with orders to use every endeavour to reach the spot before the Elector. This he succeeded in doing. Luxemburg with the rest of the army followed in the track of the Marshal as fast as circumstances would admit.

When William saw that his scheme for crossing the Scheldt before the French army had been frustrated, he wheeled about and crossed that river lower down at Oudenarde, encamping there pending the return of the heavy baggage which had been sent to Brussels when the Elector made the dash referred to.

From Oudenarde he marched to Rousselaer, where he remained until the season was too far advanced to permit of further operations.

The recapture of Huy was the only success that attended the arms of the Allies during the campaign of 1694. The town, which contained a considerable quantity of siege material, was invested on the 15th of September. The garrison made a poor show of defence, but the citadel held out until the 27th, when it capitulated. On the King receiving news of its capture he directed the army to go into winter quarters. The 23rd repaired to Bruges.

The following officers only had permission to go to England for recruiting, or otherwise to be absent during the winter quarters: Captains George Morgan, James Jones, Francis Purefoy, James Genestet, Lieutenants John Parry, Evan Lloyd, John Dickens, Ensigns Abraham Booker, Daniel Whittingham, and Richard Hemming.

1695.

The year 1695 was ushered in most inauspiciously for the French, who suffered the irreparable loss of Marshal Luxemburg. This great commander, who was adored by both officers and men and who seemed to bear a charmed life, died of pleurisy on the 4th of January in his 68th year. He was succeeded by Marshal Villeroi, who was much more the soldier than the courtier.

The King embarked at Gravesend on the 13th of April, and on reaching Holland the following day proceeded to Loo, where he determined the dispositions of the Allied army for the ensuing campaign. His plan was to recover from Louis XIV the important fortress of Namur, and in endeavouring to do so to deceive the French by a series of feints into believing that his objective was of a totally different nature.

Namur is situated at the junction of the Sambre and the Meuse. It was well defended by ditches and ravelins, while its citadel was perched upon a lofty rock seemingly inaccessible. The fortifications had been constructed by the famous Dutch engineer Cohorn, and on its capture by the French in 1692 the yet more distinguished engineer Vauban had improved on his rival. In fact it was regarded by the French monarch and his Marshals as impregnable. Its capture would, therefore, add enormously to William's prestige.

The Confederates took the field with two armies. The main army was commanded by the King in person, with the Prince de Vaudemont as his second-in-command. The other was commanded by the Elector of Bavaria, with the Duke of Holstein-Ploen as his second.

The latter army, which was to all intents and purposes a corps, was directed to form a flying camp near Brussels, under pretence of covering that part of the country. What with the English contingent, now 30,000 strong, and those of England's Allies, the King had under him about 124,000 men.

The French Marshal could command hardly more than 100,000 men, as a large number were locked up in occupying the fortified lines from Namur to the sea, which Louis had constructed during the previous winter.

The 23rd was brigaded with the 5th, 7th, 18th, Collingwood's Regiment (afterwards disbanded), and La Melonière's Regiment of Huguenots on the British establishment, under the command of Brigadier Fitzpatrick. This brigade was attached to the main army, which began to concentrate between Ghent and Deynze on the 24th of April.

On the 2nd of June the army as a whole was ready to take the field. On the same day the main army marched from Arseele to Rousselaer, and on the following day to Beccalaer in the vicinity of the French lines between Ypres and the Lys.

While at the latter place the King directed the Duke of Würtemburg to proceed with eight battalions, including the 23rd, under Major-General Churchill, together with some artillery and a supply of pontoons, to threaten Fort Knocque. The Danish General Ellenberg, who had under him nine British battalions and a regiment of dragoons, was ordered to co-operate with Würtemburg.

On the 8th of June the latter commenced operations against the fort, which were continued until the 16th, when, in accordance with his instructions, he slipped off to Dixmude. Simultaneously the Elector of Bavaria was making a pretence of attacking the French lines on the Scheldt and the Lys.

The main army being still at Beccalaer, the King on the evening of the 13th of June, with a bodyguard of cavalry and grenadiers under Major-General La Melonière and Colonel Ingoldsby of the 23rd respectively, reconnoitred the French army, which then lay at Houthem on the Lys.

The King, ascertaining on the 20th that his design to draw all the French forces between the Scheldt had been successful, ordered Würtemburg and the Elector of Bavaria to march on Namur. At the same time Vaudemont, with 20,000 men, was directed to cover the country between Ghent and Bruges and keep Villeroi in play, which he succeeded in doing most effectively for several weeks, owing to his splendid spy system. Not a movement was made by the Marshal which was not forestalled by Vaudemont, owing to the accuracy of the information supplied by three spies in particular who acted in concert.

As all the necessary cannon, mortars, ammunition, etc., required for the siege had been collected together at a convenient spot, the King started for Namur.

When Villeroi's eyes were at last opened and he perceived that William's real object was the investment of Namur, he sent an urgent order to Marshal Boufflers, who had hitherto been occupied in observing the movements of the Elector of Bavaria, to proceed post-haste to Namur and endeavour to throw himself into the town before the investment was completed. This he was successful in doing, thereby augmenting the garrison to about 16,000 picked soldiers. Ample supplies of food and ammunition were stored in the town.

On the 21st of June the King arrived before its walls. The same day Würtemburg arrived on the scene with a force which included nine English battalions, the 23rd being one of the number.

On the 28th Major-General Ramsay arrived with sixteen battalions and Lord Cutts on the 1st of July with a further five battalions, which enabled the besiegers completely to surround the town. The division commanded by the King was posted north and east of it, the Elector of Bavaria's division lay to the west of it, the whole of the south side was occupied by the Brandenburgers.

As the siege-train had now arrived, no time was lost in opening the trenches. By the 3rd of July fire was opened upon the town and on works which the French had thrown up on what was known as the Bouge Hill. On the brow of this hill stood the Cocklé, which was a dismantled tower strongly fortified with high palisadoed works surrounding it. A covered way extended from here to the bastion Balart due east of the town.

By the 8th the trenches which were manned by the English troops had approached the outer works of the Cocklé. Thereupon it was decided to attempt that evening to carry the series of works by storm and seize the covered way. Accordingly at 7 p.m. two bodies of troops moved out to the assault. The one on the right, commanded by Major-General Ramsay, consisted of the Guards' Brigade, a detachment of fifteen grenadiers from every English regiment in the camp—the 23rd being one—and a Dutch battalion. The other body on the left consisted exclusively of Dutch troops.

The Guards' Brigade advancing steadily, despite a withering fire from the French, reserved theirs until the palisades were reached, when levelling their muskets through them they poured in a volley that staggered the defenders.

Taking advantage of their disorder, Ramsay called upon his men to break through the palisades, which they succeeded in doing, tearing them up for fear they might cause an obstruction in case of retreat. The first covered way was quickly captured. The French stoutly resisted, but the Guards being reinforced at this stage by the 14th and 16th Regiments of Foot, which emerged from the trenches, carried everything before them, and not only won the second covered way but actually pursued the enemy among their own batteries, many of the French flying for refuge to some stone pits on their right.

The Dutch regiment referred to wavered somewhat, but on receiving timely support it quickly re-formed and, advancing rapidly, took its share in the capture of the covered ways.

The Netherlands troops on the left encountered fierce opposition, but on being reinforced by the 1st Battalion of The Royal Scots and the 7th Fusiliers from the trenches, and in addition being supported by three battalions, one of which was the 23rd, carried all the works which formed their objective.

In this one evening's struggle 24 officers were killed, 34 wounded, and 4 taken prisoner. Of this number the 23rd had 2 officers killed. According to Mr. Cannon's record, their names were Captain John Hamilton and Lieutenant Jasaut. No such name as Jasaut appears in the Commission Registers of the period. If Mr. Cannon quotes the name correctly, he must have been either a foreign officer attached to the regiment, or else he was serving as a volunteer in the hope of receiving a permanent commission.

The efforts of the Allies were now concentrated upon pushing forward the trenches towards Porte St. Nicolas, facing Bouge Hill. The English worked on the slope of the hill while the Dutch broke ground in the direction of the flank of the gate. By the 15th of the month the English trenches had reached the bottom of the hill, which necessitated the surrender of the Balart bastion already referred to. Its guns were immediately turned upon the town.

The capture of the Bouge Hill enabled the besiegers to plant batteries both of guns and mortars upon it, which fired without intermission on the Porte St. Nicolas. This gate was defended by the bastion St. Nicolas on its left, and by the demi-bastion St. Roch on the Meuse, with a curtain connecting them. In front was a ravelin, and farther still a counterscarp.

On the following day the trenches had approached so close to the counterscarp that it was decided to lose no time in attacking it.

Accordingly at 4 p.m. the following day the attack began. Five hundred English grenadiers selected from all the regiments in camp, except the Guards, led the way, followed by two brigades under Colonel Selwyn and Lord George Hamilton. The first-named brigade consisted of the 23rd, 25th, and the regiments of Lauder and Saunderson. Major-General Ramsay was in chief command.

The grenadiers coolly marched up to the palisades and threw their grenades over them. The 23rd and Saunderson's regiment then advanced up the glacis under a galling fire. On reaching the top, the French sprang some small mines which caused the assailants to lose a little ground. Again they gallantly pressed forward and commenced to lodge woolsacks and gabions upon the palisades of the glacis adjoining the bastion of St. Nicolas. Unfortunately the enemy managed to set fire to the woolsacks, which, the *London Gazette* states, caused Colonel Ingoldsby's regiment to suffer very much, as they were exposed for a long time to the full fire of the besieged.

The English tenaciously held their ground and effected a lodgment which necessitated the abandonment of the counterscarp by the French. In this action the 23rd lost Lieutenant Abraham Booker and Ensign Justinian Paget killed, and the following officers wounded: Captains Francis Purefoy, Jones, and David Stedman, Lieutenants Ogilvy, Henry Moor, Thomas Disney, Lloyd, and Ensigns John Patterson and William Johnson.

While the English batteries continued to fire upon the St. Nicolas bastion, the Dutch batteries played upon the demi-bastion St. Roch. During this fierce artillery duel both the English and Dutch extended their lodgments to such an extent that the besieged lost all hope of prolonging the defence. On the 24th the garrison hoisted the white flag and agreed to surrender the town.

The surrender of the town enabled the King to detach thirty battalions of the investing force, including the 23rd, and to send them to the relief of Vaudemont, who, by means of his intelligence, which never failed him, had learned that it was Villeroi's intention to march to Namur and en route to capture Brussels. Consequently he had so advantageously posted his army that, though much inferior to the French in numbers, it effectually barred their progress, but could not prevent them from bombarding the city.

On the way to relieve Vaudemont this detachment was joined by the Earl of Athlone at the head of some cavalry, and he took command of the whole force. On his reaching the then obscure village of Waterloo he became aware of the extent to which Vaudemont had been pressed by the enemy. Thereupon he hastened with ten battalions, one of which was the 23rd, to the relief of Vaudemont, and directed the rest to follow him as speedily as possible.

Villeroi, finding that the defences of Brussels were much stronger than he had anticipated, and on being apprised of the reinforcements under the Earl of Athlone that had joined Vaudemont's force, decided to raise the siege. Before doing so he subjected the city to thirty-six hours' continuous bombardment, " with red hot balls and shell." Whole streets were destroyed, and many fine buildings, churches, and convents were razed to the ground.

He then marched towards Namur in the hope of arriving in time to raise the siege of the citadel. At Soignies, however, he halted for several days pending the arrival of instructions from Paris, which enabled Vaudemont and Lord Athlone, who had started off for Namur on the relief of Brussels, to reach there ten days before him. On arriving within signalling distance of Namur he vainly probed the lines of the besiegers in the hope of discovering a weak spot through which he might break through. He was, therefore, perforce compelled to remain an unwilling spectator of the disaster which he intuitively felt to be imminent.

While these events were taking place the Elector of Bavaria with 20,000 men was rigorously carrying on the siege of the citadel, battering it with 160 siege guns and 50 mortars. So terrible was the effect of this never-ending storm of shot and shell upon the defenders that, despite all the advantages afforded by cover, in one day no less than three hundred of the garrison were either killed or wounded. Daily the trenches approached nearer and nearer to the doomed citadel, their progress being marked by the erection of fresh batteries.

On the 19th of August it was decided to make a general assault on the citadel upon the following day. Accordingly next morning, on a preconcerted signal being given, four storming parties advanced to the assault. One, led by Lord Cutts in person, consisted of a detachment of thirty-six men drawn from the grenadier company of the 23rd and from every other British regiment in the force, supported by two regiments, the 17th and Mackay's regiment, with the 18th and Buchan's regiment in reserve. Its task was to attack the counter-scarp and breach of the fort Terra Nova. Another party of 3,000 Bavarians and Spaniards under the direction of the Elector of Bavaria was ordered to attack the left of the Cohorn, which lay to the right and somewhat in the rear of the Terra Nova. A third party, consisting of 2,000 Brandenburgers and Hessians, under the direction of Prince Nassau-Saarbruck, was directed to advance against the right of the Cohorn. The fourth storming party, consisting of 2,000 Dutch troops, under Prince Holstein-Ploen, was ordered to attack the covered way about the Devil's House, which was situated slightly to the right and rear of the Terra Nova. Lord Cutts's party had to traverse an open space about 900 yards in length before the breach of the Terra Nova could be reached.

Under a galling fire the grenadiers and the two supporting regiments rapidly advanced, but, being mown down in masses, were obliged to fall back before half the distance had been traversed.

The 18th Regiment, which had been in reserve within the walls of Salsine Abbey, then made a rush for the breach and succeeded in getting within it. Fighting with incredible fury, it succeeded in planting its colours on the ramparts, only to find that the enemy had thrown up an entrenchment inside the breach which was unassailable. As they could progress no farther, Lord Cutts gave the order to retire. While they were doing so he formed the desperate resolve to call for 200 volunteers as a forlorn hope to endeavour to effect a lodgment in the covered way. His appeal was instantly responded to. Under the leadership of Lieutenant Cockle, of Mackay's regiment, the heroic band succeeded in beating the enemy back on the covered way and then trained their own guns upon the foe. The other storming parties succeeded, despite the most desperate resistance, in effecting lodgments to the extent of a mile along the covered way.

In this assault the 23rd lost one officer killed, Captain John Parry, of the grenadier company.

Marshal Boufflers, perceiving the extent of the lodgment that had been made and opining that another would soon be attempted which, if successful, would mean disaster to the garrison, signalled from the top of the citadel to Villeroi for succour. The answer of the latter was to set fire to his camp, which was an intimation to Boufflers to make the best terms possible.

On the 23rd of August negotiations were entered into for the surrender of the citadel. The stipulations of the Allies were eventually accepted by Boufflers, who, on the 26th, marched out at the head of a force variously estimated at from 5,000 to 8,000 men, with colours flying, drums beating, six pieces of cannon and as many covered waggons, under safe-conduct to Dinant. The honour of taking possession of the gates was assigned to the 23rd as a mark of appreciation of its services.

The French left behind them 109 cannon. Their loss during the siege was over 6,000, while that of the Allies was approximately 9,000. This included "Ingoldsby 92 morts, 123 blessés," as shown in the official return of casualties.

When the news of the capture of the citadel reached London, the Tower guns were fired, numerous bonfires were lit, and illuminations were general throughout the city. Nor were the garrison towns backward in expressing their joy. For instance, the *London Gazette* records that on the 1st of September the Lieutenant-Governor of Portsmouth ordered the regiments in garrison to be drawn out on parade, where they gave several volleys of small shot, the pikemen having wisps of straw on the spears of their pikes which they set fire to one after another.

The following warrant shows that a gratuity was issued to the officers of the 23rd wounded at Namur:

"*12th Aug.* 1695.

"Our Will and Pleasure is that out of such moneys as are or shall come to your hands for contingent use, you pay unto Colonel Richard Ingoldsby the sume of one thousand gilders to be distributed to the respective officers of our regiment under his command who were wounded before the town of Namur, and for so doing this . . .

"Given at the Abby of Moloigne, before the castle of Namur, this 12th of August 1695, in the 7th year of Our reign."

On the 9th of February 1910 the regiment was permitted to add "NAMUR 1695" to the battle honours already inscribed on its colours.

An official return shows that on the 4th of September 1695 the following was the state of the 23rd:

"INGOLDSBY'S

8 malade au camp.
160 malade dans l'hospital.
480 capables à faire serveux.
650 effectifs aux prima plana.
65 vacants.
— perdus ou prisoniers.
— morts.
— desertez."

Nothing more was effected this campaign. Both armies went into winter quarters in October, the 23rd wintering at Bruges as heretofore.

1696.

The following warrant, dated the 2nd of January 1696, is interesting:

"Our Will and Pleasure is that out of such moneys as are or shall come to your hands for contingent uses, you pay unto Colonel Richard Ingoldsby ye summ of three hundred and thirty pounds which we are pleased to allow for raising one hundred and tenn recruits in the room of so many men of the regiment under his command killed at Knock and Namur ye last campagne, at the rate of three pounds a man, as also the further summ of one hundred and twenty five pounds in consideration of so many men wounded at the same time, making together four hundred and fifty five pounds. And for so doing . . ."

For the campaign of 1696 the French were able to put about 120,000 men into the field. This augmentation to their fighting strength was caused by Louis XIV patching up a peace with the

Duke of Savoy, which enabled him to withdraw an army corps from Italy and to send it to the Netherlands. Two French armies took the field. The main army under Villeroi was encamped between Menin and the Scheldt. A considerable army corps under Boufflers was encamped on the canal between Bruges and Ghent. The Allies were numerically inferior to the French, owing to several English battalions having been sent home, consequent upon a scare caused by the fear of a French invasion. They also started the campaign with two army corps. One of them, which was encamped near Ghent, was commanded by Vaudemont. The other, under the command of King William, kept a close watch upon the movements of Boufflers.

On the 9th of May Villeroi marched in a north-easterly direction along the River Lys, and on arriving at Deynze halted there, sending out foraging parties who scoured the surrounding country. In order to bar his progress it was necessary to take all possible steps to guard the line of the canals. For this purpose Major-General Ramsay was directed to take thirteen battalions drawn from the garrison of Bruges, one of which was the 23rd, together with four from the field force, and proceed to Bellem on the Ghent-Bruges Canal, with the object of protecting the ford there. Twenty-five battalions in addition were employed along the canal in throwing up breastworks. On the 29th of May the King reviewed the 23rd and other regiments stationed at Bellem, and "found them compleat and in very good order."

The King, being satisfied with the arrangements that had been made to safeguard the canal, left Mariekirk on the 1st of June with a force of cavalry and infantry and marched as far as Wavre. Before leaving Mariekirk he promoted several officers to the rank of Brigadier, one of those so favoured being Colonel Ingoldsby, whose commission was dated 1st of June.

From Wavre he marched to Gembloux, and halted there to await the arrival of the Landgrave of Hesse with 15,000 troops, his object being when augmented to force the Sambre, and make his way on to French soil in the rear of Charleroi. On being informed of the approach of the Landgrave he advanced to Sombref, where they joined forces.

The King, finding that Boufflers's dispositions had been too skilfully made to permit of his achieving his object, marched to Nivelles and thence to Ath and Grammont, reaching the latter place on the 14th of August, where he remained. In the meantime Vaudemont and Villeroi had been engaged in intently watching each other's movements on the line of the Ostend-Bruges Canals. Boufflers, failing to find an opportunity for forcing the canals, abandoned the idea and retired to Wynendael on the 1st of September. In a few days both armies went into winter quarters.

Thus ended this bloodless campaign of 1696!

1697.

For the campaign of 1697—happily the concluding one in this bloody, most costly, and for all practical purposes useless war in Flanders—both armies began to take the field in April. The French monarch, although greatly hampered by the want of money, succeeded in placing an army of about 145,000 men in the field under Marshals Villeroi, Boufflers, and Catanat. Villeroi was in command of the main army. Boufflers was responsible for an army corps which was detailed for flying duties. Catanat was directed to besiege the town of Ath, situated about twelve miles to the north-east of Mons.

The advent of spring enabled the Allies to put the finishing touches to a line of defence that extended from Ostend to Namur, taking in Bruges and Brussels.

For its protection the Elector of Bavaria pitched his camp at Deynze. The main Confederate army, about 100,000 strong, rendezvoused at Bois Seigneur Issaau. The investment of Ath was commenced on the 5th of May, and by the 11th the besiegers had opened trenches. Three days later Vaudemont, who was in temporary command of the main army, marched from Bois Seigneur Issaau to Hal, where he was joined by King William, who took command. Brigadier Ingoldsby's brigade, which consisted of the 16th, 18th, 23rd, and Colonel Walter Colyear's regiment, formed part of the main army.

The King was most anxious to relieve Ath, and with that object in view marched to St. Quentin Lennock near Ninove, where he was joined by about 11,000 Germans. On reaching there he ascertained that two armies under Villeroi and Boufflers respectively were covering the siege of that town. Under these circumstances he came to the conclusion that it would be impracticable to relieve Ath. Thereupon he marched to Genappe. On the 28th of May Ath surrendered with the honours of war. The two French Marshals were now free to carry out a scheme which they had concocted—a joint march on Brussels.

Tidings of ominous movements on their part, which were speedily

I—4

conveyed to the King, caused him to come to the conclusion that it was their intention to make a dash for that city. Without a moment's delay he decided to march on Brussels. Pushing on all through the night, he reached the strong camp of Anderlecht next morning. Hasty entrenchments were thrown up which effectually protected both the city and the army. When the Marshals a few hours later reached the heights overlooking Anderlecht and saw the Allied army strongly posted there, they knew the game was up.

This was the last act in the drama. Negotiations for peace which had been proceeding for several weeks past resulted in the Peace of Ryswick, which was signed on the 11th of September.

The following is the state of two companies that were performing garrison duty during August 1697:

The Company of Lieutenant-Colonel de Montargey.—3 sergeants, 3 corporals, 2 drummers, 49 soldiers present, 4 sick, 1 absent in camp, 5 servants, 9 soldiers wanting.

The Company of Captain Jones.—3 sergeants, 3 corporals, 2 drummers, 49 soldiers present, none sick, 3 absent in camp, 5 servants, 3 soldiers wanting.

No sooner was peace concluded than a reduction was made in the 23rd, in common with all other regiments that were not disbanded. The order for this reduction, which is dated the 25th of November 1697, to take effect "four days from 9th December" in the case of the 23rd, lays down that the establishment per company shall be "42 privates (servants included), 2 sergts, 3 corpls, 1 drum (the company of grenadiers excepted, wherein 3 sergts, 2 drums are to be continued)." Each reduced sergeant, drummer, or private soldier was permitted to carry away with him his clothes, belt, knapsack, and was paid three shillings for his sword; in addition fourteen days' subsistence and a pass home were granted.

A return presented to Parliament shows that a sum of £205 8s. was paid to Brigadier Ingoldsby for disbursement to discharged N.C.O.s and men. Another return shows that down to February 1697 no less a sum than £2,587 9s. 7¾d. was due to the 23rd for subsistence in Flanders, and also £11,083 1s. as arrears of pay.

At the beginning of December the regiment was ordered to return to England. The headquarters and nine companies landed at Gravesend on the 16th of that month and marched to Dartford, Crayford, Erith, and Southwark. The other four companies landed at Deptford and also marched to Southwark.

From there the whole regiment marched as follows: six companies to Bristol and Bedminster, four to Gloucester, one to Ledbury Wickware, one to Minchinghampton and Stroud, and one to Bath.

1698.

On the 8th of February the several companies of the regiment were directed to march to Bristol to embark for Ireland. On arriving at Waterford, they marched to Clonmel and remained there until the 17th of March, when two companies were ordered to Tralee, two to Ardfert, one to Dingle, one to Ross Castle, Killarney, two to Valentia, one to Newmarket, one to Askeaton, one to Clonakilty, one to Bantry, and one to Crookhaven.

On the 5th of March the Lords Justices of Ireland were directed to deliver over to Brigadier Ingoldsby a company of Brudenell's regiment, recently disbanded, which happened to be in Ireland, the intention being to bring the 23rd up to strength.

On the 31st of March all the companies were directed to march to Limerick except the company at Ross Castle, which was to remain there until relieved. An officer and eighteen men were directed to proceed to Bilboa, Co. Limerick, where they remained until recalled to headquarters on the 31st of May. An officer and twenty men were instructed to proceed to Abington and Gorteen. On the 26th of May a warrant was issued for the delivery of half a barrel of powder to each company, being "their usual quantity for watch ammunition for six months." On the 30th of June Brigadier-General Ingoldsby was directed "to take one private man out of every [sic] twelve companies of the regiment of foot under his command, to be added to the grenadiers in same regiment to increase the company to the number of twelve men more than now."

On the 9th of July the ordnance storekeeper at Limerick was ordered to deliver "six firelocks for the use of said regiment."

On the 27th of July the company at Askeaton and Rathkeale, and the detachments at Abington, Gorteen, and Madra, were directed to join the regiment.

By an order dated the 28th of July 1698 regiments of foot were to be reduced by one company consisting of Captain, Lieutenant, Ensign or Second Lieutenant, 2 sergeants, 2 corporals, 1 drummer, and 40 private soldiers. In consequence of this reduction the sum of

£370 17s. 5d., as shown by the Parliamentary Return on the subject, was disbursed to the discharged non-commissioned officers and men of the 23rd.

On the occasion of the Lords Justices of Ireland visiting Limerick on the 1st of August they reviewed, as was customary, the regiments then quartered there, which were those of Brigadier Tiffin and Brigadier Ingoldsby.

On the 1st of August orders were issued for the regiment to march from Limerick to Drogheda. Six companies left on the 8th, marching to Birr on the 10th, Mullingar the 12th, and Trim the 13th, where they rested a day and arrived at Drogheda on the 16th. The other seven companies also left on the 8th, marching to Nenagh on the 10th, Athy the 13th, where they rested a day, and Maynooth the 17th. On the following day one company marched to Balrothery, where it remained, another to Rush, and another to Swords. The remaining four companies proceeded to Navan on the 18th, and arrived at Drogheda on the 22nd. Two of these companies remained there. One of the other two companies marched on the 23rd to Dunleer, and the remaining company proceeded to Carlingford, where it arrived on the 25th.

By an order dated the 22nd of August certain officers of Colonel John Mitchelburne's regiment (lately disbanded) were to be incorporated into the regiments of Sir Matthew Bridges and Brigadier Ingoldsby.

On the 25th of August a sergeant and ten men were instructed to guard a redoubt at Virginia, Co. Cavan, and another detachment, consisting of a sergeant and ten men, was directed to guard a redoubt at Four Mile Bridge in the Newry Mountains.

At the end of August Brigadier Ingoldsby was directed " not to admit any new men."

On the 10th of October a sergeant, corporal, and twelve men were sent to Dundalk to assist in apprehending " Rapparees," and to be under the command of Cornet Andrew Knox. On the 3rd of November a like detachment was sent from the company at Dunleer to relieve the one already at Dundalk.

Mr. William Fownes, of the city of Dublin, was appointed in November clothier to the regiment.

1699.

On the 20th of March the establishment of the regiment was shown as "Ingoldsby's 11 comps, 36 commission officers, 56 non-commission officers, private men 396, together 488."

On the 2nd of July the regiment was ordered to hold itself in readiness to march to Dublin, the sheriffs and seneschals being directed to provide quarters for officers and men in their respective "Liberties."

On the 27th the company at Carlingford marched to Dundalk and from there to Drogheda, which was reached on the 31st. The company at Dunleer reached Drogheda on the 29th, and together with the eight companies already quartered there and the one from Carlingford marched to Dublin, which was reached on the 2nd of August. The three companies at Balrothery, Rush, and Swords also reached there the same day.

On the 28th of September a warrant was issued for the payment to non-commissioned officers and men of Brigadier Ingoldsby's regiment of "an additional allowance of one penny per day for doing duty in Dublin."

A Parliamentary Return of 1699 contains the names of several foreigners—both officers and men—whom it was proposed to naturalise for good service. Amongst them appears the name of Charles Richard of Ingoldsby's regiment, who had received a commission as ensign in 1696.

1700.

On the 11th of July eleven unserviceable drums were returned to store, a like number being issued to replace them.

On the 15th of August the following movements of the companies of the regiment took place:

Three companies marched to Drogheda on the 16th, Newry the 20th, Antrim the 24th, Ballymoney the 27th, where one company remained, and the other two proceeded the next day to Coleraine.

Four companies marched to Drogheda on the 17th, Armagh the 22nd, Omagh the 27th, reaching Londonderry Barracks on the 29th.

Three companies marched to Drogheda on the 19th, Dundalk the 22nd, Armagh the 24th, Omagh the 27th, Strabane the 28th. From there one of them marched to Letterkenny; the others proceeded to Londonderry, where they arrived on the 29th.

On the 19th of December the company at Ballymoney and the two at Coleraine were ordered to go into barracks on the 26th of that month. The company at Letterkenny was ordered to march to the barrack at Culmore Fort, and to reach there on the 30th.

The war-clouds that hung so heavily over Flanders for a number of years were dispersed, as already shown, by the Peace of Ryswick, but, after what turned out to be a mere lull in the storm, again collected ominously in 1700. The burning question which then agitated the minds of the leading potentates in Europe was who should succeed the imbecile and childless King Charles II of Spain.

In March of that year, when it was noised abroad that Charles intended to nominate Philip Duke of Anjou, the grandson of Louis XIV, as his successor, the latter solemnly renounced all rights to the Spanish throne, and was, moreover, a signatory to a partition treaty whereby England, France, and Holland arranged that the Archduke Charles, the second son of the Emperor of Austria, should receive the crown of Spain together with Spanish Flanders.

France was to be the gainer by absorbing the Spanish territories in Northern Italy, while England and Holland, being essentially commercial nations, were to be compensated by receiving valuable trading privileges in the New World.

Charles II died in November 1700. Before his decease he willed his throne to Philip of Anjou, with the consent of his Council. Treating the partition treaty as a "scrap of paper," Louis, after well-feigned hesitation, accepted the throne for his grandson under the title of Philip V.

At the outset the people of England were indifferent as to who should sit upon the Spanish throne, but when they became aware that valuable trading monopolies were being granted by Spain to French companies, their commercial instincts were aroused, with the result that public opinion inclined towards war with France. Louis, perceiving that neither King William nor the United Provinces appeared to be disposed to recognise his grandson, with characteristic energy speedily brought matters to a crisis. Under previous treaties eight fortresses in Spanish Flanders were garrisoned by the Dutch. These he promptly seized without any declaration of war, and held 15,000 of Holland's picked troops prisoners of war. Thereupon that country promptly appealed to Great Britain for succour in the shape of the 10,000 foot which, by a defensive treaty of 1677, England was bound to furnish for the protection of the Low Countries.

In response to this appeal Parliament voted a force of 40,000 men, of whom 18,000 were to be English and the rest mercenaries.

King William, than whom nobody was more fully alive to the vaulting ambition and craftiness of the " Most Christian King " Louis XIV and the danger to the preservation of peace arising therefrom, had from time to time protested against the reductions that, in deference to public feeling, had been made in the English standing army since the Peace of Ryswick, and he now found himself, by the irony of fate, saddled with the unenviable task of again bringing regiments up to war strength.

The disbanded veterans of the late war, who had been shamefully treated in the matter of arrears of pay, displayed the greatest reluctance to rejoin the colours. It was only by largely increasing the levy money and sweeping all sorts of undesirables into the ranks that regiments could be brought up to their proper strength.

1701.

Twelve regiments, including the 23rd, that were stationed in Ireland, were ordered to prepare to embark at Cork for Flanders.

By an order dated the 20th of May 1701 the 23rd was directed to march to Cork. Five companies left Londonderry on the 26th, reaching Clogher on the 29th, where they found an order awaiting them to march to Carrickfergus for embarkation to the Continent.

Consequently they marched to Tanderagee on the 31st of May, rested there one day, and proceeded to Lurgan on the 2nd of June, Belfast the 4th, and Carrickfergus the 5th. The other five companies—three of which were at Coleraine, one at Londonderry, and one at Culmore—assembled at Omagh on the 30th of May, where they also found an order awaiting their arrival directing them to march to Carrickfergus. They reached Portadown on the 2nd of June, Belfast the 5th, Carrickfergus the 6th, and there embarked for Flanders with the 16th Regiment as follows:

Four companies of the 23rd on board H.M.S. *Chatham.*

Four companies of the 23rd on board H.M.S. *Jersey.*

Two companies of the 23rd on board H.M.S. *Worcester.*

The 16th Regiment embarked on H.M.S. *Worcester, Deptford,* and *Portland.*

The Squadron, which was under the command of Commodore Edward Whitaker, passed Holyhead on the 17th, Land's End on the 22nd, Portland the 24th, the Goodwins the 27th, disembarking the regiments at Helvoetsluys on the 2nd of July.

The following was the state of the regiment on embarkation:

"An account of what officers and soldiers belonging to Brigadier Ingoldsby's Regiment shipt on board the men of warr riding in Carrickfergus Bay the 11 of June 1701."

—	Captains.	Lieuts.	Ensigns.	Sergts.	Corporals.	Drums.	Centinels.	Total.
Brigadier's Co.	1	—	—	1	2	1	28	
Lt.-Col. Co.	1	1	—	1	2	1	33	
Major's Co.	1	1	1	1	1	1	38	
Capt. Jones' Co.	—	—	—	2	2	1	26	
,, Purefoy Co.	1	1	1	1	2	1	32	
,, Bennett Co.	—	1	—	1	2	1	28	
,, Lee Co.	—	—	—	1	2	1	25	
,, Mountford Co.	1	—	1	2	2	1	30	
,, Eyme Co.	1	—	1	1	2	1	34	
,, Morgan Co.	1	—	—	1	2	1	21	
	7	4	4	12	19	10	295	351

On the 30th of June the expeditionary force reached Holland. The 23rd, on landing, was told off to garrison Worcum under the command of Brigadier Ingoldsby. The remainder of the force was quartered at Heusden, Breda, and Gorcum, the whole being under the command of the Earl of Marlborough, who on the 1st of June had been appointed by King William Commander-in-Chief of the British forces in the Low Countries.

The King and Marlborough embarked at Margate on the 1st of July, and reached the Hague two days later.

Next month the 23rd was augmented by two companies, one under Captain David Stedman, with Mathew Pennyfeather as Lieutenant and William Sanderson as Ensign; the other under Captain Perkins Vaughan, with Hugh Smyth as Lieutenant and Thomas Vincent as Ensign.

On the 16th of September the 23rd marched to Breda Heath, and on the 21st of that month, together with the rest of the troops, including some Dutch regiments encamped in the neighbourhood, were reviewed by the King. His Majesty, accompanied by the Earl of Marlborough, Lord Athlone, and Overkirk, the Dutch Commander, rode down the lines, and though so weak that he could barely sit his horse, his very presence infused confidence into his troops, many of whom had served under him in previous campaigns.

As the season was then too far advanced for active operations, the troops were ordered back to their quarters and the King returned to London.

1702.

The death of King William, which occurred on the 8th of March, produced no change in the policy of the country. Queen Anne was in favour of the vigorous prosecution of the war, and with this object in view appointed the Earl of Marlborough Captain-General of the forces, both at home and in Holland.

On the 10th of March the British troops at Breda and the surrounding country broke up camp and marched to Rosendahl, where they were joined by a body of Dutch troops under Lord Athlone, who commanded the Allied army in the absence of Marlborough. The united force left Rosendahl on the 13th of April and marched to Cranenburg, which was about ten miles from Nimeguen, with the dual object of covering the siege of Kaiserswörth, which had been undertaken by the Dutch, and preserving its own communications with Nimeguen. The Duke of Burgundy, who had advanced with the object of relieving Kaiserswörth, perceiving the impossibility of succeeding in his object, determined to fall suddenly upon the small army under Athlone. With great secrecy he got almost within striking distance before his advance was discovered. The proximity of the enemy caused orders to be immediately issued for the Allied army to strike tents and make for Nimeguen. Lord Athlone, at the head of the cavalry, kept in the rear of the infantry, and held the enemy in check until the army was safely within the outworks of the town.

After much wrangling among the Allies, Marlborough was appointed Commander-in-Chief of the Allied forces. He left the Hague on the 21st of June for Nimeguen. On arrival there he concentrated his army, which brought its strength to over 60,000 men.

From the outset his movements were greatly hampered by the presence of two Dutch civilian deputies, who, according to the custom of that country, were always at the elbow of the commander in the capacity of advisers. The two parasitic individuals who, as events proved, sorely tried the temper and patience of Marlborough, were timid to a degree, fearful of risking a pitched battle, and strongly in favour of besieging each fortress and gradually pushing the enemy out of the country.

Such a policy was gall and wormwood to a man of the Commander-in-Chief's temperament. On three occasions during the following six weeks by bold and skilful manœuvres he had it in his power to inflict upon Boufflers what would probably have been a serious reverse. Each time he was thwarted by his Dutch counsellors. In disgust he resolved to confine his efforts to reducing the fortresses on the Meuse.

Early in August, when the Allied army lay at Peer, the British infantry was formed into three brigades under Brigadiers Withers, Hamilton, and Stanley respectively. The 23rd was attached to the brigade commanded by the first-mentioned general officer, which formed part of the covering army during the siege of Venloo in August and September.

After reducing Stevenswaert, Maeseyk, and Ruremonde, Marlborough determined to invest Liège. Boufflers, who commanded the French army in the absence of the Duke of Burgundy, on learning that the whole Confederate army was marching from Petersburg in the direction of Liège, pressed forward with the object of preventing it from falling into the hands of the Allies. Great, however, was his chagrin when, on nearing Liège, he beheld Marlborough's army drawn up between him and the town. Sullenly he withdrew, leaving it to its fate. The town quickly surrendered, but the citadel refused to capitulate. It was invested on the 1st of October, and a practicable breach made by the evening of the 11th. Thereupon Marlborough offered the besieged favourable terms, which were refused. Next day a general assault by eight battalions and one thousand grenadiers, including those of the 23rd, took place about noon, and in less than an hour the citadel was carried. The bravery of the storming troops was specially referred to by Marlborough in a letter from him to the Earl of Nottingham dated the 23rd of October 1702, in which he remarks: " By the extraordinary bravery of the officers and soldiers, the citadel has been carried by storm."

Shortly after the reduction of Liège all the British troops were ordered back to winter quarters in Holland.

On the 14th of December Marlborough, who had returned to London, was created Marquis of Blandford and Duke of Marlborough, in recognition of the splendid service he had rendered to the Allied cause during the campaign of 1702.

In the autumn the strength of each British regiment employed in the Low Countries was raised to 938 exclusive of officers. In a list of the forces in Holland in 1702, preserved in the British Museum, the 23rd is shown as consisting of 44 commission officers, 104 non-commission officers, and 736 private men.

The following is an extract from the *Daily Courant* of the 15th of December 1702: "Major General Ingoldsby's Regiment is to be formed into a regiment of Fusiliers, and will be called the Welsh Regiment of Fusiliers."

Fusilier regiments were originally raised with the object of protecting the artillery, for which purpose it was necessary that they should be lightly armed and quick loaders. The three first regiments so designated were the 7th (Royal Fusiliers), 21st (North British Fusiliers), and the 23rd (Royal Welch Fusiliers). Fusilier regiments were distinguished in several ways from other line regiments. In the first place, they did not have "colours" or "ensigns" to each company; consequently the title of ensign or colour-bearer was not given to the junior subalterns, but having, in consequence of the peculiar services they were called upon to perform, a care and responsibility equal to that of a lieutenant, both the subaltern officers of each company were styled "1st lieutenants" and "2nd lieutenants." In the case of the Royal Fusiliers, however, no such distinction was made, there being only "lieutenants." The officers were armed with a light fusil instead of a pike or espontoon. All the companies wore caps of the pattern of, but not so high as, those of the grenadier companies of line regiments. Their armament consisted of fusils with slings, cartridge boxes, swords, and bayonets. The fusil was shorter and of less calibre than the musket, and in consequence a handier weapon: it was fitted with a flint lock, and fired from the shoulder.

1703.

Owing to an augmentation having been made in the 23rd, the following additional arms were requisitioned from the Master-General of the Ordnance in January 1703:

"Snaphance Musquets . . 83
Cartouche Boxes . . . 83
Halberts 12
Drums 2
Hatchetts . . . . 6."

For the campaign of 1703 Marlborough arrived at the Hague on the 6th of March, and arranged with the States-General what operations were to be undertaken that year.

The British and Dutch troops were ordered to concentrate early in April at Maestricht, under the command of the Dutch Marshal Overkirk, who had taken the place of the recently deceased Lord Athlone.

Marlborough, with the Prussian, Hanoverian, and Hessian contingents, undertook the siege of Bonn. On the 8th of April Brigadier-General Withers's brigade (composed of the 1st Guards and five marching regiments of foot, including the 23rd) left its winter quarters at Breda, and on arriving at Aerschot, where the army corps assembled, formed part of the division commanded by Lieutenant-General Charles Churchill. On leaving there it proceeded to Ruremonde, and thence to Maeseyk. On reaching the latter place, Overkirk, ascertaining from his intelligence that it was the intention of Marshal Villeroi to intercept his advance on Maestricht, made a forced march which completely upset the Marshal's plan. Villeroi, being aware of the fact that Marlborough was occupied with the siege of Bonn, and knowing that the force commanded by Overkirk was inferior to him in numbers, continued his advance and appeared before Maestricht on the 3rd of May. Finding, however, that the Allies were too strongly entrenched for him to venture on an attack, he withdrew his army to Tongres. The surrender of Bonn on the 14th of May enabled Marlborough to join hands with Overkirk six days later. The united force, consisting of 136 squadrons and 66 battalions, was then reviewed by both of these commanders.

During the next three weeks Marlborough tried in vain to draw the French from their strongly fortified lines. He thereupon determined to make a dash for Antwerp, which he assumed was then, in accordance with his instructions, being lightly invested by two detachments acting in concert under the command of the Dutch Generals Cohorn and Opdam respectively. The former, however, disobeying his orders, made a raid into West Flanders, leaving Opdam's detachment entirely unsupported at Eckeren.

On the 15th of June Marlborough suddenly broke up his camp and raced for Antwerp. Villeroi, guessing his intention, followed suit, and made strenuous efforts to outstrip him. While on the march Marlborough, hearing of Opdam's precarious position, sent him urgent orders to retire, which he ignored, to his cost, for Villeroi, on learning how matters stood, detached a force under Boufflers to fall upon him.

The latter, assisted by the garrison of Antwerp, vigorously set upon Opdam. Although the Dutch gallantly stood their ground for some hours under Slangenberg, the second-in-command—their leader having fled in panic to Breda—they were eventually obliged to retreat, having suffered huge losses.

Marlborough pushed forward by forced marches, but arrived on the scene too late to avert disaster.

Despairing of success in any other undertaking this season, owing to jealousies among the Dutch commanders, Marlborough returned to the Meuse and contented himself with laying siege to Huy and Limberg in succession, both of which he succeeded in reducing. At the siege of the former the 23rd formed part of the covering force. Nothing further was attempted this year. General Churchill's division marched back to winter quarters in Dutch Brabant via Peer and Aerschot.

1704.

In February of this memorable year the 23rd, in common with the other British regiments in Brabant, furnished a detachment of 300 men for garrison duty at Maestricht.

During the winter Louis XIV had devised a scheme for uniting his troops with those of the Elector of Bavaria in the Black Forest. On the junction of the armies being effected, the Franco-Bavarian army was to march with all speed on Vienna, with the object of deposing the Emperor and placing the Elector on the vacant throne. This task was assigned to Marshal Tallard, while Marshal Villeroi was to remain in the Netherlands with the object of preventing reinforcements being sent to the Emperor.

Marlborough, who had most fortunately managed to obtain timely information of this project, resolved to move the greater part of his army to the banks of the Danube to block the advance of Tallard's army.

In order to ensure the success of this counter-movement it was essential that it should be kept a close secret until Marlborough's plan had fully matured. With this object in view the States-General were informed by the Duke that the forthcoming campaign would be conducted in the valley of the Moselle, Overkirk being left with a small force in the Low Countries to observe the movements of Villeroi. News of this simulated plan of campaign reached the ears of the

French in due course, which was what Marlborough counted upon for the furtherance of his scheme.

On the 24th of April the troops left their winter quarters, and, marching to the Meuse at Ruremonde, crossed the river there by a bridge of boats that had been constructed for the purpose. The 23rd, which had wintered at Breda, formed, for this campaign, part of the brigade under the command of Brigadier Ferguson. From Ruremonde Ferguson's brigade marched to Maestricht, and from there to Bedburg near Juliers, where the army assembled and was reviewed by Marlborough.

On the 9th of May he started on his memorable march. Proceeding up the Rhine until he arrived at Bonn, he halted there for a couple of days in order to lend colour to the Moselle campaign deception. He then marched with all speed to Coblentz, where, to the great surprise of his own troops and particularly of the French, instead of following the course of the Moselle he crossed the Rhine by a bridge of boats and continued his march to Mayence. Hastening the march of his infantry in order to counteract Tallard's movements, he crossed and recrossed the Neckar, but halted at Mannheim, where he was joined by Prince Eugene of Savoy.

Three days later they were joined by Prince Louis of Baden with a contingent of his troops. The trio then arranged that Prince Eugene should remain on the Rhine to watch the movements of Tallard, and that the main army, under Marlborough and Prince Louis, who were to command on alternate days, should seek out and attack the Franco-Bavarian army under the Elector and Marshal Marsin. Thereupon Marlborough resumed his march, and on reaching Ulm was informed that the Elector was fortifying the formidable height of Schellenberg adjoining Donauwörth on the left bank of the Danube. At the same time he ascertained that reinforcements were being collected together to strengthen the Elector. He therefore determined to storm that height without a moment's delay.

Six thousand infantry, inclusive of the 23rd, were detailed for the assault, and were placed under the command of Lieutenant-General Goor, a brave and distinguished Dutch officer.

On his giving the order to advance, the columns marched steadily up the hill, despite a galling fire from the guns in the entrenchments, to which was added, as soon as the storming party came within range, a furious musketry fire which mowed them down. Unfortunately the leading men, who were furnished with fascines to throw into the ditch of the entrenchment, by mistake pitched them into the first hollow way they reached, the consequence being that when they struggled up to the actual lines of the entrenchment, they had no means of crossing them. This check caused a certain amount of hesitation, which elated the enemy, who sallied forth, hoping to clear the slope of the height by a bayonet charge.

The situation was saved by the 1st Guards, The Royal Scots, and the 23rd, who resolutely stood their ground and beat back the counter-attack.

The conflict had been proceeding for about half an hour when Prince Louis led the Imperialists against a portion of the works that had been somewhat denuded of troops to oppose the progress of the British and Dutch. The Imperial horse, quickly overcoming all opposition, penetrated the entrenchments, causing the enemy to retire with the utmost precipitation. This paved the way for taking the enemy in flank, which was soon accomplished, ending in his complete rout. Numbers of the fugitives were either killed by the pursuing squadrons or were drowned in the Danube. Fifteen brass field-pieces were taken, together with all the enemy's tents, baggage, and ammunition.

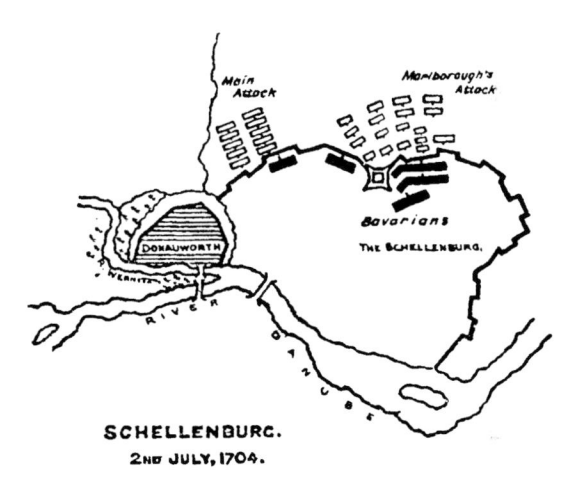

SCHELLENBURG.
2ND JULY, 1704.

The Duke of Marlborough, writing to Secretary Harley the day after the action, remarks that "The Battalion of Guards, one of my Lord Orkney's regiments and Ingoldsby's were those that suffered the most.... All our troops in general behaved themselves with great gallantry, and the English in particular have gained a great deal of honour in this action, which I believe was the warmest that has been known for many years."

The following were the casualties amongst the 23rd at Schellenberg on June 21/July 2:

Killed.

Captain Harrison.
    ,, Ogilvy.

Lieutenant Alex Fraser.
    ,, Constantine Egan.
    ,, Edward Price.

Wounded.

Colonel Joseph Sabine.
Lieutenant-Colonel — Jones.
Major Henry Ingoldsby.
Captain Isaac Eyme.
Lieutenant Isaac Jevereau.

Lieutenant — Katrick (? Carrick).
„ Charles Richard.
„ Stephen Cadroy.
„ Southwell Piggott.
„ William Aldy.
„ Griffith Jones.

Six sergeants killed, 6 wounded, 60 rank and file killed and 156 wounded.

Three days after this engagement took place the whole army crossed the Danube near Donauwörth, over several bridges that had been constructed for the purpose, and there encamped. Next day the Duke of Würtemburg, with the Danish horse, also crossed the Danube and rode into the camp.

On the 24th of June Marlborough invaded Bavaria by crossing the River Lech near Rain. Marching by easy stages, he reached Friedberg, where he encamped for several days with the dual object of watching the movements of the Elector of Bavaria, who was entrenched at Augsburg, and also covering the operations of Prince Louis, who undertook the siege of Ingoldstadt. On word being brought to Marlborough that Marshal Tallard was marching down the south bank of the Danube with the object of joining the Bavarians and then falling upon Prince Eugene, he broke up his camp and effected a junction with the troops of the latter on the small River Kessel, which empties itself into the Danube between Donauwörth and Hochstadt.

The Allied army, numbering 52,000 men, had now the choice of either attacking the Franco-Bavarian army, which was posted on rising ground near the Nebel, a sluggish stream that empties itself into the Danube at Blenheim, or falling back upon its base at Nuremberg. Marlborough was strongly in favour of the former course, which was cordially concurred in by Eugene. Their plan was for the latter to attack the Elector at Lutzingen while Marlborough, with the British troops and the rest of the Allies, crossed the Kessel and advanced against Blenheim and Oberglau.

To Lord Cutts was committed the task of attacking Blenheim. His column was formed into six lines. The first line consisted of the 1st Guards, the 10th, 21st, 23rd, and 24th Regiments under the command of Brigadier Row; the second line was composed of Hessians; the third was made up of four British regiments under the command of Brigadier Ferguson; the fourth consisted of Hanoverians. The remaining two lines were held in reserve.

At 12.45 p.m. on August 2/13 the first two lines started to cross the Nebel and encountered a heavy fire from the French guns. On reaching the opposite bank they halted to re-form under the shelter of a slight rise in the ground, leaving the Hessians there in reserve. Row's brigade, with that gallant officer leading it on foot, advanced steadily against the village. When it arrived within about thirty paces of the palisade that defended the place it was met by a withering fire that mowed down the ranks.

Row's instructions were that not a shot was to be fired until he struck the palings. The ranks quickly closed up and pressed forward. Row succeeded in reaching the palisade and drove his sword into it, whereupon his men poured in a volley and, rushing forward, endeavoured to force an entrance by uprooting the stakes. The defenders poured in a deadly volley from behind the palisade which wrought dreadful havoc. Row fell mortally wounded, and fully a third of the brigade were struck down. The survivors, thrown into disorder, began to retreat. While in the act of doing so three squadrons of French cavalry, which had galloped round the northern edge of the village, furiously charged the right flank. Pursuing their advantage too far, they were confronted by the Hessians, who gallantly held their ground and succeeded in repulsing them with the help of five English squadrons that opportunely arrived on the scene in response to Lord Cutts's appeal for a reinforcement of cavalry. The British horse in their ardour pursued too far, which exposed them to the flanking fire from Blenheim, causing them in turn to retire.

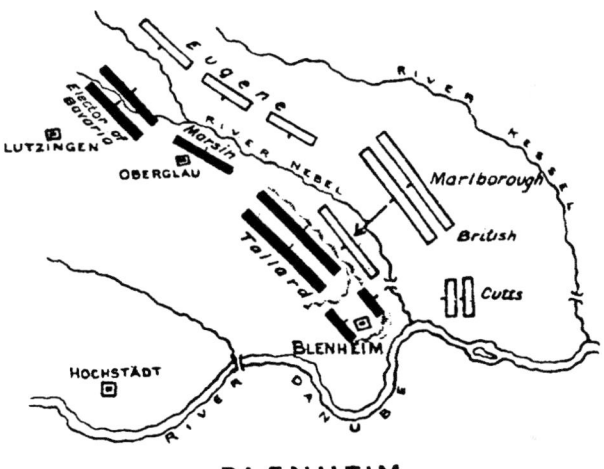

Ferguson's brigade, together with what was left of Row's, now advanced to the attack of the village, and though they succeeded in carrying the outskirts they were unable to penetrate farther, despite the fact that three times they hurled themselves against the palisade. Reluctantly they fell back, after suffering heavy loss, and sought cover under the shelter of the rising ground.

Marlborough, realising that Blenheim was too strongly held to be taken by assault, changed his plans and determined to make an attack on the centre with his main army. With great difficulty he managed eventually to get it safely across the Nebel. When this was effected he arranged his cavalry, about 8,000 sabres, in two lines, and causing the charge to be sounded he bore down upon the French infantry in irresistible style. The latter, consisting mainly of young soldiers, held their ground stoutly for a short time, but nothing could withstand the onslaught of Marlborough's horsemen, who rode them down, cutting great numbers in pieces.

This dashing charge cleared the ground for the advance of the main army under the command of General Charles Churchill. His infantry in two lines moved to the left and took up a position in the rear of Blenheim, thus effectually blocking the only avenue of escape left to the besieged. Hemmed in on all sides, and perceiving that Churchill had brought up his artillery to close range, they proposed a cessation of hostilities. While the French were wrangling among themselves over the terms of capitulation, General Churchill arrived upon the scene and informed them that if they did not at once surrender unconditionally he would renew the attack. Thereupon the garrison, which consisted of 26 battalions and 12 squadrons—in all about 12,000 men—surrendered at discretion.

The Imperialists under Prince Eugene, who were on the right of the Allied army, had been making desperate attempts to capture Oberglau and Lutzingen during the time that the events narrated had been taking place, but without success. Three successive attacks had been launched by Eugene, but all of them ended in failure, owing to the cavalry leaving the sturdy infantry in the lurch on each occasion. The collapse of Tallard's army, however, completely changed the situation. Marshal Marsin and the Elector, seeing that their position was no longer tenable, had no alternative but to retreat, pursued by Eugene for a short time only, owing to the night closing in and the danger of mistaking friend for foe.

The victory was most decisive. The enemy lost 100 guns, 24 mortars, 129 colours, 171 standards, 3,600 tents (many of which contained quantities of herbs and vegetables). Close to the Danube the carcasses of 100 fat oxen ready skinned were discovered, which must have furnished a substantial meal for many a tired and hungry soldier on that eventful night.

The enemy's loss in men was very heavy, about 40,000 killed, wounded, and prisoners, among the latter being Marshal Tallard and his staff. The casualties among the Allies amounted to 4,500 killed and 7,500 wounded. The British share was 670 killed and over 1,500 wounded, as stated by Mr. Fortescue in his *History of the British Army*.

The 23rd had the following officers killed and wounded at Blenheim on August 2/13:

Killed.

2nd Lieutenant Reginald Rowlands.

Wounded.

Major George Morgan.	1st Lieutenant Jno. Paterson.
Captain Henry Cookman.	2nd ,, Edm. Bayly.
1st Lieutenant Griffith Jones.	,, ,, Fleetwood Dormer.
,, ,, Hugh Smyth.[1]	Adjutant Jno. Powell.

On the day after the battle the English and Danish troops marched to Steinheim, where they remained four days. From there they proceeded to Seselingen, a short distance from Ulm, where they rested for several days while negotiations were being carried on with the Electress of Bavaria for the delivering up of Ulm and other strongly garrisoned places in Bavaria.

During this pourparler Ulm, which contained a garrison of nine battalions, was closely invested. Marlborough, seeing that the negotiations were likely to be protracted, left General Thurgen to carry on the siege of Ulm with the troops that had been earmarked to besiege Ingoldstadt, should it be necessary to do so, and moved his army by three different routes "for the ease of the country" towards the Rhine.

By the 28th of August the three columns had crossed the Rhine and concentrated at Philipsburg. The army then marched unmolested to Landau, greatly to the relief of Marlborough, who had expected to be strongly opposed by Villeroi.

On arriving there, the place was at once invested under the direction of Prince Louis of Baden, Marlborough and Prince Eugene

[1] Died of wounds received at Blenheim.

covering the siege from their camp at Wissemburg. While the siege dragged on, Marlborough decided to send four of his regiments to Holland for garrison duty to replace a like number of Dutch battalions that had been directed to march to the Moselle. Accordingly on the 2nd of September the four selected battalions, including the 23rd, marched from Wissemburg, under the command of Brigadier Meredith, to Germersheim on the Rhine, where they embarked, and on reaching Nimeguen landed there and proceeded to their respective destinations. That of the 23rd appears to have been Ruremonde, where they performed garrison duty for several months.

1705.

On the 1st of April, consequent upon the appointment of Lieutenant-General Richard Ingoldsby to the colonelcy of his former regiment, the 18th Royal Irish, the colonelcy of the 23rd was conferred upon Lieutenant-Colonel Joseph Sabine, who had been wounded at the battle of Schellenberg.

Marlborough's plan of campaign for this year was to divide his army into two columns. At the head of one he proposed to advance up the Moselle; the other, under the command of Prince Louis of Baden, was simultaneously to invade Lorraine and carry the war into the enemy's country.

Proceeding to Holland early in April, Marlborough lost no time in endeavouring to induce the cautious Dutch authorities to concur in the invasion of France, which he eventually succeeded in doing. No sooner had he secured their grudging acquiescence than he experienced the first taste of adverse fortune which was to make his cup very bitter during the forthcoming campaign. Prince Eugene, his great admirer and cordial co-operator in all his plans, was ordered to Northern Italy to check the progress of Marshal Vendôme.

On the 20th of April the English and Dutch troops began to march out of Holland and concentrated at Maestricht on the 1st of May, where, two days later, they were reviewed by Marlborough, who has left it on record that they "appeared all in good order." On the 4th of May the army started upon its march to the Moselle, and on arriving within eighteen miles of Trèves, encamped there for two days. It then resumed its march until it reached a position within three miles of the city, when it again encamped. At daybreak

MAJOR-GENERAL SABINE.

From a block of a mezzotint by I. Faber (after Kneller), supplied by " Country Life."

on the 22nd of May the English and Dutch troops advanced to the Moselle, near Igel, and halted there.

Resuming their march, they crossed the Saar near Consaarbrück on several improvised bridges. Proceeding the whole day through two great defiles, the head of the column arrived about 5 p.m. within less than a mile of Sierck on the Moselle. On the approach of the Allied army, the enemy retired precipitately to Ritel.

At Sierck Marlborough remained for the greater part of a month, daily expecting to be reinforced by the promised contingents of Prince Louis of Baden and the Emperor of Austria.

At the expiration of nine days of enforced inactivity he expressed his keen disappointment in a letter to St. John, the Secretary of State in London, in the following terms:

"The disappointments I have met with, and the time that is lost for want of the troops which were most concerned punctually to have complied with the measures concerted, together with the progress the enemies have taken the opportunity thereupon to make on the Meuse, give me the greatest uneasiness: and I am uncertain which way I shall be able to turn myself."

On the 6th of June he abandoned all hope of receiving the promised support, broke up his camp, and retired on the Meuse.

In the meantime Villeroi, assuming the offensive in the Low Countries, with 60,000 men captured Huy and invested the citadel of Liège. Thereupon the Dutch, in great alarm, begged Marlborough to hasten to the assistance of their Marshal Overkirk, who had been entrusted with the defence of Holland.

Although this gave the death-blow to his project of invading France, the Duke pushed forward by forced marches to join Overkirk, which caused Villeroi to withdraw from Liège and retire within his fortified lines on the Meuse. On the junction of their forces, a portion was detached to invest Huy, the garrison of which surrendered after a brief siege. A detachment of the 23rd formed part of the besieging force.

Marlborough then determined to force the formidable lines behind which Villeroi had ensconced himself. These lines, which it had taken three years to construct, extended from Namur to Antwerp along the Mehaigne, the two Geete Rivers, and the Demar to Antwerp.

The point selected for attack was close to the village of Neerhespen. In order to deceive Villeroi as to the real point of attack, Marlborough directed Overkirk to cross the Mehaigne and advance as if on Namur. Villeroi, falling into the trap, concentrated his forces several miles from the real point of attack. When Overkirk found he had effectually imposed on Villeroi, he retraced his steps with the object of reuniting with the main body.

Under cover of darkness the English troops advanced towards Villeroi's lines, but owing to a heavy fog did not reach them until daylight. The impetuosity of the infantry was so great that in a very short time they succeeded in establishing themselves within the entrenchments. They were speedily followed by the cavalry, who entered by hastily constructed bridges. The whole force had barely time to deploy before, the alarm being given, it was violently attacked by the Marquis d'Allegre with about 9,000 cavalry and infantry.

A desperate contest, lasting for two hours, ensued, which ended in the total defeat of the French. Their loss was considerable, especially in prisoners, which included d'Allegre. One regiment—that of Montluc—surrendered at discretion. The trophies taken were " ten pieces of cannon, eight whereof are with treble barrels, and a great many standards and colours."

Marlborough, writing the day after the battle to Secretary Harley, observes: " It is not possible to express the bravery and resolution which all the troops that engaged the enemy have shown on this occasion." The 23rd formed part of Ferguson's brigade in the storming of the lines and the subsequent engagement.

Villeroi, learning that his lines had been effectually penetrated, retired towards Louvain, suffering but trifling loss in his retreat owing to the refusal of the Dutch deputies to co-operate with Marlborough in a vigorous pursuit.

A persistent downpour of rain that lasted for several days, together with the opposition of the Dutch deputies and generals to his plans for further offensive movements before the season was too far advanced, prevented Marlborough from reaping any of the fruits of his victory. During the autumn the troops were employed in levelling the enemy's lines until the time came for them to go into winter quarters. In November the 23rd marched back to Holland for garrison duty during the winter.

1706.

The campaign this year was inaugurated by Marlborough giving instructions, on his arrival at the Hague towards the end of April, for the English and Dutch troops to concentrate at Bilsen, close to Tongres.

This year the 23rd was brigaded with the 1st Guards, the 1st, 8th, 28th, and Dalrymple's regiment, under the command of Brigadier Webb.

From Bilsen the army marched to the camp at Borchleon on the 10th of May, where it was joined by Marlborough, who had now about 60,000 men under his command.

His chief object was to endeavour to capture Namur by surprise, but Villeroi, who had got wind of his intentions and having under his command about an equal number of men, determined to bar his advance. To effect his purpose the Marshal drew up his army in the form of a rough crescent, extending about four miles from the village of Taviers on the right, to that of l'Autre Eglise on the left. Most of his best cavalry interspersed with infantry was drawn up in two lines on a fine plain between Taviers and Ramillies. In the latter village, which was slightly to the left of the centre, Villeroi posted twenty battalions and several guns. From Ramillies to l'Autre Eglise runs the River Geete, which makes the ground in its vicinity very swampy. Villeroi's left flank, which was weakly defended, rested on this marshy ground.

Marlborough, from a slight eminence, carefully inspected the enemy's dispositions, and arrived at the conclusion that the plain referred to would be the deciding factor in the forthcoming contest. He laid his plans accordingly. The Allied infantry was quickly drawn up in two lines, supported by cavalry on either flank. The right wing was composed of five brigades, including that of Brigadier Webb.

The first move, on the 12th of May (23rd May N.S.), on Marlborough's part was to order this wing to advance as if to attack the French left with the object of weakening the centre. The feint was most successful, as Villeroi, believing that his left was about to be seriously attacked, drew off a considerable body of troops from the plain to support it.

On seeing this, the Duke ordered the right wing, which had advanced halfway down the exterior slope of the ground it had occupied, to halt and retire slowly to the summit, while the rear line, wheeling to the left and concealed from the enemy by the rising ground, hastened to join the troops which were to make the attack upon the centre of the French position.

The Duke then rode down to the centre of his own position and sent orders to Overkirk, who was posted on the left of the Allied army, to attack the enemy's right with his Dutch infantry. At the same time four brigades of foot under General Schultz were ordered to attack the village of Ramillies, and the cavalry and infantry in the centre were directed to advance and charge the enemy in the plain.

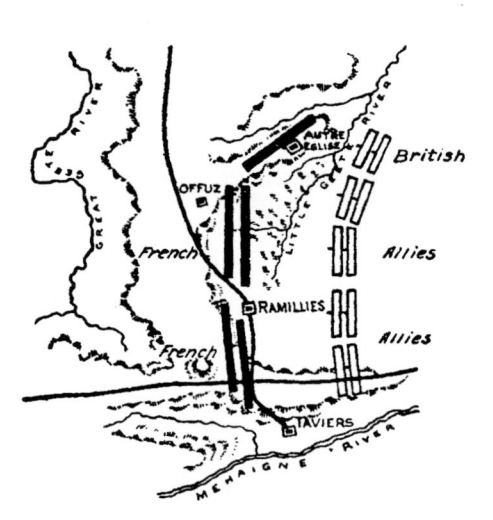

The first attack on Ramillies not being successful, the Duke withdrew Webb's and Macartney's brigades from the right wing and sent them to the assistance of Schultz, whose second attack was successful, the enemy being driven from the village at the point of the bayonet. Meanwhile the French centre was being furiously attacked, but the household troops, of which it was mainly composed, stoutly maintained their ground until their right wing was driven in by Overkirk. Then they commenced to give ground slowly. Whilst retiring they were charged by the victorious cavalry from the left wing, and thrown into great confusion, ending in complete rout. The collapse of the enemy's main body, on which so much depended, was irreparable.

RAMILLIES.
23RD MAY, 1706

The English battalions (which for four long hours had remained motionless, observing the enemy's left) at last, to their great relief, received orders to advance. Quickly descending the slope, they scrambled through the marshy ground in the neighbourhood of the Little Geete, forded the river and, penetrating into the village of Offuz, drove the defenders headlong through it.

The whole French army was by now a surging mob of panic-stricken fugitives, whose retreat was greatly hampered by the numerous baggage waggons that Villeroi had brought up too close to his centre.

The pursuit was continued relentlessly during the whole night, until through sheer fatigue the pursuers were obliged to desist when almost in sight of Louvain, whither the major portion of the beaten army betook itself.

So keen was the Duke to "press the enemy in their retreat" that, though he mounted his horse at 4 a.m. on the morning of the battle, he did not leave the saddle until noon the following day. The Allies lost 1,066 killed and 2,567 wounded. The French casualties amounted to 13,000 killed, wounded, and taken prisoners. No officer of the 23rd can be traced as having been either killed or wounded in this battle.

The Allies captured 120 standards and colours, 60 cannon, and 8 mortars. Marlborough, in writing to Queen Anne announcing the complete victory of the Allies, informed her that "all the troops, both officers and soldiers, have behaved themselves with the greatest bravery and courage."

The result of this striking victory was that fortress after fortress in Flanders surrendered to the Allies.

At the siege of Ostend, which was conducted by Overkirk, the 23rd formed part of the covering army.

Marshal Vendôme was hurried up from Piedmont to supersede Villeroi, but even he could do nothing to check Marlborough's victorious progress, owing to the *moral* of the French troops being greatly shaken in the recent battle.

A month's incessant rain following on a prolonged drought effected what the Marshal could not do by force of arms. It effectually put a stop to any further operations of the Allies this year.

The 23rd took up its winter quarters at Ghent, where it arrived in November.

In the words of Mr. Fortescue, the historian, "Thus ended the campaign of Ramillies, one of the most brilliant in the annals of war, wherein Marlborough in a single month carried his arms triumphant from the Meuse to the sea."

During the winter of 1706-7 the commanding officers of the several English regiments in the Low Countries subscribed "an allowance" towards the subsistence of the widows of such officers as were killed on service there. Marlborough was so pleased with this commendable movement that he wrote to Lord Galway, who commanded the army in Spain, bringing it to his notice and suggesting that a similar subscription should be started for the widows of his troops, who, he stated, were " very clamorous, and in great necessity."

1707.

In a letter from St. James's, dated the 10th of March 1707, the Duke of Marlborough, writing to Lieutenant-General Ingoldsby, commanding the English troops in Holland, directs him to acquaint Colonel Lalo that the officers of his regiment (21st Foot) " must conform themselves to other regiments and use pertinsans [partisans] as those of the Regiment of Welsh Fusiliers."

During the winter the prospects of the French had materially improved. This was due in great measure to the underhand dealing of the Emperor of Austria, who, to further his own ends, had concluded a secret treaty with Louis XIV, with the result that several French garrisons in Italy were released for service in Flanders.

Another contributory cause was the great success which had attended the arms of England's Allies the previous year, lulling them into a sense of false security, which caused a certain amount of reluctance to furnish their contingents.

These causes combined to enable Louis XIV to put into the field for the ensuing campaign over 80,000 men under the command of Vendôme, who received positive orders not to hazard a battle, but as far as possible to distribute his troops over a series of very strong lines along the French frontier that had been constructed during the winter. The English and Dutch troops began to leave Holland towards the end of April and concentrated at Anderlecht, near Brussels, about the 4th of May, when Marlborough found himself at the head of an army of 65,000 men.

This year the 23rd was brigaded with the 1st battalion of the 1st Guards, the 1st battalion of The Royal Scots, the 8th and 16th Regiments, under the command of Brigadier Meredith. From the 20th of May to the last day of July Marlborough's army remained stationary at Meldert, near Louvain, hoping for an opportunity of coming to close quarters with Vendôme, but all in vain. Soon afterwards, when he had shifted his camp to Soignies, the possibility of attacking the Marshal presented itself, but as the Dutch field deputies would under no circumstances consent to their troops taking part in the contemplated attack, it did not materialise. The Marshal struck his tents and cleared out of the locality as speedily as possible. Very heavy rains lasting for quite a month then set in, reducing the surrounding country to the condition of a huge bog, thus rendering further operations impossible. Marlborough had now no option but to retire and send his troops into winter quarters.

The 23rd returned to Ghent late in the autumn.

The following copy of a circular letter dated Whitehall, 25th of December 1707, addressed to Brigadier Sabine and fourteen other Colonels of regiments, is preserved at the Public Record Office:

" It being thought expedient for Her Majesty's Service in regard to the number of officers belonging to the 14 Batts broken at Almanza who are prisoners in France that a Lieut and Ensign be spared from such of the Regiments of foot in the Low Countries to give their assistance towards raising those Battalions again untill the prisoners shall be exchanged when the said Lieutenants and Ensigns if not otherwise provided for in the said Regiments in the mean time are to return to their respective posts. His Grace the Duke of Marlborough does think fitt that you cause the names of a Lieutenant and Ensign out of   Regiment of foot such as you shall think proper on this occasion, who for their encouragement on this service will be preferred to Captains and Lieutenants, to be forthwith returned to me, you taking care that they be the eldest of the Lieutenants and Ensigns serving or such who upon returning to their own Posts with a superior commission will occasion no injustice or clamour from any other the Lieutenants and Ensigns of the Regiment.

"[*signed*] H. St. John."

1708.

In accordance with the recommendations of a Board of General Officers, sanctioned by Parliament, the counties of Essex, Suffolk, Norfolk, and Cambridge were allotted as a recruiting area for the 23rd and certain other regiments early this year.

The abortive attempt of Louis XIV this spring to land the Pretender with a body of troops in Scotland led to ten regiments serving in the Low Countries being ordered to embark at Ostend and proceed to Tynemouth, there to await further orders. The 23rd was at first one of the earmarked regiments, but the order for it to proceed on the expedition was countermanded. Had it embarked, Brigadier Sabine, being "the eldest" (senior) Colonel, would have commanded the force.

The command devolved upon Major-General Withers.

For the ensuing campaign Louis made elaborate preparations. His main army, which was massed in Flanders between Mons and Tournay, numbered upwards of 100,000 men under the orders of Vendôme, but, much to his chagrin, the heir to the throne, the Duke of Burgundy, was placed in supreme command, with disastrous results as will be shown later on. On the Lower Rhine another army of 35,000 men was collected under the Elector of Bavaria, with the Duke of Berwick as his second-in-command.

Marlborough, on his arrival at the Hague in April, was met by Prince Eugene. The result of this meeting was that the Duke undertook the command of the troops in Flanders, and Eugene of the Imperial Force on the Moselle. To the Elector of Hanover, afterwards George I, was entrusted the task of holding the Elector of Bavaria in check on the Rhine.

On the return of the expeditionary force to Ghent, preparations were at once commenced for putting Marlborough's army in the field as speedily as possible. On the 11th of May the 23rd marched from Ghent to the rendezvous at Tarleask, between Louvain and Brussels.

For this campaign the 23rd was brigaded with the 8th, 18th, and 27th Regiments under the command of Brigadier Sabine.

Vendôme concentrated his army south of the River Haine in May, and advanced towards the forest of Soignies, which he considered a good jumping-off ground for swooping down upon Brussels, Louvain, and other important cities in Brabant. To counter this probable move, Marlborough concentrated some 75,000 men at Hal, and sent urgent messages to Eugene to join him without delay.

The movements of the latter were, however, greatly hampered by the usual dilatoriness of the Germans in furnishing their contingents. As the French by their movements appeared to be threatening Louvain, the Duke made a forced march to the Dyle with the object of upsetting their plans. The non-arrival of Eugene for quite a month, through no fault of his own, prevented Marlborough from taking any action during that period. The interval was made good use of by Vendôme for intriguing with the malcontent element in both Bruges and Ghent to hand these places over to him.

When towards the end of June he considered he had won them over, he silently broke up his camp and marched rapidly towards Hal, sending detachments to both Bruges and Ghent, which opened their gates on the arrival of the French. Thereupon the Duke advanced to bring Vendôme to an engagement, but the latter retired in haste to Alost, where he considered he could threaten Brussels and seriously interfere with the Allies' communications.

Marlborough then moved to Assche to cover Brussels, and sent word to Lord Chandos, the Governor of Ath, to collect every available man who could be spared from the garrisons within reach and to throw himself with them into Oudenarde, which was weakly garrisoned. On the 28th of June Vendôme sent detachments to invest Oudenarde, and then marched towards Lessines to cover the siege. Timely notice having been given the Duke of this movement, he planned with Eugene, who had now joined him, though in advance of his army, to forestall the Marshal.

Marlborough accordingly sent forward Major-General Cadogan with a strong detachment to construct bridges over the Dender and occupy Lessines, and following with all speed reached the bank of that river just as Cadogan had completed the means of crossing it. No time was lost in transporting the army to the opposite bank. Hardly had it taken up its camping-ground before the enemy's vedettes appeared in sight. Vendôme, finding that he had been checkmated, fell back on the Scheldt with the intention of crossing it at Gavre, about six miles from Oudenarde, and blocking the Allies' advance on Bruges.

The Duke, being determined to make his opponent accept battle, directed Cadogan with a force of about 11,000 cavalry and infantry, in which Sabine's brigade was included, to push forward, throw bridges across the Scheldt, and take up a position close to Oudenarde.

The French advanced guard, under the Marquis de Biron, which had leisurely crossed the Scheldt at Gavre, suddenly found itself confronted at Eyne by Cadogan's detachment. Word was at once sent to Vendôme of this unexpected move of his opponent. Riding forward to reconnoitre and perceiving that the bulk of Marlborough's army was still some distance from the river, he determined to oppose his progress. For this purpose he drew up his army in a line following the course of the Scheldt, extending from the village of Heurne to that of Mooreghem on the right.

The orders which he issued to give effect to this decision were promptly countermanded by the Duke of Burgundy, between whom and Vendôme the most pronounced disagreement was apparent. The former, with a view to thwarting Vendôme, resolved to take up a position extending from the village of Asper on the left to that of

Wanneghem on the right, about two miles to the rear of the one selected by the Marshal.

In the confusion caused by the issue of contradictory orders the French army became divided. Seven battalions together with a sprinkling of cavalry, under a misconception, occupied the village of Eyne, which was on the line selected by Vendôme, while the bulk of the army was posted on a portion of Burgundy's line behind the River Norken, to the left and rear of Eyne.

On the 30th of June the action commenced by Cadogan's three brigades making a frontal attack on this village, Sabine's brigade leading the way. While they were advancing, Hanoverian cavalry, which had crossed the river higher up, worked round to the rear of the French with the object of cutting off their retreat. So vigorously did Cadogan's men press home their attack that in a short time three of the enemy's battalions surrendered, while the remaining four, on endeavouring to retreat, were almost cut to pieces by the cavalry.

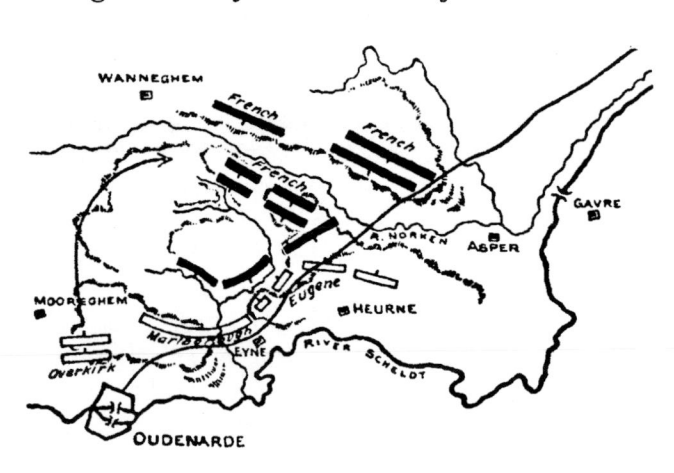

OUDENARDE.
11TH JULY, 1708.

The victorious brigades were given a brief rest in the village and were then pushed on to the village of Groenewald, there to await the advance of the main body of the allied infantry, which had by now reached the Scheldt and was in the act of crossing it.

Once again the Duke of Burgundy and Vendôme were at loggerheads, the cause of contention on this occasion being the vital question of at once advancing to oppose the progress of the Allies.

Marlborough, noticing this hesitation, and concluding that when the French advance took place it would be directed against Cadogan's corps on the extreme left, dispatched the Duke of Argyll with twenty battalions, principally British, to its support. Before, however, Argyll had time to join up with Cadogan's corps it was fiercely attacked by thirty French battalions which had crossed the Norken and advanced rapidly in perfect order.

A desperate hand-to-hand encounter took place among hedges and enclosures, the infantry on both sides greatly distinguishing themselves: eventually the French were slowly driven back.

While this struggle was progressing, Eugene, who was in command on the right, had attacked the enemy's left and was successful in piercing his first and second lines. The issue was still in doubt until Marlborough hurled twenty battalions of Dutch and Danes under Overkirk against the French right, with the result that it was completely isolated.

This bold stroke was the turning-point in the contest. Vendôme endeavoured to retrieve the situation by advancing with the infantry from the left of his position, but all to no purpose. Thrown into hopeless confusion by the numerous banks and hedges to be traversed, the infantry could make no serious impression and finally retired under cover of darkness. All was now confusion in the French ranks. The order to retreat was given by Burgundy, and such of the French soldiery as escaped the sword, or were not taken prisoner, made the best of their way to Ghent panic-stricken.

The Allied loss in this battle, fought on the 30th of June (11th July N.S.), amounted to about 3,000 killed and wounded; the French casualties were much heavier, amounting to 6,000 killed and wounded and 9,000 prisoners, including some 800 officers, several being of note. Upwards of one hundred standards, colours, and kettledrums were captured on this occasion.

The beaten army, after its retreat to Ghent, took up an entrenched position behind the canal between that city and Bruges. Despite his recent crushing defeat, Vendôme threw himself heartily into the arduous task of restoring as quickly as possible the *moral* of his troops, which was seriously impaired.

How to draw him from his entrenchments and fight a pitched battle was the problem that now confronted the Duke. While pondering over the matter, it occurred to him that by investing Lille he might accomplish his object, as he opined that Vendôme would in all probability risk an engagement sooner than permit that fortress to be invested.

On being informed of this plan, Prince Eugene assured Marlborough of his whole-hearted support. A most formidable task lay before the Confederate generals. The natural position of Lille coupled with the fact that it had been most skilfully fortified by Vauban rendered it almost impregnable. Moreover, it had a garrison of 15,000 men under the command of the veteran Boufflers.

In no way daunted by the immense difficulties of the undertaking, the Duke ordered a siege battering train to be dispatched to him from Brussels. All the waterways in Brabant being in the hands of the enemy, it required no less than 16,000 horses to haul it overland. So cleverly was it escorted by Eugene with a strong force of cavalry and infantry that the immense convoy reached its destination without any loss.

To Eugene and the Prince of Orange, who temporarily commanded the Dutch troops owing to the indisposition of Overkirk, was entrusted the investment of the town on the north and north-east sides by 40,000 men. Marlborough commanded the covering army, which was posted at Helchin on the Scheldt for the express purpose of frustrating any attempt of Vendôme from the north or the Duke of Berwick from the south to raise the siege.

For the first three weeks of its progress only five English regiments, viz. the 16th, 18th, 21st, 23rd, and 24th, occupied the trenches, and in that short period lost no less than 500 men. On the 12th of August Eugene broke ground and constructed batteries opposite the gates of St. Andrew and St. Magdalene. Fifty heavy guns were quickly got into position and opened fire upon a redoubt adjoining the latter. After a bombardment lasting one whole day it was taken by assault, but was promptly re-taken by the enemy. Next day a fortified mill opposite the St. Martin Gate was captured by assault, but was rendered untenable by the fire from the ramparts.

Thus matters stood for well-nigh a fortnight, when Vendôme and the Duke of Berwick, having joined forces, moved forward with about 110,000 men to attempt the relief of the beleaguered town. This move had been anticipated by Marlborough, who, to discount it, had taken up a strong position between the two rivers Deule and Marque.

The French generals, realising the great difficulty they would have in attempting to dislodge the Duke, decided to take no step until the Court of Versailles had been consulted. After a week's pause they made a show of attacking him, but contented themselves with a long-distance cannonade, and then retired.

While the opposing armies confronted each other, a most determined assault was made on the counterscarp close to the St. Andrew

Gate on the 27th of August by a body of 800 grenadiers, including those of the 23rd, who were followed by upwards of 2,000 workmen. This storming party attacked on the right. To the left another party, consisting of 3,000 men under the command of Monsieur Du May, a chief engineer, advanced to attack that portion of the counterscarp which was adjacent to the St. Magdalene Gate. Brigadier Sabine, with 2,000 men drawn from the English regiments of the main army, followed in support. After a desperate struggle entailing heavy loss, a lodgment was effected in the covered way. The casualties in the 23rd on this occasion amounted to 12 rank and file killed and 62 wounded.

Another determined assault was made on the 10th of September, the assailants gaining a footing three times, only to be hurled back by the brave defenders. A fourth attempt, which was led by Eugene in person, was more fruitful of result, as the Allies managed to establish themselves in the outworks, though at an appalling sacrifice. No less than 5,000 men were killed and wounded, of whom about 3,000 were English.

After a siege of sixty days the town capitulated on the 30th of September, owing to the defences commencing to crumble away as the result of the unceasing pounding they received from nearly 100 heavy guns and mortars. The casualties of the 23rd during the siege of the town amounted, according to Mr. Cannon, to " one captain, three subalterns, three sergeants, and one hundred and fifteen rank and file killed; three captains, eight subalterns, fifteen sergeants, and two hundred and thirty rank and file wounded." No record of the names of the killed and wounded officers can be traced.

On the surrender of the town, Boufflers, together with about 5,000 men, retired to the citadel to withstand a second siege. Here he held out until about the 28th of November, when, owing to his running short of both food and ammunition, he was obliged to surrender and was permitted to march out with the honours of war.

A week after the surrender of the citadel the Duke concentrated his troops and marched towards Ghent with hopes (he writes) " to reduce that place as well as Bruges before we leave the field, which will give us an opportunity of opening the next campaign with all the advantages we can desire." No time was lost in investing both of these places: the former held out until the 20th of December, but the latter capitulated on the 7th of that month. As the lateness of the season precluded the possibility of any further operations being undertaken, Marlborough sent his troops into winter quarters.

1709.

About the middle of January a number of officers—one from each unit—were ordered to proceed to England and beat up recruits for several of the regiments whose ranks had become depleted owing to the wastage of war. The 23rd being in this plight, Brigadier Sabine's mind was set at rest by his receiving in due course a batch of recruits which enabled his regiment to take the field. Negotiations for peace were opened by Louis XIV, through whose kingdom famine stalked, but the terms proposed by the Allies were so ruinous to France that he determined to fight to the last rather than agree to them: so the war continued.

The popular and resourceful Marshal Villars was placed at the head of about 90,000 men, who were determined to fight to the last rather than allow their country to be invaded. It was Marlborough's intention to concentrate his forces in March, but the backwardness of the season and the want of forage prevented the troops from marching until the beginning of May. By that time Villars had taken up a strong position extending from the Scarpe at Douay to the Lys at Béthune, which he hastened to improve in the belief that it was there the Allies would endeavour to penetrate into France. For the ensuing campaign Marlborough and Eugene were able to bring into the field about 110,000 men. On this occasion the 23rd was brigaded with the 2nd Battalion of The Royal Scots and Lord Orrery's regiment (afterwards disbanded).

The Duke determined to lure Villars if possible from his entrenchments and force him to fight a pitched battle. If that failed, he resolved upon reducing Tournay, which had been fortified by Vauban and was considered one of the strongest fortresses in the theatre of operations. On the 18th of June Marlborough and Eugene advanced seemingly as if to attack Villars in his fortified lines. Thereupon the latter drained all his garrisons within easy reach and withdrew 3,000 picked troops from Tournay to strengthen his position.

The Duke, finding that the enemy's entrenchments were too strong to be attacked, struck his tents at tattoo on the evening that the reinforcement from Tournay reached Villars, and marched off in dead silence towards that town, which was reached as daylight was appearing and immediately invested. His ruse had been highly successful. It enabled him to invest a place that had been drained of a considerable portion of its garrison without encountering any opposition. Prince Eugene carried on the siege, while Marlborough commanded the covering army, to which the 23rd was attached.

On the 26th of June the trenches were opened, and, despite constant torrential rain, the town was taken in less than a month. The Marquis de Sourville, who commanded the garrison, then retired into the citadel. The latter was famous for its underground works, which far exceeded those above ground both in number and strength. Mining, counter-mining, and desperate combats with sword and pistol became the order of the day or rather of the night, as both besiegers and besieged worked more often than not in pitch darkness. Eventually, on the 23rd of August, the garrison was forced to capitulate, and allowed to march out with the honours of war. The Allied loss in killed or died of sickness during the siege amounted to nearly 5,000 men. While the siege of the citadel was progressing, the Duke spent three days reviewing the covering army at his camp near Orchies. He was able to report that " all the troops in general and particularly H.M.'s Subjects appeared in perfect order."

On the fall of Tournay he decided to invest Mons, and accordingly made the necessary dispositions of his troops. Villars, on learning that the Prince of Hesse-Cassel had by a very rapid march crossed the River Haine about five miles to the east of Mons, and further, that Marlborough, with the object of isolating Mons from the interior of France, had seized the plateau of Jemappes, advanced rapidly from the south with 95,000 men and 80 guns, but arrived too late to prevent the investment of the town on the French side. He then drew up his army at Malplaquet slightly in the rear of two great gaps between the forest of Laignières on his right and that of Taisnières on his left, and lost not a moment in throwing up a formidable line of entrenchments all along his front. The Duke desired to attack Villars at once, but two days elapsed before he could induce the Dutch deputies to consent to this course. Villars's army, working with feverish haste, had constructed by then most formidable entrenchments. The Allied army numbered 93,000 men and 105 guns.

Eugene took command of the Allied right, which consisted of two columns of infantry under General Schulemberg and Count Lottum respectively. The 23rd was attached to that of the latter. The Duke commanded the left and centre.

The morning of the memorable 31st of August (11th September N.S.) was ushered in with dense fog which did not disperse until 7.30 a.m. A furious artillery duel then ensued, during which the columns referred to advanced against the Taisnières Wood.

At first Lottum's column could make very little headway against the crack French regiments that lined the entrenchments on the edge of the wood, but on being reinforced by three battalions from the centre and further aided by Marlborough in person charging at the head of d'Auvergne's cavalry, the regiments composing it charged impetuously and drove the "Régiment du Roi" at the point of the bayonet out of the entrenchments. Lottum's column, penetrating the wood and fighting desperately from tree to tree, joined up eventually with that of Schulemberg, which, after being driven back once, on returning to the charge had carried the entrenchments that barred its progress. The two together drove back the left wing of the enemy. On the left the Prince of Orange, contrary to the orders he had received, prematurely led his Dutch division against the French right, which was well protected by formidable works and defended by a force much superior in numbers. Although both he and his troops displayed the utmost bravery, they could make little or no impression on the enemy, the result being that his reserves were rapidly used up in the repeated desperate onslaughts he called upon his troops to make.

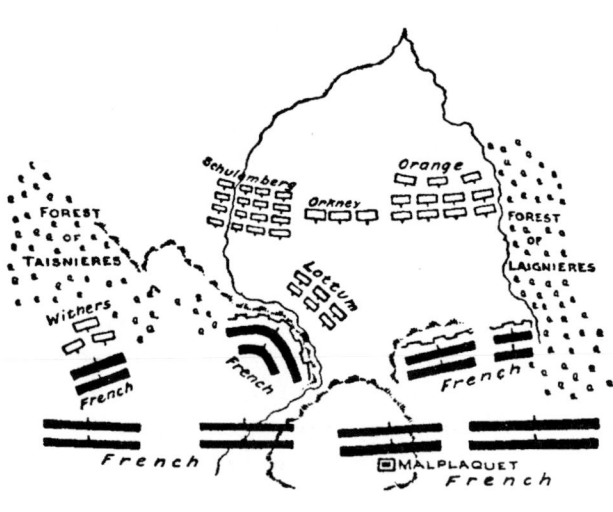

MALPLAQUET.
11TH SEPTEMBER, 1709.

Fortunately just at this crisis Villars, becoming very anxious about his left, withdrew a considerable body of troops from his centre to strengthen it. The Duke's quick eye noticed this movement, which afforded him the opportunity of turning the scale. Orkney, who commanded in the centre, received orders to move forward his troops

Dashing towards the entrenchments, they were successful in carrying them right and left.

The attack on the enemy's left was again renewed with but little success, until the English infantry, lining each trench as it was taken, contrived to keep the French cavalry in check, which contributed materially to its progress. The fate of the day was, however, decided by a brilliant charge of the whole of the Imperial Cavalry, which drove the French back over a wide area. As their left had already retired, nothing remained for Boufflers, who had assumed command owing to Villars being wounded, but to order a general retreat to Bavay.

This most sanguinary and unsatisfactory victory was purchased very dearly. No less than 20,000 of the Allies were either killed or wounded, while the French loss did not exceed 14,000. The casualties in the 23rd were as follows at Malplaquet on August 31/September 11:

Killed.

Lieutenant Joseph Bartley.
   ,,   James Fullerton.

Lieutenant Nevil Parker.

Wounded.

Captain Isaac Jevereau.
   ,,   Arthur Brett.
Lieutenant John Scawen.
   ,,   Newsham Peers.

Lieutenant Richard Ashby.
   ,,   James Gordon.
Adjutant John Powell.

Very few prisoners were taken, owing to little quarter being given on either side. The trophies taken amounted to 16 guns, 26 standards, 20 colours, and four pairs of kettle-drums. The investment of Mons was resumed as soon as the troops had had a much-needed rest: the 23rd formed part of the covering army. On the 28th of September the garrison surrendered, which wound up the campaign. The troops then marched to winter quarters, Ghent being the destination of the 23rd.

In May this year Brevet-Colonel Mathew Pennefather, who commanded the 23rd, was appointed Commissary-General of Ireland. He was M.P. for Cashel from 1716 until his decease in 1733.

On the 13th of March 1882 the following battle honours were granted: "BLENHEIM," "RAMILLIES," "OUDENARDE," "MALPLAQUET."

1710.

During the spring of this year negotiations for peace were again opened, but fell through owing to the unreasonable demands of both the Emperor and the States-General.

The Allied army once again took the field in April, and marched to the rendezvous at Tournay. By a rapid movement, Marlborough succeeded without the loss of a man in guiding his army through the formidable lines of La Bassée, which had been undertaken for the protection of Douay, and laid siege to that fortress. Leaving General Cadogan with about twenty battalions, including the 23rd, to conduct the siege, the Duke moved off with 80,000 men, and took up a very strong position near Vitry in the hope that he might be attacked there by Villars, who had recovered from his wound at Malplaquet and had again resumed command of the French army, nearly 90,000 strong.

In this he was disappointed, as both Villars and Berwick, on reconnoitring his position, agreed that it would be little short of madness to attempt to dislodge him.

Meanwhile the siege of Douay was being actively prosecuted, the besieged retaliating by making several desperate sorties. For two months the garrison held out, but was obliged to surrender on the 15th of June for lack of food and ammunition. Marlborough, in admiration of their heroic defence, allowed the garrison to march out with all the honours of war.

The 23rd suffered heavily, as is shown by the following extract from Lediard's *Life of Marlborough*: "The regiment had one captain, one lieutenant, five sergeants and forty-nine rank and file killed; and two captains, seven lieutenants, ten sergeants, and 137 rank and file wounded during the siege."

The wear and tear of siege work had told so heavily upon the company officers of the 23rd that by the month of May only two were left to carry on the regimental duties—a condition of affairs which the Duke, in several of his letters written about this time, describes as likely to bring ruin upon the regiment.

It was his intention to lay siege to Arras upon the fall of Douay, but on his ascertaining that Villars held a strong position covering that fortress, he decided to besiege Béthune instead.

Its reduction was accomplished by the 17th of August. Two

small but strategically important fortresses on the Lys—St. Venant and Aire—were then simultaneously attacked. The former fell on the 18th of September, but the latter held out until the 1st of November; the frequent torrential falls of rain greatly impeded the progress of the besiegers from first to last. The army then went into winter quarters: the 23rd marched to Courtray, where it was stationed during the winter.

1711.

During the winter the French army, whose depleted ranks had been filled up, was busily occupied in constructing most formidable lines the whole way from Namur to the coast. It was fondly hoped that these lines, which Villars proclaimed to be the "ne plus ultra" of Marlborough's career—an ironical allusion to the Duke's motto—would make the invasion of France impossible.

In April the Allied troops left their winter quarters and marched to the rendezvous at Orchies, some miles to the south-east of Lille. Here Marlborough held a review of the whole army—about 90,000 strong—and immediately afterwards marched towards the hostile lines where Villars had taken up a position between Bouchain and Oisy. For six weeks the opposing armies confronted each other, neither commander being desirous of making the first move.

Eventually, on the 3rd of June, Marlborough marched westward to Lens, where he encamped on the extensive plains in the neighbourhood of that town and took advantage of so much open country to again review his troops. As he concluded that it would be useless to endeavour to draw Villars from his almost unassailable lines, he set his great mind to evolve a scheme which would enable him to hoodwink the Marshal and thereby enable him to gain possession of them. Without divulging what was in his mind, he ostentatiously made all preparations for a determined assault upon that portion of the lines behind which Villars lay. This had the effect of causing the latter to withdraw his men all along the lines and concentrate them at the seemingly threatened point.

The Duke, having achieved this part of his plan, secretly sent off his trusty lieutenant, General Cadogan, to ask the Prussian General Hompesch, who lay at Douay with a force of about 14,000 cavalry and infantry, to attempt to penetrate without a moment's delay the enemy's lines under cover of darkness. He then issued instructions for a general attack on the following day, which greatly mystified his army, all but the veterans concluding that it was either madness or sheer recklessness that must have caused "Corporal John" to decide upon a direct attack on the enemy's lines.

Those seasoned men who had served under him during successive campaigns refrained from comment, as they rightly concluded that this was one of his brilliant inspirations, to which they had become accustomed. When the troops paraded at tattoo that night, an order was passed down the ranks that tents were to be struck and the men ready to march as speedily as possible.

In dead silence Marlborough led his men towards the River Scarpe, which had been bridged in anticipation. At daylight it was safely crossed, and the troops proceeded on the march. Presently an aide-de-camp galloped up with the intelligence that Cadogan and Hompesch had passed the causeway at Arleux about three a.m. unopposed, and were then in possession of the enemy's lines. Never was news more welcome. No spur was now needed to enable the jaded troops to complete the manœuvre of their brilliant leader. By four p.m. on the 25th of July the much-vaunted lines passed into the possession of the Allies.

Two days later the Allies laid siege to Bouchain. By the 12th of August the fortress was closely invested, the trenches having been completed by then, and the siege guns placed in position. A vigorous bombardment then ensued, which lasted until the 2nd of September, when the garrison surrendered as prisoners of war.

Twenty-six colours were captured, which were divided among the Allies by lot. As regards the part taken by the 23rd in this siege, Mr. Cannon in his Historical Record of the Regiment observes as follows: "The regiment formed part of a division of twenty battalions of infantry, commanded by Lieutenant-General the Earl of Orkney, which took post on the north and north-west side of the town and river; it shared in the duties of the trenches, and in carrying on the attacks, in which services it had several men killed and wounded."

Several days were spent by the troops in repairing the trenches, after which they set out for their winter quarters. Marlborough, taking leave of his troops at Tournay, proceeded to the Hague, where he spent some time transacting business. He then returned to England to become the victim of the basest ingratitude and shameful injustice. Before the year of one of his most brilliant feats had expired, he was deprived of all his offices, including the colonelcy of the 1st Regiment of Foot Guards.

1712.

On the 1st of January James, Duke of Ormonde, was appointed Captain-General of the British armies both at home and abroad. Early in April the English troops marched to the rendezvous at Bassieux, near Tournay, where Ormonde took command. No sooner had he done so than the Dutch refused to acknowledge him as Marlborough's successor. The difficulty was got over by Prince Eugene being placed in supreme command of the Allied armies.

While at Bassieux the right wing of the first line, consisting of all the English troops with a sprinkling of Allied cavalry, was reviewed by Ormonde. Soon afterwards the Allied army crossed the Scheldt and advanced towards Quesnoy with the object of investing it. The siege was undertaken by Eugene. During its progress the English troops lay at Cateau-Cambrésis nominally as a covering army, but in reality spectators owing to Ormonde having received secret instructions not to engage in action until he received further orders.

Quesnoy surrendered on the 22nd of June. Eugene then advanced farther into French territory and laid siege to Landrecies. Thereupon Ormonde, who had been conducting a secret correspondence with Villars, declined further to co-operate with Eugene, and, to the disgust and fierce indignation of the English troops, struck his tents and marched towards the coast.

The foreign troops in British pay, to their honour be it said, flatly refused to leave Eugene. The Dutch constantly heaped contumely upon the crestfallen troops on their backward march, and in many instances refused to admit them into their towns. Eventually they reached Bruges and Ghent, which they were obliged to take possession of in order to retain a bare foothold in Holland. The 23rd was quartered in the latter town, its Colonel, Major-General Sabine, being placed in command of the citadel until the Peace of Utrecht was signed in April 1713, and for some months afterwards.

During his tenure of office he was instrumental in suppressing a mutiny which broke out in the garrison. On July 9th he received information which induced him to send for Brigadier Sutton with all his available dragoons, who arrived at three a.m. the next morning:

these, together with the assistance of the loyal troops, soon quelled the mutiny. Seven of the ringleaders, after full evidence, were put to death. The garrison was marched round the dead bodies, and a general pardon was afterwards declared at the head of each regiment.

1713.

The question of precedence was again to the fore this year, as will be seen by the following order: " St. James's 23rd April 1713. Order for settling ye rank and preceeding of ye forces. . . . The Royl Regt. of Welsh Fuziliers, commanded by Major General Sabine. . . ." On the list appended to that order the 23rd is shown as being twenty-fourth in order of precedence. It will be observed that this is the first occasion on which the 23rd is described officially as a " Royal Regiment."

On the 13th of May fourteen regiments in Holland, including the 23rd, were reduced to forty-one private soldiers in each of the twelve companies, excepting the grenadier company, which was to have eight men more, making in all, inclusive of officers and non-commissioned officers, 613. The regiment was placed on the Irish establishment from the 24th of June.

On the 1st of July a further reduction took place, as will be seen by the following: " Regiments in Flanders about to be transferred to Ireland, Sabine's, Primrose's, Preston's, Sybourgh's and Hamilton's to be reduced to consist only of ten companies of 2 sergeants, 2 corporals, 1 drum, and 36 private soldiers, disbanding the two youngest companies with the youngest officers."

The 23rd left Flanders early in August and landed at Kinsale on the 22nd of that month, and was placed on the Irish establishment, the rate of pay and subsistence being as follows:

	Pay per diem. s. d.	Subsistence per diem. s. d.		Pay per diem. s. d.	Subsistence per diem. s. d.
*Colonel (as such)	12 0	5 0	Captain	8 0	4 0
*Lt.-Colonel (as such)	7 0	2 6	Lieutenant	4 0	2 0
*Major (as such)	4 0	1 8	2nd Lieutenant	3 0	1 6
Chaplain	6 8	3 4	Sergeant	1 6	0 9
Surgeon	4 0	2 0	Corporal	1 0	0 6
Surgeon's Mate	2 6	1 3	Drum	1 0	0 6
Quartermaster and Adjutant	4 0	2 0	Privates	0 6	0 4

* Field officers drew in addition the pay and subsistence of a captain.

From there it removed to Cork, where it remained until October, when it received orders to proceed to Wicklow and Wexford, leaving a detachment at Waterford.

1714.

On the 16th of August six companies arrived in Dublin from Wicklow, two more on the 5th of October, and two more on the 18th of the same month, where they remained until July of the following year. The title of the regiment was altered this year, as appears by the following announcement in the *London Gazette* of the 9th of November: "His Majesty has been pleased to appoint Major General Joseph Sabine to be Colonel of His Royal Highness the Prince of Wales's Own Royal Regiment of Welsh Fusiliers." This was the first opportunity that had occurred since the raising of the regiment to connect it intimately with the heir-apparent.

1715.

On the 29th of July four companies marched from Dublin, reaching Mullingar on the 2nd of August and Athlone Barracks on the 5th. Two more companies left Dublin on the 30th of July, arriving at Athlone on the 6th of August. One company left Dublin on the 29th of July, arriving at Athboy on the 1st of August and Finea Barracks on the 3rd. One company left Dublin on the 29th of July, reaching Mullingar on the 2nd of August and Lanesborough Barracks on the 5th. Two companies left Dublin on the 30th of July, reaching Drogheda Barracks on the 1st of August.

Consequent upon the raising of the standard of the Pretender by the Earl of Mar in Scotland on the 9th of September, the 23rd received orders to embark for England. So eager was the regiment to see active service again that the Lords Justices wrote to the Lord Lieutenant as follows: "Sabine's Regiment having offered to defray the charges of their own transportation we did not think proper to hinder their going off."

Six companies left Athlone on the 9th and 10th of August, one company left Lanesborough on the 9th, and one company left Finea on the same day. The two companies at Drogheda were ordered to return to Dublin by the 31st of August, the destination of the whole being Dublin, in the environs of which they were encamped. Shortly after the regiment embarked for Chester, and on arriving at Park Gate on the 9th of October it was directed to march to Hereford in three divisions.

Consequent upon the unsettled condition of affairs in Scotland, the establishment of the 23rd was this year increased to 12 companies of 50 men each: the first of the two additional companies being under the command of Captain Edward Thetford with William Gale as Lieutenant and Edward Stannard as Second Lieutenant; and the second under Captain John Powell with Roger McManus as Lieutenant and John Weldon as Second Lieutenant.

1716.

The regiment remained at Hereford until January 1716, when, on being relieved by Brigadier Grove's Regiment, 6 companies moved to Birmingham, 4 to Wolverhampton, and 2 to Bridgenorth. The establishment of the regiment was fixed at 12 companies of 61 men each. The regiment was reviewed this year by Lieutenant-General Wills.

1717.

On the 4th of April the regiment moved from the stations already mentioned to Rugby, Lutterworth, and Harborough, and on the 9th of May to Dunstable, St. Albans, and Redbourn. On the 19th of May 3 companies moved to Hackney and Bethnal Green, 1 to Stoke Newington, 2 to Islington, 1 to Hornsey, 2 to Pancras and Hampstead, 1 to Marylebone, 1 to Kensington, and 1 to "Great and Little" Chelsea and Hyde Park Corner.

From an extract from the *Weekly Journal* of the 1st June 1717 it appears that on Thursday, 30th May 1717, "the Royal Regiment of Welsh Fusileers commanded by Lieutenant General Sabine was review'd in Hyde Park by His Royal Highness the Prince of Wales," and that previously on that day "the Welsh Regiment of Fusileers were exercising at Islington when they fired one their musquets loaded with ball, shot a soldier into the thigh, and 'tis thought the wound is mortal."

After being reviewed the regiment was ordered to proceed as follows: 3 companies to Rochester and Chatham, 3 to Sheerness, 2 to Tilbury, 1 each to Upnor Castle (to relieve a company of invalids), Dover, Greenwich (to relieve a company of invalids who were there as a guard to the powder-magazine), and Harwich.

The establishment of the regiment was reduced this year to 12 companies of 52 men each.

1718.

The value of a soldier at this period can be estimated by the following order showing the time, trouble, and expense taken to bring back a deserter to his regiment :

"12th Feb. 1718. Route for 1 sergeant and 2 private men of H.R.H. The Prince of Wales' Own Royal Regiment of Welsh Fusiliers from Rochester to Hereford and back again: Gravesend, Dartford, Knightsbridge, Brentford, Colnbrook, Maidenhead, Henley, Wallingford, Abingdon, Bampton, Northleach, Cheltenham, Gloucester, Ross, Hereford where they are to take a deserter into their custody and return with him."

In compliance with a warrant of Charles II, dated the 5th of July 1672, relative to the withdrawal of the military from towns where assizes were being held, the following order was issued: "March 4, 1718, two companies at Rochester to march three days before the assizes to the next adjacent place or places: there to continue until the said assizes are over and then return to Rochester."

On the 28th of October orders were issued for the two companies at Rochester and Chatham to march to Gravesend for embarkation to Ireland, the one company at Harwich to march to Gravesend, the one at Dover to Deal, and the remaining six at Sheerness to embark for Ireland. The regiment landed at Waterford on the 2nd of December. Three companies marched to Cork Barracks; they were followed on the 4th by three more companies, and on the 6th by the four remaining. On the 24th of December the rest of the regiment, consisting of an officer and 47 men, marched from Waterford to Cork Barracks.

The establishment of the regiment was this year further reduced to 10 companies of 44 men each.

1719.

On the 2nd of May the regiment left Ireland and landed at Bristol, whence 2 companies marched to Gloucester, 1 to Ledbury, 4 to Hereford, 2 to Leominster, and 1 to Bromyard. At the end of October all the companies were directed to assemble at Bristol. During this and the two following years the regiment, although serving out of Ireland, remained on the establishment of that kingdom, owing to the fact that it was originally intended that it should take part in the expedition to Vigo along with the other regiments dispatched from Ireland for that purpose.

1720.

On the 5th of April orders were received for the regiment to march to Manchester, whence 2 companies proceeded to Bolton and 2 to Warrington.

1721.

On the 10th of February the regiment was directed to proceed as follows: 4 companies to Hereford, 4 to Ludlow, 2 to Leominster. On the 8th of August the companies at Ludlow and Leominster were instructed to march to Hereford to be reviewed by Brigadier-General Grove. On the 9th of September the regiment was marched to Chester.

1722.

On the 15th of January 5 companies marched to Manchester, leaving a small detachment at Chester; and on the 20th of February the companies at Manchester and outlying companies were directed to march to Berwick. On their arrival there they were instructed by Brigadier-General Porter to proceed to Perthshire, where they remained until September, when they concentrated in the town of Perth for winter quarters. The order to do so reads as follows: " Where they are to remain entire—'tis not intended to make detachments from them to relieve those now in the Highlands."

The establishment this year consisted of 10 companies of 44 men each with a total of 445 all ranks. The annual inspection of the troops in Scotland was this year conducted by Major-General Sabine.

1723.

In January a temporary expedient as regards the supplying of arms and accoutrements was resorted to by the assignment of off-reckonings for 18 months instead of the customary 12 months, consequent upon the augmentation.

Orders were received this month for the regiment to be augmented by the addition of 1 sergeant, 1 drum, and 19 men to each company, or a total augmentation of 10 sergeants, 10 drums, and 190 men. In April the regiment was directed to proceed to Inverness to relieve the 2nd Foot, which was destined for Fort William: all regiments to be encamped in their new quarters by the 20th of May. On the 14th of September orders to "decamp to adjacent towns" were addressed to all regiments, and in October the following disposition of the companies is found: 6 at Inverness, 2 at Elgin, 1 at Nairn, 1 at Forres.

The regiment was reviewed at Inverness by its Colonel, Major-General Joseph Sabine, on the 15th of September during his annual tour of inspection.

The following is a copy of his report:

Field Officers and Captains.	Service. Abroad.	Service. Home.	Service. Total.		Service. Abroad.	Service. Home.	Service. Total.
Lt.-Col. Peers	8	10	18	2nd Lieutenants (contd.)			
Major Wansbrough	11	11	22	2nd Lt. Hewit			
Capt. Bissell	7	14	21	,, Bissell			
,, Powell	16	12	28	,, John Bernard			
,, Wilson		5	5	,, Laton			
,, Combe	2	10	12	,, Stoke			
,, Sabine	2	10	12	,, Weaver		2	2
,, Jodrell	4	11	15	*Staff Officers*			
,, Waite		5	5	Chaplain, Mr. Key		5	5
Capt.-Lt. Hickman		6	6	Adjt. Mr. W. Bernard	3	10	13
1st Lieutenants				Q.Mr. Mr. Dudley		3	3
Lt. Dunbar	16	13	29	Surg. Mr. Harton		3	3
,, Carey	5	10	15	,, Mate, Mr. Kenny	3	10	13
,, Hickman	2	10	12				
,, Chambre		7	7	Centinells served	70	451	521
,, W. Bernard				Wanting to complete			19
,, Taylor				*Absent*			
,, Weldon				Capt. Bissell, recruiting			
,, Johnston				,, Combe, by M.G. leave			
,, Wansbrough				Lt. Johnston, recruiting			
,, Lloyd				,, Lloyd, by General leave			
2nd Lieutenants				Chaplain Key, but has a deputy serving with the regiment.			
2nd Lt. Robinson							
,, Sabine							
,, Stannard							

"*Att the Camp near Invernefs Sept: ye 15th 1723.*

"In obedience to your Excellency's command I reviewed His Royal Highness the Prince of Wales's Own Royal Regiment of Welsh Fuzileer's under my command. The bodies of the men are very good.

The Regiment is very well disciplined, performing their exercise and fireing extremely well. The cloathing, accoutrements, and Field Equipage are good. The men were regularly cleared, and had no complaint against their officers.

"Jos. Sabine."

1724.

In April orders were issued for the 23rd to be relieved at Inverness by Brigadier Grove's regiment and to proceed to Fort William. Detachments " consisting of 20 men with a regimental officer who was joined by a half-pay officer and guides " were sent to various outlying posts in the neighbourhood of Loch Laggan, Loch Ness, Glen Moriston, and Glengarry. In addition two sergeants' commands were ordered to Aumore (?) and Corran Ardgour, as " they were found to be of singular use in stopping the thieves from boating and swimming cows and horses at the said places as they had usually done."

1725.

A disposition of the cantonments of the several regiments of foot in North Britain shows that Major-General Sabine's " were to remain where they are," viz. Fort William. In February the number of effectives in each company was reduced from 54 to 42 men.

1727.

In February the 23rd was ordered to raise 206 additional men, and the Master-General of the Ordnance was directed to supply as follows : " In addition to the necessary musquets and bayonets . . . 42 tents, 6 halberts, 4 drums with cartouch boxes in proportion." So unsatisfactory was the result of the effort to raise the additional 206 men for the 23rd and other regiments that a circular letter was issued directing £120 to be paid to each regiment and a warrant for mustering it " compleat to the 24th May next." This had to be further extended to the 24th of June. At the end of May the regiment was directed to march to Berwick.

In June the two additional companies—one of which was commanded by Captain Simon Roach with Lieutenant Francis Bolton and 2nd Lieutenant Edward Gould, and the other by Captain Thomas Forth with Lieutenant Archibald Enos and 2nd Lieutenant Richard Baldwin—which had been raised in England in April of this year and which were then at Worcester, were ordered to march to Berwick and "joyn to the regiment there." Major-General Grove was directed at the same time to replace three companies of the 23rd, which were then at Glasgow and were under orders for Berwick.

Soon afterwards Major Wansbrough received orders to proceed himself with five companies to Sunderland "to be aiding and assisting to the civil magistrates (when required by them) in the preservation of the public peace and in suppressing any riots or tumults that may be raised by the keelmen [bargees] and other disorderly persons there."

It is evident that Major Wansbrough must have performed this duty to the entire satisfaction of the military authorities, as he received the following letter from the Secretary-at-War: "I am glad to find that the five companies under your command were so useful in suppressing the disorders there and putting everything into a quiet and peaceful condition. I had the honour to make the King acquainted with it, and do assure you that H.M. very much approved of your conduct upon that occasion."

In Julyt hese companies were moved from Sunderland to Newcastle, where they remained until August, when they returned to Berwick. Owing to the reduction of four regiments to the Irish establishment, a circular letter, dated the 8th of July, was addressed amongst others to Lieutenant-General Sabine, informing him that 760 men would be discharged at Bristol and a like number at Chester, and that his recruiting officers could proceed there "and furnish themselves with such men as they shall want."

1728.

In consequence of an intimation having been received by General Wade from the Secretary-at-War that the King was desirous of reviewing the 23rd, the regiment was relieved in March at Berwick by Major-General Grove's regiment and was ordered to march in four divisions to Newcastle, then to York, resting a few days at both places, then on to Lincoln and Sleaford, where it arrived on the 9th of April. Thence it marched—4 companies to Dunstable, 2 to Luton, 2 to Baldock, 2 to Hitchin, 1 to Market Street, and 1 to Redbourn.

I—7

Towards the end of March a detachment of 50 N.C.O.s and men, who travelled by sea from Berwick, on landing at the Tower, were ordered to march to Islington, rest there fourteen days, and then proceed to Dunstable to join the regiment there.

On the 6th of May the regiment marched as follows: 4 companies to Kingston, 4 to Brentford, 2 to Isleworth, and 2 to Hounslow. The *London Gazette* of the 18th of May records that "His Majesty's Own Royal Regiment of Welch Fuziliers, commanded by Lieutenant General Joseph Sabine, and the Regiment of Foot commanded by the Honourable Colonel Edward Montagu, passed in review before His Majesty, and made a very fine appearance." The following additional extract is from the *London Journal*: "On Saturday, at the Review before the King and Queen upon Hounslow-Heath, General Sabine's Regiment of Welch Fusileers made so fine an appearance and performed all their exercise with so much Regularity, Exactness and Dexterity, as was highly applauded by all the General Officers then present, and approved by his Majesty, who was pleas'd to express his particular Satisfaction on that Occasion." After the review the regiment marched as follows: 5 companies to Shrewsbury, 2 to Ludlow, 2 to Monmouth, 2 to Bridgenorth, and 1 to Wenlock. In June the regiment moved to Manchester, Warrington, and Preston. On the 29th of May Lieutenant-General Sabine was informed in reference to three deserters brought before a court-martial at Chester that they were to be "sett at liberty as this is the first Court Martial that hath been laid before Her Majesty since she hath taken upon her the administration during the King's absence."

1729.

During this year a number of minor moves took place, the regiment being located in December as follows: 3 companies were at Chester, 4 at Shrewsbury, 1 at Oswestry, 1 at Wrexham, 1 at Whitchurch, two companies and ten men from each of the other companies having been reduced the previous month. This reduction brought down the establishment to 615—one company consisting of 1 captain, 1 lieutenant, 1 ensign, 3 sergeants, 3 corporals, 2 drums, and 50 privates: total, 61. Nine more companies consisted of 549 together with a chaplain, adjutant, quartermaster, surgeon and mate. In connection with this reduction it was laid down "that if there were any old officers amongst the forces that are worn out with length of service" they could retire upon half-pay. The arms now surplus were to be handed over to the Ordnance Officer at Chester.

1730.

In March a detachment of 1 officer and 28 men was sent to Aberystwyth to relieve a like detachment of the Earl of Deloraine's regiment. The detachment rejoined headquarters in March 1731. In June the regiment was moved to Birmingham, Wolverhampton, etc., and there reviewed by Major-General Gore. Towards the end of October four companies proceeded to Portsmouth to relieve a detachment of Brigadier-General Fielding's Regiment of Invalids ordered to Jersey to quell riots.

1731.

In April 1 lieutenant, 1 sergeant, and 30 men joined the companies at Portsmouth; and in July the rest of the regiment moved there from Birmingham, etc.

1732.

Early in January the regiment left Portsmouth and marched to Manchester, Warrington, etc. From this district they moved in April as follows: 6 companies to Newcastle and 4 to Durham. At the end of May the companies at Newcastle were ordered to march " to adjacent places three days before the horse races begins." In June the regiment marched to Berwick, where it was informed it would receive instructions from General Wade as to its destination.

1733.

On the 25th of December nine men were added to each of the ten companies, and in connection therewith the following extract from a letter addressed to the Captain of each company through Colonel Peers is of interest: " His Majesty expects that each of them shall have raised seven men at least of the nine additional men for their respective companies by the 24th April next upon pain of His Majesty's displeasure."

Existing returns show that the regiment was stationed " in North Britain " this year.

1734.

On the 4th of June the Duke of Argyll was instructed to review the 23rd, whose strength was then returned as 705.

1735.

Monthly regimental returns for transmission to the Sovereign were instituted in 1735. Those for the 23rd contain the following information :

    Effectives in June . . . 760
          ,,   ,, July . . . 793
          ,,   ,, August . . 770
          ,,   ,, September . . 780

The regiment was stationed at Edinburgh in August, where it was joined, as a volunteer, by George Augustus Eliott, afterwards Lord Heathfield, the celebrated Governor of Gibraltar.

1736.

At the beginning of this year a reduction was made in the establishment of the regiment to the extent of 11 men from each of the 10 companies, the disbanded N.C.O.s and men in North Britain being paid 21 days' subsistence: they were allowed three shillings in lieu of swords and belts. The quarters of the regiment where the arms were to be delivered up was Edinburgh. On the 15th of April Captain Porteous, who commanded the Edinburgh City Guard at the execution of a smuggler named Wilson, fearing a rescue, ordered his men to fire on the mob, killing or wounding seventeen persons. He was found guilty of murder on the 22nd of June, but the Queen granted him a reprieve. This so incensed the populace that on the night of the 7th of September they broke into the prison, took Porteous out, and hanged him on a dyer's signpost in the Grass Market. In consequence of this riot a request was sent from the city magistrates for the assistance of the 23rd Regiment. The outcome of it is recorded in the following letter from Major-

General Moyle, commanding the troops in North Britain in the absence of Lieutenant-General Wade, to the Duke of Newcastle:

"EDINBURGH,
"Sept. the 9th, 1736.

"MY LORD,
I think it my duty to acquaint your Grace with what happened here last Tuesday (7th inst) night about a quarter of an hour after ten, being then in my bed, Colonel Pears who commands Lieutenant-General Sabine's Regiment in the Cannon Gate came and told me he heard there was a great disturbance in the citty [sic]. On which I immediately ordered him to assemble the six companys quartered here and to parade them near the guard in the Cannon Gate and to send for the three companys from Leath which was done with as much expedition as possible for some of the Companys are quartered a great distance from the Cannon Gate. . . ."

Colonel Peers refused to force the gates unless under legal instructions from one of the Lords of the Justiciary. This could not be obtained, and in the meantime Porteous was hanged. In consequence of this disturbance it is recorded that "the regiment are much fatigued having layn two nights on their arms." At the inquiry into the riot that took place soon afterwards, a soldier of the 23rd named Webster was able at considerable risk to supply valuable information as to the whereabouts of several of the principal rioters.

1737.

At the end of March the regiment was directed to hold itself in readiness to march to Berwick in order to relieve Brigadier Handasyd's regiment, which relief, however, was not carried out until the end of July.

On the 30th of August a warrant was issued for an allowance of 5s. a day for life to Captain Henry Masolary "for long service ever since the Revolution, age, and fatigue of war." The allowance to be raised as follows: out of Captain Carey's subsistence 3s. 6d. a day, Captain-Lieutenant Hickman's 1s. a day, and First Lieutenant John Pryce's 6d. a day.

1738.

A detachment of the 23rd was ordered at the end of January " to march to Edinburgh to attend the Paymaster with the money to Berwick which he brings for subsistence of the regiment." On the 10th of May four companies marched from Berwick to Newcastle to assist the civil magistrates in suppressing riots. At the end of May the six remaining companies proceeded in two divisions to York, whence they moved at the end of July as follows: one company to each of the following towns, Dover, Cranbrook, Battle, Lewes, Reigate, and Arundel, where they were employed on preventive work. When on the march they were halted four days at Nottingham to be reviewed by Lieutenant-Colonel Peers. The four companies that remained at Newcastle were in turn ordered to march to York, and thence one company to each of the following towns, Dover, Cranbrook, Canterbury, and Battle. They also were reviewed on their journey by Major Pole.

1739.

Preventive work this year necessitated frequent moves of the companies, but at the beginning of July they were all moved within easy distance of Kew for the purpose of being reviewed by His Majesty King George II, an account of which is contained in the following letter from the Secretary-at-War to " His Excellency General Sabine at Gibraltar":

"WAR OFFICE,
"3rd Sept., 1739.

" I have the pleasure to acquaint you that I attended His Majesty at the review of your regiment on Kew Green, they went through their manual exercises and firings greatly to His satisfaction, since which His Majesty has been pleased to say He thought it alltogether the finest regiment he had seen. On Friday last he was pleased to promote Major Pole to be Lt Col to Major General Bowle's regiment of dragoons...."

At the end of August the regiment moved in 3 divisions as follows: 3 companies to Winchester, 2 to Southampton, 2 to Farnham, 1 each to Alresford, Romsey, and Petersfield. In the autumn an augmentation of 11 men to each of the 10 companies took place, making them up to 70 "effective private men" each: the levy money being £3 10s. for each man.

On the 24th of October General Joseph Sabine died at Gibraltar, of which he was Governor, and was succeeded in the colonelcy of the regiment by his nephew Lieutenant-Colonel Newsham Peers.

At the end of December volunteers, who must not be "lame, bursten, or any way disqualified," were called upon for service in Colonel Wolfe's regiment of marines: he paying 40s. levy money per man towards again completing the 23rd.

1740.

The regiment remained in the vicinity of Southampton and Winchester till the 12th of June, when a detachment consisting of 1 captain, 2 subalterns, 3 sergeants, 2 drums, and 60 privates proceeded to Newbury to prepare a camp for the regiment, which, together with other regiments of horse and foot, were there encamped under Lieutenant-General Wade. The camp was broken up at the end of September, and the regiment marched to quarters at Marlborough, Devizes, etc.

After twenty-five years of peace following the Marlborough campaigns, an event took place that was destined to involve this country in yet another continental war, known to posterity as the "War of the Austrian Succession."

In October 1740 Charles VI, the last Prince of the House of Austria who was Emperor of Germany, King of Hungary and Bohemia, died, leaving his immense dominions to his eldest daughter, the Archduchess Maria Theresa. Her ascension to the triple throne was the signal for several of the European Princes to lay claim to her Austrian territories. The most formidable of these claimants was Charles Albert, Elector of Bavaria, who was whole-heartedly supported by Louis XV.

From the outset the English people sympathised with the young Queen, and through their mouthpiece, Parliament, voted her in April 1741 a subsidy of £300,000.

Both George II and his "peace-at-any-price" Minister, Sir Robert Walpole, strove hard to keep the country aloof, but when His Majesty perceived the possibility of his Hanoverian dominion being in jeopardy, he reluctantly gave orders for a force of cavalry and infantry to be held in readiness for foreign service, the 23rd being one of the selected regiments. Beyond these preparations nothing, however, was done.

The following estimate for the supply of camp necessaries for a regiment of 10 companies shows the articles then authorised for this service.

Bell tents for arms	12
Camp colours (silk)	11
Drum cases	20
Tin kettles and bags	160
Hand hatchetts	160
Tin waterflasks	780
Haversacks	780
Knapsacks	780
Powder baggs	10

1741.

In February a draft of 50 men and 2 drums was called for from each of the 11 regiments in Great Britain, grenadier companies excepted, for incorporation in the four newly raised Marine Regiments. The draft from the 23rd was directed to join Colonel Jeffrey's regiment at Marlborough. During the summer of this year the 23rd and certain other regiments destined for the Continent were encamped on Lexden Heath, near Colchester.

1742.

The resignation of all his offices by Walpole in the spring of 1742 brought his peace policy to an end. The country soon rang with warlike preparations, and a decision was arrived at to send an army to the Continent under the command of the veteran Field-Marshal the Earl of Stair.

The expeditionary force, which consisted of eight regiments of Dragoons, the Brigade of Guards, and twelve regiments of the line, including the 23rd, was now being got ready for active service. The following interesting item, under date 22nd April, is contained in the *London Evening Post*. " The bell tents for the stands of arms, and two of the officers' tents belonging to Colonel Peers's Regiment of Welsh Fuzileers, were rais'd in St. James's Park, as a Pattern or Sample for others that are to be sent abroad."

The following extract from the *Daily Post* of Thursday, 29th April, refers to a Review which took place the previous day. "Yesterday morning Colonel Peers's Regiment of Welsh Fuzileers and Handasyd's Regiment were reviewed by His Majesty on Kew Green, from whence they marched directly for Deptford and Greenwich, in order to embark forthwith for Flanders." The force, which consisted of about 16,000 men, embarked at Deptford in May and landed at Ostend. From there it marched to Ghent and thence to Dieghem. The dilatoriness of the Dutch in furnishing their contingent prevented any operations being undertaken before it became necessary to send the troops into winter quarters.

1743.

The Allies planned for the ensuing campaign that the British and Dutch troops should march rapidly across the Rhine, head for Frankfort-on-the-Main, and effect a junction with the Austrians under Count d'Aremberg. Maestricht was fixed upon as the rendezvous.

The British contingent, leaving its winter quarters early in February, arrived there about the 10th of the month, where it remained inactive for two months owing to the reluctance of the Dutch to take the field. Lord Stair, becoming impatient at their non-arrival, gave the order to advance. On reaching Höchst, on the Main between Mayence and Frankfort, he was joined by the Austrians and some Hanoverians, which brought the total of his force to about 40,000 men.

He then advanced to Aschaffenburg with the idea of interposing between the French and their Bavarian Allies. Here he was joined by King George II, who assumed the command of the army on the 8th of June. No commander could have joined an army under more unpromising circumstances. It was suffering from semi-starvation, having had little or no bread for days; relations between Stair and d'Aremberg had become strained; it was confronted on the opposite side of the Main by an army numerically much superior; and to crown all, both sides of the Main at Aschaffenburg were occupied by the enemy, with the result that no supplies could reach the Allies.

The King perceived at once that there was no alternative but to retire as fast as possible by the right bank of the river to Hanau, where supplies and reinforcements were collected. No sooner was intelligence of this retrograde move conveyed to Noailles than he lost no time in crossing the Main above Aschaffenburg with the object of harassing the rear of the allies. At the same time he detached 30,000 of his men, under his nephew the Duc de Gramont, with orders to cross the Main at Seligenstadt, three miles in advance of the Allies, and occupy the defiles of Dettingen. The river barred the progress of the Allies on the left, impenetrable woods served the same purpose on the right. Is it, therefore, to be wondered at that Noailles should exclaim that he had his enemy in a "mousetrap," and gloat over what seemed inevitable? In all probability his plan would have succeeded admirably had not his impatient nephew abandoned an almost impregnable position, to take up another on the plain where he would be opposed by a force superior in numbers.

The King, on being informed that de Gramont barred his progress in the open, took steps to set his army in battle array. He drew it up in two lines of infantry, his left resting on the river, his right supported by nine regiments of British cavalry. The 23rd was posted slightly to the left of the first line. On the King waving his sword and shouting words of encouragement, the whole of the first line advanced.

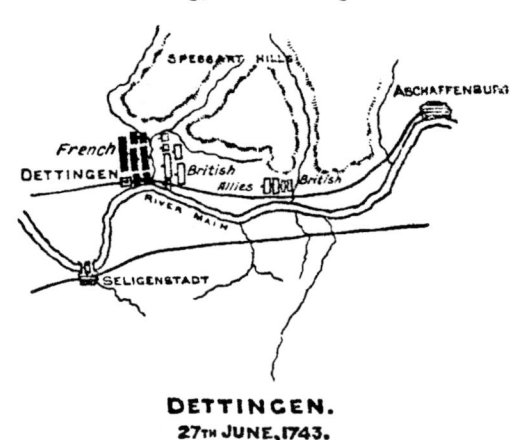

DETTINGEN.
27TH JUNE, 1743.

The following extract from the journal of "an officer in Col. Piers's Foot, of Welsh Fusiliers," gives a graphic account of the part taken by the 23rd in this battle:

"Our men were eager to come to action, and did not at all like the long bullets (as they term'd 'em) for indeed they swept off ranks and files. However, when we came to the small ones, they held them in such contempt, that they really kept the same order as at any other time. . . . Our army gave such shouts before we were engaged, when we were about 100 paces apart before the action began, that, we hear by deserters, it brought a pannick amongst them. We attack'd the Regiment of Navarre, one of their prime Regiments. Our people imitated their predecessors in the last War gloriously, marching in close order, as firm as a wall, and did not fire till we came within 60 paces, and still kept advancing: so that we had soon closed with the enemy, if they had not retreated: for when the smoak blew off a little, instead of being among their living, we found the dead in heaps by us: and the second fire turn'd them to the right about, and upon a long trot. We engaged two other Regiments afterwards, one after the other, who stood but one fire each: and their Blue French Foot Guards made the best of their way without firing a shot. Our Colonel fell in the first attack, shot in the mouth, and out at the neck: but there are hopes of his recovery. The Gens d'Armes are quite ruin'd, who are their chief Dependance, and intended to cut us to pieces without firing a shot. Our Regiment sustain'd little loss, tho' much engaged: and indeed our whole army gives us great honour. Brigadier Huske, who behaved gloriously, and quite cool, was shot thro' the foot at the time that our Colonel fell, yet continued his post. We have no more than 50 killed and wounded, and one Officer besides the Colonel. What preserved us, was our keeping close order, and advancing near the enemy ere we fir'd. Several that popp'd at 100 paces lost more of their men, and did less execution: for the French will stand fire at a distance, tho' 'tis plain they cannot look men in the face. 'Till we obtained this victory we wanted bread, and 'tis not to be imagined what fatigues the Army underwent by continual alarms. 'Till now, I assure you, I have not been under cover above two nights in 14. The night after the action, it rain'd without intermission, 'till 8 next morning, and very violent."

The Allies continued their victorious career by charging the French foot, which they utterly routed and thereby decided the fate of a battle which was waged furiously for four hours. The French lost about 6,000 in killed, wounded, and drowned in their retreat. The Allies' loss did not fall far short of 2,500. The 23rd had 15 men killed and 27 wounded. Two officers were wounded—Colonel Peers and Lieutenant Richard Price—the former succumbed to his wound a few hours after the battle was over. Twelve standards were brought home and conveyed to St. James's.

In this battle, which was fought on the 16th of June (27th June N.S.), the *London Gazette* records that " the British troops and all the Allied army, who were engaged in this action, behaved with the utmost resolution, bravery, and intrepidity."

The Allies passed the night under arms on the field of battle and continued their march next day in torrents of rain towards Hanau.

The French followed suit on the opposite side of the Main towards Offenbach.

Dettingen was the last occasion on which a British Sovereign took the field in person.

It was only on the 11th September 1882 that the regiment was permitted to bear on its colour the word "DETTINGEN" in commemoration of that battle.

In July Brigadier John Huske, having recovered from a wound in the leg which he received at Dettingen, was appointed Colonel of the 23rd in lieu of Colonel Peers, deceased. The keen interest he took in his men and everything that tended to promote their comfort soon earned for him the affectionate nickname of "Daddy Huske."

The dissensions between Stair and d'Aremberg, which were in abeyance while the Allied army was in deadly peril, broke out afresh with renewed vigour when all present danger had been removed, with the result that no further operations could be undertaken against the common enemy. Lord Stair, at his own request, was permitted to throw up the command. The army then retired into winter quarters.

1744.

At the beginning of May the Allied army, which consisted of 22,000 British troops under Marshal Wade, who had succeeded the Earl of Stair, 16,000 Hanoverians, and 20,000 Dutch, took the field and assembled at Assche, a few miles from Brussels. The French had already taken the field, a force of 120,000 men being massed on the Austrian frontier under the Duc de Noailles, with Prince Maurice of Saxe as second-in-command.

For several weeks the Allies remained inactive at Assche, the precious time being frittered away in useless and never-ending discussions about a plan of campaign on which no two of their leaders could agree, the Austrian General d'Aremberg rendering himself particularly obnoxious. At last, on the 20th of July, the Allies moved out of the town and crossed the Scheldt, where they came to a halt and remained motionless for another prolonged period, Marshal Wade's hands being tied by the indecision of some of his colleagues and the timidity of others. Full advantage of this fatal inactivity was taken by the French, who overran Western Flanders, capturing Courtray, Menin, Ypres, and other strong fortresses. The continued divided counsels of the Allies prevented any concerted action being taken. Purposeless marches and counter-marches became the order of the day. Finally, early in October, the Allies crossed the Lys and retired into winter quarters. Marshal Wade, in utter disgust, requested the King's permission to resign his command in Flanders and return to England, which H.M. was pleased to grant.

At the end of June the regiments of foot serving in Flanders were ordered to be augmented by two companies: each to consist of 1 captain, 1 lieutenant, 1 ensign, 3 sergeants, 3 corporals, 2 drums, and 70 private men. In September these two additional companies of the 23rd were formed and were quartered at Cambridge.

On the 13th of December 1745 the two additional companies of Huske's, Wolfe's, Ligonier's, Bligh's, Fleming's, and Skelton's regiments were ordered to march to Portsmouth to be formed into a battalion under Colonel Cotterell. In the case of the 23rd this does not appear to have been carried out, as the companies were still stationed in the vicinity of Cambridge, St. Neots, and St. Ives.

During the next few years these companies appear to have marched and counter-marched, performing miscellaneous duties, such as preventive work, garrison duty at Landguard Fort, etc.

At the beginning of January 1748 these companies furnished a draft of 1 captain, 1 subaltern, 2 sergeants, and 60 privates, who marched to Harwich for embarkation to Holland.

On the 27th of September 1748 the O.C. of the additional companies at St. Neots was ordered to draft all men between 18 and 28 years of age and not under 5 feet 6 inches, and to march them to Colchester, to be inspected and examined by Major-General Cholmondley. No men in future to be enlisted under 5 feet 7 inches. On the 8th of November orders were issued for the two additional companies to be disbanded and paid 14 days' subsistence, with the usual allowance of 3s. for their sword.

1745.

In March this year H.R.H. the Duke of Cumberland was made Captain-General of all the forces in Flanders. On the 5th of April he set out for Holland, and arrived at Anderlecht, a suburb of Brussels, on the 10th, where the British and Dutch troops were assembled. He immediately set to work to improve the discipline of his troops. It is recorded of the British troops that " they being new-cloth'd made a fine appearance and were very desirous of engaging yᵉ enemy."

It was apparent that Marshal Saxe with his numerically superior army of 76,000 men intended to attack one of the frontier fortresses, but the question was, which would he select. The Duke maintained that Mons would be invested, this being the result of a skilful feint on the part of Saxe to induce him to arrive at this conclusion. Faulty intelligence work was also instrumental in keeping the Duke in the dark for several days as to the real object of the Marshal.

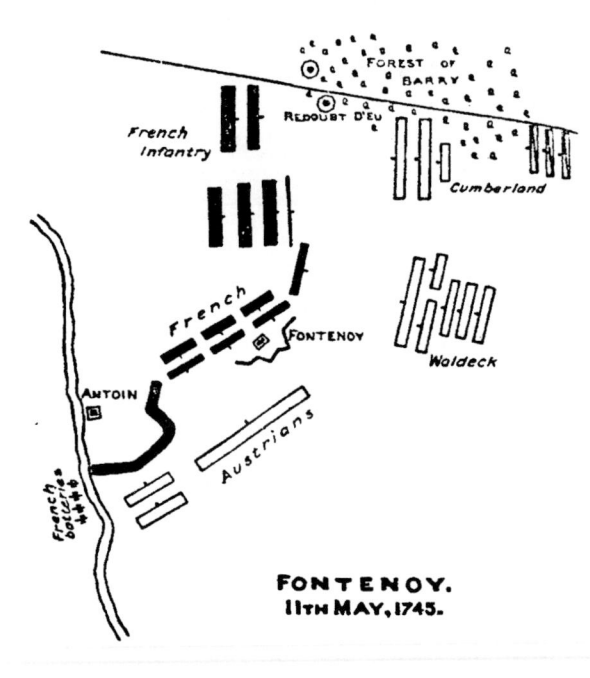

On the 19th of April the latter swooped down upon Tournay and invested it. The same day Cumberland left Brussels and, advancing leisurely by Hal, Cambron, and Leuse, reached Brissoel, about fifteen miles south-west of Tournay, on the 28th of April. Here he came within sight of Saxe's outposts and encamped for the night. The following morning he advanced to attack the French, who had taken up a position at Fontenoy to bar the road to Tournay. After marching for two hours the troops were halted to take up their ground preparatory to a general attack on the enemy.

The Duke drew up his British infantry with the exception of four regiments in two lines to the right, this being the post of honour. The 23rd formed part of the second line. Both flanks were protected by cavalry, the British being on the right and the Dutch on the left. The four regiments referred to, viz. the 12th, 13th, 42nd, and a Hanoverian battalion, were brigaded under Brigadier Ingoldsby, who had orders to lose no time in attacking a field-work called the Redoubt d'Eu, which guarded the edge of a forest that lay to the right of the British column. The Austrians and Dutch, under the Prince of Waldeck, were posted in the centre and on the left of the line.

Soon after 9 o'clock on the morning of the 30th of April (11th May N.S.) the order for the general advance was given. The British infantry, stepping out with all its wonted steadiness, soon came under a cross-fire from Fontenoy and the Redoubt d'Eu which exacted heavy toll of the advancing column. In no way daunted, the men moved forward as if on parade, and, successfully storming the entrenchments, though with greatly depleted ranks, actually penetrated into the French camp.

Nothing now was wanted to ensure complete success but the silencing of the fire from the redoubt in question and the timely support of the Austrians and Dutch, who, unknown to the British troops, had fallen back, being unable to stand the flanking fire of a battery that was posted on the other side of the Scheldt. A murderous fire from all sides was now poured into the brave British troops, who had come to a halt and were anxiously gazing on all sides for their allies. No help being forthcoming, the order was given to retire some distance and re-form. Most unaccountably, so far Brigadier Ingoldsby had made no attempt to capture the Redoubt d'Eu. The Duke, having received an assurance from the Dutch that they would make a second attack on Fontenoy, ordered his British infantry to advance again. The same ground was once more traversed with heavy loss—thanks in great measure to Ingoldsby's continued inactivity—and the French camp penetrated as before, when it was noised abroad that the Dutch, on whom so much depended, had obstinately refused to advance on the order to do so being given. Nothing now remained but to beat a general retreat, which was conducted in an orderly fashion.

The 23rd was one of the heaviest sufferers in this battle. Its losses were as follows:

Killed.—Lieutenants John Weaver, Arthur Forster, John Pryce, — Isaac, 4 sergeants, and 181 privates.

Wounded.—Captains William Hickman, James Carey, John Bernard, James Drysdale, Lieutenants William Izard, William Awbry, Esme Clarke, Henry Eyre, William Roberts, Thomas Rodd, 6 sergeants, and 71 privates.

Missing.—Major Roger Lort, Captains Arthur Taylor, Joseph Sabine, Alexander Johnston, Lieutenants Gregory Berners, Edward Gregg, Nathaniel Hawes and Roger Lort, 5 sergeants, and 34 privates.

In Tenby Church there is a monument to the memory of " Roger Lort Esq. youngest son of George Lort of Prickeston in this county, Esq., who, being major of the regiment of Royal Welsh Fusiliers, was killed at the battle of Fontenoy near Lisle A.D. 1745, aged 51 years."

The Allies retired first to Ath, where they encamped under the guns of the fortress for a short time, and then proceeded to Lessines.

In consequence of the very heavy losses sustained by the 23rd, 12th, and 21st regiments they were sent, under command of Colonel Ligonier, to perform garrison duty—the 23rd at Ghent, and the 12th and 21st at Ostend. A return, dated 11th June (N.S.), gives the following particulars respecting the regiment—Present fit, 1 Lieut.-Colonel, 2 captains, 3 lieutenants, 3 second lieutenants, 5 staff, 18 sergeants, 15 drummers, 289 fit, 59 sick present, 92 sick in hospital; total, 440. Wanting to complete: 12 sergeants, 5 drummers, 260 men.

On 6th July Cumberland dispatched Lieut.-General Molke with a force consisting of 10 squadrons and three battalions—The Royals, 16th and 20th regiments—to strengthen the garrison of Ghent. When three miles short of Melle they were attacked by the enemy, with the result that the 16th and 20th retired on Alost, whilst Molke with The Royals and the cavalry pushed their way on to Ghent.

This gallant effort was abortive, as they were hardly a day there before the garrison was surprised by the enemy appearing in force, and compelled to surrender, being marched as prisoners of war to Lille.

In a *state* of the regiments in the Low Countries taken on the 16th of July, the following appears: "Royal Welch Fuzileers—taken in the Cittadel of Ghent."

Towards the end of September the regiment was exchanged, rejoined Cumberland's forces on the 7th of October, and proceeded to the coast for embarkation, in the first of two divisions into which the 11 battalions destined for England were divided.

The 23rd landed at Harwich towards the end of October, and marching to Hertfordshire were billeted at Hertford, Ware, etc. On the 4th of November a detachment, consisting of a sergeant and 12 men of the 3rd Foot Guards, was ordered to "escort the Paymaster of Major-General Huske's regiment from London to Ware." A small detachment of two sergeants and two corporals was sent to Kensington "to receive such recruits as shall be delivered to them from time to time from the vestrys of St. Martin's and St. James's Parishes."

On the 9th of December the regiment marched to Paddington, Tottenham Court, Kentish Town, etc., where it remained until the 14th, when it moved to Newington, Camberwell, and Peckham, "where they are to be quartered on the public houses till the barns and empty houses can be got ready for them, there to lye on straw, and you are to direct the Quartermaster to proceed immediately to Peckham, and apply himself to the Commissary who is to furnish wood and straw and is to be heard of at the Red Cow in Peckham."

On the 20th the regiment moved to Rochester, Stroud, and Chatham.

At the beginning of this month the 23rd was one of six regiments which were ordered to take the field, presumably in connection with the Jacobite Rebellion. In addition to the usual military stores, transport, etc., furnished, the Quakers, to show their loyalty, " agreed by voluntary contribution to furnish flannel waistcoats for the use of the soldiers in this severe season." This example was followed by the merchants in London, who furnished " a blanket and two canvas paliasses for every tent, and thirty waistcoats for every battalion as well as a pair of worsted gloves for each non-commissioned officer and private man."

Sergeant Peter Hewitt on the 29th of May was granted a commission in the regiment for gallant conduct at Fontenoy. This is the first occasion on which a non-commissioned officer was granted a commission in the regiment, so far as can be ascertained. He was wounded at the battle of Lauffeld. He was promoted Lieutenant on the 2nd of June 1748; promoted Captain in the 2nd Battalion on the 30th of August 1756; Captain in the 68th Regiment (on the 2nd Battalion of the 23rd Regiment being made a separate corps and being given a number).

Thomas Stevenson, " trooper," evidently from a cavalry regiment, received a commission in the regiment on the same day, 29th of May. He exchanged with Ensign Richard Lloyd of Bragg's regiment (28th Foot) on the 16th of April 1746.

1746.

From Rochester the regiment moved in three divisions on the 13th, 14th, and 15th of January to Guildford and Godalming. On the 13th of March a detachment of 2 officers, 4 sergeants, 4 corporals, and 70 men proceeded from Godalming to Harwich, " where the private men are to be incorporated into the additional companies to the said regiment, and a draught of 100 private men is to be made from the said corps who are to march to Godalming and their join the regiment."

On the 2nd of April the Secretary-at-War, in a letter to the O.C. Troops at Carlisle, intimated that he had received a letter from the Mayor of Kendal informing him that he had amongst other arms and gunpowder captured from the rebels the following: "one firelock with slings marked on the barrell 'Royal Welsh' on butt 'Captain Cary 9/58.'" Conjecture is rife as to how this musket got into the hands of the rebels, considering that, so far as is known, the regiment was never within 200 miles of the line of march of the Young Pretender.

On the 17th of April 6 companies moved to Reading and 4 to Newbury, being relieved by Colonel Murray's regiment. On the 7th of June 5 companies were ordered "to march with all possible expedition to Exeter, there to follow such orders as they shall receive from Major General Read." This move was evidently undertaken in view of yet another of the many expected descents of the French upon the coast.

On the 10th of June Major-General Huske was directed to instruct his recruiting officers to obtain such recruits as they required from the nine regiments then being disbanded. As showing the interest the King continued to take in everything connected with the 23rd, the Secretary-at-War wrote to Lieutenant-Colonel Waite on the 21st of June, "that as 40 to 50 men in Major General Huske's regiment are thought to be of too small size to serve therein you are to take care not to discharge same when replaced in the regiment by other recruits. His Majesty directs they shall be incorporated into some other corps whose standard is of a lesser size than the men in General Huske's regiment."

The high opinion of Major-General Huske which the King entertained is shown by the following letter from the Secretary-at-War to the General:

"WAR OFFICE,
23rd June, 1746.

"When I moved His Majesty to make the Adjutant you recommended, in room of Mr. Izard promoted, he asked me if it was your recommendation, and told me that I might always rely upon what you said for you was a very honest man as well as an exceeding good officer."

On the 5th of August a detachment equal to an entire company was ordered to march from Bristol on the 25th to Bath to attend on H.R.H. the Princess Caroline during her residence there, but remained for a very short time, being relieved by a dismounted detachment from Lieutenant-General Sir Robert Rich's regiment of Dragoons in September. The detachment returned to Bristol, whence the regiment proceeded to Plymouth, where they embarked on board the transports.

At the end of October the 23rd was disembarked at Gravesend and marched to Southwark; thence 6 companies proceeded to Reading and 4 to Newbury. Early in November a detachment as before was ordered from Reading to Bath to take over the duties of guard to H.R.H. the Princess Caroline, and rejoined the regiment in the middle of December on the departure of the Princess.

Hitherto it was the practice to recover deserters by having them conveyed by the same escort from point to point, but from now onwards the practice was to hand over the deserters from unit to unit for conveyance to their destination.

1747.

On the 12th of January the regiment moved from Reading and Newbury to London, where it was reviewed on the 17th by His Majesty. The following account of the review is extracted from the *Penny London Post*: "Last Saturday his Majesty reviewed the two battalions of Foot Guards, and the Regiment of Welch Fuzileers, commanded by General Husk in the Green Park, facing the Library. His Majesty was attended by his Royal Highness the Prince of Wales, the Duke of Cumberland, the Dukes of Montagu, Bolton and Richmond, the Earls of Pembroke and Cadogan, and several other of the nobility. They made a very fine appearance and it is said will embark next Friday. His Royal Highness the Prince of Wales, dressed in regimentals, walked through the Park afterwards behind the Battalions." On the 27th the regiment marched as follows: 5 companies to Greenwich, 3 to Woolwich, and 2 to Charlton.

On the 28th of January the 23rd sailed from Gravesend for the Netherlands, where the war undertaken on behalf of Maria Theresa was still being waged. The regiment embarked 800 strong, with 60 horses and 25 tons of baggage. On landing at Wilhelmstadt, the regiment marched to Tilburg, near Breda, where the Allies were concentrating their forces. The Duke of Cumberland, who was again chosen to take command of the whole, found himself in due course at the head of about 110,000 men.

No movement was possible for several weeks, owing to the inclemency of the weather. When at last a forward movement was feasible, the Duke was hampered at every turn by Waldeck, who commanded the Dutch contingent, and by Batthyani, who commanded the Austrians. They were furiously jealous of each other, but united in opposing him as far as they dared.

At last, on the 1st of May, the Allied army marched towards Antwerp with the object of recapturing it, but found themselves forestalled by Marshal Löwendahl, who, by direction of Marshal Saxe, had thrown himself with a considerable force into the citadel.

A period of inactivity followed consequent upon discord in the Allied camp, during which the Duke was reduced to the helpless position of watching Saxe's movements. On ascertaining, however, that all appearances pointed to an attack on Maestricht, Cumberland induced his worthless colleagues to consent to advance with the object of interposing between that town and the French army.

A rapid and skilful movement by Saxe, which resulted in his capturing the Herdeeren Heights, reversed the situation, as it enabled the French to interpose between the Allies and Maestricht. On the 21st of June both armies made ready for battle. The Allies were drawn up in three lines, the Austrians to the right, the Dutch in the centre, and the British and Germans on the left. The straggling village of Lauffeld, which was occupied by five British and Hanoverian regiments and had cannon planted for its protection on both front and flanks, was the key to the Allied position.

At 10 a.m. the ball was opened by a determined assault upon this village. Three times it was taken, but as often recaptured. A fourth assault made about noon was more fortunate, as it enabled the enemy to gain a footing from which it was impossible to dislodge him. Seeing the uselessness of continuing to make counter-attacks upon Lauffeld, the Duke, hoping to gain more favourable results in other quarters, launched from the centre of the position the Dutch cavalry, which, after advancing for some distance, was suddenly seized with uncontrollable panic. Wheeling about, it bore down direct upon the 21st and 23rd Regiments. The former fired a volley into the Dutchmen which to a considerable extent saved it from the worst consequences, but the Welshmen, less fortunate, were knocked down in scores and trampled upon by the affrighted horsemen. This left the Allied centre open to attack, which was an opportunity too good to be lost by the Marshal, who launched his carabiniers upon it, with the result that Cumberland's army was rent in twain.

Seeing that the day was lost, the Duke ordered a retirement upon Maestricht. Great havoc would have been wrought in the ranks of the retiring infantry, who were beginning to feel the pressure of the enemy cavalry on their rear, had not Sir John Ligonier at the head of three cavalry regiments most gallantly charged the pursuing French, with the result that they recoiled in confusion and lost five standards. Thereafter the retreat was effected in good order with trifling loss. In addition to the five standards captured by Ligonier, nine colours were also taken. The Allies lost about 6,000 men and were obliged to abandon 16 guns. The French loss was considerably more, amounting to over 9,000 men.

The casualties of the 23rd were as follows:

Killed.—Captain Alexander Johnston and one man.

Wounded.—Captains Fortescue, William Izard, and Thomas Baldwin; Lieutenants Eyre, Rich, Gregg, William Adey, Archibald McLaughlin, Peter Hewitt, and 42 men.

Missing.—Lieutenant Hildebrand Oakes and 187 men.

The Allies managed to cross the Meuse, but were then held in check by the French until the arrival of winter, which put an end to any further operations this year.

Volunteer William Lowes was granted a commission as 2nd Lieutenant in the regiment on 25th of June 1747, and was promoted 1st Lieutenant on the 19th of February 1754.

1748.

During the winter negotiations for peace were being conducted at Aix-la-Chapelle in a very half-hearted manner, owing to the mutual mistrust of the Allies, preventing them from accepting the terms offered by Louis XV, which must be considered as advantageous.

The war therefore dragged on, the allied rendezvous for the approaching campaign being fixed at Eyndhoven. Once more the Duke of Cumberland was appointed Commander-in-Chief. Saxe was first in the field and lost no time in investing Maestricht at the beginning of April. As Cumberland's army was much inferior in numbers, he could only be described as holding a " watching brief."

On his ascertaining that preliminaries for peace had been signed at Aix-la-Chapelle on the 19th of April, he made overtures to Saxe for an armistice and for the surrender of Maestricht, which were accepted by Louis XV.

The last act in the drama was the opening of the gates of that fortress to Marshal Löwendahl on the 30th of April. Hostilities altogether ceased on the signing of the Treaty of Aix-la-Chapelle on the 7th of October. Early in December the British troops embarked for home, but encountered on the passage a severe storm that dispersed the transports; those, however, conveying the 23rd appear to have safely reached Leith.

A compassionate warrant was issued this year granting 7s. a day to Lieutenant-Colonel John Wait for life, made up as follows: from the pay of the Lieutenant-Colonel 2s. a day, from the pay of the Major 5s. a day.

Volunteer Samuel Leslie was granted a commission as 2nd Lieutenant on the 2nd of June 1748. He was promoted 1st Lieutenant on the 5th of July 1755. His name does not appear as being in the regiment in any Army List after 1757.

Volunteer Benjamin Bernard, from the dates available in all probability a son of Captain John Bernard of the regiment, was promoted 2nd Lieutenant therein on the 3rd of June 1748; promoted 1st Lieutenant on the 2nd of October 1755; appointed Adjutant on the 23rd of March 1756; promoted Captain on the 20th of December 1760; promoted Major on the 24th of January 1764; and Lieutenant-Colonel on the 28th of August 1771. He was succeeded on the 31st of January 1778 by Lieutenant-Colonel Nesbit Balfour.

1749.

The inspection returns show that the regiment was stationed at Aberdeen from the 1st of January to the end of April, the effective strength being 659 rank and file, wanting 71.

Although the regiment was stationed in the north of Scotland, a party under Lieutenant Lowe was recruiting this year as far south as Sheffield.

1750.

In consequence of the arduous duties that had to be performed by the troops serving in the Highlands, a special gratuity of one pair of shoes and one pair of stockings, or in lieu thereof 4s. and 2s., was granted on the 2nd of February. In March Rich's regiment was directed to hand over its tents to the 23rd at Inverness for their summer encampment, as the regiment had moved in May to Banff, and in June to Elgin, Forres, and Nairn, arriving at Fort George at the end of that month. Their winter quarters are indicated by the following extract from the *Scot's Magazine* for September 1750: "Towards the end of September the Welch Fusiliers encamped at Ardersier Point, struck their tents, and marched to Inverness etc. for winter quarters."

1751.

At the end of February a tragic occurrence took place. A party consisting of 1 sergeant, 1 corporal, and 16 men crossing Dornoch Firth on their way to Caithness "were unfortunately cast away: five men only being saved, and 1 halbert, 17 firelocks, slings and bayonets, and 11 cartouch boxes were at the same time lost."

The regiment was stationed in Inverness till June, when it encamped at Maryburgh, arriving in Glasgow at the end of September. On the 1st of July a Royal Warrant consolidating the various clothing warrants that had been issued from time to time was promulgated. It will be referred to in the chapter on clothing and equipment in Vol. II. This is the first occasion on which regiments were known by their numbers, but the practice of distinguishing them by their Colonels' names was not dropped for some years to come.

1752.

At the end of July orders were issued for the 23rd to proceed at the end of the camping season to Carlisle, where two companies were to be left until relieved by Pulteney's: the remaining companies were directed to march to St. Albans, where they appear to have arrived about the middle of October, as orders were sent to them there on the 5th of October to proceed to Reading in three divisions, where they were reviewed by Lieutenant-General Campbell. From Reading they marched at the end of November as follows:

The Colonel's, Lieutenant-Colonel's, Major's, and Captain Poole's companies to Dover, Captain Napier's to Deal, Captain Baldwin's to Canterbury, Captain Proby's to Bromley, Captain Izard's to Sevenoaks, Captain Marlay's to Maidstone, and Captain Adey's to Cranbrook, where they were stationed and were mostly employed on preventive work.

1753.

Early in April the 23rd was reviewed at Guildford by Lieutenant-General Campbell, after which five companies proceeded to Exeter, the other five remaining in Sussex to assist the Excise. One of the companies was directed to proceed to Colehampton and observe the following instructions: "You take care a civill officer be always present, when repelling force with force may be necessary, that the proceedings may be legall."

On the 22nd of August the five companies in Sussex received orders to march to Bristol. On arriving there a detachment consisting of "officers, non-commissioned officers and 25 privates" was dispatched to Aberistwith (sic) "to assist in preserving the King's warehouses, the mine of Esgaer Emnyen and whatever is necessary in suppressing all disturbances."

The regiment was reviewed on the 23rd of October at Bristol by Sir John Mordaunt.

1754.

On the 25th and 26th of March five companies of the regiment marched from Bristol to Plymouth, and on the 29th the other five companies left their quarters for the same destination, the regiment being under orders to embark for Minorca.

The 23rd embarked in April for Minorca, relieving the 37th Regiment. The garrison of the island consisted on its arrival of the 4th, 23rd, 24th, and 34th Regiments, together with a company of artillery. In North America, Great Britain and France were striving for supremacy, but although hostilities had been carried on for some time, no declaration of war had so far been made by either country.

1756.

Early in January 1756 the French Government decided to make a descent upon Minorca, which was valuable to England both for guarding its Mediterranean trade and also as possessing a fine harbour where ships could comfortably refit. Preparations for this expedition were being openly made at Toulon and its destination noised abroad. Nothing, however, would persuade the infatuated English Ministry that its object could be other than an intended invasion of England. As late as March it appears to have dawned upon them that it was a Mediterranean port which, after all, was likely to be attacked.

Consequently, an ill-manned fleet, consisting of ten ships, was equipped and dispatched on the 7th of April under the command of Admiral Byng to the Mediterranean, having the 7th Regiment on board. On the following day a French fleet, carrying 16,000 troops under the command of the Duc de Richelieu, sailed from Toulon and reached Minorca on the 18th of April.

General Blakeney, the governor of the island, a gallant old soldier but almost crippled with gout, had in all about 2,800 men to oppose the French. The fighting value of this force was to a certain extent discounted by the fact that there was a serious shortage of officers at the moment, especially those of superior rank. The French landed unopposed, whereupon General Blakeney withdrew his force into Fort St. Philip, which was immediately invested. For seventy days he gallantly withstood the fire of nearly ninety guns, howitzers, and mortars.

Once during this memorable siege the devoted garrison rejoiced at the sight of the tardy appearance of Admiral Byng's fleet in the offing. Their joy was, however, short-lived, as a French fleet bore down upon Byng, who, to the amazement and consternation of the anxious watchers, contented himself with putting up a "mock fight," ending in his showing the enemy a clean pair of heels, with the result, so far as he was concerned, that his earthly career soon came to an abrupt termination.

For some time the French batteries could make little or no impression upon the fortifications, but by the first week in June they had increased to such an extent that very soon a considerable breach was caused by the fire of over one hundred guns and mortars. The besieged repaired the breach as far as possible, and manfully stuck to their guns. On the 14th of June a party sallied from the fortress and succeeded in spiking several guns, but, pursuing their success too far, were surrounded and taken prisoner almost to a man.

At 10 p.m. on the night of the 27th of June the enemy made a determined attack upon the "Inner Covert Way," but was repulsed. During the attack the quarters of the working party of the 23rd were taken, with the result that most of the men lost their knapsacks, waistbelts, pouches, swords, etc. Fuller particulars of this attack are contained in the report of the Inspecting General of February 1757.

In no way daunted, the garrison heroically held out, and it was not until three of the principal outworks known as the Queen's Redoubt and the Argyll and Anstruther batteries were captured that Blakeney felt he and his devoted band had now to face the inevitable. A council of war was called, which unanimously decided that as there were hardly enough men left to man the guns, there was no alternative but to propose terms of capitulation, which in the main were accepted by Richelieu.

The French writer Cesternes, in describing the capitulation, makes the following statement about the 23rd: "1 battalion of fusiliers royal or of Wales, commanded by Major Pool, the General Husk, colonel being absent and the Lieut.-Colonel being dead."

All the honours of war were accorded to the vanquished for their "noble and vigorous defence." By the terms of the capitulation the British troops were conveyed to Gibraltar. During the siege the 23rd lost 28 killed, and 90 wounded, including 1 officer, Lieutenant John Pryce. Two men died of disease.

In November the 23rd left Gibraltar and landed at Southampton at the end of the month. From there it proceeded to Winchester, Oxford, and Leicester, where it was stationed, together with the newly raised second battalion.

On the 25th of August fifteen regiments, of which the 23rd was one, were augmented with a second battalion, consisting of 10 companies of 70 privates each, making, with officers included, 815 per battalion at a daily cost of £40 4s. 8d. Brevet Lieutenant-Colonel John Lambton commanded the 2nd battalion of the 23rd. It is interesting to note that the medical work was performed by two surgeon's mates instead of a surgeon and surgeon's mate.

The company officers were as follows:

Captain William Rowley	. . .	From 78th Company of Marines.
,, William Fowler	. . .	,, 27th Foot.
,, George Bingham	. . .	,, ,, ,,
,, John Fox	. . .	,, 1st Battalion, 23rd Regiment.
,, William Dundas	. . .	,, 59th Foot.
,, Peter Hewitt	. . .	,, 1st Battalion, 23rd Regiment.
,, Richard Lloyd	. . .	,, ,, ,, ,, ,,
,, Tristram Revell	. . .	,, 9th Foot.
,, John Blacquire	. . .	,, 11th Dragoons.
,, Robert Ridley	. . .	,, 1st Foot Guards.
1st Lieutenant Charles Reynell	. .	From 27th Foot.
,, ,, Joseph Patterson	. .	,, ,, ,,
,, ,, James Sutherland	. .	,, Scotch Dutch.
,, ,, Arthur Barber	. .	,, 30th Foot.
,, ,, Philip Mercier	. .	,, 14th Dragoons.
,, ,, Arthur Hawthorne	.	Q.M., 23rd Foot.
,, ,, Lewis Bellew	. .	Sergeant, 18th Foot.
,, ,, Robert Young	.	Sergeant, 23rd Foot.
,, ,, — Porter	. . .	,, ,, ,,
,, ,, Edward Evans	.	From 1st Troop, Horse Guards.
,, ,, John Haswell	. .	,, ,, ,, ,, ,,
2nd Lieutenant George Orpin	.	Not known.
,, ,, William Blakeney	.	From 27th Foot.
,, ,, Robert Gibbins	.	Not known.
,, ,, Joseph Ferguson	.	,, ,,
,, ,, — Whaley	.	,, ,,
,, ,, John Hunt	. .	,, ,,
,, ,, William Alderton	.	,, ,,
,, ,, William Teesdale		,, ,,
,, ,, Owen Hodgson	.	,, ,,

In October the 2nd battalion was quartered at Leicester and Loughborough. Sixteen men drawn from three regiments of Dragoon Guards joined it at the former place, and were appointed non-commissioned officers.

In the following month the Commissioners for Recruiting decided to allot "all impressed men from Leicestershire and Northamptonshire to General Huske's Regiment."

Another great continental war was started this year. It is known in history as the "Seven Years' War." At a later period it will be explained in due course how Great Britain was drawn into it.

1757.

In February the invalids belonging to the garrison at Minorca, who had been left behind in charge of 1st Lieutenant Benjamin Young of the 23rd, were landed at Deal. He was instructed to obtain the services of a surgeon, and carts (if necessary) for their conveyance to Chelsea Hospital.

On the 14th the 1st battalion and those companies of the 2nd battalion which had been formed were ordered to rendezvous at Leicester, so that they might have a field-day before the review on the 16th by Major-General the Earl of Ancram.

The Inspecting General in his report furnishes the following particulars of the regiment:

"Under Arms

"Lieutenant-Colonel Pole and 22 officers, 17 sergeants, 30 corporals, 15 drummers, 520 privates fit, total 630, wanting to complete 70, 11 officers absent."

The nationality of the officers was as follows: 17 English, 3 Scotch (Captain Napier, 2nd Lieutenants Monro and Farquison [sic]), and 10 Irish (Major Marlay, Captains Rainey and Rowley, Lieutenants Leslie, Bernard, Pattison, and Hawthorne, 2nd Lieutenants Orpin, Blakeney, and Gibbins).

The N.C.O.s and men were divided as follows: 602 English, 79 Scotch, 29 Irish. As regards size, ten were over 6 feet, the majority being 5 feet 8 inches with 10 years' service.

"Return of Arms

"Wanting 9 halberts, 8 drums, 70 firelocks, 144 bayonets, 283 cartridge boxes, 70 ramrods. The several species of arms and accoutrements wanting (excepting some few destroyed during the siege) were all lost the night of the attack. The sergeants (as all of them carried arms) lost nine halberts and the drummers (as all carried arms that were able) lost 8 drums, and the rest (12) all damaged, tho' not many years delivered to them (March 1752). The officers by Lord Blakeney's order carried fuzees, and lost all their espontoons and in general most of their baggage and cloathes except what they had on that night."

"Return of Accoutrements

"Colours 2 bad. Wanting 662 swords, 206 waistbelts, 577 pouches with shoulder belts, 299 slings, 35 grenadier match cases, 7 pioneers axes, 3 saws, 10 aprons.

"The working men the night of the attack (the 27th of June,

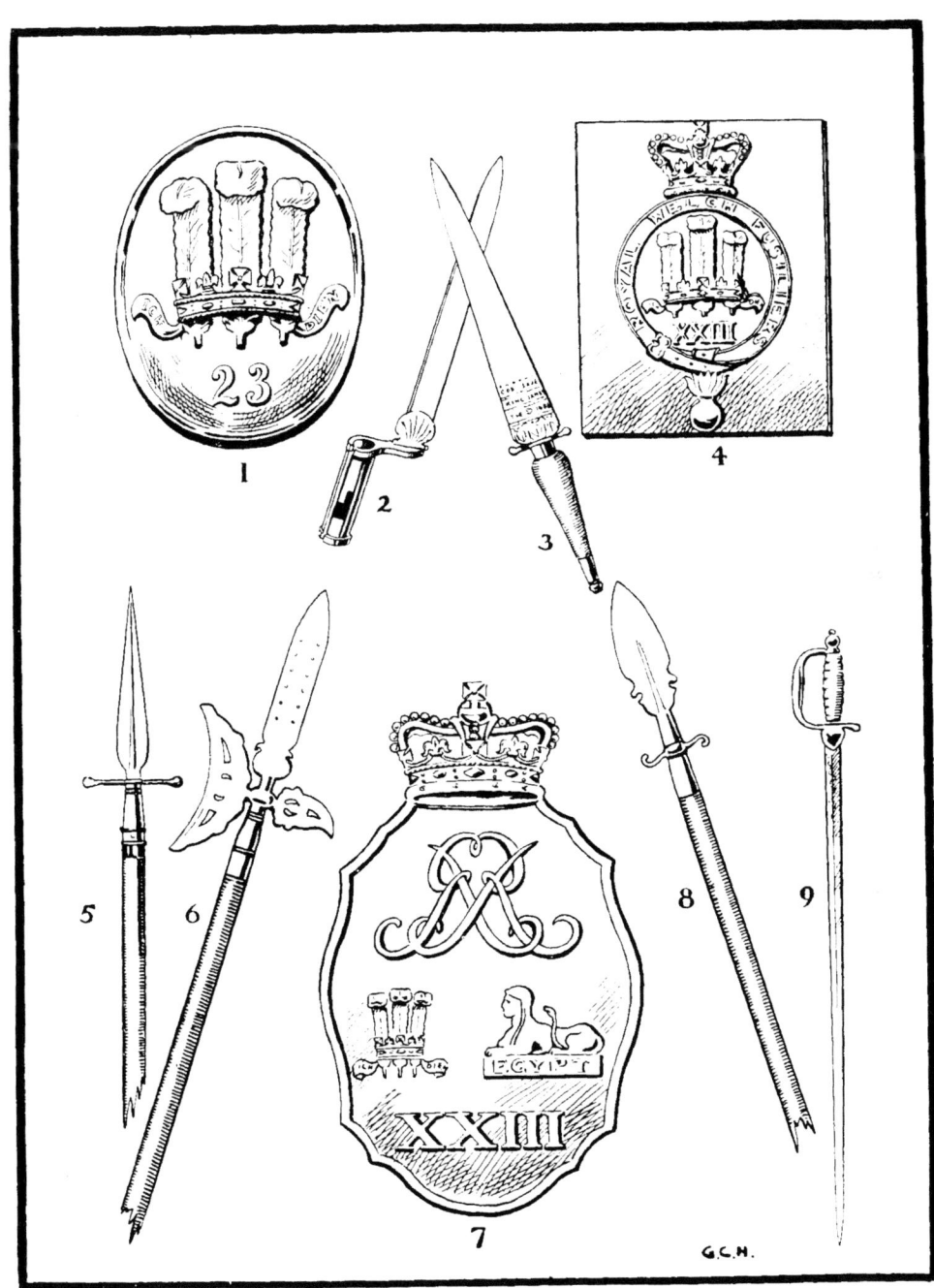

1. OFFICER'S SHOULDER-BELT PLATE, ABOUT 1800.
2. SOCKET BAYONET, 1700.
3. PLUG BAYONET, 1689.
4. OFFICER'S SHOULDER-BELT PLATE, 1815.
5. SERGEANT'S PIKE, 1792.
6. SERGEANT'S HALBERT, 1700.
7. OFFICER'S HAT PLATE, 1811—1815.
8. ESPONTOON, 1786.
9. OFFICER'S SWORD, 1800.

Siege of Minorca) lost all their pouches and almost all of their waistbelts and swords. The Hatchet men's tools were all lost the same evening, and most of the men lost their knapsacks with their necessaries, as their quarters were storm'd and took while they defended the Inner covert way: on which amount the regiment is indebted to the Captains betwixt two and three hundred pounds. Almost all the spare cloathing by Lord Blakeney's orders were delivered for the use of the Greeks and sailors.

"Officers—Salute very well.

"Men—Strong and well made—very well sized under arms. The N.C.O.s alert on their duty. The sergeants have sashes.

"In general—It is a very fine regiment."

In anticipation of the 1st battalion of the regiment being called upon to take the field, all the old arms were called in by the Board of Ordnance, and a fresh issue of 730 firelocks and bayonets, iron ramrods, cartouch boxes and straps, 36 halberts, and 20 drums substituted in lieu.

On the 23rd of May the 1st battalion left Leicester, arriving at Newbury on the 31st; the 2nd battalion left Loughborough on the 23rd, reaching Reading on the 1st of June. On the 27th of June the 1st battalion left Newbury and arrived at Chatham, "and encamped within the lines encompassing the dock" on the 5th and 6th of July, the 2nd battalion also reaching there on the 7th of the month. On the 9th of August a draft of 80 men from the two battalions was ordered to reach Winchester on the 11th of September for embarkation to America to assist in making good the wastage in the regiments then serving there. Each detachment of 40 men to be in charge of a lieutenant, who was allowed 5s. a day for this extra duty; the regiment to receive £5 for each man furnished, together with £1 18s. 3d. for his clothing. At the end of September both battalions of the regiment moved to Dover Castle and Folkestone.

On the 24th of September the 1st battalion was inspected at Chatham by Major-General George Sackville. He reported as follows: "Colours: 2 bad. Arms: good, having been received in July 1757. Men: A tall, well made strong body of men, clean and well dressed under arms. Accoutrements: Well put on. Caps: Good and well put on. Uniform: Red, lapelled and faced with blue, with a red, blue, yellow and white striped worsted lace."

The 2nd battalion was inspected the same day and at the same place. General Sackville reported as follows: "Under arms, 23 officers, 18 sergeants, 16 drummers, 468 privates. Colours: 2 good. Officers: uniform only frocks faced with blue and bound with a narrow gold lace. Men: a low body of men very few old. Caps: good in general but too big. Cloathing: Very good, but few white gaiters. Brown gaiters compleat in number and tolerably good."

Towards the end of September a reduction in the regiment took place. The establishment of the 1st battalion was fixed at 9 companies of 100 men each. The 2nd battalion lost its 10th or "youngest" company, which was ordered, under the youngest lieutenant and 2nd lieutenant, to march to Chelmsford to form part of a newly raised regiment under Lieutenant-Colonel Draper for service in the East Indies.

1758.

On the 1st and 2nd of May the two battalions of the regiment moved from Dover to the Isle of Wight, being ordered to encamp there by the 16th and 17th of the month and prepare for foreign service. This warning proved to be the precursor of one of the many minor expeditions to which Mr. Pitt was partial.

The scene selected for operations was St. Malo, the object being to destroy the arsenal and shipping there, and at the same time divert the French from sending troops to America and Germany. The force collected in the Isle of Wight for this undertaking amounted to about 13,000 men. Both battalions of the 23rd were employed on this enterprise, and together with the 33rd and 68th Regiments formed the 3rd Brigade. The second Duke of Marlborough was Commander-in-Chief.

On the 1st of June the convoy sailed from St. Helens, but a strong gale having sprung up soon after land had been lost sight of, it was not until it had subsided on the 5th that a landing could be effected at Cancale Bay, about eight miles from St. Malo. The grenadier companies of the regiments taking part in the expedition landed at the little village of Layhoule after the guns of the fleet had silenced a battery there.

The "Welch Grenadiers" were the first to land under a sharp fire from a force posted in a windmill. When the whole of the grenadiers had safely landed, a detachment of them was ordered to dislodge the enemy from the windmill. The first fire of the assaulting party caused the enemy to evacuate it and retreat in haste. The grenadiers were then ordered to post themselves on the adjacent hills, with the object of assisting in covering the landing of the troops, "which they Bravely did."

The entire army was soon landed, and immediately seized the village of Cancale, where the 3rd Brigade was left to guard the landing-place.

On the 7th the remainder of the army marched towards St. Malo and encamped within a mile of the town. That night Brigadier Elliott, with 200 cavalry and an equal number of infantry en croupe, carrying hand grenades, stole down to the harbour and succeeded in setting on fire a 50-gun ship, two 36-gun frigates, about 116 privateers and merchantmen, and several naval storehouses containing great quantities of pitch, tar, etc., which burnt furiously. No attempt was made by the garrison of St. Malo to beat off the daring band. On the following day preparations were made to besiege St. Malo, but on the Duke of Marlborough learning that a superior force was marching to cut off his retreat, he gave orders for the troops to re-embark. By the 12th all were on board. After lying at anchor for some days the convoy sailed with the object of attacking Granville, but at the last moment the naval and military authorities decided not to risk the attempt.

A westerly gale springing up drove the fleet within sight of the Isle of Wight. Owing to the wind abating, the fleet was enabled on the 25th to stand back for the French coast. The next day it reached the mouth of the Seine, and sailing close in shore reached Cherbourg on the 29th and anchored about two miles from the shore. Preparations were then made for landing, and a portion of the Guards had taken their places in the boats, when an on-shore wind sprang up suddenly and soon blew so hard that Marlborough decided to abandon the enterprise. The fleet made the best of its way back to the Isle of Wight, and on the 1st of July the troops disembarked at St. Helens. The two battalions of the 23rd returned to their previous encampment.

On the 15th of June orders were issued for the fifteen second battalions raised on the 25th of August 1756 to be regimented, "from and after the 25th day of June." The 2nd battalion of the 23rd therefore became the 68th Regiment, under the command of Colonel Lambton.

In June William Pitt, the Prime Minister, decided to throw the weight of England gradually into the war that was then raging on the Continent, already referred to as "The Seven Years' War." Commencing in 1756 and carried on until 1763, it was the third, last, and most sanguinary of the contests undertaken for the possession of Silesia, which had been snatched from Maria Theresa of Austria in 1748, when she was in sore straits.

To recover the lost province from her hated rival Frederick the Great of Prussia became the great object of her life. Allying herself with France and Russia in 1756, she was about to strike the first blow for its recovery when the confederates found themselves forestalled by Frederick, who, by a rapid march on Dresden, took possession of Saxony and cooped up the Saxon army, which some weeks later was obliged to surrender. This brought the first campaign to a close.

The second campaign (1757) opened more auspiciously for the Austrian coalition, but both sides having experienced reverses during its progress, matters were left in December, when it was brought to a close, very much as they were at its commencement.

In the third campaign (1758) Frederick was about holding his own, thanks to that able General Prince Ferdinand of Brunswick, when Pitt arrived at his momentous decision to send British troops to Germany. The strength and composition of the contingent were then determined upon, and the troops comprising it warned for active service. At the last moment the King decided to increase it by three other regiments, viz. the 20th, 23rd, and 27th Regiments of Foot, as "they are actually in compleat readiness to embark as soon as they receive their new clothing."

The contingent, under the command of the second Duke of Marlborough, sailed from the Thames in two divisions and landed at Hartsum, about eight miles up the Ems from Emden, where the disembarkation of the force from the "large transports of 400 tons" was completed by the first week in August. Leaving four companies of invalids at the base (Emden), the Duke, having received a route from Prince Ferdinand, lost no time in setting out to join the latter, with whose army he effected a junction at Koesfeld, near Münster, on the 21st of August. The weather was so broken during this march, that the foot "marched always near their middles in water."

Mauvillon, who was an historian of the war and took part in this campaign, gives the British first place in fighting qualities among the different elements of which Ferdinand's army was composed, but adds that they are careless in outpost duty and neglect the ordinary precautions that should make surprise impossible.

On the 22nd of August Ferdinand inspected the British auxiliaries, and remarked respecting them: "It is impossible for me to express the satisfaction I felt at the good order in which I found these fine troops."

The addition of the British contingent brought Ferdinand's total strength up to 40,000 men. In the brigading of the British troops that now took place, the 12th, 23rd, and 37th Regiments were formed into the 1st Infantry Brigade, under Major-General Waldegrave. On the 29th of August the Allied army reached Dülman, where it encamped. The Duke of Marlborough, writing from there to the Duke of Newcastle, informs him that he found himself with "9,000 men in a barren country wanting the absolute necessities of life, with no commissary to act for us, and no contractors for bread, forage, and wagons. Prince Ferdinand has done all in his power to assist, but has little enough for himself." On the 1st of September Marlborough informed Newcastle that "the English and Hanoverians live in the greatest harmony."

For several weeks to come Ferdinand contented himself with marching and counter-marching mainly in the vicinity of the River Lippe, for the purpose of keeping open his communications with Münster and Hanover. On his ascertaining on the 26th of October that a French army had invested Münster, he marched there with all haste, which had the effect of causing the French to raise the siege and retire on Hanem. In the meantime the Duke of Marlborough had died at Münster of a "fever and flux": he was succeeded by Lord George Sackville with the rank of General.

On the 13th of November the French began to disperse to their winter quarters. Ferdinand's army followed suit four days later. The British headquarters and the 12th, 20th, 23rd, and 37th Regiments were cantoned at Münster during the winter.

1759.

In February the total strength of the Allied army was 66,621 men.

During the spring and the early part of summer, while Ferdinand was first of all operating against the Austrians and later on attempting to drive the French out of Hesse and Frankfort, in which undertaking he received a severe check at Bergen, the British contingent formed part of a corps that lay near Münster under the command of the Hanoverian General von Spörcken, its object being to guard Westphalia. The affair at Bergen is interesting as being the first occasion on which British troops—under the command of Lord Granby—took an active part in the Seven Years' War, happily with the trifling loss of one officer and four men wounded.

Towards the end of May Ferdinand joined forces with von Spörcken, and the united army then cantoned along the Lippe from Cresfeld to Hamm. For several weeks to come certain movements were at the outset made by Marshal Contades, of which Ferdinand was successful in obtaining information, but later when the configuration of the country prevented his whereabouts from being ascertained, the Allied commander was completely puzzled, and it greatly added to his anxiety, as he was left in the helpless position of not knowing from day to day when and where the enemy would strike the next blow.

All doubts as to the enemy's intention were removed when, on the 10th of July, Ferdinand learned that Count de Broglie (brother of the Marshal) had seized Minden the night before, with the alarming result that a bridge over the Weser had been secured and the road lay open to Hanover. After some hesitation he decided to retire to the Lower Weser.

On the 16th of July Contades effected a junction with Marshal de Broglie, which increased the strength of the French army to about 60,000 men as compared with 45,000 under the command of Ferdinand. Thereupon the latter, though his army was numerically much inferior, advanced to offer Contades battle, which, however, the latter declined and, withdrawing, took up an unassailable position to the south of Minden.

Ferdinand's situation was a most trying one, as the French had only to hold on to the bridge at Minden in order to ruin by their exactions a large tract of country. Besides, the position they had taken up was much too well protected on the flanks and too strong on the front to hope for success by a direct attack.

In no way daunted by the difficulties that beset him, Ferdinand drew up his army before the French front and countered their plundering raid by threatening their communications with Cassel; further, in order to induce Contades to attack him, he detached a corps, which included a British grenadier battalion consisting of the grenadier company of each regiment, under Wangenheim, with orders to entrench in such a position as to cover the only outlet by which the French right could debouch from behind the extensive morass that lay between the Weser and a small river some 16 feet wide named the Bastau. Ferdinand's hope that this move on the part of Wangenheim would act as a bait to draw Contades from his position was realised.

During the early hours of the 1st of August the whole French army moved out to attack Wangenheim. Ferdinand's order issued overnight was that the troops should be under arms at one a.m. It was not, however, until quite two hours later that he definitely learned of the French move. Foreseeing the possibility of a sudden march becoming necessary, he had issued another order to the effect that, on the army taking up its position, when a signal was given, an advance should be made in eight columns, infantry in the centre and cavalry on either flank. The column, under the command of Major-General Spörcken, comprised the 12th, 20th, 23rd, 25th, 37th, and 51st British infantry Regiments. Tory, in his *Journal*, records that the 23rd entered into the action 505 strong—24 officers, 23 sergeants, and 458 rank and file.

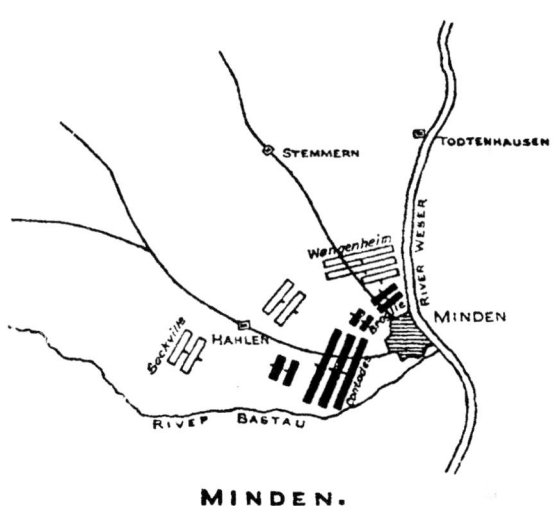

MINDEN.
AUGUST, 1759.

The first line, counting from right to left, was made up of the 12th, 37th, and 23rd Regiments under Brigadier Waldegrave. The second line consisted of the 20th, 51st, and 25th Regiments under Brigadier Kingsley; and was flanked by Hardenberg's Hanoverian regiment and two battalions of Hanoverian foot guards.

The French line of battle was made up of 63 squadrons of cavalry in the centre, with 18 squadrons in reserve, and infantry on either wing.

Ferdinand ordered the columns to advance to their appointed stations, and then rode off to direct the Prince of Anhalt to drive the French from the village of Hahlen which lay to his right. The first column, which consisted of cavalry under the command of Lord George Sackville, had so far shown no sign of obeying the order to advance, the fact being that several of the regiments composing it were ready to move forward when the signal was given, and others quite unready and the commander nowhere to be found.

As Ferdinand cantered back from Anhalt's position he noticed that Spörcken's column of British infantry was in the act of deploying. Thereupon he sent Count Taube to inform Spörcken that when the time to advance had arrived, it was to be made with drums beating. Taube misinterpreted the message, and made it to appear that Spörcken was to advance with drums beating and attack everything on his front. To Ferdinand's intense surprise, he saw the leading British brigade commencing to advance. No less than five A.D.C.s galloped off with orders to stop it until the formation of the remainder of the army was complete.

Accordingly, the line halted for a short time under cover of a small wood while the deployment was being completed. Suddenly, to the general amazement, the drums began to roll and the first brigade commenced to march rapidly, so much so as to outpace their battalion guns and all but outdistance the second line. The Anglo-Hanoverian infantry advanced with the cool precision of a review in peace time, despite the fact that they were exposed to a cross-fire of some sixty guns and were unsupported. With erect mien they strode for the left of the mass of French cavalry. Presently eleven squadrons from the first line of the enemy's cavalry were launched against them. The line halted and, reserving its fire until the horsemen were almost on top of it, poured in such a volley that in a trice the ground was strewn with men and horses. Very few daring riders reached the first rank of the infantry, and such as did were quickly bayoneted.

Ferdinand, perceiving the disorder into which these squadrons had been thrown, ordered Lord George Sackville, who had by now taken his allotted position, to advance and complete their rout, but, to his surprise, no notice was taken of the command. Once again the sorely tried battalions had to withstand not only a second charge of cavalry, consisting of fourteen squadrons drawn from the French second line, but also, following it, an attack from four brigades of infantry which endeavoured to enfilade them. For a moment the line wavered, but quickly closing up its ranks it poured a deadly volley of musketry into the charging squadrons that practically wiped them out of existence; then, fiercely turning upon the French infantry, it drove them back with great loss.

Once again Sackville was importuned to charge with his British squadrons and complete this success, but the powers of man would not make him budge an inch. Yet a third charge was made by the French reserve cavalry, consisting of the Carabiniers and the Gendarmerie, but with no better success than the previous attempts. Once again an urgent order to advance was dispatched to Lord George, which he ignored, and had the effrontery to ride leisurely forward to Ferdinand, and request him to say what exactly he required him to do! Ferdinand, scornfully replied that the time for him to do anything had gone for ever.

At this stage of the battle seven battalions of Saxons fell upon the right of the British infantry and inflicted considerable loss upon it—the 20th Foot in particular suffering severely. A charge, however, of German cavalry scattered this force in all directions. It was now nine a.m., and Contades, realising that the day was lost, gave orders to retire. A vigorous pursuit of the enemy was kept up until the Rhine was almost reached. Forty-three guns, ten colours, and seven standards were captured by the Allies.

The French loss in killed, wounded, and prisoners is officially recorded as being 7,086; while that of the Allies, which fell to a considerable extent on the British infantry, amounted to 2,797 killed and wounded. The loss sustained by the 23rd was as follows:

Killed.—Four sergeants and 31 rank and file.

Wounded.—Lieutenant-Colonel Edward Sacheverel Pole, Captains William Fowler and John Fox, Captain-Lieutenant Richard Bolton, Lieutenants Charles Reynell, Joseph Patterson, Arthur Barber, Grey Grove, and George Orpin, 2nd Lieutenant David Ferguson, 6 sergeants, 3 drummers, and 153 rank and file.

Missing.—Ten rank and file.

The following extract from the General Order issued by Ferdinand on the day following the battle shows the high opinion he entertained of the valour of the British infantry:

" His Serene Highness orders his greatest thanks to be given the whole army for their bearing and good behaviour yesterday, particularly to the British infantry and the two battalions of Hanoverian Guards. . . .

" His Serene Highness declares publickly that, next to God, he attributes the glory of the day to the intrepidity and extraordinary good behaviour of these troops, which, he assures them, he shall retain the strongest sense of as long as he lives. . . ."

It was not, however, until 1801 that the 23rd was authorised to bear the word "MINDEN" on its colour and appointments in commemoration of its gallant conduct at that battle.

On the morning of the 2nd of August M. Dagieu, Lieutenant-Colonel of the Régiment d'Aquitaine and Commandant of Minden, offered to surrender the fortress at discretion. At noon it was taken over by Ferdinand, who thereby gained possession of a large quantity of baggage, supplies, and stores of all kinds. For several days the pursuit of the French was vigorously kept up by the Hereditary Prince of Brunswick, but despite his utmost efforts, they managed to effect their retreat without serious loss, such as there was being mainly by desertion among their German and Saxon allies.

On the 19th of September the Allied army reached Krofdorf, where it remained until December. A long rest had become necessary, owing to an epidemic of dysentery having broken out among the troops.

1760.

From Krofdorf Ferdinand marched to Marburg, which was reached on the 5th of January 1760. The army then went into winter quarters, the British being sent to Fribertshausen and Nesselborn in the Bishopric of Osnaburg.

Ferdinand contemplated making an early start this year, but was unable to do so owing to the dilatory methods of the British Treasury, which prevented the army from having magazines or money to provide and stock them.

For the forthcoming campaign Ferdinand had an army of nearly 75,000 men—34,000 being British—while de Broglie had no fewer then 130,000 men available to oppose him. In the brigading of the Allied army that took place preparatory to its getting into motion, the 23rd was brigaded with the 12th and 37th Regiments under the command of Major-General Howard.

On the 5th of May the army commenced to march towards Hesse, leaving Granby, who was now the British Commander-in-Chief, in bed suffering from fever. It reached Paderborn on the 14th and Fritzlar on the 19th, where it encamped and remained for some weeks.

On the 21st a welcome reinforcement of six British infantry regiments—"six of our best regiments," to quote the words of the Duke of Newcastle—reached Ferdinand. This augmentation necessitated a re-brigading of the British contingent. The 23rd was now brigaded with the 11th, 33rd, and 51st Regiments constituting the 2nd Infantry Brigade under the command of Major-General Griffin.

During the protracted stay of the army at Fritzlar the weather was excellent, and the country people readily brought their produce to the camp; but there was one order issued by Ferdinand that made the British hate the place, as it jarred upon their sporting instincts. It read thus: "It is forbid on pain of death to all and every one to go a sporting or to kill game of any kind."

On the 24th of June the Allied army quitted Fritzlar and marched to Neustadt, where it ran up against de Broglie's army. Although not more than six miles apart, both armies, except for sharp skirmishes between picquets and advanced guards, sat watching each other for quite a fortnight. This period of inactivity was brought to an end by de Broglie striking his tents late on the night of the 7th of July and marching in the direction of Corbach, with the object, as it turned out, of seizing the heights there and effecting a junction with St. Germans.

Ferdinand, on learning of de Broglie's movement, broke up his camp and marched after him post haste, sending in advance a strong corps under the Hereditary Prince—reinforced en route by four British battalions, including the 23rd, under Major-General Griffin—with orders to push forward for Corbach. On the Hereditary Prince arriving there, he found the enemy drawn up on the heights. Being under the impression that its deployment had not been completed, he attacked without delay, but, owing to the greatly superior numbers of the French, he vainly endeavoured to dislodge them. Eventually he was forced to retire with the loss of 824 men killed, wounded, and missing, and 16 guns, of which 7 were British.

On the 23rd of July de Broglie made certain movements evidently with the object of cutting off the Allied army from the city of Cassel and at the same time preventing General Spörcken's corps from effecting a junction with the main army under Ferdinand. This action on the part of de Broglie necessitated the retreat of the Allied army to Celle, which was reached on the 27th.

The French greatly harassed Ferdinand's rear during this trying period, making repeated efforts to break in upon him which were invariably repulsed with considerable loss to the enemy. The retreat of Ferdinand afforded de Broglie the opportunity of detaching the Chevalier de Muy, who commanded the reserve of the French army, across the Diemel to Warburg, with the object of cutting off the communications of the Allied army from Westphalia, while de Broglie himself advanced with the main body towards Ferdinand's camp. The latter at once resolved to attack de Muy.

On ascertaining on the 30th that the Chevalier had taken up an advantageous position in front of Warburg, he decided that the Hereditary Prince and General Spörcken should endeavour to turn the enemy's left while he advanced upon its front. The next day the Hereditary Prince and Spörcken, timing their movements to a nicety, almost simultaneously attacked the French flank, with the result that de Muy was obliged to fall back upon Warburg. The crossing of the Diemel delayed Ferdinand to such an extent as to prevent him from seconding the attack upon de Muy's position as fully as he wished. General Waldegrave at the head of the British infantry did all in his power to encourage his men to put their best foot forward, and right royally they responded to his call. The heat of the day, combined with the physical strain caused by floundering through morasses, made scores of the men drop insensible on the march.

Ferdinand, seeing the impossibility of the infantry being in time to take part in the battle, ordered the Marquis of Granby, and General Mostyn, his second-in-command, to press forward with the British cavalry of the right wing. At a full trot Granby covered the five miles that separated Ferdinand's army from the combatants so speedily as to enable his corps to share in the glory of the day. The French cavalry, with the exception of three squadrons that stood their ground but were quickly overwhelmed, fled precipitately on the approach of Granby, who bore down upon them at the head of the Blues. General Mostyn then charged the French infantry, which suffered severely, one regiment in particular—composed of Swiss—being cut to pieces.

De Muy's army, finding that both its flanks were enveloped, retired in the utmost confusion and crossed the Diemel, hotly pursued by Granby, many of the fugitives being drowned in the act of crossing the river. Maxwell's grenadier battalion—of which the grenadier company of the 23rd formed part—being in the thick of the fight, "greatly distinguished itself, performing wonders." The trophies taken were ten cannon and several colours.

In this action Maxwell's battalion lost no less than 240 men. The casualties of the grenadier company of the 23rd were 1 sergeant and 11 privates killed, Captain Patrick Rainey and Lieutenant Philip Mercier together with 19 privates wounded.

After the battle Ferdinand's army encamped in the vicinity of Warburg. While there he formed the project of attempting to capture Wesel in the Duchy of Cleves, which was the base of the French Army of the Rhine. To achieve his object he quietly collected during September a powerful train of siege artillery, which, when ready, he dispatched towards Wesel, followed by the Hereditary Prince with 10,000 German troops. Four days later he ordered 1 Hanoverian and 10 British battalions, inclusive of the 23rd, under the command of Generals Howard and Waldegrave, also to proceed to Wesel and assist in its investment.

The siege began on the 3rd of October, but progressed very slowly, owing to torrents of rain and a succession of gales of wind. On the 12th the alarming news reached the Hereditary Prince that a powerful French force under M. de Castries was advancing to raise the siege and had reached Rheinberg, where it was encamped behind the convent of Campen. Thereupon the Prince decided to march on the night of the 15th of October from before Wesel and, if possible, surprise de Castries in his camp. To reach there it was necessary to dislodge a corps which occupied the convent, as it lay in front of the enemy's main army. The noise of the unavoidable firing, being heard by de Castries, put him on his guard. From five a.m. until noon repeated attempts were vainly made to dislodge him from a wood which had been taken possession of by his army. Eventually the Prince's infantry, having expended all its ammunition, was obliged to retreat, and would have been very roughly handled had it not been for a dashing charge of the 15th Light Dragoons, which enabled it to retire in good order. One gun, fourteen ammunition waggons, and a British colour were captured by the enemy.

The casualties of the 23rd were as follows:

Killed.—Two sergeants and 19 rank and file.

Wounded.—Major Thomas Marlay, Captain Paston Gould (taken prisoner), Captain William Fowler (taken prisoner), Lieutenants Joseph Ferguson, Grey Grove, George Orpin, William Blakeney, Thomas Mecan, 4 sergeants, and 97 rank and file.

Prisoners.—Lieutenant-Colonel Edward Sacheverel Pole, the two officers mentioned above, and 44 rank and file.

On the 14th of November the Allied army was ordered to go into mourning for the death of King George II. It took the form of black crape on the colours, drums, and banners. The officers covered their swords, knots, and sashes with black crape, which was also worn round the arm. Plain hats with crape hat-bands were also worn.

The drenching rains that fell about this time, lasting well into December, rendered the roads almost impracticable and prevented supplies of provisions and forage from reaching the troops. Ferdinand was in consequence reluctantly compelled to raise the siege of Göttingen, which he had undertaken, and lead his troops into winter quarters. The 23rd was cantoned on the 29th of November at Wreden, in the Upper Bishopric of Münster.

1761.

To the great grief of the regiment, General Huske expired on the 16th of January, and was succeeded by Lieutenant-General the Honourable George Boscawen, who was transferred from the colonelcy of the 29th Regiment for that purpose.

During midwinter Ferdinand devised a plan for wresting the Landgravate of Hesse from the French. His army, leaving its winter quarters early in February, assembled on the Diemel by the 11th of March. In four columns it advanced towards Cassel. On the 16th the Marquis of Granby captured Gudersberg, and on the following day Melsungen and Ober-Morschen fell to him. Considerable quantities of meal and forage were found in all three places.

The army continued its advance, leaving Cassel, Ziegenhain, and Marburg invested, and took up a strong position on the Ohm, which, although excellent from a military operations point of view, had this disadvantage, that it was in the centre of a region which had been drained of its resources.

Before long the stores of food and forage became dangerously depleted, and as there was no possibility of their being speedily replenished, Ferdinand was reluctantly compelled, after driving the French from Hesse, to raise the investment of the three fortresses named and evacuate the country. On reaching the Bishopric of Paderborn he again dispersed his army in winter quarters, the greater part being cantoned north of the Diemel, and the remainder posted along that river to secure the passages.

So much marching and counter-marching in deep snow, alternating with heavy rain, had thinned the ranks of the effectives to such an extent as to render the army unfit again to take the field for several weeks to come.

On the 19th of April Marshal de Soubise, who was to command this year a separate army on the Lower Rhine, met de Broglie at Frankfort with the object of concerting measures relating to the future operations of both armies.

On the 19th of June Ferdinand's army concentrated at Paderborn, and on the 21st struck its tents and marched in six columns to Gesecke. In the column commanded by Lieutenant-General Conway, the 11th, 23rd, and 51st Regiments were brigaded under Major-General Lord Frederick Cavendish. Then followed several marches which it would be tedious and unprofitable to narrate; suffice it to say that on the 28th the army reached Werle, where General Mostyn took over command of General Conway's corps.

Ferdinand's main army, continuing its marching, took up on the 11th of July a position on the north bank of the River Ase near Hamm, which was strengthened in every possible way. On the same day a council of war was held at the French headquarters at Soest, about seven miles as the crow flies from Ferdinand's position, at which Soubise decided to attack the Allies, as he considered that Ferdinand's army could not well exceed 65,000, while his force combined with that of de Broglie amounted to 92,000 men.

During the next three days valuable information respecting the enemy's movements reached Ferdinand from his intelligence officers, especially from Captain John Fox of the 23rd, who was in command at Werle, where he had the advantage of being able to ascertain, from the tower of a little fortress there, a great deal of what was going on in Soubise's camp. Many of his excellent reports in both English and French are contained in Westphalen's *Campaigns of Duke Ferdinand*. In the *Memoirs of James Campbell of Ardkinglas* this same Fox is described as "a tall, thin, hard-favoured man, reckoned in the army as a very stern soldier."

On the 14th Ferdinand issued his orders for the disposition of the troops in anticipation of the attack that was seen to be imminent. His main army occupied the heights of Wambeln, where from right to left the Brigade of Guards under Major-General Caesar and the

Brigades commanded by Generals Townshend, Conway, Howard, and the Prince of Anhalt were posted. Howard's troops consisted of Major-General Cavendish's brigade of the 11th, 23rd, 33rd, and 51st Regiments. The troops of the Hereditary Prince occupied the extreme right. Lord Granby's corps was posted on the heights of Kirch Dünckern to the left of the position. Across the River Ase and a little to the left and rear of Granby stood General Wutginau's corps.

About six p.m. on the 15th of July Captain Fox sent word to Ferdinand that de Broglie had struck his tents and was advancing in force upon the left of the Allied position. Thereupon Ferdinand ordered Granby "to maintain his ground to the last extremity." For some time the latter clung tenaciously to his position, but, weight of numbers telling upon him, he was pushed back to the village of Vellinghausen, in which the French succeeded in obtaining a bare foothold. Wutginau's corps, coming to the assistance of Granby's hard-pressed troops, attacked the enemy in flank, and when darkness had put an end to the fighting for the time being, not an inch more ground had been gained by de Broglie.

Soubise was unaccountably supine during the whole evening, and paid no heed whatever to the repeated appeals of his brother Marshal to put his army in motion. During the night Granby was reinforced by Howard's corps and that of the Prince of Anhalt, as Ferdinand felt confident that the enemy's greatest effort on the morrow would be directed against his left.

At three a.m. on the 16th de Broglie deployed his columns and fiercely attacked Wutginau's corps, which stood its ground with the greatest firmness, so much so that after five hours of fighting it remained immovable. Broglie had arranged with Soubise that while he was attacking the Allied left, the latter was to advance against its centre and right. Soubise made a few faint-hearted attacks that were easily repulsed. Ferdinand, on learning that to all appearance the enemy was about to attempt to plant two batteries on an eminence whence they would make havoc of Granby's corps, decided to have it carried at all cost. Maxwell's grenadiers, two battalions of Highlanders, and five foreign battalions were ordered to storm it. Advancing with the greatest intrepidity, they had barely come to close quarters before the French gave way and retreated with precipitation, abandoning their dead, wounded, and several cannon, some of which were sixteen-pounders.

Maxwell's grenadiers took the Régiment de Rouge, consisting of four battalions, prisoner with its cannon and colours. The enemy was pursued as far as Haltrup, but the nature of the ground did not permit of Ferdinand employing cavalry in the pursuit. The Allied loss in killed, wounded, and missing amounted to 1,400. Three guns were captured by the enemy on the 15th of July.

The casualties of the 23rd were very slight, amounting to no more than 3 privates killed; 1 sergeant, 4 privates wounded; First Lieutenant Wood, 1 sergeant, 28 rank and file prisoners. The French loss as given by de Broglie was 2,400, but was computed to be more than double that number. Nine guns and six colours were taken by the Allies.

The 23rd remained in the neighbourhood of Kirch Dünckern until the 27th, when it moved with the main army to Büren, which Ferdinand opined would be a good centre from which to operate in the event of de Broglie invading Hesse.

On the 1st of August a Monthly Return gave the following particulars: Present, 1 lieutenant-colonel, 1 major, 4 captains, 14 lieutenants, 5 second lieutenants, 1 quartermaster, 1 surgeon, 1 mate, 30 sergeants, 19 drummers, 632 privates fit, 33 sick present, 129 sick in hospital, 34 on command: total, 828. Wanting to complete, 72 privates.

Thenceforward, while the Hereditary Prince maintained a watchful eye on Soubise and countered his movements whenever possible, Ferdinand kept de Broglie fully occupied, and by a series of skilful marches so completely upset his plans that, seeing he could make no headway, the Marshal led his troops into winter quarters early in December. Ferdinand lost no time in following his example: the British infantry were quartered in the Bishopric of Osnaburg, the 23rd being cantoned on the 12th of November in the neighbourhood of Postenhagen.

The Monthly Return of the regiment for November is as follows: Present, 26 officers, 28 sergeants, 28 drums, 547 privates fit for duty, 38 sick present, 122 sick in hospital, 37 on command: total, 744. Wanting to complete, 156.

A General Return of the sick in the British hospital in Bremen on the 1st of January 1762 gives the following particulars as regards the 23rd: 113 sick on the 1st of December, 29 admitted since, 77 discharged, 4 dead; remaining on the 1st of January, 61.

1762.

An unusually late start was made this year by the Allies in taking the field, due in great measure to the " want of green forage," the term " forage " being evidently applicable to both man and beast. On the 4th of June the British troops which had been cantoned near Bielevelt joined the corps under General Spörcken near Blomberg, and marched to Brakel, where the army concentrated. The 11th, 23rd, 33rd, and 51st Regiments had for brigade commander this year Lieutenant-Colonel E. S. Pole, of the 23rd.

On the 22nd the entire French army, under the command of Marshals d'Estrées and Soubise, advanced from Cassel and encamped at Gröbenstein, fixing their headquarters at Wilhelmstahl. On the 24th Ferdinand determined to surprise them. He directed General Spörcken and Lieutenant-General Lückner to advance against the enemy's right, Granby was by a detour to work round his left, while Ferdinand himself with the bulk of the force, which now included Pole's brigade, advanced against the centre. Lückner fell upon the French right flank, and the turning movement was progressing favourably when unfortunately Spörcken's corps, having taken a wrong turn, ran up against Lückner's corps, and mistaking it for the enemy, fired into the ranks. The sound of the firing aroused the French main army from its sleep. All was confusion for the moment, but quickly forming on the heights, it began slowly to fall back upon Wilhelmstahl.

M. de Stainville with the Grenadiers of France, the Royal Grenadiers, and several other regiments that were considered the cream of the French infantry, took up a strong position in a wood and endeavoured by every means in his power to cover the retreat of the main body. Slowly but surely Granby's corps, fighting desperately, attacked both flanks. Ferdinand's troops, whose progress had hitherto been very slow, now arrived upon the scene, and between the two Stainville's corps was practically annihilated, which terminated the conflict.

As the 23rd does not appear to have sustained any loss in this engagement, it seems probable that the part it played in it was, for once in a way, a minor one. The trophies taken were 1 standard, 6 colours, and 2 guns. All the enemy's transport and baggage fell into the hands of the Allies.

During the remainder of the campaign, which terminated with the taking of Cassel by the Allies on the 1st of November, the 23rd, although taking part in several operations, does not seem to have been seriously engaged. On the 8th of November Ferdinand was informed by the two French Marshals that on the 3rd of the month peace had been signed at Fontainebleau between England, France, and Spain.

On the 19th the Allies began to disperse to their winter quarters, those of the 23rd being at Belem and Schledehausen.

The Monthly Returns are as follows:

	January.	April.	June.	October.
Effectives	477	499	470	525
Sick present	65	30	14	17
,, in hospital	38	19	33	35
On command	96	82	80	109

On the 25th of December the establishment of the regiment was fixed at 9 companies of 3 sergeants, 3 corporals, 3 drums, 2 fifers to the grenadier company, and 47 privates, making a total of 529.

1763.

The Monthly Return for January shows 1 lieutenant-colonel, 1 major, 7 captains, 14 lieutenants, 5 second lieutenants, 1 adjutant, 1 quartermaster, 1 surgeon, 2 mates, 35 sergeants, 18 drums, 604 privates fit, 29 sick present, 50 sick in hospital, 15 on command, 3 on furlough: total, 701. Wanting 1 drum and 199 privates.

Towards the end of February the regiment marched through Holland to Wilhelmstadt, where it embarked for England.

Another General Return of the sick in the British Hospital at Bremen on the 15th of March shows: Lieutenant George Pettener on hospital duty, 1 corporal, 1 drummer, 34 privates in quarters, 6 privates in hospital, 1 sergeant and 3 privates on store duty: total, 1 sergeant, 1 corporal, 1 drummer, 43 privates, 4 discharged.

Early in March the 23rd landed at Harwich: 5 companies proceeded to Windsor, 2 to Hampton, 1 to Kingston, and 1 to Chertsey. At the end of April 3 of the companies at Windsor were directed to " march immediately to Winchester to assist the 20th regiment there." This "assistance" seems to have been merely a case of relieving the 20th, as the latter regiment proceeded to Gibraltar at the end of March. On the 27th of May the company at Chertsey proceeded to the Isle of Wight to relieve a detachment of the 33rd guarding the sick at Carisbrook Castle. On the 7th of June 2 companies at Windsor were dispatched "with all possible expedition to Bristol to relieve the 70th regiment in the duty on the French prisoners and to assist the Invalids in that duty." On the 28th the remaining companies left Windsor for Hilsea, leaving a detachment to do duty at Hampton Court and Windsor, being joined at Hilsea Barracks by the company from Bristol which had escorted the French prisoners to Porchester Castle. From Hilsea the regiment marched in three columns on the 18th, 19th, and 20th of July to Exeter, whence a detachment of 2 subalterns, 1 sergeant, 2 drums, and 32 rank and file was sent to Padstow to assist in quelling riots occasioned by the "tinners" from the local mines.

In April a letter was received from the Secretary-at-War intimating that "the necessaries of life greatly increased in value, have raised the wages of every artificer in the Kingdom but the soldier's pay remains the same: his weekly subsistence after deductions amounts only to 3s. with that sum he is to fill his belly, wash his linnen, shave his beard, powder his hair, black his shoes, colour his accoutrements etc. etc. His Majesty . . . thinks fit that the private men of the infantry should be exempt from the deduction of 1s. in the pound that has always been made by the Paymaster General of the forces from the pay of the whole army." This, together with the abolition of the allowance per man for the regimental paymaster and surgeon, meant an increase per annum of 16s. 6d. for each private. The latter concession only was granted to sergeants, corporals, and drummers.

1764.

On the 6th of April the regiment was reviewed at Exeter by Major-General Charles Jeffreys.

Under arms: 20 officers, 23 sergeants, 23 corporals, 17 drummers, 354 privates, 27 wanting.

The nationality of the N.C.O.s and men was as follows:

        380 English.   31 Irish.
        56 Scotch.   3 foreigners.

As regards size, 13 were over 6 feet, the majority being between 5 feet 7½ inches and 5 feet 8½ inches, and with 8 to 10 years' service.

> "*Colours.*—2 good.
> *Officers.*—Made a good appearance, saluted with carbines, having no espontoons.
> *N.C.O.s.*—Very good and well dressed.
> *Men.*—A very fine body.
> *Exercise.*—Great steadiness and attention both in officers and men.
> *Accoutrements.*—Good, well put on, coloured white.
> *Clothing.*—Good. The Fusilier caps much worn, but they are to have new ones with the next clothing.
>
> "A very good regiment, excepting a few old men, well disciplined and fit for service."

On the 7th and 9th the 23rd proceeded in two divisions to Plymouth, arriving there on the 12th. Thenceforward during the remainder of the year detachments were stationed at Penzance, Padstow, St. Colomb, and other haunts of smugglers, doing preventive work. About the end of October the regiment was reviewed by Major-General the Duke of Richmond.

1765.

In January the company at Penzance, under Captain William Blakeney, Lieutenants Davison and Cochrane, with 2 sergeants and 50 private men, were called upon to "assist in preserving the ship *Dolphin*, which was stranded in the Port of Penzance." For this duty the following award was made by the Justices of the Peace: Captain Blakeney 10 guineas, the two lieutenants 5 guineas each, the sergeants and men 1½ guineas each—a total of £102 18s. 0d.

On the 22nd of February the ship *Neptune* was wrecked and the company was again called upon to assist in saving part of the cargo. For this service the sum of 10 guineas was paid to Captain Blakeney for distribution.

On the 3rd of May the detachment at St. Agnes was directed to assist in guarding the cargo of the *Hannover*—a Lisbon packet which had run ashore. In June Lieutenant and Adjutant Mackenzie, with

4 sergeants, 6 corporals, and 2 privates, marched to Ockingham (? Wokingham) " to undergo instruction in the new exercises," moving to Greenwich in July, and returning to the regiment in September.

In the middle of June Captain John Fox was allowed to dispose of his commission " in consideration of your distinguished service, but it must be offered in the regiment." It will be remembered that this is the Captain Fox whose intelligence reports in the Seven Years' War were so accurate and so promptly rendered as to call for warm commendation from His Serene Highness Duke Ferdinand of Brunswick, under whom he served.

Towards the end of the month the regiment marched in two divisions, 7 companies to Exeter and 2 to Tiverton; and on the 22nd and 23rd of July the whole moved to Rochester, being reviewed there in October by Major-General Parslow.

1766.

In March the regiment proceeded to Cirencester to be reviewed there, and on the 31st of that month left for Berwick and Newcastle to relieve the 7th Regiment. Before leaving, it furnished a draft of 31 privates for the 53rd and 54th Regiments at Gibraltar, which embarked at Southampton. In July a recruiting party was sent to Wakefield to assist Ensign Nicholls of the 54th Regiment to recruit, " he having no party of his own regiment."

1767.

In April the 23rd left Berwick and Newcastle for Edinburgh, the winter cantonments being as follows:

6 companies at Edinburgh Castle, with detachments at Inversnaid and Leith.

1 company at Dundee, with a detachment at Arbroath.

1 company at Montrose, with detachments at Stonehaven and Johnshaven.

1 company at Aberdeen, with detachments at Newburgh and Petershead.

1768.

On the 27th of May the regiment was reviewed at Edinburgh by Major-General Oughton.

Under Arms.

Lieutenant-Colonel Hemmington.
28 officers.
24 sergeants.
25 corporals.
17 drummers.
350 privates.
Total effective, privates 393.
Wanting 12.

A detachment consisting of 1 officer, 23 N.C.O.s and men was stationed at Inversnaid.

Officers.

11 English.   3 Scotch.   13 Irish.

N.C.O.s and Men.

394 English.   24 Irish.
45 Scotch.   3 foreigners.

"*Colours.*—2 good.

Officers.—Their arms good, uniforms new, well acquainted with their business and thoroughly attentive, salute remarkably well, and made a very good appearance.

N.C.O.s.—The sergeants well armed, and pretty well looked, attentive and diligent. The drummers and fifers play extremely well. The band of musick very fine. The whole perfectly well cloathed and appointed.

Men.—Of a good size and soldierlike appearance, extremely silent and steady under arms.

Exercise.—The whole of their manual, evolutions, marching and wheeling exceptionally good.

Firing.—They locked, levelled and fired remarkably well.

Cloathing.—Very good, their caps tolerably good and very well put on.

"Their conduct in quarters being as good as their appearance in the field."

In July 5 companies were at Glasgow, their principal duty being the repairing of roads, the other 4 companies being at Perth. The strength was then 488, the establishment being the same as in April.

1769.

In April the regiment was still stationed at Glasgow and Perth, but in July 8 companies had moved to Fort George, and 1 company under Captain Horsfall, to Aberdeen.

The companies at Fort George were inspected by Lieutenant-General the Marquis of Lorne, and in his report he states: "The musick, drummers and fifes beat and played extremely well. . . . Men: well dressed, of a good size, steady and attentive, made a fine appearance. . . . Evolutions, performed remarkably well considering it blew very hard. . . . It is a very fine regiment, perfectly well disciplined, well cloathed and very fit for service."

A document preserved at the Public Record Office, London, contains the following return of recruits who joined the 23rd during a series of years:

1765	102
1766	65
1767	70
1768	40
1769	50
Total	327

The establishment from the 25th of December was 9 companies of 42 men each, making with officers a total of 484, at a daily charge of £29 10s. 4d.

1770.

On the 8th of June the regiment was inspected at Fort George by Lieutenant-General Oughton. Under arms were Lieutenant-Colonel Hemmington, 22 officers, 283 non-commissioned officers and men. On detachment duty there were:

At Braemar Castle	. .	1 officer,	9 N.C.O.s and men.
„ Corgarff Barracks	. .	1 „	19 „ „ „
„ Dumbarton	. .	1 „	33 „ „ „
„ Banff	. .	2 officers,	38 „ „ „
„ Portsoy	. .	1 officer,	26 „ „ „

The detachments at Banff and Portsoy were stated to be there "on account of the distemper among the horned cattle."

The total establishment at this period was 434 non-commissioned officers and men. The Inspecting General reported as follows:

> *Officers.*—A genteel corps, saluted gracefully and very perfectly attentive.
> *Non-Commissioned Officers.*—Very good.
> *Drums and fifers.*—Beat and played well. They had neither swords or caps, the band of musick very good.
> *Men.*—A fine Corps well limbed and square shouldered.
> *Recruits.*—Very fine, of a great size.
> *Marching.*—In quick time, remarkably good.
> *Arms.*—In good repair, the grenadier sergeants had no fusees.
> *Accoutrements.*—Not extraordinarily good, appearing to be much burnt with the white colouring."

In August 5 companies were stationed at Fort William and 4 at Fort Augustus.

On the 11th of October the regiment was ordered to proceed to Berwick and relieve the 17th Regiment. On the 25th of December an augmentation took place by the addition of a light company, which consisted of 1 captain, 2 lieutenants, 3 sergeants, 3 corporals, 2 drums, and 62 privates; also 20 additional men to each company: total, 737 all ranks.

1771.

In the early part of January the regiment proceeded to Manchester. At the end of the month a reduction was ordered in the establishment, which was fixed at 10 companies of 47 all ranks, 5 staff officers, and 2 fifers for the grenadier company. In March it moved to Lincoln and in May to Bedford; from there it marched to Highgate and Hampstead, proceeding on the 19th of June to Chatham, where, together with the 7th, 15th, and 37th Regiments, it was reviewed on the 1st of August by Lieutenant-General Robert Monckton.

The outcome of his inspection return was that the Board of Ordnance was directed to issue the following from store to make good deficiencies: 6 halberts, 18 drums, 36 sticks, 73 firelocks, 127 bayonets, and 243 cartouch boxes.

On the 5th of August the regiment received orders to move to Deptford, Lewisham, and Lee, to be reviewed by the King at Blackheath.

The Gazetteer for Monday, the 12th of August, records as follows:

"On Saturday morning His Majesty accompanied by His Royal Highness the Duke of Gloucester, Lord Ligonier in his new regimentals, as Colonel of the 9th Regiment of Foot, Lord Ancram and other General Officers reviewed the two royal regiments of English and Welch Fuzileers on Blackheath Common. They made a fine and very martial appearance, both regiments wearing black bearskin caps, and as the men are remarkably tall, are equal to a detachment of the same number of Grenadiers. These regiments of fuzileers are regiments that have distinguished themselves on all occasions, and their caps and other trophies were given them on that account. The royal regiment of Welch Fuziliers is as well known to all veterans in Europe, as any regiment in their respective nations."

The London Evening Post of the 10th states that a detachment of the Guards had marched early on the morning of that day to Blackheath "to prevent obstructions."

In October anonymous complaints reached the War Office from Chatham respecting soldiers assisting in harvest work. The Secretary-at-War wrote to Major Bernard, temporarily in command of the 23rd, informing him that he "had never disapproved of men being employed at harvest work under proper inspection and with leave of the commanding officer."

1772.

In May the King decided to give the captain-lieutenant the rank of captain "on all occasions as well in the Army as in their respective regiments."

On the 10th of June the regiment was reviewed at Chatham by Major-General McKay. Present: Lieutenant-Colonel Bernard, 28 officers, 378 non-commissioned officers and men. The nationality of the non-commissioned officers and men was as follows: English 357, Scotch 43, Irish 16, "Foreigners" 2. There were 14 over 6 feet, 260 over 5 feet 8 inches; 115 men had over 10 years' service. The Inspecting General remarked that "This regiment beats the grenadier march on all occasions, the regiment has a band of musick."

On the 4th of August 5 companies of the regiment marched to Kingston and 5 to Putney and Wimbledon, where they were reviewed by the King and afterwards proceeded to Southampton.

About the end of September the regiment marched to Plymouth, to relieve the 6th Regiment. Detachments were sent to Penzance, St. Nicholas Island, Helston, and St. Ives. On the 23rd of December the regiment received orders to hold itself in readiness to proceed to America in the following April with the object of relieving the 29th Regiment: not less than 1 field officer, 4 captains, and 11 subalterns to embark with the regiment; a party to be left for recruiting; 3d. a day to be deducted from every officer, non-commissioned officer, and private towards the expense of provisions on board; and 60 women, 12 servants, and 60 tons of baggage to be allowed.

1773.

In February the turbulent "tinners" were the cause of no less than three companies of the regiment being sent to Penryn, Truro, Falmouth, etc., to restore order. On the 15th of April the 23rd embarked for America, and disembarked at New York on Monday the 14th of June at nine a.m., marching to the Upper Barracks and mounting guards as follows: 1 subaltern, 1 sergeant, 1 corporal, and 20 privates at the Upper Barracks, 1 sergeant, 2 corporals, and 18 privates at the Fort Guard, 1 corporal and 6 privates at the Lower Barracks.

On the 30th of June the regiment was reviewed by the Commander-in-Chief at 5.30 a.m., when he expressed himself as "highly pleased with the fine appearance of His Majesty's Twenty-third or Royal Welch Regiment of Fusiliers reviewed this morning, and returns his thanks to Lieutenant-Colonel Bernard, the Officers and men for their great attention, alertness and soldier-like performance under arms."

A field-day was held on the 29th of October, on which occasion the Commander-in-Chief expressed his appreciation of their attention and alertness.

1774.

On the 16th of May the regiment was reviewed by the Commander-in-Chief, who was "much pleased with its fine appearance, soldier-like performance, steadiness, alertness and attention."

Saturday the 4th of June being the anniversary of his Majesty's birthday, the Royal Regiment of Welch Fusiliers with a detachment of the Royal Artillery and two field-pieces were under arms at 11.30 a.m. on the road near Vauxhall leading to Greenwich, the artillery firing a royal salute at 12 o'clock which was followed by three volleys from the regiment.

On the 27th of July the regiment embarked for Boston on the transports *Wentworth, Ocean,* and *Sea Venture,* and arrived there on the 7th of August, going into camp on Fort Hill. Owing to its proximity to the Admiral's quarters, it was ordered to post two sentries there.

The Governor, considering it advisable to place a guard at the narrow isthmus, known as the Boston Neck, connecting the town with the mainland, the 23rd was directed to furnish its proportion of that guard, consisting of 1 captain, 2 subalterns, 2 sergeants, 2 corporals, 1 drummer, and 50 privates, four light 12-pounders being also posted there.

In September the Commander-in-Chief issued an order that regiments "will look out for leggins and mittens against the severity of the winter."

The following was the state of the regiment on the 26th of October: 306 present fit for duty, 17 sick, 30 servants, 7 musicians: total, 360; 30 wanting to complete.

In November, the troops were redistributed in brigades, the first brigade, under Brigadier-General Earl Percy, being composed of the 4th, 23rd, and 47th Regiments.

To prevent accidents during the frosty weather, orders were issued that bayonets should not be fixed on the firelocks. This instruction did not affect sentries.

In the disposition of the garrison in the event of alarm being given, the 23rd with the 10th and 38th Regiments were to form up in the street from the General's house to Liberty Tree, and if at night the troops were on no condition to fire even should they be fired upon, "but are to oppose and put to rout anybody (that shall dare to attack them) with their bayonets."

1775.

Unfortunately political differences which had been steadily growing for some years between the mother-country and the North American colonies culminated this year in an open rupture leading to actual hostilities.

In February, the self-constituted Congress which took upon itself the direction of affairs in Massachusetts issued an address which was well calculated to arouse the passions of the people. In it they exhorted the militia to perfect themselves in military discipline. This was followed by resolutions for providing and manufacturing arms.

The Commander-in-Chief, Lieutenant-General Gage, felt that the time had now come when it was necessary to take stern measures for maintaining the supremacy of the mother-country. An opportunity for so doing speedily presented itself. Being informed that the revolutionaries had collected a quantity of military stores at the town of Concord, about twenty miles from Boston, he dispatched on the night of the 18th of April the grenadier and light infantry companies of the 5th, 10th, 18th, 23rd, 38th, 43rd, 52nd, and 59th Regiments, under the command of Lieutenant-Colonel Francis Smith of the 10th Regiment, to destroy them. Although every precaution was taken to keep the destination of the detachment secret, it had not proceeded many miles before the firing of guns and the ringing of bells showed plainly that the countryside was aroused.

On arriving at Lexington, about fifteen miles from Boston, the advanced guard of the detachment encountered an armed body of men drawn up on a green adjoining the high-road. On being called upon to disperse, the assemblage scattered. The main body having now joined the advanced guard, as the detachment moved off, several shots were fired, which luckily only wounded one man. On their arriving at Concord, such of the military stores as could be seized were quickly destroyed, and the force set out upon its return march. The whole way to Lexington the weary troops were sniped at from behind stone walls, trees, houses, and rocks. There, fortunately, they were met by Lord Percy with a detachment consisting of eight companies of each of the 4th, 23rd, and 47th Regiments, together with a battalion of marines and two guns.

The following is Lord Percy's dispatch to General Gage in reference to the expedition:

"BOSTON, *April* 20, 1775.

"SIR,

"In obedience to your excellency's orders I marched yesterday morning at 9 o'clock with the 1st Brigade and two field pieces in order to cover the retreat of the Grenadier and Light Infantry in their return from their expedition to Concord. As all the houses were shut up and there was not the appearance of a single inhabitant, I could get no intelligence concerning them till I had passed Menotoring, where I was informed that the rebels had attacked H.M.'s troops who were retiring overpowered by numbers, greatly exhausted and fatigued, and having expended almost all their ammunition: and about two o'clock I met them retiring thro' the town of Lexington. I immediately ordered the two field pieces to fire at the rebels, and drew up the brigade on a height. The shot from the cannon had the desired effect and stopped the rebels for a little time, who immediately dispersed and endeavoured to surround us, being very numerous. As it began now to grow pretty late and we had 15 miles to retire, and only our 36 rounds, I ordered the grenadiers and light infantry to move off first, and covered them with my brigade, sending out very strong flanking parties, which were absolutely necessary, as there was not a stone wall or house tho' before in appearance evacuated, from whence the rebels did not fire upon us. As soon as they saw us begin to retire they pressed very much upon our rear guard, which for that reason I relieved every now and then. In this manner we retired for fifteen miles under an incessant fire all round us till we arrived at Charlestown between seven and eight in the evening, very much fatigued with a march of above thirty miles, and having expended almost all our ammunition. We had the misfortune in losing a good many men in the retreat, tho' nothing like the number which from many circumstances I have reason to believe were killed of the rebels. His Majesty's troops during the whole of the affair behaved with their usual intrepidity and spirit. Nor were they a little exasperated at the cruelty and barbarity of the rebels who scalped and cut off the ears of some of the wounded men that fell into their hands.

"I am, Sir,

"PERCY, *Acting Brigadier-General.*"

Of the 1,800 men who took part in this ill-fated expedition, no less than 65 were killed, 136 wounded, and 49 returned as missing. The 23rd lost: 4 rank and file killed; Lieutenant-Colonel Ben-

MAJOR-GENERAL THE HON. SIR WM. HOWE, K.B.
From a block of a mezzotint by Corbatt, supplied by "Country Life."

jamin Bernard and 26 rank and file wounded ; 6 rank and file missing. The American loss, as estimated by themselves, amounted to 60 killed and wounded, but was probably quite one-third more.

On the 8th of May the following General Order was issued:

"The Commander-in-Chief having received advice that three soldiers of the Royal Welch Fusiliers and twelve marines are prisoners in the gaol at Worcester, and have nobly despised the offers, and defied the threats of the rebels, who have tried to seduce them to take arms against their King and fight against their brother soldiers: it is the Governor's orders that money be given by said corps to Major of Brigade Moncrieffe who has an opportunity of conveying it to the above men to prevent such brave spirited soldiers from suffering."

On the 11th of May Major-General the Honourable Sir William Howe was transferred from the colonelcy of the 46th Regiment to that of the 23rd in succession to Lieutenant-General George Boscawen, who had died in London on the 3rd of that month.

Towards the end of May a welcome reinforcement under Sir William Howe reached Boston, thereby bringing the garrison up to about 10,000 men.

The jubilation of the Americans over their victory at Lexington, as they were pleased to describe the result of this fracas, was great, and their spirits were, if possible, still more elated by the arrival of a considerable body of troops from Connecticut under Colonel Putnam, an experienced officer who had served in two previous wars.

Boston was now blockaded, but the Neck was so well protected by fortified lines and cannon that the revolutionaries dared not risk an attack upon it. The timely arrival of the reinforcement referred to, enabled Gage to carry out a plan which he had devised for occupying an eminence in the peninsula of Charleston, that was separated from the Boston peninsula (in British occupation) by the River Charles, his object being to prevent the enemy from dominating Boston by artillery fire from that height. By means of their spies the Americans were informed of Gage's project, which they immediately set about forestalling. Late on the evening of the 16th of June a strong detachment stole noiselessly over Charleston Neck and reached the top of Breed's Hill, adjoining Bunker's Hill but nearer to Boston than the latter. The party, having provided themselves with entrenching tools, worked unceasingly during the entire night, and by daylight had constructed a formidable redoubt on their right, and a line of trenches reaching from it to the River Mystic on the left.

H.M.S. *Lively*, on discovering the enemy, fired upon his entrenchments; presently a battery of guns posted on Cops Hill in Boston followed suit. About noon a detachment from the British Army, consisting of ten grenadier and a like number of light infantry companies drawn from the ten senior regiments, including the 23rd, under General Howe, and two battalions under General Pigot, landed without opposition upon the peninsula of Charleston. The two Generals, being impressed by the formidable nature of the task that confronted them, decided to send for reinforcements before attempting to storm the works. On the arrival of the reinforcements the force moved on towards the enemy's position, the light infantry forming the right wing, and the grenadiers the left. The former were directed to attack the fortified lines and the latter the redoubt.

The Provincials, resting securely behind their entrenchments, reserved their fire until the British had approached to within about forty yards, when they poured in such a withering volley as to make the line recoil and give way in several places. General Clinton at Boston, observing this disorder, hurried across the intervening water and rallied the troops so effectually that, advancing with fixed bayonets, they drove the Americans, who ran short of ammunition, headlong from their works and took possession of the hill. The British loss was terrible. Of the force, which consisted of about 2,500 men, nearly one-half was either killed or wounded.

The flank companies of the 23rd lost the following: 2 sergeants, 1 drummer, and 11 privates killed or died of wounds; Captain William Blakeney, Lieutenants Onslow Beckwith, Thomas Cochrane, John Lenthall, 2 sergeants, 1 drummer, and 35 privates wounded. The American acknowledged loss was 450 killed and wounded.

In July the garrison under the command of Major-General Howe was re-brigaded, the 23rd forming part of the 1st Brigade under Brigadier-General Percy, along with the 4th, 44th, and 59th Regiments, 2 squadrons of the 17th Dragoons, and the 1st Brigade of Artillery.

On the 31st of August the Secretary-at-War wrote to General Gage informing him that from the 25th of that month the 23rd would be augmented with 10 sergeants, 10 drummers, and 180 men; also with two additional companies of 1 captain, 1 lieutenant, 1 second lieutenant, 3 sergeants, 3 corporals, 2 drummers, and 56 privates; 1 additional company to remain to recruit in Ireland, and the other in

Great Britain. Officers from half-pay and non-commissioned officers had been appointed to one company, the other to be formed by regular regimental promotion. The establishment would then consist of 12 companies of 3 sergeants, 3 corporals, 2 drummers, and 56 privates each, with officers, staff, and 2 fifers, making a total of 811. A return of artificers in the 23rd dated the 7th of September gives the following particulars respecting them: 13 carpenters, 2 smiths, 1 mason, 2 bricklayers, 1 cooper, and 1 harness maker.

As the medical authorities were fearful of an outbreak of scurvy among the garrison, they recommended as an antidote an allowance of three pints of spruce beer daily, to be paid for by the soldier at the rate of a dollar per barrel of about 32 gallons.

On the 10th of November the 23rd quitted its encampment on Fort Hill and went into barracks which had been prepared for its reception.

On the 2nd of December Lieutenant Richard Bailey, of the 23rd, who had been appointed Assistant Deputy Quartermaster-General, was sent home to provide necessaries for the army.

During the winter 1775-6 the blockade of Boston was carried on under the direction of General George Washington, who had been appointed Commander-in-Chief of the American armies in June.

The following is the first authenticated reference to the regimental custom of being preceded at a review by its goat. It is extracted from Major Donkin's *Military Recollections*, 1777:

"The royal regiment of welch Fuzileers has a privilegeous honour of passing in review preceded by a Goat with gilded horns, and adorned with ringlets of flowers: and although this may not come immediately under the denomination of a reward for Merit, yet the corps values itself much on the ancientness of the custom.

"Every 1st March, being the anniversary of their tutelar Saint, David, the officers give a splendid entertainment to all their welch brethren: and after the cloth is taken away, a bumper is filled round to his royal highness the Prince of Wales, (whose health is always drunk to first that day) the band playing the old tune of 'The noble race of Shenkin,' when an handsome drum-boy, elegantly dressed, mounted on the goat richly caparisoned for the occasion, is led thrice round the table in procession by the drum-major. It happened in 1775 at Boston, that the animal gave such a spring from the floor, that he dropped his rider upon the table, and then bouncing over the heads of some officers, he ran to the barracks with all his trappings, to the no small joy of the garrison and populace."

1776.

So closely was the blockade maintained by Washington that during this most trying period the besieged, who were on short rations, suffered greatly from inanition and fatigue. With the advent of spring Washington redoubled his efforts to capture the town before the arrival of reinforcements from England.

On the 2nd of March a battery opened fire on the western side of the town, doing considerable damage. On the 5th another, which had been erected on the eastern shore, commenced to play upon the town. For fourteen days a constant fire was maintained from both, which the garrison bore unflinchingly. No alternative now remained for the besieged but to dislodge the Provincials from their works on Dorchester Hill, or to evacuate Boston. These works had been seized by them on the 4th of March and had been rendered almost impregnable. In addition to earthworks the ingenious Americans had chained together a considerable number of hogsheads filled with stones, which would have been let loose upon the British as they mounted the hill.

Seeing that under these circumstances it would be impossible to carry the hill, Howe decided before it was too late to evacuate the town. By the 17th of March the garrison and such of the inhabitants as remained loyal—about 2,000—were got on board ship and sailed for Halifax, Nova Scotia, which was reached on the 2nd of April.

The effective strength of the 23rd on embarkation was as follows: 26 officers, 27 sergeants, 11 drummers, and 297 privates. A return prepared in April shows that the regiment then consisted of 28 officers, 27 sergeants, 11 drummers, and 324 privates: total strength, 388.

On the 28th of May 404 German recruits embarked from home for service in North America. Forty of these were assigned to the 23rd.

Early in June Howe considered that his troops had sufficiently recovered from sickness and fatigue to permit of their embarking for Sandy Hook, at the mouth of the Hudson River, where he expected to be shortly joined by reinforcements from England. On the 4th of

June the troops began to embark. The embarkation return, dated the same date, gives the following particulars of the 23rd (which, together with the 44th and 64th Regiments, formed the 6th Brigade under the command of Brigadier-General Agnew): 16 officers, 22 sergeants, 9 drummers, and 257 rank and file.

By the 7th of the month all the troops and stores were on board ship, but owing to the wind being unfavourable, the transports did not leave Halifax until the 11th. The 23rd embarked upon the *Elinor* and *Hudson* of 303 and 311 tons respectively. Sandy Hook was reached on the 29th of June.

General Howe, on being informed that the Americans were taking steps to block the channels leading to New York, decided to proceed to Staten Island, where the troops were landed on the 3rd of July, no attempt being made by the enemy to oppose their landing. From the 1st of July onwards the transports with the reinforcements from England began to arrive and land their complement of troops on Staten Island.

On the 1st of August General Clinton, with a small expeditionary force under his command, joined Howe. He had been engaged in an unsuccessful attempt to capture Fort Moultrie, which commanded the harbour of Charleston. Howe then proceeded to organise his army for an attack upon New York. He divided it into seven brigades, of which the sixth was composed of the 23rd, 44th, 57th, and 64th Regiments. The Reserve was made up of the grenadier and light infantry companies together with the 33rd and 42nd Regiments.

Howe's army, which included some Hessians, amounted to about 25,000 men, as compared with 18,000 under the command of General Washington. About 5,000 Americans were told off to man the forts and other defences of New York. General Putnam with about 10,000 men occupied an entrenched position on Brooklyn Heights to bar the passage to New York through Long Island. Another force of about 3,000 men under a General styling himself Lord Stirling lay astride Gowan's Road to the right of Putnam between Brooklyn Heights and the channel known as the Narrows.

On the 22nd of August a division 4,000 strong under General Clinton landed at Gravesend Bay, Long Island, adjacent to the Narrows. The rest of the army, together with the artillery, were landed close to the same spot as soon as Clinton's division had moved forward sufficiently to permit of their doing so. The village of Flat Bush lay in the plain facing Putnam's entrenched position.

To it the Hessians under General de Heister were pushed forward as an advanced post.

After three days spent in reconnoitring, Howe directed Clinton to advance along the Jamaica Road with his division, which constituted the right wing of the army, against the left wing of the enemy, as he opined that if it was turned, the enemy must risk a general engagement or retire under disadvantageous circumstances. Fortunately for Clinton an important pass over the heights leading to Bedford in rear of the American main position had not been secured, which enabled him to reach that town before the enemy was aware of his proximity.

De Heister, on hearing of the success of this turning move, advanced with the Hessians and attacked the enemy's central position. After a short but sharp encounter the Americans were utterly routed, losing three guns. While the centre and right were engaged as described, the column on the left, which consisted of the 4th and 6th Divisions, the 42nd Foot, two companies of New York Provincials, and ten guns under the command of General Grant, advanced along the road traversing the shore of the bay with the object of diverting the enemy's attention from the main attack on the right.

About midnight he encountered some advanced parties in a pass and quickly drove them back. These proved to be the advanced guard of General Stirling's army, which was advantageously posted. At daybreak, on Grant advancing, a furious cannonade commenced on both sides, which was continued until Stirling, hearing the firing at Bedford, and being fearful that his retreat might be cut off, made a sudden retrograde movement across a morass that lay to the right of the entrenchments of the American main army.

While doing so, his corps was attacked by the 2nd battalion of Grenadiers and the 71st Regiment, which caused it to suffer considerable loss. Many of his men in their hurried retreat were either suffocated or drowned, while he himself was taken prisoner. Thus ended a day when " victory was certainly on the side of the English."

The American loss in killed, drowned, or taken prisoner was quite 2,000. Among the latter, in addition to Stirling, were Generals Sullivan and Udell. The British casualties in killed, wounded, and missing were under four hundred.

The 23rd loss was as follows :

Killed.—1 sergeant and 6 rank and file.

Wounded.—1 officer (Captain Grey Grove), 1 sergeant, and 26 rank and file.

Six brass field-guns and 26 heavy guns were captured from the enemy.

Late in the afternoon of the 27th of August the British advanced, and encamped in front of the enemy's lines. Two days later Washington, concluding that his position on Long Island was untenable, effected a masterly retreat across a stretch of water fully a mile wide to New York, without the loss of a man.

Howe's first task after the evacuation of Long Island was to cut off communication with New York by sea, which was accomplished in a few days. He then decided to make a descent upon the island on which New York stood. Under cover of the fire of five men-of-war, a division, consisting of 4,000 men under General Clinton, was landed at Kips Bay, about three miles above New York, and occupied a height from which the enemy was easily driven by the furious fire of the ships.

In the meantime Washington had withdrawn most of his army from New York and had posted a portion of it at Haarlem Heights, about five miles to the north of Kips Bay, but the greater part he stationed at Kingsbridge, which he fortified in order to secure his retreat. While Clinton's division was landing at Kips Bay, the Hessians advanced upon New York, which was speedily evacuated, the garrison retreating to the main American army. So strongly was the enemy entrenched upon the Haarlem Heights with his flanks protected by batteries from attacks by the fleet, that a frontal attack was out of the question. Howe therefore contented himself with merely constructing several redoubts across his position at Macgowan's Hill to cover New York from the north, but beyond this he did nothing for several weeks, probably owing to his being temperamentally of a procrastinating disposition, and possibly also to his conjecturing, with some show of reason, that the American army would disrupt if left to itself. Such hopes, if they were entertained, were not realised.

Eventually he determined to cut off the enemy's supplies from Connecticut, and at the same time threaten his fortified rear at Kingsbridge. To carry out his purpose it was necessary to embark his troops on flat-bottomed boats and pilot them through an intricate and dangerous passage before a landing could be effected. His plan was, however, neutralised by Washington, who, on getting wind of it, detached 2,000 men from his army to strengthen the garrison at Fort Washington, and then retired north, taking up a position at White

Plains, where he entrenched himself, leaving a series of entrenched camps on the heights as he retired north.

On the 21st of October Howe advanced to New Rochelle, where he was joined by a division of Hessians from England under General Knyphausen. On the following day the 6th Division, commanded by Brigadier-General Agnew, proceeded to Mamaroneck to establish a post there. Howe, continuing his advance, arrived on the 25th within four miles of White Plains. Preparations were then made for assaulting Washington's position, but a prolonged and very heavy downpour of rain made the ground so slippery as to render any attempt impossible. Washington, taking advantage of Howe's enforced inactivity, retired behind the River Crotton, and took up so strong a position that any attempt to dislodge him would have been futile.

Thereupon Howe decided to reduce Fort Washington, which was an important post as it was almost exactly opposite Fort Lee, on the other shore of the Hudson or North River, thus establishing a cross-fire which would effectually obstruct the navigation of the North River.

On the 15th of November he summoned it to surrender, to which a defiant answer was returned by the commandant, Colonel Magaw. The following morning four columns, advancing from opposite directions, converged upon the fort. The one from the south, of which the 23rd formed part, under the command of Lord Percy, surmounted the greatest difficulties and carried the outer works confronting it, having 1 sergeant wounded. A like good service was rendered by the other columns, especially by the one under Colonel Stirling, consisting of the 42nd and two other regiments, which stormed a redoubt and took 200 prisoners. All the columns having penetrated through the enemy's lines, Magaw, seeing that further resistance was useless, surrendered the fort.

The British loss amounted to 458 killed and wounded. The 23rd loss was confined to one sergeant wounded. Of the Americans 2,818 were captured on the surrender of the fort. The winter setting in soon after caused a suspension of hostilities; thereupon the armies went into winter quarters, the British being cantoned between the Hakensack and Delaware Rivers.

1777.

The campaign opened this year by the Commander-in-Chief on the 23rd of March sending a detachment of 500 men, under the command of Lieutenant-Colonel Bird of the 15th Regiment, from New York up the North River to a place called Peek's Hill, to destroy a quantity of stores which he was informed were deposited there. Meeting with no opposition, the detachment burnt such stores as they came across, set fire to a barracks and several storehouses, and returned unmolested to New York.

The following month another expedition on a larger scale was undertaken with a similar object. On its coming to the ears of Sir William Howe that an accumulation of stores had been made in the town of Danbury in Connecticut, he dispatched a force of 1,800 men drawn from the 4th, 15th, 23rd, 27th, 44th, and 64th Regiments, with six guns, under the command of Governor Tryon of New York, with orders to carry away any stores that were removable. Tryon had been given the rank of Major-General of Provincials, and had under him Brigadier-Generals Agnew and Erskine, whom Howe thought it advisable to attach to his staff, as Tryon's keenness to be on active service was as great as his knowledge of soldiers and all that appertains to campaigning was small.

On the 25th of April the detachment sailed from New York, and proceeding up the East River to Camps Point on Norwalk Bay, disembarked there, and marched twenty miles to Danbury, which was reached without opposition on the afternoon of the following day. As no carriages could be obtained to remove the stores, both the town and all supplies therein were set on fire.

During the time occupied in burning Danbury, the Americans had assembled at a village called Ridgefield, where under the command of General Arnold they had entrenched themselves. As it was necessary for the British to pass through Ridgefield on their return journey, they attacked the enemy's entrenchments with intrepidity and carried them after a sharp struggle. The retreat was continued until nightfall, when the weary troops formed themselves into a square and lay on their arms until morning. The march was then resumed.

During the day the rear of the column was greatly harassed by repeated attacks upon it led by General Worcester. This continued until the troops reached a height within half a mile of the transports, that were ready to convey them back to New York, when General Erskine, placing himself at the head of 400 of the least fatigued members of the detachment, charged Worcester's corps with fixed bayonets, put it to flight, and embarked without further molestation.

What happened is described by Major Broughton-Mainwaring as follows: "The Royal Welsh Fusiliers were ordered by Brigadier-General Erskine to charge: this they did, after firing a volley so effectually, aided by the other regiment, which had rallied, that, after killing and wounding a great number of the Americans, the latter dispersed, and did not fire another shot, but allowed the rear guard to embark without further molestation." Here we have an exact parallel on a small scale of what took place at the retreat to Corunna in 1809 and its finale.

In this expedition, the British loss in killed, wounded, and missing amounted to 165, including 10 officers. Similar loss on the American side amounted to 407 of all ranks. General Worcester and several field officers were included among their slain. The casualties of the 23rd were as follows:

Killed.—5 rank and file.

Wounded.—Second Lieutenant Edward Price, Volunteer W. Richard Veale, 1 sergeant, and 18 rank and file.

Missing.—10 rank and file.

A state of the regiment dated New York, 5th May, shows that it then, together with the 4th, 38th, and 49th Regiments, formed the first brigade under the command of Major-General Vaughan. It mustered 3 captains, 6 lieutenants, 5 second lieutenants, adjutant, quartermaster, surgeon, surgeon's mate, 20 sergeants, 14 drummers, and 301 rank and file.

The arrival early in June of British and German recruits together with camp equipage "greatly wanted for the opening of the campaign" enabled Howe to carry out a plan, which he had communicated to the authorities at home, for penetrating into Pennsylvania through New Jersey.

Accordingly in the second week of June he transported his army over to Staten Island, and set to work to entice Washington to leave a strongly entrenched position which he had occupied upon the heights at Middlebrook, thus barring Howe's progress. The efforts of the latter met with a certain amount of success, but no tangible result ensued—do what he might he could not induce Washington to hazard a general engagement. Seeing that it would be fruitless to persevere,

Howe returned with his army to New York, the 23rd again taking up its quarters there. Foiled in his attempt to penetrate to Philadelphia through New Jersey, Howe resolved to reach there by sailing up the Delaware River.

On the 5th of July his army, numbering about 14,000 men, embarked on board the transports, the 23rd, 416 strong, being accommodated on the *Eleanor* of 303 tons and the *Saville* of 355 tons. Owing to the wind being contrary for eighteen days, the men were pent up in the ships in sweltering heat. A shift of wind on the 23rd enabled the transports to get under way, but they had not proceeded far, when they encountered a head wind which prevented them from reaching the mouth of the Delaware until the 30th.

At this stage the naval officers intimated to the Commander-in-Chief that they would not be responsible for navigating the ships up the river, as they had good reason to believe that the enemy had obstructed the passage in several places. Howe thereupon abandoned his original idea, and decided to proceed to the Chesapeake River. Once again the wind was unfavourable, so much so that the middle of August had arrived before the transports entered that river.

On the 25th of that month the army landed at the west side of the Elk River, when it was divided in two columns commanded by Lord Cornwallis and Lieutenant-General Knyphausen respectively. The 23rd, which was brigaded with the 4th, 5th, and 49th Regiments under Major-General Vaughan, formed the 1st Brigade of Knyphausen's column. The two columns, advancing slowly, reached Newcastle on the evening of the 8th of September, where they encamped for the night. The enemy, who was then but four miles off, retired under cover of darkness to a selected position on the heights behind Brandywine Creek, thereby blocking the road to Philadelphia, where it crossed the Creek at Chad's Ford. Two days later the British reached Kennett Square, which brought them within less than four miles of the ford.

On the 11th the army again advanced in two columns: the one commanded by Knyphausen moving direct upon Chad's Ford, the other, under Lord Cornwallis, making a detour of twelve miles with a view to turning the enemy's right at Chad's Ford.

Knyphausen's column reached the ford at 10 a.m., and during the time that his troops were deploying he managed to plant several guns in advantageous positions. A fierce cannonade then ensued which occupied the attention of the Americans while Lord Cornwallis was effecting his turning movement. Knyphausen, noticing the confusion of the enemy evidently caused by the progress of Lord Cornwallis, gave orders for the column to advance. The ford was quickly traversed and the entrenchments carried. Thereupon the enemy retreated, leaving five guns and a howitzer behind him.

By this time Lord Cornwallis had crossed two forks of the Brandywine River, and had taken the road to Dilworth, which enabled him to operate upon the enemy's right. This caused Washington to detach General Sullivan with a considerable force to oppose him.

At 4 p.m. Cornwallis began the attack. The Americans for a while obstinately maintained their ground, but the ardour of the British troops was so great that they were eventually driven into the woods. There they made another stand, but after a further desperate resistance were dislodged, and utterly routed.

The British loss in killed and wounded amounted to over 500. The American loss was considerably heavier, 300 being killed, 600 wounded, and about 400 taken prisoners. The 23rd loss was slight, amounting to 1 sergeant and 1 private killed, 4 privates wounded. Captain Mecan of the regiment, who was temporarily serving with the 1st battalion Light Infantry, was also wounded. Eleven guns were captured.

While the British army remained on the battlefield, General Washington, with such of his troops as he could keep together, retreated to Philadelphia, where he spent three days replenishing his depleted stores, and collecting as many troops as possible, and having done so, marched to Lancaster.

The road being now open to Philadelphia, Howe crossed the Schuylkill River on the 22nd of September, and reached Germantown, seven miles from there, on the 24th. The following day Lord Cornwallis with a strong detachment occupied Philadelphia without opposition. The Commander-in-Chief now busied himself with removing obstructions to navigation, which the Americans had placed in the channel a short distance below the spot where the Schuylkill empties itself into the Delaware. This blocking of the waterway necessitated his detaching a portion of his army to assist in removing the obstruction, and also sending a considerable force to escort his supplies overland from the Chesapeake.

Washington, on being informed of the causes that combined to weaken Howe's army, determined to make a surprise attack upon Germantown, which he carried out on the morning of the 4th of October. After nearly three hours' hard fighting, for the most part in a thick fog, he was repulsed with considerable loss. The 23rd does not appear to have taken part in this battle, as the day before it left the camp at Germantown and proceeded to Philadelphia. From there it marched to Chester, where it was joined by the 10th and 42nd Regiments. All three regiments then formed the escort to a large convoy of provisions destined for the camp at Germantown. Beyond assisting in reducing two forts on the Delaware that interfered with the navigation—which proved to be a most arduous task—and taking part in skirmishes, the 23rd was not seriously engaged before going into winter quarters at Philadelphia, after a prolonged and trying campaign.

1778.

During the period, October 1777–June 1778, that the British army was quartered at Philadelphia, no military operation of any importance was undertaken by Sir William Howe, who contented himself with sending out detachments to collect forage and provisions; also small parties to protect as far as possible the loyalists from outrage. Brushes with the enemy frequently occurred, but were of little account.

On the 8th of May Sir Henry Clinton arrived at Philadelphia, and took over from Sir William Howe the command of the "forces in America from Nova Scotia to West Florida." The latter General had requested and obtained the King's permission to resign his post of Commander-in-Chief, mainly on account of serious differences which he had with Lord George Germaine, the Secretary of State for the American Department at Whitehall, regarding the conduct of operations against the revolting colonists.

A return containing a state and distribution of the Royal army at Philadelphia, dated the 23rd of May, shows that the 1st Brigade was composed of the 4th, 23rd, 28th, and 49th Regiments.

The state of the 23rd was as follows: 3 captains, 8 lieutenants, 6 second lieutenants, adjutant, quartermaster, surgeon, surgeon's mate, 20 sergeants, 12 drummers, 347 rank and file, 12 prisoners. Sick—3 sergeants, 3 drummers, 34 rank and file. Total effectives: 24 sergeants, 16 drummers, 399 rank and file.

On the 17th of June a council of war was held at which it was decided to evacuate the city and remove the troops to New York. Accordingly at three o'clock on the morning of the 18th Clinton's army in two divisions set out on its perilous journey.

Lieutenant-General Knyphausen commanded the van, which included the 1st and 2nd Infantry Brigades. To him was confided the task of taking charge of the baggage of the whole army, which formed a train well-nigh 12 miles in length. Lord Cornwallis with his division followed in rear.

The lengthy column succeeded in crossing the Delaware at Gloucester Point without being followed by the enemy. Fortune continued to favour Clinton, as a strong corps of the enemy abandoned on his approach the difficult pass of Mount Holly, which was safely traversed. Then his troubles began in earnest, as he found bridge after bridge over river or creek broken down by the enemy. A torrential downpour of rain, followed by excessive heat, unequalled in living memory, rendered the task of repairing them a most difficult one, and made marching over roads deep in sand a terrible ordeal.

Clinton's original intention was to make for Staten Island, by the route through New Brunswick and Perth Amboy, but on learning that General Gates was approaching from the north to bar his passage over the River Rariton, he decided to branch off to the right and take the road leading through Freehold to the Navesink, which was a highland close to Sandy Hook.

On the 27th Cornwallis's division (which Clinton accompanied) encamped on the heights at Freehold court-house, county of Monmouth. On the following day, as it was descending into the plain, Clinton noticed the enemy occupying the ground barely vacated by him. Thereupon he directed Lord Cornwallis to wheel about and attack the Americans. The Brigade of Guards and four battalions of Grenadiers, although heavily clothed for such scorching weather, attacked so vigorously that the first line of the enemy soon gave way. A second line was then encountered, which also fell back after a stubborn defence. The rest of the division at this stage joined in the action, with the result that the Americans were driven from the field. The grenadier company of the 23rd, which formed part of the 1st battalion of Grenadiers, was greatly commended by Brigadier-General Medows, who commanded the Grenadier Brigade, for its gallant conduct on this occasion.

Major Broughton-Mainwaring, in his *History of the Royal Welch Fusiliers*, eulogises the conduct of the flank companies in the following terms :

" The flank companies of the Royal Welsh Fusiliers distinguished themselves on this occasion, particularly the right flank company, which received the warmest thanks of Brigadier-General Sir William Medows, who commanded the grenadier brigade: that company had one-third of its officers and men killed and wounded: among the latter was Captain Thomas Wills, who had his thigh carried away by a cannon-shot, of which he died a few days after: he was assisted off the field by his subaltern, Lieutenant Saumarez."

The British loss in killed, wounded, and missing was 294, including 20 officers. In addition 3 sergeants and 56 rank and file dropped dead from heat apoplexy. The American loss amounted to 361, including 32 officers.

The remainder of the retreat was accomplished without molestation. At Sandy Hook the fleet lay at anchor awaiting the arrival of the army.

The state of the 23rd prior to embarkation was as follows: 1 lieutenant-colonel, 3 majors, 8 captains, 4 lieutenants, adjutant, quartermaster, surgeon, surgeon's mate, 18 sergeants, 11 drummers, 367 rank and file, 14 prisoners. Sick: 3 sergeants, 4 drummers, 40 rank and file. Total effectives: 24 sergeants, 16 drummers, 430 rank and file.

All the troops being on board by the 5th of July, Admiral Howe set sail for New York which was reached the same day.

France having now thrown in her lot with the Americans, a powerful French fleet from Toulon under Count d'Estaing appeared off the harbour of New York at the beginning of August. A report that this squadron was on its way caused a mild panic, as it was known that the British fleet was much undermanned. Offers to assist in manning the fleet poured in from all directions, one of the first being from the 23rd in honour of their Colonel, who was Admiral Viscount Howe's brother.

Owing to contrary winds followed by a severe storm, Lord Howe's squadron was unable to bring on a general engagement, but on the evening of the 14th of August the *Renown*, a 50-gun ship, commanded by Captain George Dawson, having on board Lieutenant John Wilkinson, 1 sergeant, 1 corporal, 1 drummer, and 17 privates of the 23rd, fell in with the *Languedoc* of 90 guns, D'Estaing's flagship, but had to break off the action on account of the arrival on the scene of six sail of the French squadron.

On the same day the *Preston*, a 50-gun ship, under Captain Hotham, engaged the *Tonnant* of 80 guns for nearly one hour, when, the captain records, " we was at too great a distance to fire with effect, at 9 wore ship, and lost sight of the enemy." On her return to port, Admiral Lord Howe on the 18th visited the ship and "returned his thanks to the officers and company for their spirited conduct in the engagement on the 14th." The detachment of the 23rd on board the *Preston* consisted of 1 officer, 1 sergeant, 1 corporal, and 18 men.

On the 16th the *Isis*, also a 50-gun ship, commanded by Captain John Raynor, encountered the *Cæsar*, a French 74-gun ship. An account of the fight is contained in the following extract from Captain Raynor's dispatch to the Admiral:

"'Isis,' off Sandy Hook,
"18th August, 1778.

"My Lord,

"I beg leave to acquaint you that on Sunday last the 16th instant about 4 o'clock in the afternoon on my return to New York after having been separated from your Lordship by the late gale of wind . . . we fell in with a French ship of 74 guns with whom an action commenced, which lasted one hour and a half, at the expiration of which time the French ship put before the wind, leaving us in a situation by the damage to our masts and rigging that disabled us from pursuing her. . . . The *Isis* has suffered much in her masts, yards, sails, and rigging, but I have the pleasure to inform your Lordship little in her hull, and had only one man killed and fifteen wounded in the action. I cannot express too much my great satisfaction on the conduct and bravery of the officers and seamen belonging to the ship: the volunteer seamen from the Transports commanded by the agent Lieutenant Robert Parry: and the light infantry company of the 23rd Regiment under Captain Smith. . . .

"John Raynor."

The entry in Captain Raynor's log of the 17th of August respecting the casualties is slightly different from what is recorded in the foregoing dispatch. It reads as follows: "Had killed in the action one man a corporal of the light infantry, and 13 seamen and 3 marines wounded."

The corporal referred to was John Fowler, who, it is stated, was "killed in the tops."

The detachment of the light infantry company on board the *Isis* consisted of Captain the Honourable Lionel Smythe, Lieutenant Francis Erskine, 1 sergeant, 2 corporals, and 30 privates.

An entry in the log on the following day is as follows: "Lord Viscount Howe came on board and returned his public thanks to Captain Raynor, his officers, and ship's company for their gallant behaviour on the 16th instant, which was received with three cheers."

On the greater part of the regiment disembarking on the 14th of September, Admiral Viscount Howe addressed a letter to the commanding officer, of which the following is an extract: "Presents his most particular thanks to the officers and soldiers of the three companies of the Royal Welsh Fusiliers for their spirited and gallant behaviour on board the ships that had engaged the enemy, and to the whole regiment for its conduct during the time it served on board the fleet."

The following table shows how the 23rd was distributed on board the fleet:

	Captains.	Lieutenants.	Staff.	Sergeants.	Corporals.	Drummers.	R. and File.	Total.	From
Eagle			Colonel Nesbit Balfour				8	9	1 Aug.–13 Sept.
Trident	T. Peter	C. Apthorpe		1	3	1	12	19	1 Aug.–14 Sept.
Preston		A Lieutenant		1	1		18	21	2 Aug.–14 Sept.
Cornwall	T. Mecan	Thos. Chapman	Surgeon W. Robertson	3	1	1	47	55	1 Aug.–13 Sept.
Nonsuch		Timothy Tuckey		2	3		33	40	1 Aug.–14 Sept.
Raisonable		John Heighington Thos. Saumarez		1	1		28	31	30 July–14 Oct.
Somerset		" a volunteer company	of the 23rd."						2 Aug.–14 Aug.
St. Albans	T. Gibbons	W. O. Wallis	Surgeon's mate Hugh Orr	3	2		43	51	1 Aug.–14 Sept.
Ardent		John Browne		2	1		24	28	1 Aug.–13 Sept.
Centurion		W. G. Bayntun		1	1	1	18	22	2 Aug.–19 Sept.
Experiment		Ingram Nichols		1	1		9	12	15 Aug.–11 Oct.
		John Campbell		2	1		23	27	1 Aug.–12 Oct.
Isis	Hon. Lionel Smythe	Francis Erskine		1	2		30	35	29 July–26 Aug.
Renown		John Wilkinson		1	1	1	17	21	1 Aug.–14 Sept.
Phœnix		Ed. Price		1	1		18	21	1 Aug.–14 Sept.
Roebuck		John Blucke		1	1		30	33	1 Aug.–4 Oct.
Venus		Geo. Allanson		3	2		21	27	1 Aug.–14 Sept.
Pearl		Thos. Eyres		1			15	17	2 Aug.–8 Sept.
	4	17	3	25	22	4	394	469	

The total effective strength early in December was 472 all ranks. On the 25th of that month 14 regiments serving in North America, one being the 23rd, were augmented by the addition of 2 companies consisting of 3 sergeants, 4 corporals, 2 drummers, and 70 privates each.

1779.

On the 26th of March the additional companies embarked on board the troopship *Ann* of 271 tons at Chatham, their destination being New York. Three officers recently appointed to the regiment, viz. Second Lieutenants —— Innes, Harry Calvert, and Stephen Guyon, together with 36 rank and file, and 13 impressed men "required to complete," also travelled by the same vessel. General Clinton, who, much against his will, had been compelled to remain inactive at New York during the winter and spring, mainly owing to the want of men, on the arrival of the usual spring drafts planned an expedition having for its object the attacking of two strong forts on the Hudson River, known as Verplank's Neck, and Stony Point, about sixty miles above New York.

Accordingly, on the 27th of May a division from the army at New York, in which the 23rd was included, embarked on board transports and three days later sailed up the Hudson River under his own command. The major portion of the division under Major-General Vaughan disembarked on the east side of the river at Verplank's Neck, about seven miles from Fort Lafayette. The remainder, under Clinton, were landed higher up on the opposite bank at a spot about three miles from Stony Point, which was an eminence of strategic importance.

The Americans, who were then engaged in constructing works on its summit, retired on the approach of the flotilla towards evening. No time was lost in landing heavy guns and mortars, which with infinite labour were hauled up the hill during the night, and at five o'clock the following morning commenced to play upon Fort Lafayette on the opposite side of the river. The commanding height of Stony Point was a decided advantage, as it enabled the artillery to rain shot and shell upon the fort with telling effect in a short space of time.

While the cannonading was proceeding, General Vaughan had time to advance and invest the fort from the land side. Armed vessels prevented the escape of the garrison by water. Being surrounded on all sides, it had no alternative but to surrender at discretion. A vast quantity of stores and several small vessels were taken and burnt at the cost of only one man wounded! Leaving a garrison at both posts, Clinton returned to New York.

A state of the regiment taken there on the 15th of June reads as follows: "17 officers, 17 sergeants, 12 drummers, 316 rank and file fit; sick, 29; required to compleat, 40 rank and file."

An expedition against the coast towns of Connecticut was next planned by the Commander-in-Chief, its object being the destruction of stores and provisions, which it was hoped would overawe the rebels and lukewarm loyalists.

On the 3rd of July a force of 2,600 men, under the command of Major-General Tryon, embarked at New York for this purpose. On the following day the transports weighed anchor, and, escorted by a frigate and three smaller vessels, set sail for Newhaven, the capital of Connecticut, which was reached on the following day.

The troops were then landed in two divisions. While one proceeded to take the town—which was not accomplished without opposition—the other seized a fort on the opposite side of the harbour which commanded the entrance to it. A vast quantity of ammunition and stores of all kinds was carried away or destroyed. The troops then re-embarked and sailed from Newhaven.

In this affair the 23rd had 1 drummer and 1 rank and file wounded.

Fairfield was next visited, where the troops again landed and destroyed stores and vessels in the harbour.

Norwalk and Greenfield were successively visited with a like result. At the former place, where the troops arrived on the 11th of July, the 23rd had two rank and file wounded, probably sniped from windows, for which the inhabitants paid dearly, as the town was set on fire by order and entirely consumed.

Major-General Tryon had also contemplated a raid upon New London, which was a regular nest of privateers, but running short of ammunition and anticipating considerable opposition, he wisely determined to return to New York.

A state of the regiment taken there on the 15th of September furnishes the following information: "17 officers, 18 sergeants, 14 drummers, 348 rank and file; 88 sick; wanting to complete, 58."

On the 30th of September an expeditionary force, consisting of the 7th, 23rd, 33rd, and 57th Regiments, the Queen's Rangers, and the Volunteers of Ireland, under the command of Lord Cornwallis, embarked at New York with the object of raiding the French West Indian Islands. The fleet had not proceeded far when it was hailed by an English frigate, which communicated the alarming news that a greatly superior French fleet was within a few days' sail. The course was immediately altered, and a run made for New York, which was safely reached.

For several weeks after its return to New York the 23rd was quartered on Long Island, and was "hutted near Bedford" when the winter regularly set in. On the 23rd of December its effective strength was 409 of all ranks.

Sir Henry Clinton, considering it advisable to carry the war into South Carolina, sailed from Sandy Hook on the 26th of December in command of an expeditionary force not far short of 8,000 men, the 23rd being one of the regiments composing it. The fleet sailed for Charleston, where Clinton hoped to establish a base.

1780.

A succession of heavy gales signalised the passage of the transports, with the result that they were soon dispersed in all directions. Some were lost, one of these containing the heavy guns, a few were captured by enemy privateers, and all were more or less damaged. Hardly an artillery or cavalry horse survived the voyage. It was not until the end of January that a few of the transports managed to reach Tybee in Georgia, which was the appointed place of rendezvous. Unfortunately this delay enabled the enemy to strengthen the fortifications of Charleston to such an extent as to render the capture of it a formidable task.

On the 10th of February Sir Henry Clinton sailed from Tybee with such of the transports as had succeeded in reaching there and had been refitted. After a rapid passage he reached the Edisto River on the following day, and disembarked on John's Island, about thirty miles from Charleston. While a portion of the fleet was employed in blocking up the harbour of Charleston, the troops, advancing slowly, reached James's Island. From there they marched over Wappoo Cut to the mainland, finally establishing themselves on the banks of the Ashley River opposite to Charleston.

On the 1st of April ground was broken about 800 yards from the enemy's works. On the 9th Admiral Arbuthnot, taking advantage of a strong favourable wind and tide, succeeded in steering his squadron past Fort Moultrie on Sullivan's Island with trifling loss. The following day Clinton and Arbuthnot sent a joint summons to General Lincoln, the Governor of the city, to surrender, which he answered by a short but firm refusal. Thereupon certain of the batteries that were already in position opened fire, which soon caused "the fire of the enemy's advanced works to abate considerably."

The co-operation of the Navy enabled Clinton to detach 1,400 men, under Lieutenant-Colonel Webster of the 33rd Regiment, with the object of severing the enemy's communication inland. A daring surprise of American cavalry and militia by an advanced detachment of this force under a leader whose name was to become famous in this war—Lieutenant-Colonel Banastre Tarleton—on the night of the 14th of April met with complete success, one hundred prisoners being taken, together with all stores, camp equipage, and baggage. This brilliant affair enabled Webster to clear the country north of the River Cooper and gain large supplies of provisions.

On the 18th a considerable reinforcement reached Clinton from New York, which enabled him to strengthen the force above the Cooper, and thus effectually cut off the enemy's retreat should he attempt to do so. On the 6th of May fresh batteries were opened, and "a manifest superiority of fire was soon obtained." On the 11th General Lincoln capitulated. The prisoners taken, including 1,000 American and French seamen, amounted to 5,618 men. Nearly 400 guns were captured.

In a return of British troops killed or wounded, from the landing on the 11th of February to the surrender of Charleston, the 23rd is shown as having had four rank and file wounded.

Clinton now hastened to return to New York, leaving Lord Cornwallis in South Carolina with a force of 4,000 men, so distributed in cantonments as to preserve order internally, and on the frontiers of South Carolina and Georgia. The principal force, under the command of Lord Rawdon, was in the neighbourhood of Camden, "where huts of proper materials to resist the hot weather were constructed," or occupying advanced posts. It consisted of the 23rd and 33rd Regiments, the Volunteers of Ireland, and a few other Provincial corps.

While the Americans were collecting their forces with the object of ousting the King's troops from South Carolina, Lord Rawdon made certain alterations in the distribution of the troops on the frontier, with the object of making the posts they occupied more compact. The 23rd fell back, from an isolated post it was holding, to Colonel Rugeley's Mills about fifteen miles north of Camden.

Daring guerilla bands now began to appear upon the scene under able and active partisan leaders. One of the most daring of them was a Colonel Sumter, who hailed from Virginia. On the 6th of August Sumter made a most determined attack upon one of these outlying posts named Hanging Rock, which was only saved by a stratagem. Rawdon, on hearing of this attack, directed the 23rd under Major Mecan to proceed there from Rugeley's Mills, and make the post secure.

The approach of General Gates with an army of 6,000 men, by the main road to Camden, caused Rawdon to contract his posts upon the frontier with the object of greater concentration. The 23rd was in consequence recalled from Hanging Rock. Rawdon, leaving a weak guard at Camden to protect the hospital and stores, advanced with his corps to the left bank of Lynch's Creek, where he posted it. Gates moved forward to the opposite bank of the creek, but dared not attack Rawdon, as he considered his position too strong. The latter, taking advantage of Gates's inactivity, fell back to Camden.

On the 13th Gates moved his army to Rugeley's Mills, and on the same evening Cornwallis arrived at Camden from Charleston with reinforcements. Although he had only about 1,400 effective regulars and Provincials available, he determined, relying upon the valour and discipline of his troops, to attack Gates with the least possible delay.

On the night of the 15th he set out on his march, the 23rd being in the first division, which was commanded by Lieutenant-Colonel Webster. By a strange coincidence Gates left Rugeley's Mills the same night, and about the same hour, with the intention of surprising Cornwallis. About 2 a.m. the advanced guards encountered each other. Both armies halted and were then formed, the firing ceasing by mutual consent. Cornwallis posted Webster's division on the right and Rawdon's on the left. At break of day Cornwallis, noticing that Gates was proceeding to alter his position, gave orders for both divisions to advance simultaneously and charge the enemy.

The light infantry and the 23rd, which were opposed to the Virginia Militia, attacked with such impetuosity that it quickly broke, " ran at first like a torrent, and afterwards spread through the woods in every direction." Instead of pursuing the fugitives, both wheeled to the left and bore down upon the enemy's flank, which was soon thrown into confusion. The Maryland Brigades and the Delaware Regiment stood their ground manfully for the best part of an hour, but a charge of the cavalry under Lieutenant-Colonel Tarleton and

Major Hanger forced them to flee from the field, which completed the rout.

The American Army was practically annihilated, over 800 being either killed in action or during the pursuit. About 1,000 prisoners were taken. The British loss in killed, wounded, or missing amounted to 325 of all ranks. The 23rd had 6 rank and file killed; Captain James Drury and 17 rank and file wounded. Seven guns, several colours, and all the enemy's stores, ammunition, and baggage fell into the hands of the British.

The field return of the troops under Lord Cornwallis on the eve of the battle shows that the 23rd went into action as follows: 3 captains, 6 lieutenants, adjutant, 13 sergeants, 8 drummers, and 261 rank and file.

Cornwallis, considering it expedient to undertake without delay the reduction of North Carolina, on the arrival of reinforcements from Charleston, advanced from Camden on the 7th of September in two columns. The principal column under his own command consisted of the 7th, 23rd, 33rd, and 71st Regiments, three provincial corps, a sprinkling of cavalry, and four guns. His progress being slow owing to the scarcity of food and forage, "both parties having made a desert of the country," he did not reach Charlottetown until the 22nd of the month. The town abounded in mills, which were picketed by the British troops. One in particular, Colonel Polk's mill, which contained a great quantity of flour and wheat, was held by Lieutenant Stephen Guyon, a very young officer of the 23rd whose departure from England to join his regiment has already been referred to. A determined attack was made upon his post by a much superior force of Americans, but a well-sustained fire from a loopholed building adjoining the mill mowed down the assailants, who were obliged to retire.

The gallant conduct of this youthful officer was much appreciated by Lord Cornwallis. A variety of circumstances compelled his Lordship on the 14th of October to evacuate Charlottetown, and fall back upon Winnsborough, where he encamped and remained until the beginning of the New Year.

A board of field officers which inspected a number of recruits who reached Long Island towards the end of October, reported on those of the 23rd that the "cloathing of some was good, and of others very bad."

The want of recruits caused the 23rd and fourteen other regiments to be reduced from the 25th of December 1780 to 12 companies of

3 sergeants, 4 corporals, 2 drummers, and 56 privates, with 2 fifers to the grenadier company, as it was found impossible to maintain the establishment fixed on the 25th of December 1778.

1781.

It was the intention of Cornwallis to invade North Carolina as early as practicable this year, but his plans had to be modified owing to the unexpected and disastrous defeat of Lieutenant-Colonel Tarleton at Cowpens on the 17th of January by the American General Morgan, who had made an incursion into South Carolina with the object of capturing the post Ninety-six, so called owing to its being exactly 96 miles from the principal town of the Cherokee Indians.

On the following day Cornwallis was joined by a reinforcement under Major-General Leslie. This augmentation of strength decided him to march in a north-westerly direction in the hope of intercepting Morgan, who he thought would be encumbered by the number of prisoners he had taken. Although he halted on the 25th for a brief space to destroy all baggage and waggons that were not absolutely required, and then marched night and day with the fewest possible halts, he did not succeed in reaching the fords of the Catawba River until the evening of the 30th of January, just two hours after Morgan had safely crossed it with his force.

He halted there with the intention of giving his fatigued troops a few hours' greatly needed rest. During the night torrents of rain fell, which so swelled the river as to render it impassable for two days.

At dawn on the 1st of February, the river having rapidly fallen, he determined to attempt the passage. With the object of deceiving the enemy as to where the real crossing would be made, he directed Lieutenant-Colonel Webster with one division of the army to march to a public ford called Beatty's, and make a feint of crossing there, while he proceeded to a private one, known as McCowan's Ford, about six miles down the river.

On his way thither, owing to the narrow road and the darkness of the morning, a gun was overturned which temporarily caused a break in his force. The Guards and the Hessian Regiment of Bose, being in front of the obstacle, were not delayed, but the cavalry, artillery, and the 23rd Regiment were obliged to halt for the time being.

The Brigade of Guards and the Hessians on reaching the bank of the river saw, by the numerous fires on the opposite side, that the passage would be contested. The Guards, leading the way, plunged into the river, which was about five hundred yards wide at this spot, and although up to their waists in the swift-running current, and exposed to the fire of the enemy, they forged ahead with the utmost steadiness, and reserved their fire until the opposite bank was gained. They then poured a volley into the Militia, under a Colonel Davidson, which disputed their advance, with the result that the Americans gave way at once, with the loss of their General killed and about forty others killed or wounded. As soon as the whole of the division had completed the crossing, Cornwallis sent Tarleton with the cavalry and the 23rd Regiment to attack the rear of the American force at Beatty's Ford.

While on the march word was brought to Tarleton that the Americans were beating a hasty retreat. As it was raining heavily at the time and the condition of the roads being very bad for a rapid advance, he decided to post the 23rd upon the main road to Salisbury, and take up the pursuit with his cavalry. Overtaking the enemy at a place called Tarrant's Tavern, where they had halted evidently with the object of making a stand, he furiously charged a body of about 500, and bursting through their centre, scattered them like sheep.

The pursuit of Morgan was then resumed by Cornwallis with vigour, but once again the elements fought for him, as he managed to cross the River Yadkin a few hours before a torrential rain, which lasted for about eighteen hours, rendered it impassable.

It was not until the 8th of February that it was possible to resume the pursuit of Morgan. Two days later, when only twenty-five miles separated Cornwallis from the retreating Americans, he learned that Morgan and General Greene had joined forces at Guildford, but had continued the retreat. Hotly pursuing them, he had the mortification to find that they had succeeded in crossing the River Dan, and had only just broken down the bridge at Reedy Fork, when he appeared on the southern bank.

His pursuit was, however, not altogether fruitless, as he had succeeded in drawing the enemy out of North Carolina. His Lordship then fell back by easy stages to Hillsborough, where he hoisted the Royal Standard, and issued a proclamation inviting all loyal subjects to repair to it. The dearth of provisions compelled him to evacuate it after a few days' occupation. Marching in a south-westerly direction, he encamped at an important cross-roads about twelve miles from Guildford.

This retrograde step enabled General Greene, who now commanded the American Army, to re-enter North Carolina, where, on being joined by strong reinforcements from Virginia, he decided to advance to Guildford Court-house with the object of offering Cornwallis battle. Previous, however, to his doing so, a skirmish took place at Wetzell Mill on the Reedy Creek, between a brigade, of which the 23rd formed part, under Lieutenant-Colonel Webster, and some American light troops, which were routed with considerable loss. The 23rd casualties on this occasion were confined to 1 officer (Lieutenant Thomas Chapman) and 9 rank and file wounded.

Cornwallis, though his small army did not exceed 2,000, as compared with quite 4,000 Americans, was in no way reluctant to join issue with Greene. At daybreak on the 15th of March he left his encampment and directed his march to Guildford. On arriving within half a mile of the Court-house there, he deployed his troops. The 23rd and 33rd Regiments, under Lieutenant-Colonel Webster, formed the left of the British line, supported by the grenadiers, and 2nd battalion of the Guards under Brigadier-General O'Hara.

The part taken by the 23rd in this action is vividly described by Sir Thomas Saumarez, then a company officer in the regiment, in his journal. His narrative reads as follows:

" About one o'clock the action commenced. The Royal Welsh Fusiliers had to attack the enemy in front, under every disadvantage, having to march over a field lately ploughed, which was wet and muddy from the rains which had recently fallen. The enemy, greatly superior in numbers, were most advantageously posted on a rising ground and behind rails. The regiment marched to the attack under a most galling and destructive fire, which it could only return by an occasional volley. No troops could behave better than the regiment and the little army did at this period, as they never returned the enemy's fire but on word of command, and marched on with the most undaunted courage. When at length they got within a few yards of the Americans' first line, they gave a volley, and charged with such impetuosity as to cause them to retreat, which they did to the right and left flanks, leaving the front of the British troops exposed to the fire of a second line of the enemy, which was formed behind brushwood. Not being able to attack in front, the Fusiliers were obliged to take ground to their left to get clear of the brushwood. They then attacked the enemy with the bayonet in so cool and deliberate a manner as to throw the Americans into the greatest confusion, and disperse them. After this the Royal Welsh attacked and captured two brass six-pounders, having assisted in the attack and defeat of the third line and reserve of the Americans. Such men of the Fusiliers and Seventy-first as had strength remaining were ordered to pursue the dispersed enemy. This they did in so persevering a manner, that they killed or wounded as many as they could overtake, until, being completely exhausted, they were obliged to halt, after which they returned as they could to rejoin the army at Guildford Court-house.

"This action was unquestionably the hardest, and best-contested, fought during the American War. The Royal Welsh Fusiliers had about one-third of the officers and soldiers killed or wounded."

The actual loss sustained by the 23rd was as follows: killed, Lieutenant William Robinson and 12 rank and file; wounded, Captain Thomas Peter, 1 sergeant, and 53 rank and file.

Owing to the want of provisions Cornwallis was unfortunately in no condition to follow up his victory. After resting his troops for three days at Guildford, he decided to retire southwards, to Wilmington, where he hoped to replenish his stock of provisions. He reached there on the 7th of April. On the way to Wilmington Lieutenant-Colonel Webster (of the 33rd Regiment), who had so often led the 23rd to victory, succumbed to wounds which he received at Guildford. His death was a great loss to the Royal cause.

After a halt of eighteen days at Wilmington, during which large quantities of rum, salt, and flour were collected, Cornwallis arrived at the fateful decision to march through North Carolina into Virginia, in the hope that by so doing he would be successful in drawing off General Greene from South Carolina, whither the latter had proceeded with the object of overwhelming Lord Rawdon, who commanded at Camden.

When he began his march on the 25th of April he had under his command about 1,600 men, of whom the 23rd formed part, the state of the regiment being then 11 officers, 19 sergeants, 15 drummers, 314 rank and file fit, 44 sick, 17 prisoners, 9 wounded, and 178 wanting to complete.

At Petersburg, which was reached on the 20th of May, Cornwallis was met by General Arnold with a detachment of 2,000 men. He then took command of the whole. A few days later he received a reinforcement of 1,800 men, which Clinton had dispatched to his assistance.

From Petersburg Cornwallis marched to Richmond, and thence to Williamsburg, destroying at both these towns considerable supplies of arms and ammunition.

On hearing that the general assembly of Virginia was in session at Charlotteville, Cornwallis directed Tarleton to make a dash for there, and break up the meeting. Tarleton, with 180 dragoons and 70 men of the 23rd, under Captain Forbes Champagné, as mounted infantry, riding post haste, swept down upon the town, took seven members of the assembly prisoner, and destroyed " one thousand new firelocks," several hundred barrels of gunpowder, and many hogsheads of tobacco.

Whilst at Williamsburg Cornwallis received orders from Clinton to establish a defensive post in any healthy situation he chose, " be it at Williamsburg or York Town," and after retaining such troops as he judged " necessary for an ample defence," to send back the remainder with all possible speed to New York, which was weakly garrisoned, and which Clinton believed would be attacked in force by Washington. This reduction of strength necessitated his falling back upon Portsmouth, where, on the troops reaching their camping ground, they constructed huts to protect them from the fierce heat of the sun.

On the 20th of August Portsmouth was evacuated, and two days later Cornwallis concentrated his force at York and Gloucester—on opposite sides of the York River—employing his infantry in constructing defences at both places. The 23rd was employed in constructing an advanced redoubt on the right flank, which it was directed to hold when ready.

Towards the end of the month it dawned upon Clinton that Washington's movement was, after all, not directed against himself, but against the army in Virginia. This tardy discovery prompted him to send on the 6th of September a strong force under Brigadier-General Arnold against New London in Connecticut, in the hope of " drawing General Washington's attention that way."

Although Arnold took two forts, burnt several enemy ships, captured or spiked about 50 guns, and destroyed vast quantities of military stores, as a diversion it was a complete failure, owing to its not being of sufficient importance to stop Washington, who had been joined by a French force under the Count de Rochambeau, from advancing through Virginia. This united force passed through Philadelphia, and marching to the head of the Elk River, was there taken on board French transports, which conveyed it to Williamsburg in Virginia, which was reached on the 26th of September.

On the 28th the Franco-American force of 20,000 men arrived within sight of Yorktown, which was immediately invested. To defend Yorktown, Cornwallis had but 5,950 men, of whom only 4,017 were fit for duty. On the night of the 6th of October the enemy constructed his first parallel and " erected batteries with great regularity." On the 9th firing commenced from about forty heavy guns, and fourteen mortars, against the British left. At the same time other batteries opened upon the redoubt on the right, which had been constructed by the 23rd Regiment, and was now defended by a detachment of 130 men of that regiment and 40 marines " with uncommon gallantry."

On the 11th a second parallel was constructed. At this stage Cornwallis informed Clinton in cypher that " we continue to lose men very fast." On the 14th two redoubts were stormed and captured.

On the 16th a sortie was made by about 350 men under Lieutenant-Colonel Abercrombie, with the object of attacking two batteries and spiking the guns. In the hurry the guns were imperfectly spiked and some hours later were again firing upon the besieged. By now the British works on the left were beginning to crumble, and could not stand such pounding much longer.

Cornwallis, seeing the futility of attempting to maintain his position with a force that had been greatly reduced in numbers both by the fire of the enemy and by sickness, resolved to attempt to escape with the greater part of his infantry after dark by crossing over to the Gloucester side of the York River. With the utmost secrecy sixteen large boats were collected for transferring all but the sick and wounded of the garrison to the opposite bank.

The light infantry, the greater part of the Guards, and a portion of the 23rd, had been safely ferried across when a violent gale sprung up, sweeping the boats down-stream. Fortunately, all these troops were able to return to Yorktown the following morning with little loss.

Foiled in his attempt to evacuate Yorktown, and being advised by his chief engineer that the crumbling works could not be maintained with the present garrison, Cornwallis, in order to avoid further useless shedding of blood, decided to capitulate upon terms which were agreed to on the 19th of October. In his dispatch of the following day to Sir Henry Clinton giving a detailed account of the siege, he states that "the detachment of the 23rd Regiment and of the marines in the redoubt on the right commanded by Captain Apthorpe (of the 23rd) . . . deserve particular commendation." Captain Thomas Saumarez (afterwards Lieutenant-General Sir Thomas Saumarez), of the 23rd Royal Welsh Fusiliers, in a journal which he kept at this period, observes as follows:

"For the gallant defence made by the troops which defended the right redoubt they received the particular thanks of Earl Cornwallis, and also the most flattering testimonies of approbation from the general officers of the army, for their persevering and intrepid conduct during the siege and on all former occasions. Even the French general officers, after the termination of the siege, gave the Royal Welsh Fusiliers their unqualified approbation and praise for their intrepidity and firmness in repulsing the three attacks made by such vastly superior numbers on the redoubt, and could not easily believe that so few men had defended it."

By the terms of the capitulation the garrison surrendered prisoners of war. The colours were saved by Captain Peter and another officer wrapping them round their bodies. The following casualties of the 23rd were reported as occurring during the period of the siege: killed, 2 officers (Lieutenants Charles Mair and Stephen Guyon), 1 sergeant, and 8 rank and file; wounded, 3 sergeants, 2 drummers, and 15 rank and file.

The following surrendered prisoners of war: 3 captains, 6 lieutenants, adjutant, surgeon, surgeon's mate, 16 sergeants, 205 rank and file: total, 233.

On the 29th of October the regiment left Yorktown, and on the 15th of November reached Winchester in the back settlements of Virginia, where it was confined in barracks, surrounded by a stockade.

1782.

On the 12th of January the regiment started to march from Winchester through Maryland to Lancaster in Pennsylvania, a long and most trying march, owing to the severity of the weather. Many of the men were frost-bitten en route.

On the evacuation of Galveston in December 118 men of the 23rd, who formed part of the garrison there, were conveyed on board the transport *Thetis*, of 367 tons burthen, to Long Island.

1783.

On the 7th of January this detachment disembarked at New York. It then consisted of 1 captain, 4 lieutenants, 4 sergeants, 59 rank and file fit; sick, 1 sergeant and 20 rank and file; also 25 women and 23 children. On disembarkation it moved to the headquarters of the regiment at Springfield, Long Island.

A return of the army at New York on the 1st of March contains the following information respecting the regiment: " 10 companies— 10 officers, 10 sergeants, 4 drummers, 142 rank and file. Sick and wounded, 14. On command, 6 sergeants, 14 drummers, 48 rank and file. Prisoners, 12 sergeants, 4 drummers, 193 rank and file. 175 privates wanting." During the month of May there "returned from captivity" 1 captain, 3 lieutenants, 9 sergeants, 1 drummer, 115 rank and file.

On the 12th of October the regiment was informed that it would be " removed at the first evacuation." On the 5th of December it sailed for England.

In April and May of this year the recruiting parties of the regiment that were stationed at Edmonton and Southgate, near London, received orders to proceed to Manchester.

1784.

On the 17th of January the 23rd disembarked at Portsmouth, and was quartered at Hilsea. On the 19th of February it proceeded to Winchester. On the 16th of March it was moved to Doncaster, where it was joined by the recruiting parties from Manchester.

A state of the regiment rendered in April contains the following particulars: Present 9 officers, 128 non-commissioned officers and men, 76 fit for duty, 306 wanting to complete—a silent but enduring record of the manner in which the gallant Royal Welch Fusiliers fought on many a field in North America to uphold the authority of their Sovereign. In consequence of this depletion of the ranks, when the regiment was reviewed this year by Lieutenant-General Johnston, the officers and recruiting parties were not ordered to rejoin it for inspection.

The regiment was reviewed on the 14th of May at Doncaster by Lieutenant-General James Johnston. Under arms were Lieutenant-Colonel Nesbit Balfour, 15 officers, 86 non-commissioned officers and men. Of the officers 13 were English, 4 Scotch, 7 Irish, and 4 "foreigners," viz. Captain Apthorpe, Second Lieutenants McEvers, Skinner, and Winslow. Recruiting parties were engaged at Manchester, Preston, Blackburn, and Greenock.

General Johnston's remarks were as follows:

> "*Colours.*—2, bad.
> *Officers.*—Those which I saw were very genteel young men, well dressed, with a great deal of airs, saluting very genteelly.
> *Non-Commissioned Officers.*—The few present were very good looking young men with much air.
> *Drums and fifers.*—Very good and some boys soldiers' sons, and a very good band of musick.
> *Privates.*—Well looking with a great deal of airs, Light Infantry and Grenadiers remarkably good for their numbers.
> *Recruits.*—20 in number, very unexceptionable promising young lads.
> *Marching.*—In very good time, with a firm step and much air.
> *Accoutrements.*—Although bad were well put on and very clean, new ones have been ordered."

1785.

So low in April was the effective strength that the Secretary-at-War decided to reduce the subsistence allowance for private men by one-half from the 25th of that month. The following entry in the Army records, dated the 13th of June, shows that several commissions in the regiment must have been vacant prior to that date: "Pay to Lord Ed. Fitzgerald late 90th Regiment the pay of the several commissions in the 23rd Regiment of Foot in succession to him during the time the same remained vacant."

The regiment was reviewed at Doncaster on the 16th of May by Major-General Smith.

On the 5th of August an order was issued for the regiment to move out of Doncaster during the races there.

It is evident that the effective strength must have increased since April, as the subsistence for the private men rose to two-thirds per man in August and three-fourths in November.

1786.

On the 10th of January the Mayor of Doncaster was informed that it was the intention of the military authorities to remove the 23rd from there. During the following week it moved to Leeds. On the 26th six companies marched to Tynemouth and two to Sunderland to relieve the 12th Regiment. On the 21st of April Major-General Richard Grenville was appointed Colonel of the regiment in succession to Lieutenant-General the Honourable Sir William Howe, who was transferred to the colonelcy of the 19th Light Dragoons.

The regiment was reviewed at Tynemouth Barracks on the 20th of July by Major-General Wynyard. Present, Major Mackenzie, 16 officers, 215 non-commissioned officers and men. Recruiting parties were engaged at Manchester, Glasgow, Birmingham, Bradford, and Darlington.

At the beginning of August a detachment was sent to Newcastle to quell disturbances there.

1787.

In March the regiment was ordered to be relieved by the 35th. On the arrival of the latter the 23rd proceeded to Berwick with instructions to be billeted there, if the barracks was not ready for its reception.

On the 23rd of April the regiment was reviewed at Tynemouth by Major-General Sir William Erskine. The nationality of the non-commissioned officers and men was as follows: 287 English, 35 Scotch, 11 Irish, 8 "foreigners."

Towards the end of September the regiment marched to Chatham.

In consequence of the difficulty in obtaining recruits, the standard was generally lowered to 5 feet 6 inches, and the recruiting parties were again excused from returning for the half-yearly inspection.

1788.

On the 5th of April those regiments which had Irish officers were directed to send them with parties to Ireland for recruiting purposes.

Lieutenant-General Sir George Osborne, Bart., reviewed the regiment at Chatham on the 22nd of May. He reports as follows:

"*Men.*—A good body of men well set up, many old soldiers of last war and still serviceable.

"*General Observations.*—Well behaved and orderly regiment, only four men punished this year. Have lost fewer men in four years by desertion or otherwise than any regiment upon this establishment."

On the 5th of September the regiment moved to Greenwich. On the following day it marched to Staines, and on the 7th five companies proceeded to Slough and Datchet and five to Windsor to relieve the 33rd Regiment on duty with their Majesties. The following extract is taken from a daily paper dated the 25th of November 1788: "This morning the Prince of Wales and the Dukes of York and Cumberland were present at the mounting of the guard. The whole of the regiment (the 23rd Royal Welch Fuzileers) were under arms, and went through their manœuvres and exercises."

During the autumn it was employed in forming the rides in Windsor Park.

1789.

On the 10th of March the King and Queen paid a flying visit from Kew to Windsor, with the object of giving the inhabitants of the royal borough the opportunity of seeing His Majesty, after recovering from severe indisposition. "The twenty-third regiment was also drawn up before the Lodge, properly officered, in order to testify their joy on the happy occasion."

Again, on the 17th of that month, Windsor was revisited by their Majesties. In addition to illuminations, etc., "About eight o'clock the Welch Fuziliers were posted in the batteries in the Round Tower, and fired three feu de joys, which had a great effect." In June the regiment was encamped in Windsor Forest, where it was reviewed by Major-General George Scott, who, in his general observations, remarks,

"*Colours*, 2 good." (As the colours were described as "bad" in May 1788, the presumption is that the regiment had received new colours since that date.) "Some of the men have served long, but are yet fit for further service, and from the difficulty there is procuring recruits, of the size of this regiment wishes to be kept to, the discharge of them is regulated as success. may attend the recruiting service."

In July it proceeded to camp on Egham Common, where it remained until the 3rd of October when it marched to Guildford, and thence to Portsmouth, which was reached on the 6th, being relieved by the 17th Regiment. In December the 22nd and 23rd Regiments received orders to proceed to Ireland to relieve the 47th and 62nd Regiments, which were ordered to Nova Scotia.

1790.

On the 3rd of April part of the 23rd embarked at Spithead on board H.M.S. *Actæon*, a 44-gun frigate, and the rest on the following day, the destination being Cork. On the 6th Cork Harbour was reached, but it was not until the 12th that the regiment disembarked, being mustered in the interim by the "clerk of the cheque." On the departure of the regiment the captain of the ship laconically records in his log: "Smoked ship with tobacco."

On landing, the regiment mustered 1 major, 6 captains, 9 lieutenants, 1 second lieutenant, adjutant, quartermaster, surgeon, surgeon's mate, 19 sergeants, 26 corporals, 9 drummers, 310 men, 60 women, and 48 children.

During the period 14th of June—14th of November, 183 recruits joined the regiment, of whom no less than 111 enlisted in Ireland.

1791.

In January the regiment marched from Cork to Waterford, sending five companies to Wexford, with detachments to Arklow, Wicklow, Enniscorthy, and Duncannon, being chiefly employed on preventive work.

On the 26th of July the regiment was reviewed by Major-General John Leland at Waterford, and at the end of that month marched to Dublin, where it remained.

1792.

In February a proposal to level up the pay of the soldier on the Irish establishment to that of the English was brought before the Irish House of Commons, and was unanimously approved.

In May, "there being 10 firelocks, 33 bayonets bad or wanting, and 60 magazines wanting," application was made to the Board of Ordnance to make good these deficiencies: this was the result of the inspection of the regiment by Major-General John Leland on the 12th of May.

In August the headquarters was moved to Armagh, with detachments at Tanderagee, Monaghan, Poyntz Pass.

The monthly return for October shows the strength of the regiment as follows: 1 major, 4 captains, 3 lieutenants, 6 second lieutenants, adjutant, quartermaster, surgeon, surgeon's mate, 16 sergeants. 9 drummers, 273 present fit, 10 sick, 33 on command, 10 recruiting, 24 furlough: total, 350.

1793.

The headquarters remained at Armagh, with detachments at Cootehill, Kingscourt, and Charlemont.

On the 7th of February Captain Thomas Peter was appointed Aide-de-Camp to General Sir William Howe.

On the 23rd of October a return of the flank companies of certain regiments, which were to be formed into grenadier and light infantry battalions, shows the 23rd as supplying a company of 3 officers, 4 sergeants, 4 corporals, 2 drummers, and 66 rank and file for each battalion. These battalions were intended for service against the French in the West Indies.

On the 13th of November the grenadier company of the regiment, under Captain Apthorpe, Lieutenants A. Halkeit and Evan Jones, forming part of the 1st battalion grenadiers under Lieutenant-Colonel Sir Charles Gordon, embarked at Monkstown, Cork, on the *Hope*. In addition, six women and three children embarked.

The same day the light infantry company under Captain Campbell, Lieutenants W. Polhill and Wynne Garnons, forming part of the 1st battalion light infantry under Brevet Major Ross of the 31st Regiment, embarked at Monkstown on the *Berwick*. In addition, thirteen women and three children embarked.

PRIVATE, 1689.

THE COLOURS.

The Regimental Colour for 1742 is reproduced from Napier's original sketch, but the blue dragon on a red ground is evidently an artist's error, and the colour should probably be reversed.

GRENADIER, 1753.

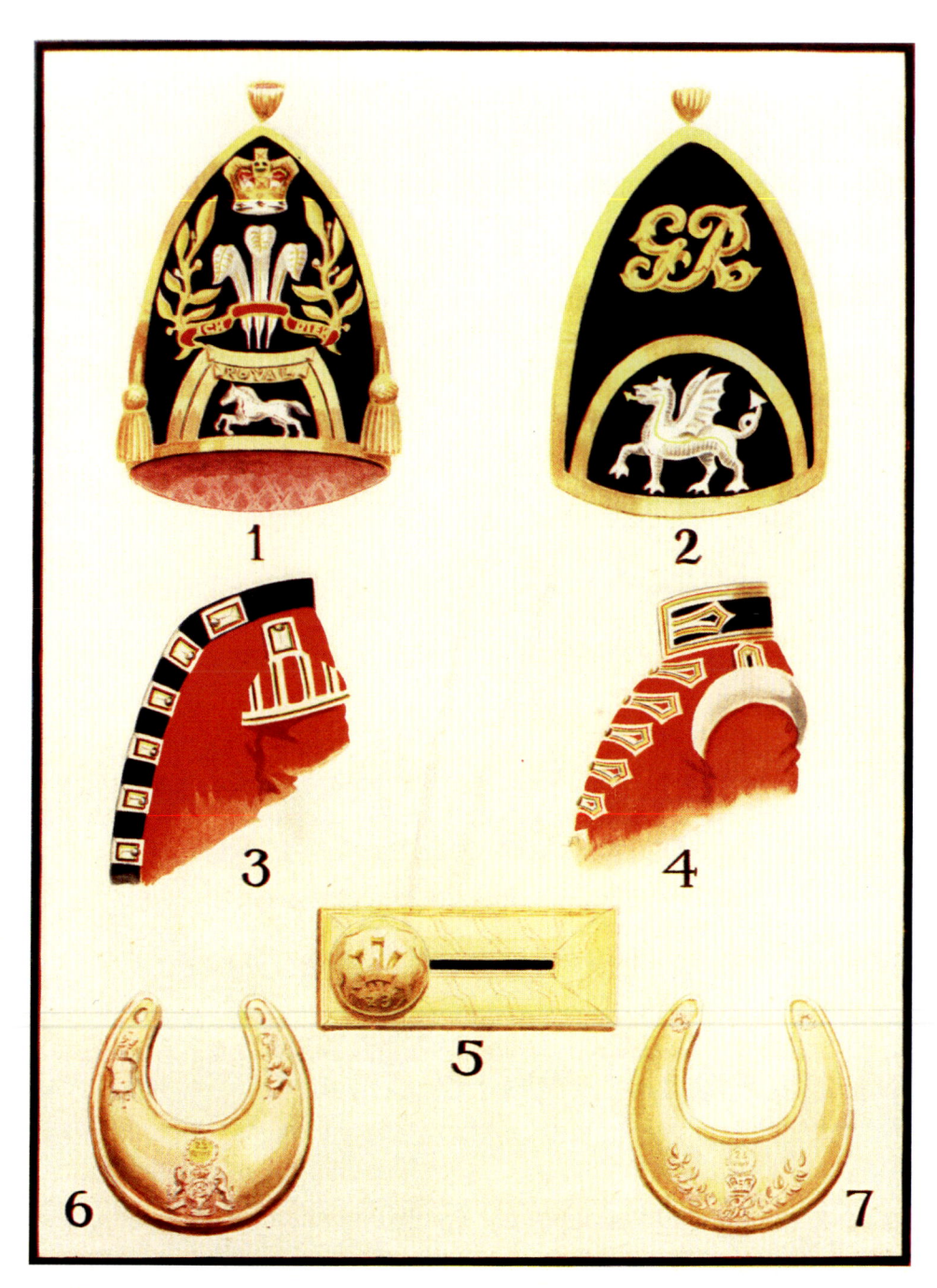

1. OFFICER'S CAP, FRONT, ABOUT 1740.
2. OFFICER'S CAP, BACK, ABOUT 1740.
3. PRIVATE'S COAT, 1768.
4. PRIVATE'S COAT, 1836.
5. OFFICER'S BUTTON AND LACE, 1802.
6. OFFICER'S GORGET, BEFORE 1802.
7. OFFICER'S GORGET, AFTER 1802.

OFFICER AND PRIVATE, 1791.

OFFICER, 1800.

OFFICER AND SERGEANT, 1808.

OFFICER AND SERGEANT-MAJOR, 1814.

1794.

On General Sir Adam Williamson, the Governor of Jamaica, representing to the home authorities that the officials and mercantile community of St. Domingo were desirous of being temporarily annexed to the British Crown, Henry Dundas, the then Secretary of the Home Department, authorised the dispatch of an expedition there in 1793.

So great was the mortality anong the troops, owing mainly to the ravages of yellow fever, that continuous calls were made for reinforcements. In response to one such made early in 1794, the battalion companies of the 23rd were ordered to prepare for foreign service.

Owing to the then unsettled condition of affairs in Ireland, the Lord Lieutenant was very loath to allow the 23rd and 35th Regiments to leave the country until their reliefs had arrived. His objection being overruled, the regiment was marched to Cork and there received four months' subsistence in advance, embarking on the 8th and 9th of March as follows:

Transport.	Officers.	Sergts.	Corporals.	Drummers.	Privates.	Women.	Children.
Leighton	6	9	9	4	141	12	12
Trelawney	4	8	6	6	130	12	12
Hercules	3	6	6	2	127	12	12
Campion	4	6	6	4	126	12	12
Recruiting, etc.	7	5	5	2	2		
Sick					21		
Total	24	34	32	18	547	48	48
Wanting					53		

On the 19th of May the battalion companies landed at the harbour of Mole St. Nicholas, St. Domingo, along with the 22nd and 41st Regiments under Major-General Whyte, having touched at Martinique and Jamaica. After strengthening the defences there, the force proceeded to the Bay of Port-au-Prince, where it arrived on the 31st of May.

After the guns of the fleet had silenced Fort Bizothon, a landing was effected, and the fort stormed under cover of a tremendous hurricane, accompanied by a deluge of rain. Troops were then landed on the north side of Port-au-Prince, which was evacuated by the enemy on the 4th of June.

The following return, dated from there on the 1st of July, shows the state of the battalion companies: 11 officers, 16 sergeants, 10 drummers.

Present, fit 162, sick 197. On command: at Tiburon, Captain Blair, Lieutenant Bradford, 4 sergeants, 76 men; at Bizothon, 2 sergeants, 8 men. Flank companies: 4 officers, 8 sergeants, 4 drummers, 106 rank and file.

As illustrating the very heavy mortality due to the climate, the monthly return for August shows no less than 10 commissions rendered vacant by the death of the following officers. *At Port-au-Prince*—Captains Thomas Chapman, John McEvers, Lieutenant and Quartermaster A. Garden, Lieutenant Watkin Lloyd, Second Lieutenants F. Steele, P. Baggott, and J. Morris. *At Guadeloupe*—Lieutenants William Polhill and Wynne Garnons. *At Mole St. Nicholas*—Surgeon's Mate William Service.

It is now necessary to revert to the doings of the flank companies which left Ireland on the 13th of November 1793. Barbadoes was reached on the 6th of January 1794, and after a month's stay there the expedition sailed, under General Grey, for Martinique, where a landing was effected at three different points. Within the next few weeks Gros Morne, Morne Bruneau, Fort Mathilde, and Colon were taken. The grenadier and light infantry companies, being in the 1st grenadier battalion and 1st light infantry battalion, under Colonel Colin Campbell and Colonel Myers respectively, took their full share in this campaign, the result of which was that on the capture of Fort Bourbon and Fort Royal the island became a British possession for the second time in thirty years.

It is impossible to distinguish the movements and losses of the flank companies of the 23rd, as they are not differentiated in the battalion returns.

On the 30th of March Grey's force, which included the grenadier and light infantry battalions, sailed for St. Lucia, which was reached on the 1st of April. The 1st battalion of the grenadiers, under Prince Edward, Duke of Kent, disembarked at Marigot des Roseaux, and was included in one of the four columns in which the army advanced on Morne Fortuné. The latter was successfully stormed on the 2nd. After leaving a garrison there consisting of the 6th and 9th Regiments, Grey re-embarked on the 4th of April, returning to Martinique, whence he sailed again on the 8th for Guadeloupe.

On the 11th the grenadier and light infantry battalions landed at Grand Bay. Fort La Fleur d'Épée was successfully assaulted, giving Grey possession of Point-à-Pitre in the north half of the island. The subjugation of the southern half of the island was speedily accomplished,

General Collot capitulating on the 21st. The very small loss—amounting to no more than 86—incurred by Grey's force, which was less than half that of his opponent, was due in great measure to the cordial co-operation of Admiral John Jervis in this combined naval and military operation.

On the 6th of May the battalion companies of the 22nd, 23rd, 35th, and 41st Regiments arrived at Martinique, where the 35th remained, the other three regiments proceeding to Jamaica under General Whyte, and thence to St. Domingo, arriving there on the 19th of May, where they were shortly afterwards joined by their respective flank companies.

The Monthly Return dated 1st December gives the state of each company and shows how they had become almost non-existent.

Companies.	Sergeants.	Drummers.	R. and File.	On Command.
Colonel	—	1	—	3
Lieutenant-Colonel J. J. Ellis	1	2	5	4
Major S. Foot	2	—	3	2
Captain C. Apthorpe	—	—	3	6
,, J. H. Campbell	—	1	3	8
,, G. Adderley	1	—	1	8
,, C. Blair	—	—	—	28
,, P. Skinner	—	—	—	24
,, A. Halkeit	2	2	2	2
,, T. Chapman	1	2	4	9
	7	8	21	94

Early in the morning of the 5th of December a revolted mulatto named Rigaud, at the head of 2,000 men, made a most determined attack upon two posts that formed the defence of Fort Bizothon. The garrison, however, having been under arms for some hours, was quite prepared for what was intended to be a surprise operation. After a fierce attack lasting for nearly an hour, Rigaud, finding that he could make no headway, retired with the survivors of his band. The 23rd, which was one of three skeleton regiments holding these posts, had one sergeant killed and one rank and file wounded.

Rigaud, undismayed by the failure of his attempt to capture Fort Bizothon, essayed a harder task in attempting, very early on Christmas morning, to carry by storm the post of Tiburon, which was held by Lieutenant John G. Bradford of the 23rd, who had under him 480 men, chiefly black troops. The discharges from a mortar which threw a fifty-pound shell, combined with increasing musketry fire, very soon had the effect of dismounting the guns of the fort and decimating the gunners. Despite this almost overwhelming disadvantage, the brave garrison held out for four days, until a shell from the mortar exploded in a ditch which was occupied by the greater part of the black troops. Thereupon a panic ensued, resulting in a wild race for the drawbridge, which the disorderly troops lowered by main force, and streaming across it they fled to Jérémie. Lieutenant Bradford, with the remainder of his force, including the wounded, succeeded in evacuating the post, and though compelled to force his way through an ambuscade of the enemy, reached Jérémie without further loss.

1795.

During the whole of this year the regiment remained in the pestilential island of St. Domingo, the result being that it was never able to muster more than 30 to 40 men when the Monthly Return was taken.

1796.

In the official records of 1796 it is stated that by "sword of the enemy" the whole British loss in St. Domingo since landing, up to November 1795, was between 90 and 100, whereas by death up to March 1796 the loss was 129 officers, 5,720 men, of which the 23rd lost 12 officers and 600 men.

The following table shows at a glance the heavy mortality due to disease suffered by the regiment from July 1794 to February 1796:

	1794.				1795.					1796.	
	July.	Aug.	Oct.	Dec.	Jan.	Feb.	July.	Sept.	Dec.	Jan.	Feb.
Officers	11	9	9	8	9	9	9	10	9	9	10
Sergeants	16	11	4	7	8	5	3	9	12	9	9
Drums	10	10	7	8	10	10	5	6	7	7	7
Fit	162	110	52	21	36	54	33	24	37	10	8
Sick	197	136	162	139	115	87	79	75	45	15	17
Dead	133	151	33	58	33	16	16	22	9	1	10
On command	202	166	142	94	71	64	66	43	18	22	13
Total	572	421	365	263	231	215	197	166	131	70[1]	60
Wanting	218	369	235	337	369	385	403	434	469	530	540

[1] 60 drafted into 1st Foot.

On the 22nd of February, according to the captain's log of H.M.S. *Regulus*, " came on board a captain and 45 of the 23rd regiment " at Port-au-Prince. The ship left there on the 19th of March, touching at Bermuda on the 31st of March, and the entry in the log on Wednesday, the 27th of April, reads as follows : " Spithead, sent on shore the troops belonging to the 23rd regiment." On landing, orders were received to proceed to Worcester, and on the 28th of May to Kidderminster.

In the Monthly Return for the 1st of June 12 companies are stated to be at Upton with a total strength of 103, including 56 " recruiting "; and in the return for the 1st of August Captain Thomas Bury, Captain James Richardson, with Quartermaster Hart, are stated to be " still in the West Indies." These officers arrived at Deptford on the *King George* transport on the 9th of September with 13 sergeants, 7 drummers, and 10 rank and file, and received orders to proceed to Chatham.

From July to October the regiment was stationed at Kidderminster with recruiting parties at Manchester, Carnarvon, Worcester, Preston, Halifax, Bolton, and Abergavenny. The regiment left Kidderminster on the 14th of October, arrived at Uxbridge on the 24th, and reached Chatham on the 29th, where it remained until March of the following year.

The November Monthly Return shows the strength of the regiment as 229, a slow but steady progress towards the full establishment of 1,010 men.

1797.

In April the 23rd moved to Chelmsford, where it remained until September, when it moved to Deal, being stationed there until December, leaving a detachment of 2 officers, 3 sergeants, 2 drummers, and 63 rank and file at Purfleet.

The following is of regimental interest, as well as being an example of the system which was even then in vogue of giving commissions to infants : at this time both Lieutenant-Colonel J. Joyner Ellis and his distinguished son Captain Henry Walton Ellis were serving in the regiment. The former had served successively in the 18th, 89th, and 41st Regiments, and became Lieutenant-Colonel of the 23rd in 1793, his ensigncy dating from 1761. The latter, born at Cambray in 1783, had on the 26th of March that year been appointed by purchase to an ensigncy in the 89th Regiment. On its being disbanded a few months later, the baby was placed upon half-pay, but brought on full pay again as ensign, at the age of six, on the 21st of September 1789, in the 41st Foot; Captain in the 23rd, the 6th of April 1797, at the age of fourteen.

1798.

The Monthly Returns show that the regiment had moved to Norwich in January, where it remained until the end of April and then it moved to Canterbury.

On the 2nd of that month Sir Charles Grey selected for the expeditionary force which it had been decided to dispatch to Ostend, with the object of destroying the sluice-gates there, the 11th Regiment and " detachments from the 49th and 23rd Regiments, not wishing to embark them, but to make up the number of troops wanted from the flank corps, my reason for this is the 49th are composed of raw recruits . . . and the 23rd have a great many Dutchmen in the regiment which I do not think exactly calculated for the intended service."

In disregard of Sir Charles Grey's discrimination, the 23rd was moved to Margate, and embarked together with the flank companies as part of the expeditionary force, which assembled off the North Foreland on the 15th of May; a portion of the 23rd being on board H.M. sloop *Harpy*.

Ostend was reached on the 19th. Information having been received that the town was lightly held, the naval and military authorities decided to effect an immediate landing, despite the threatening condition of the weather.

The disembarkation began on the sandhills to the east of Ostend Harbour. By five a.m. the following troops had landed: 23rd and 49th Regiments—flank companies only; two companies Light Infantry Coldstream and 3rd Guards; sergeant's party 17th Light Dragoons, 11th Regiment, and 6 guns, also a party of seamen. The ships which carried the 23rd, with the exception of the flank companies, were stationed at the west of Ostend, to make a demonstration on that side. H.M.S. *Wolverine* embarked on the 12th of May a detachment of the 23rd consisting of 1 sergeant, 1 corporal, 1 drummer, and 61 privates under Captain H. Edwards and Lieutenants A. MacLean and W. Offley, and took up a position so close to the enemy's batteries on that side, that in a very short time no less than 11 seamen were killed and wounded, and of the 23rd 1 private was killed and 5 wounded. The grenadiers of the 11th and 23rd Regiments, under Major Skinner of the latter regiment, were posted at the lower ferry to prevent the enemy crossing the harbour from Ostend. The light infantry of the 11th, 23rd, and 49th Regiments, under Major Donkin of the 44th, occupied the village of Bredene.

A summons to surrender was forwarded to the commandant of Ostend, to which he returned a firm refusal, although the garrison numbered no more than 400 men. The mines which had been laid at the lock gates of the canal were successfully exploded, the object of the expedition being thereby attained. The expected storm suddenly springing up prevented the re-embarkation of the troops.

General Coote, finding his retreat was cut off, took up a position on the sandhills, and then threw up breastworks. At four o'clock on the 20th of May two strong French columns were seen advancing on the front, and several others on the flanks. For two hours the British made a desperate resistance, but finally were overwhelmed by weight of numbers and compelled to surrender. Both Major Skinner and Captain Halkeit of the 23rd light infantry company were specially mentioned, as also the following : " Mr. Lowen attached the 23rd light infantry was twice wounded, and was particularly conspicuous, and marked as a most promising soldier."

The following was the return of casualties in the 23rd : 4 rank and file killed, 11 rank and file wounded. Volunteer Lowen wounded severely. The prisoners of war included the following from the 23rd : Lieutenant-Colonel R. Talbot, Major P. K. Skinner ; Captains J. G. Bradford, Thomas Bury (grenadiers), A. Halkeit (light infantry) ; Lieutenants H. H. Hanson, H. Vischer, Charles Lloyd (grenadiers), L. Cotton, J. V. Cortland, Richard Roberts, Edward Hill, 8 sergeants, 4 drummers, 160 rank and file. They were marched to Lille and interned there, and did not rejoin the regiment until June in the following year.

This expedition was a pet scheme of Captain (afterwards Admiral) Sir Home Popham, his idea being to prevent Ostend from being made a base, not only for the invasion of England but also for privateers.

From June 1798 to February 1799 the regiment was stationed at Amherst Barracks, Guernsey, relieving the Nottingham and Glengarry Fencible Regiments ordered to Ireland.

On the 4th of October the regiment was inspected by Major-General Sir Hew Dalrymple. Under arms : Major J. Hall, 16 officers, 34 sergeants, 36 corporals, 24 drummers, 291 men. There were still

3 "foreigners" among the officers, viz. Major Skinner, Lieutenants H. Vischer and J. V. Cortland, and 34 among the non-commissioned officers and men. The inspecting General remarked as follows: "The regiment is extremely steady, the whole seem to possess the proper esprit de corps which leaves no room for doubt, that, in a short time, the regiment will be as excellent as possible. This regiment has excellent interior regulations admitting of no idlers, and of course turns out strong on all occasions."

1799.

In January a detachment under Captain H. Edwards with 3 lieutenants, 3 second lieutenants, 1 assistant surgeon, 13 sergeants, 7 drummers, 180 rank and file proceeded to Eling Barracks, Southampton, leaving four companies in Guernsey. These companies moved over to Eling Barracks next month, where they were inspected on the 18th of May by Lieutenant-General Stevens.

In June the following prisoners of war rejoined the regiment: 13 sergeants, 4 drummers, 172 rank and file, leaving 3 rank and file sick at Lille. On the 27th of July the regiment arrived at Barham Down Camp, preparatory to embarking on the Helder Expedition, which was undertaken with the dual object of capturing the Dutch fleet and arsenals, and re-establishing the power of the Stadtholder.

On the 9th of August the 23rd and 55th embarked at Ramsgate, but the expedition, under Sir Ralph Abercromby, did not sail till the 13th; no landing could be effected until daybreak on the 27th, owing to unfavourable weather. The disembarkation was unopposed, but the advanced guard had scarcely begun to move forward before it was attacked.

The British position was on a ridge of sandhills stretching along the coast from north to south. The right flank was unavoidably exposed. Although there was not sufficient ground to form more than one battalion in line, the 23rd and 55th Regiments forming the reserve brigade, under Colonel Macdonald, stubbornly held their ground. About 3 p.m. the Dutch retired to Petten. The 23rd had 18 rank and file killed; Captains Bury, Ellis, and the Hon. Godfrey McDonald, 5 sergeants, 69 rank and file wounded. The following day the whole of the troops were on shore.

The result of this action was the capture of two line-of-battle ships, five frigates (one of them being the *Valk*, to which reference will soon be made), and 13 Indiamen, as well as possession of the Helder, giving entrance to the Zuyder Zee.

From the 27th of August to the 1st of September Abercromby remained stationary, waiting for reinforcements. General Brune, aware of the cause of this delay, determined to forestall Abercromby by attacking him at daybreak on the 10th of September. By 10 a.m. the enemy was beaten off at all points, and fell back on Alkmaar, hotly pursued by the 23rd and 55th Regiments under Macdonald.

Between the 12th and 15th of September strong reinforcements reached Abercromby. The Duke of York landed on the 15th of September and assumed command of the army, which now numbered about 30,000 men and 1,200 cavalry. On the 19th the Duke of York's army moved forward in four columns, the 23rd in reserve, with the 55th Regiment forming part of the detached column under Lieutenant-General Sir Ralph Abercromby. This column took no direct part in the action fought on this day.

The state of the weather and roads compelled the Duke to defer operations until the 2nd of October, when he advanced with the object of forcing the enemy to evacuate North Holland. The attack was made in four columns, the 23rd being again in Colonel Macdonald's reserve, forming part of the first or right column under Abercromby. This column moved along the beach against Egmont-aan-Zee. Macdonald's reserve together with the 1st battalion of the Grenadiers and Light Infantry of the line, drove the enemy from Campe, and from the sandhills above that village.

The division under Sir Ralph Abercromby met with little resistance at first, and arrived within a mile of Egmont, where they found a large body of French infantry posted on the sandhills in front of the town. The enemy attacked with great determination, but were unable to drive back the English, who by nightfall had pushed their advance to within a short distance of Egmont.

The 23rd lost in this battle: 7 rank and file killed; Lieutenants McLean and Keith, 1 sergeant, 3 drummers, and 49 rank and file wounded; 7 rank and file missing.

Brune retired that night from Egmont to another and stronger position, at Beverwyk and Wyk-aan-Zee, which the Duke of York was desirous of forcing. His advanced posts were pushed forward on the 6th of October, and by the evening the Allies obtained possession of Bakkum and Castricum.

The losses sustained by the 23rd in this useless action were 6 men killed, 1 sergeant and 33 men wounded.

The approach of winter, the unfavourable nature of the advanced line as a defensive position, and the fact that the Dutch people had not risen in favour of the invaders, rendered it evident that no advance could be made with any chance of success. The Duke of York therefore decided to retire to the Zype position. The troops began to retire on the 7th of October, the movement being completed by the 12th. Negotiations were entered into with the French for the evacuation of the country, the agreement being concluded on the 18th. The Allies were to evacuate the country before the 30th, retaining however possession of the captured fleet. The 23rd marched to the Helder and embarked on the 29th of October—the embarkation strength being given as 630 all ranks—on some canal boats for conveyance to the fleet in the offing.

The following is Mr. Cannon's account of what befell three companies of the regiment:

"The wind dying away they were unable to proceed, and were ordered on board some Dutch frigates, when it was the fate of Lieutenants Hill, Hanson, Vischer, MacLean, and Hoggard, with the grenadier and two other companies, amounting to two hundred and sixty-two men, and twenty-five women and children, to embark in the *Valk*. This ship was prevented from sailing at the same time with those which conveyed the rest of the regiment, but she got out with the next tide. On the following evening they were, by reckoning, within thirty miles of Yarmouth, but would not come nearer the shore during the night. Next morning the wind was contrary, and soon increasing to a storm, drove the *Valk* towards the coast of Norway. She now beat about for several days, till all idea of her position was lost. On the morning of the 10th of November the ship struck on a sand-bank, as was afterwards ascertained, within six miles of the Dutch coast, from which the captain had conceived he was many leagues distant, supposing himself to be at least equally near to that of England; the crew, of whom, indeed, scarcely twenty had ever been at sea before, abandoned themselves to despair, and trusted more to their prayers than to their exertions.

"The spirit of the Englishmen was not, however, dismayed by their appalling situation. Lieutenant Hoggard, who had some little knowledge of nautical affairs, took some of the soldiers down to the pumps, and Lieutenant Hill, having failed in an attempt to break open the powder-magazine, fired several rounds from a soldier's musket; the ship guns had all been drawn, and the gunner could not be found. The ship now beat over the bank and drifted among some breakers, the mainmast went overboard, severing the long-boat in two in its fall; the mizen and foremasts soon followed, carrying with them numbers of people who had crowded into the rigging. Lieutenant Hill now hearing the ship going to pieces, took his station on the forecastle, where he lay down, and from whence he witnessed the unhappy fate of most of his companions, the afterpart of the ship having soon broken away. The forecastle seemed to be fast bedded in the sand, but it soon fell over, when Lieutenant Hill quitted it, and after many fruitless and fatiguing efforts, succeeded in fastening himself with his braces to a fragment of the wreck, on which he at length reached the shore, when he found that of four hundred and forty-six souls which had sailed in the *Valk*, only twenty-five survived—himself, nineteen men of the Royal Welsh Fusiliers, and five Dutch sailors.

" The land on which they were cast proved to be the island of Ameland, on the coast of Holland. The inhabitants had hoisted the colours of the House of Orange, and cut off all communication with the main-land; they received the survivors in the kindest manner, and performed the last offices to those who were washed ashore, with as much decency as their poverty would permit.

" Having fulfilled these melancholy duties, Lieutenant Hill hired a fishing-boat, in which he and his companions were conveyed to the Helder, from whence they returned to England in the *Success* frigate."

. The Monthly Return for December as regards the shipwreck is " 11 sergeants, 6 drummers, 218 rank and file were lost at sea 10th of November."

On its return to England the regiment, landing at Yarmouth on the 5th of November, arrived at Sudbury on the 13th, left there on the 15th, and arrived at Battle Barracks on the 23rd.

1800.

On the 28th of February the regiment was inspected by Major-General Lord Charles Somerset. He reported as follows: " There are 283 firelocks and bayonets wanting to complete to the present strength of the 23rd. I am happy to have it in my power to state that the 23rd Regiment is extremely correct and expert in the field, and in every respect except the want of arms, it is in high order."

The regiment was stationed at Battle until April. In the previous month the 23rd supplied 1 subaltern, 2 sergeants, 1 drummer, and 32 privates towards the formation of "the Rifle Corps at Horsham." This experimental corps was numbered the 95th, and as such rendered most distinguished service in the Peninsula.

In May the regiment moved to Honiton, Chard, and Crewkerne, and in June to Plymouth.

Certain overtures which Buonaparte addressed to the Spanish Court with the object of winning over that country to his side in the contest which he was now waging with this country having been favourably entertained, the Government, through their mouthpiece Dundas, decided on the 1st of August to dispatch a force of about 13,000 men under Sir Ralph Abercromby to destroy the Spanish arsenals, dockyards, and fortifications at Ferrol, Vigo, and Cadiz.

The 23rd Regiment embarked on the 1st of July at Plymouth in the *Naiad* and *Alcmene* frigates, and landed on the island of Houat off Quiberon Bay, where they remained for over a month, being joined by the 31st, 1st battalion 52nd, and 63rd Regiments. The rest of Abercromby's army was composed of regiments from home which proceeded to the rendezvous in Quiberon Bay, where the whole was picked up by Lieutenant-General Sir James Pulteney, who was selected to command the expedition.

On the 19th of August Major Mackenzie, together with 9 officers, 1 volunteer, and 200 N.C.O.s and men, embarked on H.M.S. *Amethyst*, and on the 20th Major Edward Jones, 10 officers, and 300 N.C.O.s and men embarked on H.M.S. *Amelia* and *Stag*.

On the 25th of August the fleet reached Ferrol, and immediately attacked a fort manned by eight 24-pounder guns, whose fire was soon silenced.

That night the disembarkation began, and was so skilfully conducted by the Navy, that not a single man was lost by the time that the operation was completed. The troops on landing ascended a ridge of hills adjacent to the bay, and took possession of the crest. The following morning they were attacked by a large force of the enemy, which was driven back, with the result that the British were left in complete possession of the heights overlooking the town and harbour. Pulteney, after minutely inspecting the situation of the place, and being able from reports of prisoners to form some idea of the strength of the enemy, decided to proceed no further with the enterprise, a decision which was unanimously concurred in by his brigadiers. The casualties of the 23rd were 1 man killed and 3 wounded.

The re-embarkation of the army was satisfactorily effected on the night of the 27th, thanks to the Navy. Pulteney then proceeded to Vigo, but coming to the conclusion that nothing was to be gained by landing troops there, he sailed for Gibraltar, which was reached on the 19th of September.

Before leaving Vigo, 211 officers and men of the 23rd were transhipped from the *Amethyst* to the *Heroine*, and 310 officers and men from the *Amelia* and *Stag* to the *Astrea*.

On the 11th of that month Abercromby had arrived at Gibraltar from Minorca with 10,000 men; as he was senior to Pulteney the command of the united force devolved upon him.

On the arrival of Pulteney the desirability of making a descent upon Cadiz was considered by the naval and military commanders, and was the subject of acrimonious discussion for several days. It was finally decided on the 7th of October to embark 3,000 men on flat-boats, and land them on the northern end of the Bay of Cadiz. On Admiral Keith representing that this detachment would be isolated in the event of the fleet being blown off the coast—a contingency always to be reckoned with—before further troops could be landed, Abercromby decided to abandon the attempt and return to Gibraltar.

The regiment, after leaving Vigo, spent most of September and all October on board ship, landing a party on the 21st of September from the *Astrea* under Captain Bradford, 2 lieutenants and 65 N.C.O.s and men, to guard the watering-place i Tetuan Bay. A similar party landed there from the *Heroine* under Lieutenant Hill on the 25th.

A private of the regiment on board the *Heroine* received twelve lashes for "selling his grog."

Towards the end of October Abercromby was directed to send a division of his army to Minorca, and with the rest of his army, to which the 23rd was attached, to proceed to Malta, which was not reached until the middle of November, consequent upon the great trouble experienced by the transports, when anchored off Gibraltar, in taking fresh water on board owing to a succession of gales.

On the 24th of November the regiment disembarked at Malta from the two ships.

Towards the end of the month the division which had proceeded to Minorca rejoined Abercromby.

While the transports were being overhauled—an operation lasting nearly a month—the troops were stationed on shore. On the 20th of December the 23rd re-embarked. Dundas having decided upon a campaign against France in Egypt, directed Abercromby to proceed to the rendezvous in Marmorice Bay in Asia Minor, about forty miles north of Rhodes, which was reached on the 30th of December.

1801.

A state of the regiment on the 11th of January 1801 at Marmorice Bay was as follows: 1 lieutenant-colonel, 2 majors, 6 captains, 19 lieutenants, 4 staff, 42 sergeants, 13 drummers, 427 privates present fit, 54 sick, 72 absent: total, 553.

The expedition was unable for various reasons to leave Marmorice Bay until the 22nd of February. Good use was, however, made of the interval in practising trial landings and evolutions on shore.

On the 2nd of March the fleet anchored in Aboukir Bay. Owing to the heavy swell the landing could not be effected until the morning of the 8th, when the 23rd landed from the *Astrea* and *Heroine*. In the composition of the expeditionary force the 23rd formed part of the Reserve, under Major-General John Moore.

After being rowed for nearly six miles the troops made good their landing, although "exposed to a very severe cannonade and fire of grape," which churned up the water like hail. The Reserve leaped out of the boats, and formed up as they advanced. Fronting it was a hill which Abercromby described as "almost inaccessible." The taking of this hill was entrusted to the 23rd, and the four flank companies of the 1st and 2nd battalions of the 40th Regiment, who rushed up it with "almost supernatural energy, never firing a shot but charging with the bayonet two battalions which crowned it, breaking them and pursuing till they carried the two Nole [sic] hills in the rear, which commanded the plain to the left, taking at the same time three pieces of cannon."

For this brilliant feat both the 23rd and their gallant comrades of the 40th were highly commended by Major-General Moore. In less than two hours the whole range of heights was in possession of the British.

The loss sustained by the 23rd in this action was:

Killed.—Six rank and file.

Wounded.—Two officers (Captains Lloyd and Pearson) [Note.—Cannon says Captain Ellis was wounded—making 3 officers wounded], 1 sergeant, 37 rank and file.

Missing.—One rank and file.

In addition to the foregoing casualties Lieutenant the Hon. Edward Meade was killed. He had been an ensign in the 40th Regiment, but the War Office Army List, now at the Public Record Office, shows that he had been promoted lieutenant in the 23rd Regiment, and records " Killed at Aboukir on 8th March." He was doubtless unaware of his promotion and transfer to the 23rd, as his name is shown in Captain Smythies's *History of the 40th Regiment*.

On the 12th the whole army moved forward through deep sand, and soon came in sight of the French, who occupied an advantageous ridge known as the Roman Camp. Abercromby decided to wait until the following morning before attacking them. Accordingly at 5 a.m. on the 13th the British army moved forward in three parallel columns, the Reserve forming the right column. The troops had not been long in motion before the enemy descended from the heights, and fiercely attacked the leading brigades of the centre and left columns. This attack on the other columns enabled the Reserve to push forward with the object of turning the enemy's left. In due course the heights of the Roman Camp were gained by it, whereupon Moore halted his men until he was joined by the rest of the army.

As night was rapidly approaching, Abercromby decided to suspend operations, and encamped on the position which had been occupied by the French the previous evening.

In this engagement the 23rd lost 2 rank and file killed and 4 rank and file wounded.

Abercromby remained in this position until the 21st, when the enemy, about 12,000 strong, essayed at 3.30 a.m. a surprise attack, not knowing that the British had been under arms for at least half an hour.

General Menou, who commanded the French, planned a false attack upon Abercromby's left, while driving it home against the centre and right. General Craddock's column on the left soon repulsed the enemy's effort in that quarter. The attacks on the right and centre columns were, however, fiercely maintained for some time, the one against the right column, consisting of the Reserve, particularly so.

General Hutchinson, in his dispatch of the 5th of April, narrating the events of the day, comments on the gallant conduct of the Reserve in the following terms : " The Reserve, against whom the principal attack of the enemy was directed, conducted themselves with un-exampled spirit. They resisted the impetuosity of the French infantry, and repulsed several charges of cavalry."

In this part of the field the French left a prodigious number of dead and wounded. To the inexpressible grief of the army, Sir Ralph Abercromby died on the 28th of March of a wound received in this battle.

The casualties of the 23rd were :

Killed.—Five rank and file.

Wounded.—One officer (Lieutenant Samuel Cooke), 2 sergeants, 12 rank and file.

A state of the army taken on the 30th of March supplies the following information respecting the 23rd Regiment : " 1 major, 5 captains, 15 lieutenants, 4 staff, 34 sergeants, 12 drummers, 362 rank and file fit for duty, 116 sick present : total, 591."

Beyond the taking of Fort Rahmanieh on the 10th of May, followed a week later by the surrender to Brigadier-General Doyle of 600 of the " best troops of France," the evacuation of Cairo by the French and their auxiliary troops on the 27th of June, winding up with the surrender of Alexandria on the 2nd of September, which shattered Napoleon's aims in Egypt, nothing of importance remains to be narrated.

In a re-brigading of the army that took place on the 9th of August, but did not affect the 23rd, the effective rank and file strength of that regiment is shown as 343.

The following extract from a General Order, dated the 16th of May 1801, furnishes eloquent testimony to H.R.H. the Commander-in-Chief's appreciation of the manner in which the landing at Aboukir Bay on the 8th of March was carried out, viz. :

" His Royal Highness the Commander-in-Chief cannot forbear to avail himself of this opportunity of recapitulating the leading features of a series of operations so honorable to the British arms.

" The boldness of the approach to the coast of Aboukir, in defiance of a powerful and well-directed artillery, the orderly formation upon the beach, under the heaviest fire of grape and musketry, the reception and repulse of the enemy's cavalry and infantry, the subsequent charge of our troops, which decided the victory, and established a footing on the shores of Egypt, are circumstances of glory never surpassed in the military annals of the world."

In October the regiment embarked for Malta; a state taken there on the 22nd of October is as follows: 2 majors, 5 captains, 15 lieutenants, 3 second lieutenants, 4 staff, 40 sergeants, 13 drummers, 316 privates fit present; 115 sick present; 106 sick absent: total, 537. On the 12th of December the regiment, with the 2nd battalion The Royals, 8th and 25th Regiments, was on its way to Gibraltar.

A state of the regiment in December shows: Present, 29 officers, 34 sergeants, 12 drummers, 294 fit; sick, 70; in England, 150: total, 519. Wanting to complete, 481.

1802.

On the 27th of January a recruiting party, including the band, which had been stationed at Worcester, left there, and on arriving at Southampton crossed to the Isle of Wight on the 6th of February to join the depôt.

In March recruiting parties were stationed at Stourbridge under Captain H. Edwards, and in Ireland under Lieutenant A. Leekey.

The following circular letter, dated the 6th of July, was addressed to such regiments as had served in the campaign of the previous year:

"I have the honour to inform you that His Majesty has been graciously pleased to grant permission to the several regiments of His Army, which served during the late campaign in Egypt, to assume and wear in their Colours a badge as a distinguished mark of His Majesty's Royal approbation, and as a lasting memorial of the glory acquired to His Majesty's arms by the zeal, discipline and intrepidity of His troops in that audacious and important campaign."

The badge in question was the Sphinx with the word "Eygypt" beneath; this was seemingly altered about 1825 to "The Sphinx superscribed 'Egypt.'"

In recognition of the services rendered to the Ottoman Empire the Grand Signior Selim III presented large gold medals to all field officers, smaller ones to captains, and still smaller ones to subalterns.

The following is a description of this medal, known as the "Order of the Crescent," viz.:

The obverse bears a crescent and star of eight points, surrounded by an ornamental border. The reverse has a similar border, surrounding the Sultan's cipher, with the date, 1801, below. It was struck in four sizes, the design being the same in all cases.

Owing to a difference in the dies, these medals were struck with the crescent on different sides of the star, sometimes on the right and sometimes on the left side.

The medal given to admirals and general officers was $2\frac{1}{10}$ in. in diameter, and weighed 10 oz. 8 dwt. 3 gr. That given to field officers of the army, and their equivalent rank in the navy, was $1\frac{9}{10}$ in. in diameter, and weighed 19 dwt. 4 gr. The third, given to captains in the army, and their equivalent rank in the navy, was $1\frac{7}{10}$ in. in diameter, and weighed 12 dwt. 18 gr.; and the smallest size was $1\frac{4}{10}$ in. in diameter, and weighed 8 dwt. 18 gr. It was given to commissioned officers of both services below the rank of captain in the army and the corresponding naval rank.

The medal was worn with an orange ribbon, to which it was attached by means of a small gold chain and hook.

On the 1st of September the Monthly Return shows that the establishment had been lowered to 750, as it is stated that the total effectives were 430, "wanting to complete, 320."

By then the recruiting parties had been moved to Wrexham, Worcester, and Liverpool.

1803.

On the 4th of March the regiment was inspected at Gibraltar by H.R.H. the Duke of Kent. He observed with regard to the men that they were "low but stout and active and fit for any service"; "Arms: all bad but clean and kept in best possible order." His general remarks include the following: "The Adjutant of this regiment and the Sergeant Major having both particularly distinguished themselves by their persevering attention to the instruction of the men at the different periods of drill, claim that I should name them to the commander-in-chief accordingly, and I feel I should be wanting in what is due to them were I not to state that they merit any mark of favour which he may choose to bestow upon them." The total effectives, non-commissioned officers and men, were 460, wanting to complete 346.

On the 21st of June the regiment embarked at Gibraltar, and returned to England, arriving at the Motherbank anchorage between Ryde and Cowes at the beginning of August. Owing to its returning to England with the 8th and 25th Regiments, and 26th Light Dragoons, and their being on board troopships which at that date were nearly all French or Dutch built, they were mistaken by the Danish ship *Moucherron* when off Scilly for French, and reported as an enemy force to the Commander-in-Chief in Ireland, the helmets and blue clothing of the Light Dragoons accentuating the mistake. In September the regiment was stationed at Portsmouth, and moved to Freshwater Gate, Isle of Wight, in October.

The following is an extract from a General Order dated the 6th of June 1803, abolishing the command of companies by field officers :

"It being His Majesty's pleasure, that in future each Troop and Company throughout the army shall have an effective Captain, and consequently that the Field Officers of the several regiments of Cavalry, Foot Guards, and Infantry of the Line shall no longer have Troops or Companies, the following arrangement, in regard to the appointment of the additional Captains, is to take place.

"The Captain Lieutenant of each Corps succeeds to the Colonel's Troop or Company : the rank of Captain Lieutenant being abolished.

"The Lieutenant Colonel's Troop or Company in each Corps will be filled by a Captain from the Half Pay Establishment, or in some very particular cases by a Lieutenant on Full Pay.

"The Major's Troop or Company by a Lieutenant on Full Pay, who is to raise thirty men for his promotion : or by a Captain from Half Pay, who will also be required to raise the same number of men."

1804.

On the 1st of January the state of the regiment was as follows : Present, 21 officers, 28 sergeants, 15 drummers, 325 rank and file, 41 sick : total, 389. Wanting to complete, 361. Recruiting parties were stationed at Wrexham, Yeovil, Worcester, and Manchester.

In May the 23rd moved to Hailsham and Eastbourne.

So alarmed was the Addington Ministry in 1803 and well into 1804 at the dearth of recruits for the regular army—the casualties, mainly from desertions, considerably exceeding the enlistments—that various expedients were resorted to, in order to fill up the depleted ranks.

One expedient in particular, known as "raising men for rank," was revived. Under it an officer could gain one or more steps according to the number of recruits he was able to produce. On this occasion it was laid down by the Commander-in-Chief that only one step of promotion would be sanctioned, no matter how many recruits were procured, and a further provision was to the effect that unless the recruits were forthcoming within six months, no step could be obtained. Permission was given for the officers of the 23rd and ten other regiments to enlist men under these conditions for service in second battalions of their regiments.

So meagre were the results obtained that Pitt, succeeding Addington in May, devised a scheme for augmenting the army, the main feature of which was that recruits enlisted for home service, and for a period of five years, for which they were to be paid a bounty of ten guineas, would, on accepting service in the regular army, receive a second bounty of ten guineas; the men so raised were to be formed into second battalions of regular regiments. This measure, which was known as the Permanent Additional Forces Act, became law on the 29th of June, and under it a second battalion was added to the 23rd from the 25th of December. The recruiting areas allotted to the 23rd were Anglesea, Carnarvon, Denbigh, Flint, and Merioneth.

On the 25th of August H.R.H. the Duke of York arrived at Eastbourne with his staff to review the two brigades encamped there. The one under General Lennox was reviewed that day; the other under General Maitland, which was encamped on the heights and included the 23rd, and had been under arms since the early morning, was dismissed and reviewed the following morning. "They went through their business with great precision and steadiness, particularly the 8th, 23rd, and 88th Regiments, and although last, not least, the North Hants Militia. A small corps of Caravan [sic] Artillery surprised the spectators by the rapidity of their motions, always changing their position in full gallop."

On the 28th of October the regiment was reviewed by Brigadier-General Maitland, who remarked as follows: "This regiment has been taught to drill out of the King's Regulations, according to the mode adopted at Gibraltar." He adds as follows: "The men of this regiment are low, and it has not been successful in recruiting for a second battalion. All their London recruits having deserted, and being now only 550 strong."

1805.

1st Battalion.

In May 3 captains, 5 lieutenants, and 5 second lieutenants were "receiving volunteers from the Militia," the result of which appeared in the return for June, where the strength is shown as 27 officers, 28 sergeants, 16 drummers, 604 present, 143 on command, 31 sick: total, 788.

In the autumn Pitt decided to send a mixed force, consisting of the King's German Legion, now fully organised, together with certain British regiments, including the 23rd—the whole under Lieutenant-General Don—to co-operate in the expulsion of the French from Hanover. Accordingly the 23rd, 726 strong, forming part of Major-General Paget's brigade of the 1st Division, marched from Eastbourne to Deal on the 23rd of October, thence to Ramsgate, where it embarked and sailed from there on the 29th of October for the Elbe. Owing to contrary winds, Cuxhaven was not reached until the 17th of November. The troops on landing, after a severe march, were cantoned on the banks of the Lower Weser.

1805.

2nd Battalion.

On the 1st of February the headquarters were at Wrexham, but so far it had not been possible to form the battalion into companies, as the effective strength on that date numbered no more than 1 lieutenant-colonel, 2 majors, adjutant, 2 sergeants, 28 rank and file, 1 sick in quarters, 2 in hospital, and 3 on furlough: total, 36 non-commissioned officers and men.

The Monthly Return, in which the foregoing is recorded, holds out hopes of better things to come, as it states that Lieutenant C. Mills was on his road to join with a party from the 1st battalion, and that Captain Hurford was recruiting at Beaumaris.

That this hope was partly justified is shown by the fact that the strength on the 1st of March had increased to 1 lieutenant-colonel, 2 majors, 2 captains, 1 lieutenant, 3 staff, 12 sergeants, 4 drummers, 70 privates, and 4 sick. There were still, however, 29 sergeants, 22 corporals, and 722 privates wanting to complete. Captain Hurford was recruiting at Carnarvon, and Captain Coulthurst was similarly employed at Holywell.

On the 1st of June eight companies were formed on paper, but the privates had only increased by five! As, however, it is recorded that 307 were wanting to complete, the authorities evidently decided to lower the establishment to 400, owing to the paucity of recruits. Doubtless great efforts were being made to secure them, as Captain Hurford was still recruiting at Carnarvon and Captain Coulthurst at Holywell, while Captain J. T. Leahy was recruiting at Llanwrst, Captain Brown at Bala, and Captain Green at Mold. The united efforts of these officers secured 13 recruits during the following two months!

Although the strength is not shown in the October Monthly Return, it may reasonably be assumed that the recruiting officers were meeting with more success, as it is recorded that a detachment consisting of 1 captain, 3 lieutenants, 4 sergeants, 2 drummers, and 50 men were at Chester.

In November the regiment was at Chester Castle. The effective strength was 147, while 253 were wanting to complete.

The recruiting area had been extended to England, as Captain Leahy was engaged on this work at Birmingham, Captain Pierse at Wigan, Lieutenant Midhurst at Stockport, and Lieutenant Griffith at Stourbridge. In the Principality Holywell, Wrexham, and Mold were still regarded as happy hunting-grounds.

1806.

1st Battalion.

Early in January the expedition occupied Bremen and Verden, the 23rd being stationed at Ostendon, Lisajenhonjen, and Hasted, with its headquarters at Leesam near Bremen, where they remained until the 13th of February, when, having received orders to re-embark for home, they marched to Cuxhaven and embarked for England on the 15th under Lord Cathcart, who had succeeded Don in command of the expedition. The strength on embarkation was 36 officers, 30 sergeants, 18 corporals, 678 fit privates, 39 in hospital, 29 on command: total, 746.

The regiment landed at Harwich, being stationed at Woodbridge in March, April, and May, whence it moved to Colchester in June.

On the 12th of September the battalion, under Lieutenant-Colonel

James Losack, was inspected at Colchester Barracks by Major-General Thomas Grosvenor. The total effective strength, non-commissioned officers and men, 768; wanting to complete, 308.

On the 8th of November Sergeant-Major William Buckley was granted a commission and transferred to the 2nd battalion The Royals as adjutant, in which regiment he rose to the rank of captain, and was killed in action at Quatre Bras on the 16th of June 1815.

1806.

2ND BATTALION.

During this year the battalion was stationed at Chester, Wrexham, etc., the strength rising from 177 privates, present fit, in April to 267 in October.

On the 5th of December this year the battalion, under Major T. Pearson, was inspected at Chester by Major-General G. Fisher. He observed as follows:

"In consequence of the late rains and the wetness of the ground everywhere I was under the necessity of seeing the battalion on its Parade in the Castle, where it had not room to manœuvre ... the greatest part of this battalion being in Billets upon the town their messing could not go on so regularly as it does, from the circumstance of having about 56 in the Castle Barrack where the whole are obliged to mess, including those billeted in the town."

The total effectives were 400; wanting to complete, 48. The nationality was divided as follows:

	Sergeants.	Corporals.	Drums.	Privates.
English	13	9	10	189
Scotch	1	—	—	7
Irish	10	2	—	85
Welch	—	5	13	56
	24	16	23	337

N.B.—This is the first occasion on which men of "Welch" nationality are specifically mentioned.

1807.

1st Battalion.

In February the battalion received a draft of 257 men from the 2nd battalion.

On the 26th of March it was inspected by Major-General Thomas Grosvenor at Colchester. His report states that 257 non-commissioned officers and men had been received from the 2nd battalion, bringing the total effective strength up to 991, wanting 89. Of the non-commissioned officers and men, 2 sergeants, 2 corporals, and 142 privates were "Welch."

By a secret clause in the Treaty of Tilsit, which was concluded between France and Russia on the 7th of July 1807, it was arranged by the "high contracting" parties that the navies of Denmark and Portugal were to be demanded from their respective sovereigns, and taken by force if not voluntarily surrendered. No time was lost by Napoleon in presenting this demand at the Danish Court; at the same time he dispatched troops into Holstein in such numbers as would overawe the Danes into acquiescence.

The menace from a combination of the navies of Europe was so threatening, that the British Cabinet decided to demand the "temporary deposit of the Danish ships of the Line in one of His Majesty's Ports," and to enforce it by sending an expeditionary force to Copenhagen.

This was made up of 7,000 men of the German Legion, who were dispatched to Stralsund in May and June under Lieutenant-General Lord Cathcart, to be ready for any emergency, and were presently to be withdrawn from there to co-operate in the expedition.

The balance of the force left England for the Baltic in three divisions, officially described as the Right, Left, and Reserve Divisions, towards the end of July, embarking from the Downs, Harwich, and Hull respectively. The 23rd, forming with the 4th Regiment Major-General Grosvenor's Brigade of the Left Division under Lieutenant-General Sir David Baird, embarked at Harwich on the 25th of July and sailed on the 30th, 925 strong, under Lieutenant-Colonel Evan Jones.

On the 9th of August the three divisions were assembled in the Elsinore roadstead, where they were joined three days later by Lord Cathcart, who had been appointed Commander of His Majesty's Military Forces in the Baltic, and who had left Lieutenant-General Lord

Rosslyn to follow him with the German Legion in due course. On the 16th of August the army disembarked at the village of Vedbeck, in the bay of the same name, situated nearly midway between Copenhagen and Elsinore, without encountering the slightest opposition.

The same evening the army advanced in three columns towards Copenhagen. The left column, which contained the 23rd Regiment, marched by the coast to Charlottenlund, and then " lay upon their arms." The following day Copenhagen was completely invested, the left column under Sir David Baird resting upon the sea. On the 18th a summons was dispatched to Major-General Peymaun, who defended the city, to surrender, but it produced no effect.

Great progress was now being made in the erection of batteries and the construction of trenches, which work was carried on by parties of 600 men relieved every four hours. On the 21st of August Lord Rosslyn's corps, consisting of eight infantry battalions, two regiments of Light Dragoons, a garrison and a depot company, all of the German Legion, which had moved from Stralsund to the island of Rugen, arrived upon the scene and, disembarking in Kjoge Bay a few miles to the south-west of Copenhagen, took its position in the second line covering the centre.

The same day a brigade consisting of the 7th and 8th Infantry Regiments under Brigadier-General Macfarlane arrived, and landed at Skorreshard. The combined British and German force now amounted to 25,319 men.

On the 24th Sir David Baird's division carried a redoubt, which the enemy had been constructing for some days past, and which was that night converted into a work against them.

On the 26th the regiment lost one private killed and one wounded in repelling a sortie, and again on the following day one private killed.

On the 31st of August General Peymaun, who was alarmed at the rapid progress of the works, made a sortie. The advanced picket, supported by the pickets of Baird's division, led by him in person, gallantly opposed the enemy, and drove him back in confusion through the gates of the citadel. In this affair the 23rd had two privates wounded; one of these, Private Charles Bent, dying soon afterwards, his widow was awarded a sum of £30 on the 22nd of December from Lloyd's Patriotic Fund.

On the 1st of September a draft of 76 men was received from the 2nd battalion, which brought the strength up to 977.

On that day terms were again offered to General Peymaun, which were rejected. At half-past seven on the following evening the English batteries, being now ready, opened fire upon Copenhagen, which was continued for three days and nights, to which the enemy replied in the feeblest manner possible. One shot, however, fired by the enemy on the 4th of September, unfortunately killed 2nd Lieutenant Jennings and two men of the 23rd, besides wounding two others of the same regiment. These appear to be the only casualties suffered by the regiment.

On the following day Peymaun proposed an armistice for twenty-four hours to settle the preliminaries of capitulation, which was ratified on the morning of the 7th of September. The British troops then took possession of the citadel, dockyard, and arsenal.

Between the 22nd of September and the 5th of October a working party of the 23rd was employed in the naval arsenal, in the equipment of the captured Danish men-of-war, under Lieutenant J. E. A. Griffiths, the rate of pay being 4s. for a lieutenant, 1s. for a sergeant, 9d. for a corporal, and 6d. for a private. It is noticeable that at this period so many Welshmen of the same name were serving, that they had to be distinguished as " David Davis 3rd," " Robert Roberts 3rd," " John Jones 6th."

On the 18th of October the 23rd embarked for home, but owing to a heavy gale their departure from Copenhagen was postponed until the 21st of the month. They embarked in the *Brunswick*, *Surveillante*, and *Heir-Apparent Frederick* (a Danish prize), and after a stormy voyage landed at Yarmouth, with the exception of Captain Shaw's company, which " had been ordered round to Portsmouth with the *Heir-Apparent* prize ship."

This order does not appear to have been acted upon, as Captain Shaw's company landed at Deal on the 6th of November, marched to Canterbury, and rejoined the battalion at Colchester on the 28th of that month.

A Danish lad was so taken with the 23rd that he smuggled himself on board, was taken on the strength by mistake, but had to be discharged.

1807.

2ND BATTALION.

On the 3rd of June the battalion was inspected at Chester by Brigadier-General Peter Heron. His remarks were as follows: "Much improved in point of height and appearance. Consists of 646 rank and file, and 94 volunteers from militia on march to join it."

The following orders were issued:

"(1) Officers will cease to appear in grey trousers when in uniform.

"(2) The surgeon is to be dressed in uniform.

"(3) The officer on guard will not wear blue pantaloons.

"(4) Windows to be frequently open to procure a thorough draught of air. Soldiers are not to remain in their bedrooms during the daytime.

"(5) Men to be drilled for one hour in the morning, viz. from half-past seven till half-past eight in squads (when they are to breakfast), and again from two to three in squads or otherwise. The non-commissioned officers to be drilled once a day under the direction either of the adjutant or sergeant-major.

"(6) At every parade some manœuvring or marching is to take place.

"(7) The pendulum and taps of the drum to be resorted to to ensure correct marching, and pacing sticks to ensure the length of step."

The battalion remained at Chester until the end of September, and had in the interim supplied drafts of 257 men and 76 men respectively to the 1st battalion, and had recruiting parties at Cork, Liverpool, York, Darlington, Manchester, and Magherafelt. On the 1st of October the battalion was on the march to Ashford Barracks with a total strength of 305.

Transfer from the militia to the regular army being no longer prohibited, the result, so far as the 23rd is concerned, is shown in the Monthly Return for November, which states that 385 men were received from the English and Welsh Militia, bringing the strength of the battalion on the 1st of November up to 654 present fit, 41 sick, recruiting 29: total, 724.

On the 23rd of November the battalion embarked at Portsmouth for Ireland, but does not seem to have disembarked, under Lieutenant-Colonel W. E. Wyatt, at Monkstown, Cork, until the 17th of December, when the return shows as follows:

On the *George*, 8 officers, 223 N.C.O.s and men, 14 women, 6 children.
On the *Mary*, 7 officers, 179 N.C.O.s and men, 10 women, 6 children.
On the *Request*, 4 officers, 155 N.C.O.s and men, 10 women, 4 children.
On the *Phylleria*, 5 officers, 117 N.C.O.s and men, 8 women, 4 children.
On the *Rebecca*, 1 officer, 3 privates.

Recruiting parties were left behind at Stockport, Manchester, Evesham, Faversham, Malpas, Warrington, and St. Albans.

1808.

1st Battalion.

In January 59 men were received from the 2nd battalion, which raised the effective strength to a total of 1,029.

At the end of the month the battalion marched to Portsmouth, and in the beginning of February embarked on board the following transports for Nova Scotia, viz. on the *Lord Collingwood* (headquarters), *Robert*, *Sea Horse*, *Traveller*, *Albion*, and *Harriot*. The last, being a very slow sailor, and thereby encountering storms which the faster sailing transports escaped, did not reach Halifax until the end of May, having on board Captain Van Courtland's and Captain J. T. Leahy's companies.

The battalion, under Lieutenant-Colonel H. W. Ellis, on landing on the 16th of April was composed of 49 sergeants, 22 drummers, 682 rank and file "service for life," 326 rank and file "service for limited period," and was stationed at Annapolis Royal, Halifax, and Digby.

The battalion was inspected on the 10th of August at Annapolis by Lieutenant-General Sir George Prevost. Present under arms, 16 officers, 271 non-commissioned officers and men; on duty, 23 officers, 744 non-commissioned officers and men. A draft of 168 had been received from the 2nd battalion, and 3 sergeants, 1 corporal, 4 drummers, and 192 privates were returned as "Welch."

Curious to relate, in the Monthly Return for November two men are shown as "prisoners of war." While there part of the battalion was armed with the Baker rifle.

In December the battalion left Nova Scotia in company with the 7th and 8th Regiments for Martinique. The convoy sailed on the 6th of December under the *Penelope* frigate, with Sir George Prevost and staff, and arrived safely at the rendezvous, Carlisle Bay, Barbadoes, on the 29th of December.

1808.

2nd Battalion.

In January the battalion was stationed at Loughrea, where it remained until June, with a strength of 610 rank and file fit present: total, 680; "wanting to complete, 120."

At the end of June it moved to the Curragh, thence to Carlow, and on the 1st of September was stationed at Cork.

In August the British Government decided to send a reinforcement of 10,000 men from Great Britain to assist in certain operations about to be undertaken in North Spain, for further assisting that country in her efforts to free herself from the yoke of Napoleon.

On the 9th of September the battalion, being one of those selected for this service, embarked under Lieutenant-Colonel W. E. Wyatt at Cork with the following strength: 3 field officers, 10 captains, 20 subalterns, 4 staff, 40 sergeants, 19 drummers, and 575 privates, and sailed for the general rendezvous at Falmouth as follows:

On the *Lenshill*, 10 officers, 143 N.C.O.s and men, 10 women, 2 children.

On the *Boreas*, 6 officers, 131 N.C.O.s and men, 7 women, 3 children.

On the *Good Intent*, 6 officers, 122 N.C.O.s and men, 13 women, 7 children.

On the *Laurel*, 7 officers, 110 N.C.O.s and men, 9 women, 5 children.

On the *Patriot*, 7 officers, 123 N.C.O.s and men, 9 women, 3 children.

The assembled troops, under the command of Lieutenant-General Sir David Baird, were then organised into four infantry brigades. The one commanded by Brigadier-General Craufurd consisted of the 2nd battalion of the 14th, 2nd battalion of the 23rd, 2nd battalion of the 43rd, and the 2nd battalion of the 95th Regiments.

On the 8th of October the force sailed from Falmouth, and reached Corunna on the 13th. On arriving there, Baird found that the troops could not be landed until the permission of the central Junta had been obtained. Over a fortnight elapsed before the necessary permit was forthcoming on the 29th of that month.

On landing, Baird was handed an order from Lieutenant-General Sir John Moore to proceed with all speed to Astorga—a distance of

140 miles—and join him there. After encountering the greatest difficulties in organising his transport and procuring supplies, he set out for his objective, marching his men in successive columns of 2,000—Craufurd's "always leading"—in order to subsist them. It thus came about that for a short time his whole force was echeloned the entire way from Corunna to Astorga.

On reaching his destination on the 22nd of November he was surprised to learn that the Spanish army, which he believed was covering his advance, had been badly beaten by Marshal Soult on the 11th of November, and that his further advance to join Sir John Moore at Salamanca was threatened by two French corps under Soult and Lefebvre.

On the 29th of November Moore decided on a general retreat on Portugal, and sent orders to Baird to fall back on Corunna and sail for the Tagus. Leaving his cavalry at Astorga to cover his retreat, Baird set out for Villafranca, about 50 miles on the road to Corunna. Moore, on ascertaining that Napoleon, who was at Madrid, was maturing his plans to advance upon Portugal and seize Lisbon, determined on the 5th of December to make a raid upon Valladolid, or if possible upon Burgos, with the object of threatening Napoleon's line of communication with France.

On the 11th he began his march and advanced on Toro, situated on the Douro. From an interrupted dispatch he learned that Soult was isolated at Sahagun; thereupon he decided to fall upon him, and for this purpose marched northward. At Mayorga he joined forces with Baird, who, some days prior to this junction, had received orders countermanding his retreat, and had consequently returned to Astorga, pending the receipt of further orders respecting his movements.

On the concentration of the army it was redistributed by Moore into four divisions and two light brigades. The 3rd Division, commanded by Lieutenant-General Mackenzie Fraser, consisted of the brigades of Colonel William Beresford (afterwards the Portuguese Marshal) and Brigadier-General John Fane, to the former of which the 2nd battalion of the 23rd was attached.

Despite the severity of the weather and the long and trying marches, Napier in his History remarks with regard to Moore's army at this period that "a more robust set of men never took the field: the discipline was admirable, and there were but few stragglers."

Moore reached Sahagun on the 21st of December, and there learned that Napoleon had, through three British deserters, become aware of his daring move, and was rapidly advancing at the head of 80,000 men to overwhelm his small force of barely 26,000 cavalry and infantry. Moore instantly decided to retreat, which decision was bitterly resented by the great mass of officers and men, who considered themselves vastly superior to the French in fighting qualities. On the 24th of December he commenced his retreat through mountains covered with snow, Hope's and Mackenzie Fraser's divisions being in advance.

Astorga was reached on the 30th of December. At 4 a.m. on the following morning the retreat was continued in very severe weather, wind, rain, and snow alternating. The stragglers increasing with every mile marched, necessitated frequent halts.

1809.

1st Battalion.

A state of the regiment taken on the 1st of January, when on board ship in Carlisle Bay, shows that the following were on active service: 35 officers, 43 sergeants, 37 corporals, 18 drummers, and 853 privates. In England there were 12 officers, 4 sergeants, 1 corporal, 2 drummers, and 20 men. At Halifax, Nova Scotia, 3 officers, 5 sergeants, 7 corporals, 2 drummers, and 80 men.

The island of Martinique, which served as a base for French activity in the West Indies, had in consequence been blockaded by a British fleet for some months past. Despite the activity of the cruisers, a considerable reinforcement of men, and quantities of stores, were safely landed on the island in December 1808.

Thereupon the naval and military commanders on the spot decided to organise a force with the object of capturing the island, and thus strike a heavy blow at French naval power in that direction. The necessary preparations for an expedition under Lieutenant-General George Beckwith having been completed by the 28th of January, the army sailed from Carlisle Bay and landed at Martinique on the 30th and 31st in two divisions; the 7th and 23rd formed the Fusilier Brigade of the 1st Division, together with the 1st West India Regiment.

Four thousand five hundred men of the 1st Division—not, however, including the 23rd, which formed part of it—together with a proportion of horses and artillery, under Lieutenant-General Sir George Prevost, landed at Malgré Tout, Bay Robert, on the north-east side of the island, at 4 p.m. on the afternoon of the 30th, without meeting with any opposition. As soon as darkness had set in, Prevost marched seven miles, through a difficult country, and halted to refresh his troops at De Manceaux's estate on the banks of the Grande Lézarde River. Then, pushing on with the advance, which consisted of the 7th Regiment and the grenadier company of the 1st West India Regiment, he reached the heights of De Bork's estate towards evening, the enemy retiring before him as he advanced.

At daylight on the 1st of February he was joined by Brigadier-General Hoghton with the 23rd Regiment, and the light infantry battalion under the command of Major Campbell of the Royal West India Rangers. Without a moment's delay Lieutenant-Colonel Pakenham was pushed forward with the 7th Regiment, the " rifle company " of the 23rd, and the grenadier company of the 1st West India Regiment, to seize Morne Bruneau. At the same time Brigadier-General Hoghton was ordered to support this movement with the light infantry battalion, and having done so to effect a junction with Pakenham, and proceed to force the heights of Des Sourier, the 23rd being held in reserve by Prevost to strengthen such points of attack as might require it.

The junction having been effected on the heights of Bruneau as arranged, the column moved forward towards its next objective, as stated above. It had not proceeded far before a considerable body of the enemy's regular forces was discovered, advantageously posted on the declivity of a hill, having the River Monsieur in front and one or two guns posted on the left. Hoghton, having decided to dislodge it, although the light artillery had not yet reached the column, directed Pakenham with the rifle and grenadier companies of the 7th and the rifle company of the 23rd to turn the right, and Major Campbell with the light infantry battalion the left, of the enemy's position. The frontal attack was undertaken by Hoghton himself with the battalion companies of the 7th, and the grenadier company of the 1st West India Regiment. All these attacks were well executed, resulting in the enemy being driven with considerable loss from every part of his position and retiring in confusion.

When Pakenham had turned the right flank of the enemy, he pushed forward towards the heights of Sourier, supported in the first instance by the right wing of the 23rd under Lieutenant-Colonel Ellis, and subsequently by the remainder of that regiment, which Sir George Prevost had ordered forward. The enemy had collected a considerable force, mainly drawn from Fort Bourbon, advantageously posted to defend the approaches to the heights of Sourier; but Pakenham, ably seconded by Lieutenant-Colonel Ellis, Majors Pearson and Offley of the 23rd, and the "determined bravery of the whole detachment," by a spirited charge succeeded in driving the enemy from his position, compelling him to take shelter under his redoubts.

At this point Beckwith rode up and inquired of Lieutenant-Colonel Ellis if he thought he could rely on his grenadiers to storm the redoubts. "Sir," replied Colonel Ellis, "I will take the flints out of their firelocks and they shall take them." Beckwith, however, would not allow of the attempt being made.

Pakenham then established his position on the heights which commanded Fort Bourbon. Sir George Prevost, in reporting this action to Lieutenant-General Beckwith, remarks as follows:

"On my coming on the heights of Sourier, I had innumerable proofs of the valour and judgment of the Honourable Lieutenant-Colonel Pakenham, of the excellence of the Fusilier Brigade, and of the spirited and judicious exertions of Lieutenant-Colonel Ellis and Majors Pearson and Offley of the 23rd or Royal Welch Fusiliers, also of the bravery of Major Campbell and the light infantry battalion all of which have enabled me to retain this valuable position without artillery, within three hundred yards of the enemy's entrenched camp covered with guns."

In the action of the 1st of February the 1st battalion of the 23rd suffered the following loss:

Killed.—1 sergeant, 14 rank and file.

Wounded.—2 sergeants, 79 rank and file.

Missing.—1 sergeant, 5 rank and file.

The casualties of the battalion next day upon the heights of Sourier were as follows:

Killed.—1 sergeant, 3 rank and file.

Wounded.—1 subaltern (Lieutenant Roskelly), 1 staff (Surgeon Power), 19 rank and file.

Missing.—1 sergeant.

The loss of the heights necessitated the abandonment by the enemy of the fort known as Fort de France. Before doing so the guns were spiked and dismounted, and the magazines blown up.

The 2nd Division, under General Maitland, which had landed at Saint Luce on the 30th of January, now joined up with the 1st

Division. The capture of Pigeon Island by the fleet enabled the Navy to co-operate with the Army in preparing for the bombardment of Fort Bourbon. The preparations for this undertaking necessitated the incessant employment of both soldiers and sailors for over a fortnight in the construction of gun and mortar batteries, landing of cannon, mortars, howitzers, etc., and in mounting the ordnance.

During this period the enemy constantly fired upon the encampments with shot and shell, but luckily with little effect. On the 19th of February fire was opened upon Fort Bourbon, from six points, with fourteen heavy guns and twenty-eight mortars and howitzers, and was continued without intermission until noon of the 23rd, when the commandant, Admiral Villaret Joyeuse, sent a trumpet with a letter proposing terms of capitulation. As they were considered inadmissible, the bombardment recommenced at ten o'clock at night, and was continued without intermission until nine the next morning, when three white flags were hoisted on the fortress, which caused the fire from the batteries to cease immediately. The articles of capitulation were signed on the 24th of February.

Lieutenant-General Beckwith's pride in the force under his command is expressed in almost the concluding line of his dispatch to the Secretary of State, which reads as follows: " The command of such an army will constitute the pride of my future life."

From a return of sick and wounded in the General Hospital at Martinique between the 1st and 27th of February, the following particulars respecting the 23rd are ascertained:

Admissions.—Gunshot wounds 88, fevers 9, fluxes 44, casualties 3: total 144.

Discharged cured.—Gunshot wounds 28, fevers 6, fluxes 15, casualties 3: total 52.

Died.—Gunshot wounds 5, flux 1.

Remaining in hospital.—Gunshot wounds 55, fevers 3, fluxes 28: total 86.

For its distinguished conduct in this campaign the regiment was permitted on the 30th of October 1816 to bear the word " MARTINIQUE " on its colour and appointments; to which was added the date " 1809 " by Army Order 295 of 1909.

The Monthly Return for the 1st of March shows: Privates present 736, sick 104, dead 23; wanting to complete, 25. Total all ranks, 975. General Prevost's division, in which the 23rd was included, returned to Nova Scotia on the 9th of March. The Monthly Return for the following month—" the regiment being at sea," on board the transports *Albion*, *Ajax*, *Navigator*, *British Tar*, and *Royal Yeoman* destined for Halifax, Nova Scotia—gives: Privates present 753, sick present 54, sick at St. Christopher and Martinique 21; on command at Halifax 80; in England 22: total, 930; wanting to complete, 20.

The battalion was inspected on the 14th of June at Halifax by Lieutenant-General Sir George Prevost. The aftermath of the expedition to Martinique is evident from the following: " Sick, 1 sergeant, 1 drummer, and 126 privates."

The Monthly Return dated the 25th of June gives the following distribution of the regiment in Nova Scotia:

Headquarters at Halifax.—20 officers, 25 sergeants, 32 corporals, 18 drummers, 376 privates.

Fort Clarence.—4 officers, 8 sergeants, 4 corporals, 1 drummer, 123 privates.

Melville Island.—3 officers, 3 sergeants, 3 corporals, 1 drummer, 69 privates.

York Redoubt.—1 officer, 1 sergeant, 1 corporal, 20 privates.

Sackville Fort.—1 officer, 1 sergeant, 30 privates.

Point Pleasant.—2 officers, 5 sergeants, 3 corporals, 65 privates.

George Island.—4 officers, 3 sergeants, 4 corporals, 93 privates.

West Indies.—1 officer and 13 privates.

Total, 844; wanting to complete, 107.

1809.

2ND BATTALION.

On the 1st of January 1809 Napoleon reached Astorga barely twenty-four hours behind Moore's army. There he learned that Austria was about to take up arms once again, which decided him to return to Paris with all haste, leaving the pursuit of the British to Soult and Ney. On the same day the main body of the retreating army reached Villafranca, which was, unfortunately, the scene of pillage and drunkenness for the time being.

On the evening of the 5th of January Moore reached Lugo—just fifty miles from Corunna—and after resting his troops for two days, took up a strong position in front of that town awaiting Soult's attack, which, however, he appeared indisposed to deliver.

Through the action of an orderly dragoon getting drunk, and losing an order which he was conveying to Fraser to halt at Lugo, that officer with his division had proceeded a day's march beyond there before he learned that he should have halted at that town. He immediately countermarched, but two days' greatly needed rest was, through the conduct of this drunken soldier, denied to the 23rd and other battalions composing the division.

On the night of the 8th of January the retreat recommenced in a terrific storm. By 10 a.m. the following morning the men were thoroughly worn out and a halt was made. Their sufferings were now appalling; "they lay scattered over a bleak and desolate heath with nothing to protect them . . . many perished, regiments got mixed up together." Late that night the retreat of what was now a disorderly mob was continued. Corunna was reached on the night of the 11th of January. Moore began at once to fortify the landward front of Corunna, and to demolish the defences on the seaward side.

After two days' rest the several divisions, about 15,000 strong, occupied a position on a ridge about two miles from the town and prepared to give battle to Soult, who had repaired the broken bridge of El Burgo, and whose army, consisting of over 16,000 of all arms, was advancing in three columns.

Moore's disposition for the battle was as follows: Hope's division was posted on the left of the ridge referred to—known as Monte Mero. Baird's occupied the right. To the rear, but somewhat to the right of Baird, Paget's reserve was massed. Farther still to the right of the rear Fraser's division was drawn up on the heights of Santa Margarita, with the object of guarding the main road to Corunna.

At 2 p.m. on the 16th of January the French, advancing in three columns, carried the village of Elvina and then divided. One portion attacked Baird in front, and the other attempted to turn his right. Moore quickly discerned that this was the pivot of the battle, and that if the attack succeeded here, disaster would befall his army. He ordered the 4th Regiment, which was on the right of Baird's line, to swing round and open a flank fire on the advancing column, at the same time directing Paget with the reserve to check its advance, and Fraser's division to make a counterstroke at the French left.

The 42nd and 50th Regiments, followed by the 1st battalion of the 1st Guards, were then launched against the column which had occupied Elvina. The village was quickly carried. Both Baird and Hope succeeded in driving back with loss the columns that had attacked

THE KEYS OF CORUNNA.
From a photograph by Algernon Smith, Wrexham.

them. At this moment a round shot struck Moore on the shoulder and hurled him from his horse. About 5 p.m. the French confined themselves to a distant cannonade, which ceased altogether an hour later.

At 10 p.m. the embarkation of the troops began and was continued throughout the night. To the inexpressible grief of the whole army the terrible wound sustained by the gallant Sir John Moore proved to be mortal during the night following the battle. He was buried at 8 a.m. the following morning on a bastion of the citadel by a party of the 9th Regiment. The only British troops on shore by the morning of the 17th of January were the brigades of Hill and Beresford, which had covered the embarkation and were now exposed to the fire of a battery which the enemy had brought to a height commanding the harbour. Their embarkation was successfully accomplished during the afternoon and night of 17th-18th of January, the 2nd battalion of the 23rd being the last battalion to leave this portion of Spanish soil.

The following is an extract from a letter written by Miss Fletcher, of Nerquis Hall, co. Flint, to Major R. T. Webber, dated Wrexham, the 22nd of February 1889:

"The rear-guard was commanded by Captain Thomas Lloyd Fletcher, of the Twenty-third Royal Welch Fusiliers. He, with his corporal, were the last to leave the town. On their way to embark, and as they passed through the gates, Captain Fletcher turned and locked them. The key not turning easily, they thrust in a bayonet, and between them managed it. Captain Fletcher brought away the keys, and they are now in the possession of his son, Phillips Lloyd Fletcher, Esq., of Nerquis Hall, co. Flint, a relic, we need not say, highly prized and cherished by a soldier's children.

"The keys are held together by a ring, from which is suspended a steel plate, with the inscription 'Postigo de Puerta de Abajo' ('Postern of lower gate'). One key still shows the wrench of the bayonet.

"Weight of bunch, $1\frac{3}{4}$ pounds.
"Length of larger key, $6\frac{1}{2}$ inches.
"Length of smaller ditto, $5\frac{1}{2}$ inches."

On the death of P. L. Fletcher the keys passed into the possession of his cousin Captain L. W. H. Tringham, of the 23rd Regiment and 21st Lancers, who died on service in India with the latter regiment on the 22nd of November 1918. The keys then became the property of Mrs. Elwes, of Gwernhayled, Ellesmere.

For its services in this campaign the regiment was permitted in February 1835 to bear the word "CORUNNA" on the regimental colour and appointments.

Lieutenant-Colonel Wyatt received the honorary distinction of a medal.

The following is an extract from a letter written to his parents by Lieutenant Samuel Thorp of the Light Company of the 2nd battalion. This officer served afterwards in the Walcheren Expedition, and was present at the battle of Albuera on the 16th of May 1811, where he was twice severely wounded. Promoted captain and transferred to the 39th Regiment, he was again severely wounded at the battle of Toulouse on the 10th of April 1814.

"ASTORGA,
"27 *November*, 1808.

"I have not seen or heard from Rowland since I left Corunna as our Regiment is in General Craufurd's or 'The Light Brigade' and always in advance. I shall now, as I think you would wish to know, inform you of our strength and situation. Our small army consists of five brigades:

"(a) The First or Light Brigade under Brigadier-General Craufurd.
 2nd Battalion 14th Foot Infantry.
 2nd Battalion 23rd Royal Welsh Fusiliers.
 The 43rd. The whole light troops.
 The 95th or The Rifle Corps.
 One brigade of flying artillery consisting of 12 Light sixes.

"(b) Second Brigade, Colonel Cheyney 1st Guards.
 1st Battalion, 1st Regiment of Foot Guards.
 2nd Battalion, 3rd Regiment of Foot Guards.
 Brigade of Artillery.

"(c) Third Brigade, Brigadier-General Manningham.
 3rd Battalion, 1st Foot or Royals.
 1st Battalion, 26th or Cameronians.
 The 81st.
 Brigade of Foot Artillery.

"(d) Fourth Brigade, no Commander at present.
 51st, 59th, and 76th: also one Brigade of Artillery.

"(e) Fifth Brigade (Cavalry), Major-General Lord Paget.
    7th, 10th, and 15th Light Dragoons. One Brigade of Horse Artillery.

"Our first day's march was to a place called Batancos, four leagues from Corunna, each Spanish league is four British miles: we halted four days at Batancos as the troops could not get provisions till after that time. Our next march was to a place (only one house) called Cavallo Torto, four leagues from the other: here we encamped and marched the next mo ning five leagues more to a number of nameless huts, marched the next day four leagues to Lugo, one of their capital towns, remained here one day.

"Marched in four different stages of one day each, sleeping in camp and huts, to Villa Franca seventeen leagues from Lugo. In four more stages seventeen leagues further to Astorga, this was only the march of the Light Brigade. The next day the Rifle Corps was ordered to advance on the road to Benavente. The 43rd received orders the next day to advance, but before they left the town we were all surprised by the sudden return of the Rifle Corps who had made a rapid retreat from Benavente: hearing that an advance guard of 7,000 French were some leagues on their right they had retreated fearing they might be cut off. The whole Light Brigade were now in Astorga a place not so large as Dartford in Kent. An express was sent off to Sir David Baird who immediately advanced with most of the army, leaving the Fourth Brigade to secure the strong passes in the snow mountains near Villa Franca. We soon afterwards received news of the defeat of General Blake's army who was surprised in a thick fog, which we have several times experienced especially in the snow mountains.

"Shortly afterwards an express arrived from Blake's army to Sir David Baird with some important information: he immediately ordered the whole of the Heavy Brigades in advance to fall back to Villa Franca which the General has ordered to be fortified and all the strong posts strongly guarded. The Light Brigade are left in Astorga.

"The inhabitants are in great consternation, and if the alarm bell rings even for a fire the whole cry is ' *les francoises, les francoises.*' We send out a picquet of an hundred men each Regiment every night, also a strong guard is mounted in the Grand Square.

"All rum, brandy, and wine is now entirely exhausted in this town and the adjacent country. A few hours before the army retreated all the rum puncheons, port and biscuit were staved in the street: rum pouring down the canals mixed with dirty water and filth.

"Three regiments of cavalry and some artillery have just arrived: if the French come now, which is not probable that they can be very near, we shall show them a little fun they may not much like.

"Sir John Moore with twenty-seven thousand English is now in Salamanca: if the two armies can make a junction we shall immediately attack the French.

"I am happy to hear that Colonel Wyatt approves of my conduct in the Regiment and shall always strive to meet his approbation.

. . . . . .

"I shall certainly take your advice respecting eating fruit, as I am sure it is very unwholesome, and many of our officers have the flux: and also the wine as it is wretched stuff called claret and a sort of white wine, eight quartos or halfpence per bottle: but that is here put out of our power to drink as it is all gone.

"I am billeted with another Lieutenant at the house of an industrious tailor with a large family: they are remarkably attentive and as far as lies in their small capacity would make us comfortable. We have for the first time since we left Corunna enjoyed the luxury of plates, as at the other places they either had none or else hid them when we came. As to the eatables there are plenty at this place though very dear: a good turkey seven pistrines or shillings, a fowl half a dollar, hares two pistrines: partridges are the only cheap thing here, four for a shilling.

"I can now speak enough of Spanish to ask for anything I want, the names of animals, etc., etc.

"We have all bought ponies to carry our baggage: most of them have died through fatigue: mine is not in the best state, it cost me twenty dollars. I have with me three blankets, two coats, one great coat, one beaver light infantry cap and one large fur cap for piquet. I was forced, though reluctantly, to throw away my trunk, as my choice was to leave that, or all its contents, and the rest of my baggage: the small leather portmanteau is now of the greatest use, for if we retreat rapidly, or the pony dies, I can carry my best jacket and valuables on my back. . . ."

On arriving home the battalion disembarked at Portsmouth in February and marched to Horsham, 109 sick being left at Plymouth and Portsmouth. Recruiting parties were sent to Stockport, Manchester, Beccles, Belfast, and Dundee.

The battalion was reviewed at Horsham on the 26th of March by Lieutenant-General Lord Charles Somerset, and again at the same place on the 11th of May by Major-General the Earl of Dalhousie. Out of a total of 788 non-commissioned officers and men there were 12 sergeants, 17 corporals, 11 drummers, and 398 men " Welch." He reports as follows : " The men are young and stout, rather tall than otherwise, the regimental Courts Martials are very few indeed, not having had a man punished since the return of the battalion from Spain. It is a very good steady battalion, well commanded and well officered. Ninety-seven men are volunteers from the Militia."

The June Monthly Return shows 460 present fit, 111 sick, and 150 prisoners of war in Spain : a total of 752 ; wanting, 56.

Napoleon was straining every nerve this year to materialise the hope uppermost in his mind for some time past, of establishing a successful maritime rivalry to this country. The possession of Holland and the Scheldt would place considerable naval resources at his disposal and would also enable him to establish at Antwerp a commercial rival to London.

With a view to defeating his object, the British Cabinet decided to attempt to make the Scheldt not navigable for ships-of-war, and also to attack and destroy the naval forces and establishments at Flushing, Antwerp, Terneuse, and in the Island of Walcheren.

For this purpose an expeditionary force numbering 40,679 all ranks was collected in July, under the command of Lieutenant-General the Earl of Chatham, K.G., with Lieutenant-General Sir Eyre Coote, K.B., second-in-command. The army was made up of four divisions, a light division, and a reserve division, divided into a right and left wing. The 2nd battalion of the 23rd, together with the 1st battalion of the 5th, 1st battalion of the 26th, and 1st battalion of the 32nd, under Brigadier-General Browne, formed part of the 4th Division (left wing) commanded by Lieutenant-General Mackenzie Fraser. The five companies of the battalion which had been detached for this expedition arrived at Portsmouth on the 28th and 29th of June, and embarked the following month with a strength of 22 officers, 31 N.C.O.s, and 403 rank and file.

On the 27th of July the left wing of the army, under Lieutenant-General Sir Eyre Coote, which had embarked at Portsmouth, arrived in the Downs and sailed for the island of Walcheren at 4 a.m. on the following morning, reaching there at 3 p.m. the same day.

As a fresh gale was blowing which raised a heavy surf, the fleet was obliged to run for smooth water, which was found off the Bree-Zand, where the 1st, 4th, and 5th Divisions under Coote were landed on the sandhills facing Oost Kapelle.

The 4th Division on landing was detached to the left against Fort-den-Haake and the town of Veere. The fort was evacuated on the approach of the division, but Veere, which was occupied by a garrison of 600 Dutch, held out until 4 a.m. on the morning of the 1st of August.

On the 31st of July a rearrangement of divisions took place. The army was now composed of a right and left wing, centre, and reserve. The battalion formed part of the centre under Lieutenant-General Lord Paget.

On the following day the army moved forward in three columns for the investment of Flushing. The enemy made a firm stand, but were driven within their lines.

On the 4th of August artillery, stores, etc., intended for the siege were landed and forwarded to their destination. Although constant heavy rain greatly interfered with the working parties who were constructing the batteries, they were ready and the guns mounted by the morning of the 13th of August. At 1.30 p.m. on that afternoon the bombardment of Flushing was begun by land and sea. The following day the French garrison, numbering 4,379, capitulated, and was immediately embarked for England.

By the fall of Flushing the British became masters of Walcheren. It had hardly surrendered before the low fever to which the inhabitants of the island were annually subject broke out among the troops, and " spread with unexampled rapidity," so much so that by the 28th of the month no less than 4,000 men were on the sick-list. On the previous day a meeting of the lieutenant-generals was convened to consider possible future operations. The conclusion arrived at was that the siege of Antwerp was impracticable " and that no possible advantage could result from engaging in any minor expedition."

So rapidly had the fever spread that on the 3rd of September, of the five companies of the 2nd battalion of the 23rd, consisting of 398 rank and file, no less than 244 were sick, and three days later not a single man was able " to take any share of duty."

On the 9th of September Lord Chatham handed over the command in Walcheren to Lieutenant-General Sir Eyre Coote, and sailed for England on the 14th with his staff.

On the 23rd of the month Coote wrote home stating that " the

23rd Regiment had been so weakened by the fever" that he had ordered it home at once. On the 6th of October the companies started from Middelburg to embark at Flushing, but being unable to march were conveyed in waggons.

On the 27th of October Coote resigned his command, and was succeeded by General Don, who impressed upon the military authorities at home the impossibility of his being able to continue to hold the island. In response to his report an order was received to destroy the works and docks at Flushing, and evacuate Walcheren as soon as possible.

Out of a total of 35,000 officers and men who returned from the expedition, no less than 11,500 were in hospital, numbers of whom subsequently died, and of those who recovered the greater part carried ruined constitutions to their graves—" the legacy left by the fever fens of Walcheren."

In a return of casualties which took place between the embarkation of the force and the 10th of January 1810, the companies' losses were as follows:

Killed.—None.

Died on service.—9 non-commissioned officers, 100 rank and file.

Died since being sent home.—3 non-commissioned officers, 71 rank and file.

Deserted.—None.

1810.

1ST BATTALION.

On the 2nd of August the battalion was inspected by Lieutenant-General Sir George Prevost, whose " general remarks " are as follows: " Unanimity and good understanding prevails in this corps. The regiment is a good serviceable body of men, with a general appearance of health, though many are under the fixed standard. The officers mess together, and the regimental mess is established on a proper system of prudence and moderation."

The battalion remained in Nova Scotia until the 10th of November, when it embarked, under Lieutenant-Colonel H. W. Ellis, 814 strong (leaving 20 sick at Halifax) to join Wellington's army in Portugal.

It arrived in the Tagus on the 11th of December and disembarked the following day. On the 16th it set out to join Wellington at Santarem, where he was engaged in watching the movements of Marshal Masséna; the latter with three corps faced him, and was in the unenviable position of being unable to advance and yet very loath to retire. On the 18th of December the battalion reached Sobral, joining the 4th Division under Major-General the Honourable Lowry Cole, and was attached to the brigade commanded by Major-General Pakenham, taking the place of a portion of the Brunswick-Oels Corps, which was transferred to another division.

Cole, on joining Wellington, found that on the 1st of December the latter had been obliged to place his divisions in cantonments, in the neighbourhood of Cartaxo, owing to heavy and prolonged rains having rendered the manœuvring of masses of troops an impossibility for some time to come. The battalion was, therefore, directed to canton at Azambuja.

This year a pensioner in Chelsea Hospital named John Wickers, late a private in the Royal Welch Fusiliers, died, bequeathing a sum of £400 to the Female Orphans of the Royal Military Asylum. This philanthropic act of a humble soldier deserves to be recorded as an example.

1810.

2ND BATTALION.

In January the battalion was stationed at Horsham, moving in February to Lewes, and in March to Portsmouth, the return for that month showing present fit 255, sick in hospital 133, with a total of 458; wanting to complete, 142.

In April the battalion moved to Fort George, Guernsey, where it remained until December. No less than fifteen recruiting parties were stationed at London, Denbigh, Leeds, Carmarthen, Downpatrick, etc. Captain the Hon. F. J. Percy was acting as A.D.C. to Sir John Doyle, while Major C. Sutton and Captain R. G. Hare were on the staff in Portugal.

The battalion was inspected on the 16th of May by Lieutenant-General Sir J. Doyle at Fort George, and again by him on the 4th of October.

In the latter report officers of "Welch" nationality are mentioned separately for the first time—namely, Captain Henry Wynne, 1st Lieutenants T. E. Tucker, George Farmer, 2nd Lieutenants John Enoch, Grismond Philipps, B. Llewelyn, and Adjutant W. H. Jones.

Sir John Doyle's general remarks were as follows:

"That those corps which had served and suffered at Walcheren have nearly got rid of the remains of the fever of that country, the medical people impute the recovery of the men in a great degree to their being very much in the air, under canvas, and being moderately exercised in working on the public roads, the very few relapses that have occurred were amongst the men who remained in barracks, and were not so employed."

1811.

1st Battalion.

The battalion remained at Azambuja until the 24th of January, when it moved to Aveiras de Cima, the state of the battalion being then:

Present.—1 lieutenant-colonel, 1 major, 9 captains, 15 lieutenants, 3 2nd lieutenants, paymaster, adjutant, quartermaster, surgeon, assistant surgeon, 35 sergeants, 18 drummers, 600 rank and file.

Sick present.—18.

Sick at Lisbon.—1 officer (Lieutenant Wynne), 5 sergeants, 122 rank and file.

On command.—At Villanova, 1 officer (Captain Macdonald), 2 rank and file.

At Belem also on command.—1 officer (Lieutenant T. Browne), 5 sergeants, 3 drummers, 31 rank and file.

Officers on duty with other corps.—Major Offley attached to Marshal Beresford; 3 lieutenants, 5 2nd lieutenants, and 1 assistant surgeon with the 2nd battalion.

Recruiting.—8 sergeants, 4 drummers, and 8 privates.

Invalids sent home.—5 sergeants, 2 drummers, 66 privates.

Twenty privates left *sick at Halifax*, Nova Scotia, as already stated.

Total.—50 officers, 54 sergeants, 22 drummers, and 1,000 rank and file.

On the 23rd of January Major-General Pakenham was succeeded in the command of the brigade by Major-General Houston, who in turn was succeeded on the 5th of March by Colonel Myers.

Towards the end of February Masséna's situation had become most critical. His supplies were almost exhausted, his foragers, despite their ingenuity, could no longer unearth magazines of food, and to crown all, hunger, cold, and fatigue had produced disease which was increasing at an alarming rate. His secret agents having informed him that British reinforcements had reached the Tagus on the 2nd and 3rd of February, he decided at once to retire from before the British lines.

With infinite skill Masséna began moving his divisions on the 3rd of March and the two following days. It was not until the morning of the 6th that Wellington became aware of the French having evacuated their position. He immediately started in pursuit, being completely in the dark as to Masséna's true movements.

On the 8th of March, however, he felt assured that Masséna was retiring as fast as possible to the Spanish frontier. Thereupon he ordered the 2nd and 4th Divisions to join up with Marshal Beresford, who was directed to march at once to Badajoz.

The following extract from a letter written by an officer of the 23rd, dated "Thomar, March 17, 1811," narrates the movements of the 4th Division from the 1st to the 15th of March, viz. :

"About the 1st instant the French began to move their sick and baggage, and continued to file off until the 6th at night, when our light division entered Santarem, and found it vacant, but nearly demolished, it being set on fire. At day-light on the 5th, we marched from Avevras de Lima to Cartaxo: but from the strength of Santarem, and not having exact information, whether the enemy had abandoned the place or not, his Lordship was cautious and we returned to our old quarters for the night. We again marched at day-break on the 6th, and entered Santarem in the evening, where we found the division above mentioned had felt their way the night before. Our second day's march was to Golegao, where we found boiled beans left by the enemy, who had quitted in the morning.

"The third day we reached Thomar in the evening, and found that Ney had only left it in the morning—so close did we follow them up, by hard and long marches over the worst road in the world. The next night we took up our abode in the open air, in constant rain, and had nothing to cover us but our great coats and blankets—hard times! From this ground we had a forced march of thirty miles, and found nearly the whole of the British army assembled on a large plain near Pombal—our division with the light division became the advanced guard of the army. At Pombal we came up with the enemy, and drove them out that evening, but not until they had set it on fire and destroyed it completely. From this town, they posted themselves very judiciously on a range of heights, with a broad river and a marsh in their front. Notwithstanding these obstacles, it was determined to attack them, and although we had marched thirty miles, it being nearly dark alone prevented us from doing it immediately. Every disposition was made to do it at day-break but they decamped in the night, leaving large fires in order to deceive us : we came up with them on a plain, close upon Redinha, where they made a stand, and a very smart skirmish ensued. Ney commanded. His line and artillery were posted on the ridge of a hill, from whence he threw a vast deal of round shot. Our cavalry made several desperate charges, to little or no effect. Our division filled into the plain, consisting of the following regiments :

" 1st Line, 3rd Battalion of the 27th, 1/40th and 97th, and 11th and 23rd Portuguese Regiments. 2nd Line, 16th Portuguese Regiment on the right : 23rd Welsh Fuzileers, and 7th regiment, 2 battalions. The Light Companies of the brigade (the 1st line) were thrown out in front, and skirmished.

" The enemy's artillery played on us in high style, and many shot passed close to me. Our first line lost about 20 men killed and wounded. To have seen us deploy and march in line, as we did, you would have been highly pleased. I never saw better. The troops in the highest spirits, and to do justice to the Portuguese, they equalled us. When our first line had approached within about 400 yards, without firing but marching as steady as a rock, in ordinary time, the enemy's infantry began to retire, in double quick time, and the artillery and cavalry followed their example. They again formed on a very advantageous ground, in rear of the town which was in flames. His Lordship detached three divisions to outflank them, who cut off 3 officers and 140 men, and killed and wounded about 250. Our loss was about 40. Lord Wellington has shewn himself a skilful General, and Ney has manœuvred with great judgment. It was a beautiful sight, and everything so regular, as at a review in St. James's Park. The next day we had another skirmish at Condeixa, which was very warm. Our division did not fire but was detached over the mountains to the left of the enemy, and had as hard a march as ever we experienced. We had to climb the most difficult places, and what with the heat of the weather, and being without provisions, I was nearly exhausted. About four we entered a lovely little place, Panella, and marched on for Espinhel, where we arrived about six p.m. and found that General

Nightingall's brigade had passed close to the place where Reynier was posted with 3,000 men, to prevent our outflanking Ney. Every oven in the place was full of Indian corn bread, which was very acceptable to Gen. Nightingall's brigade. The enemy had even cut wood for fires, and brushwood to hut themselves, which fell to our lot. Reynier hurried over the mountain as quick as he could.

"On the 15th at 3 p.m. we received a dispatch from the Commander in Chief, ordering us to march for the relief of Badajoz, but that place has fallen it is said by treachery. I wish we had been in time to have saved it. On receiving the order, we marched until dark, when we slept on the ground, and a rainy night we had of it. Yesterday we marched into this town about 7 p.m. having performed a march of 35 miles. We halt here to-day and to-morrow move on towards Portalegre. Marshal Beresford goes with us. It is supposed Masséna is retiring on the Ponte de Murcella, not being able to pass by Coimbra, as the bridge is destroyed, and Colonel Trant is there with 15,000 irregulars. An orderly book was found, containing an order to burn every town through which the rear guard passed. Our being without provisions was not owing to any neglect; the rapid marching was the sole cause. A ship biscuit lasted me for four days, when I was necessitated to eat boiled Indian corn: it was the same with the men. To-day, however, I shall make up for it, having salt fish and fresh beef soup for dinner, with two bottles of wine between four of us. How I have stood the fatigue and continually sleeping out, I am astonished to think. Thank God, in the midst of all I am very well. On the road from Santarem, I saw a great many dead Frenchmen, and a vast number of horses, mules, and asses. This retreat is equal to a victory."

Wellington then decided to continue the pursuit of Masséna and to dispatch Beresford with a considerable force, including the 4th Division, to recapture Badajoz, which had been taken by the French on the 11th of March. Accordingly, on the 15th of the month, Beresford's troops started to march to that fortress. On the 20th the greater part of them reached Portalegre, but it was not until the 22nd of March that the 4th Division reached there in sorry plight. Many of the men were without shoes, and several hundred had fallen out during the march. After resting for two days the 4th Division followed the remainder of the army, arriving at Aronches on the 24th, and Campo-Mayor on the following day.

A state of the battalion taken on that date shows that there were present fit 32 officers, 25 sergeants, 13 drummers, and 503 rank and file. On the march from Aveiras de Cima were 4 sergeants, 3 drummers, and 128 rank and file. Sick at Lisbon, 3 sergeants, 98 rank and file. At Belem, 3 officers (Lieutenant Mercer, 2nd Lieutenant Harris, and Assistant Surgeon Barr), 8 sergeants, 4 drummers, 40 rank and file. In charge of sick, 3 officers, 2 sergeants, and 3 rank and file.

On obtaining possession of Campo-Mayor, Beresford cantoned his troops in Elvas and the surrounding country for a brief but badly needed rest, the 4th Division suffering greatly from sore feet owing to their having to march barefooted for the want of shoes.

On the 9th of April the army appeared before the small fortress of Olivença, which was garrisoned by about 400 French. Two days later the main body started for Albuera, leaving the 4th Division, of which the 23rd formed part, to carry on the siege. On the 15th Olivença surrendered, and on the following day the 4th Division joined up with Beresford at Zafra. On the 25th of April the battalion was at Valverde.

A state taken there records that between that date and the 25th of March the following had joined from the 2nd battalion: Captain Patten, Lieutenants G. Browne, Whalley, and Thorp, 2nd Lieutenants Palmer, Hall, Enoch, Philipps, Joiner, 5 sergeants, and 198 rank and file.

On the 8th of May the investment of Badajoz was completed, but on the night of the 13th Beresford gave orders for the siege to be abandoned, as he received reliable information that Soult had arrived at Llerena with a strong force to raise the siege.

While the greater part of the army marched to Valverde, the 4th Division remained behind to protect the train and stores during their removal to Elvas. So well was this duty performed that not a single article fell into the hands of the enemy.

On the 15th of May the main portion of Beresford's force from Valverde reached Albuera, and took up a position along the heights north of the Albuera River, awaiting attack by Soult which Beresford confidently expected. The British and Portuguese formed the centre and left, on either side of the high-road from Albuera to Badajoz and Valverde, the village and bridge at Albuera being held by the brigade of Germans under Major-General Charles von Alten. The Spaniards were posted on the right.

Soult, hearing that the 4th Division had been left behind at Badajoz, determined to attack Beresford's position the following morning. As a matter of fact, however, the 4th Division arrived upon the scene about 7.30 a.m. on the morning of the battle. About 8 a.m. the enemy was seen to be in motion, his main attack being directed against the Spaniards, with the object of securing the high ground to their right front, which would enable him to rake the rest of the Allied line. At the same time he assaulted the village of Albuera, which was successfully held, but the Spaniards were driven from their ground. The British from the centre, under Major-General Stewart, then advanced with the object of recovering the lost ground, and at the outset met with a serious check.

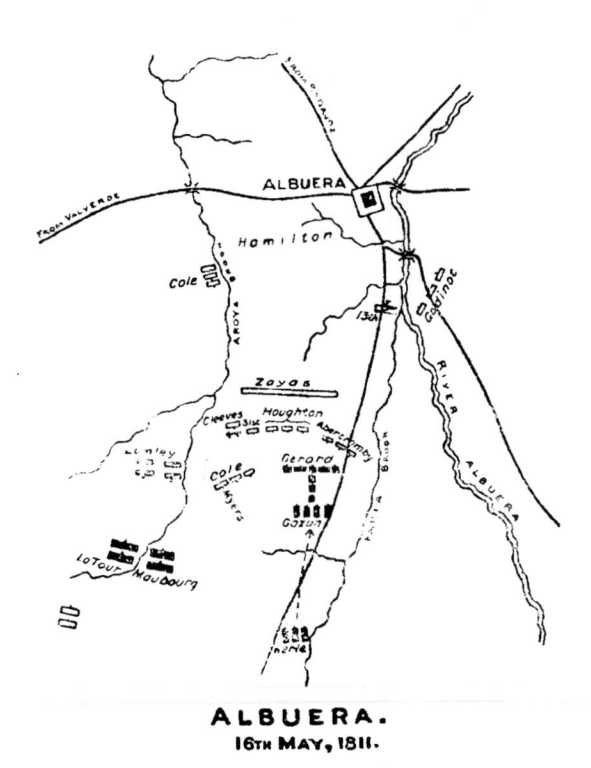

While some of the regiments were deploying in a thick mist, they were suddenly attacked by Polish Lancers, who inflicted heavy loss upon them, capturing for the time being six guns.

Hoghton's brigade next arrived upon the scene, and was met by showers of grape at half-range that spread havoc among the ranks. All was now confusion, " and the unhappy thought of a retreat rose in his [Beresford's] troubled mind." The day, however, was redeemed by the 4th Division, of which only two brigades were in the field, the one, Portuguese, under General Harvey, the other, the " Fuzilier brigade," consisting of the 1st and 2nd battalions of the 7th and the 1st battalion of the 23rd Regiments, commanded by Sir W. Myers. Major-General Lowry Cole, leading the Fusilier brigade in person, having the Portuguese on his right flank, charged the heights. What followed is vividly described in the words of Napier the historian :

ALBUERA.
16TH MAY, 1811.

"Such a gallant line, issuing from the midst of the smoke and rapidly separating itself from the confused and broken multitude, startled the enemy's heavy masses, which were increasing and pressing onwards as to an assured victory: they wavered, hesitated, and then vomiting forth a storm of fire, hastily endeavoured to enlarge their front, while a fearful discharge of grape from all their artillery whistled through the British ranks. Myers was killed; Cole, and the three colonels, Ellis, Blakeney, and Hawkshawe, fell wounded; and the Fusilier battalions, struck by the iron tempest, reeled and staggered like sinking ships. Suddenly and sternly recovering, they closed on their terrible enemies, and then was seen with what a strength and majesty the British soldier fights. In vain did Soult, by voice and gesture, animate his Frenchmen; in vain did the hardiest veterans, extricating themselves from the crowded columns, sacrifice their lives to gain time for the mass to open out on such a fair field; in vain did the mass itself bear up, and, fiercely striving, fire indiscriminately upon friends and foes, while the horsemen hovering on the flank threatened to charge the advancing line. Nothing could stop that astonishing infantry. No sudden burst of undisciplined valour, no nervous enthusiasm, weakened the stability of their order; their flashing eyes were bent on the dark columns in their front; their measured tread shook the ground; their dreadful volleys swept away the head of every formation; their deafening shouts overpowered the dissonant cries that broke from all parts of the tumultuous crowd, as foot by foot and with a horrid carnage it was driven by the incessant vigour of the attack to the farthest edge of the hill. In vain did the French reserves, joining with the struggling multitude, endeavour to sustain the fight; their efforts only increased the irremediable confusion, and the mighty mass giving way like a loosened cliff, went headlong down the ascent. The rain flowed after in streams discoloured with blood, and fifteen hundred unwounded men, the remnant of six thousand unconquerable British soldiers, stood triumphant on the fatal hill!"

Five of the six captured guns were recovered by the Fusilier brigade.

The loss of the Royal Welch Fusiliers in this terrible battle fought on the 16th of May was very severe. Captain Montagu and Lieutenant Hall, 1 sergeant, and 73 rank and file killed; Lieutenant-Colonel Ellis, Captains Hurford, Macdonald, and Stainforth, Lieutenants Harrison, Treeve, Booker, Thorp, Castle, Harris, Ledwith, and McLellan (adjutant), 12 sergeants, 1 drummer, 232 rank and file wounded; and 1 sergeant and 5 rank and file missing. Captain Macdonald and Lieutenant Castle died of their wounds. So numerous were the casualties among the officers and sergeants, that Captain Stainforth's company was, at the conclusion of the action, commanded by a corporal, named Thomas Robinson.

For its gallant conduct in this battle the regiment was permitted to add the word "ALBUHERA" to its colour and appointments on the 30th of October 1816.

On the 18th of May Soult retreated towards Llerena, escorting a large convoy of wounded. The same day the investment of Badajoz was resumed by the 3rd and 7th Divisions, together with the Portuguese, and completed by the 25th of May.

On the 27th Beresford left the army and proceeded to Lisbon. His successor, Major-General Rowland Hill, reached Almendralejo on the 31st, and received a most cordial welcome from the 4th Division, which had proceeded there to cover the siege operations. The battalion had now 21 officers, 19 sergeants, 9 drummers, and 327 rank and file at headquarters fit for duty. Thirteen wounded officers and 232 rank and file had gone to the rear. Captain Potter and Lieutenant the Hon. Thomas Jocelyn had left for England to join the 2nd battalion.

Although a practicable breach was made by the 10th of June, Wellington, on hearing that Marmont was marching southward, decided to raise the siege and proceed towards Elvas, where he was joined by General Brent Spencer's corps. He then prepared to bar the entry of the combined forces of Soult and Marmont into Portugal by the Badajoz road.

In the disposition of his army the battalion was posted on the 21st of June at Torre de Mouro. Its effective strength at headquarters was 463 all ranks. Two sergeants and 33 rank and file had died since the 25th of May.

In consequence of commissions in General Hoghton's brigade having been granted to non-commissioned officers who had distinguished themselves in action, Major-General Lowry Cole, commanding the 4th Division, applied for similar recognition for his Fusilier brigade, with the result that Sergeant David Scott of the 1st battalion of the 23rd Regiment was promoted to an ensigncy in the 11th Foot on the 18th of July; Quartermaster-Sergeant Arthur Bymes of the 7th Regiment to an ensigncy in the 27th Regiment on the 17th of July;

and Sergeant William Johnston from the 7th Regiment to an ensigncy in the 57th Regiment on the 18th of July.

The following is the official correspondence on the subject:

"ELVAS,
"11 *June* 1811.

"SIR,

"Major-Genl Wm Stewart having informed me that your Excellency had been pleased to permit his recommending for promotion to an Ensigncy a Sergeant from each of the Regiments which composed the late Major-General Hoghton's Brigade in the 2nd division for their distinguished gallantry in the action of the 16th ult. at Albuera, I trust you will not conceive I am assuming too much in claiming for the Fuzileer Brigade a similar mark of your Excellency's approbation of their conduct on that day, which I may venture to assert was as distinguished for gallantry and steadiness as that of their rivals. Under that impression I have taken the liberty of transmitting to your Excellency the name of a Sergeant from each of the Battalions composing that Brigade, and recommended to me by the respective commanding officers.

"I have the honour to be

"G. L. COLE, *Major-General.*

"To His Excellency Marshal Sir Wm. C. Beresford."

"QUINTA DE BERBO,
"13 *June*, 1811.

"SIR,

"I have been favoured with your letter of the 11th inst. recommending a Sergeant of each of the Battalions of the Fuzileer Brigade for an Ensigncy as a mark of approbation to the Conduct of that Brigade on the 16th ult. at Albuera. I will have much pleasure in submitting to Lord Wellington for favourable consideration the names of the Sergeants for promotion with my best recommendation, and it will give me infinite pleasure to have an opportunity of testifying to that Brigade my approbation of the excellent conduct on that day on which in the noblest sense of the word it can be said to have rivalled the best.

"It had my best approbation and I am glad the occasion is presented of making it in a way that will be agreeable to the Brigade.

"I have, etc.,

"WM. C. BERESFORD."

On the 18th of July Wellington ascertained that the French Marshals had abandoned their attempt to cross the Portuguese frontier and had separated, Soult marching towards Seville, and Marmont in the direction of Salamanca. Accordingly he issued orders for his troops to go into cantonments from Castello Branco in the north, to Estremoz in the south, distant from each other about seventy-five miles. At the latter town the battalion was cantoned. Lieutenant Watkin Wynne died on the 1st of August.

On the following day Wellington decided to blockade Ciudad Rodrigo in the hope of compelling it to surrender for want of provisions. To carry out his purpose he directed the 3rd Division and the Light Division to march northward to the River Agueda, and blockade the fortress on the south. The Spanish guerilla band under Julian Sanchez was directed to blockade the northern side.

The remaining divisions were distributed over a broad front, the 4th being located at Pedrogao. While there the following officers from the 2nd battalion joined the 1st—Major T. Dalmer, Lieutenant H. Walker, 2nd Lieutenants R. Butler, W. Curties, G. Fielding, B. Llewelyn, together with 6 sergeants, 2 corporals, and 246 rank and file. The effective strength of the battalion at headquarters was 597 towards the end of August.

On the 23rd of September General Dorsenne's corps joined Marmont, their united forces amounting to nearly 60,000 men. Marmont then advanced to raise the blockade of Ciudad Rodrigo, which caused Wellington to fall back upon the ridge of Fuente Guinaldo, the 4th Division being posted there, and the rest of the army, excepting the 5th Division, he drew up in echelon between that place and Fuentes de Oñoro.

The Monthly Return of the battalion, dated the 25th of September, records that Captain Keith had died since the date of the last return; Captain Hill had joined the Portuguese Army; and 6 sergeants, 1 drummer, and 51 rank and file had been invalided home.

On the night of the 26th of September the Allied forces fell back upon Alfaiates, the light companies of Pakenham's brigade being left as a rearguard at Aldea da Ponte. Here, on the 27th, a sharp engagement took place between them and the French advanced guard. The village was twice lost and twice retaken, on the second occasion with the assistance of Pakenham's brigade, supported by a Portuguese regiment.

At nightfall the village was left in the hands of the French. Pakenham's brigade then set out to join the 4th Division at Boucafarinha, and the Portuguese regiment to join Pack's Portuguese brigade at Villaboa.

In repelling the attack on Aldea da Ponte on the 27th of September, the battalion lost Captain Van Courtland killed; Brevet Lieutenant-Colonel Pearson, commanding the light companies of the brigade, and Captain James Cane and 13 rank and file were wounded; 1 missing.

Captain John Van Courtland, frequently described in the Returns as a "foreigner," is another instance of a commission being granted to a child, his age when killed being given as "34" and service as "30 years."

The following account of his death is contained in an extract from a letter written by a brother-officer, dated September 1811, from Sabugal:

"Among those who lost their lives in the late engagement, none can be more truly lamented than our excellent friend Capt. Van Cortlandt, of the 23rd Royal Welsh Fuzileers. He was killed by a cannon-ball on the day of the 27th, and fell, covered with laurels, universally lamented by those who knew him: his death has thrown a gloom over all friends here, for I believe there are none who do not sincerely lament him. Thus fell, in the prime of life, a deserving and excellent young officer, who signalled himself in 28 different engagements. He has left his aged parents, a wife, and two children, and extensive connexions to mourn their irreparable loss. He was second son to Col. Van Cortlandt, of the manor of Cortlandt."

Major Broughton-Mainwaring, in his account of this affair, states that "Viscount Wellington, having asked Major-General Pakenham for a 'stop-gap regiment' to cover the retreat of the division, the latter replied, 'That he had already placed the Royal Welsh Fusiliers there.' 'Ah,' said his Lordship, 'that is the very thing.'"

On the 1st of October the French forces separated; Dorsenne returned to Salamanca and Marmont to the valley of the Tagus. Thereupon Wellington put his troops into winter quarters on both banks of the Coa, the 4th Division being cantoned in the neighbourhood of Gallegos. The present fit on the 25th of that month were as follows: 13 officers, 30 sergeants, 16 drummers, 445 rank and file.

1811.

2ND BATTALION.

The battalion was inspected on the 14th of May by Major-General A. Gledstanes. He reported that although the 2nd battalion had sent 5 sergeants and 200 of its best men to the 1st, many of the remainder were fit for service, the total effectives being 379.

In June the battalion moved to Alderney, and received from the Denbigh and Glamorgan Militia 43 men. In July it furnished a draft to the 1st battalion of 6 sergeants, 2 corporals, 246 rank and file, with Major T. Dalmer, Lieutenant H. Walker, 2nd Lieutenants R. Butler, W. Curties, G. Fielding, and B. Llewelyn; and returned to Guernsey in the same month.

In August the battalion moved to Carmarthen, being stationed either there, or at Milford, or Haverford West during the remainder of the year.

1812.

1ST BATTALION.

On the 1st of January Wellington issued orders for the attack on Ciudad Rodrigo. The 4th Division, being one of those selected for the work of the siege, moved from its cantonments to San Felices, and on the 8th of January the fortress was invested.

On the 19th, the breaches being deemed practicable, the assault was fixed for 7 o'clock that night. The 4th Division, being on duty in the trenches all day, did not participate in the storming of the fortress, which fell that night. Colonel Garwood, afterwards well known as the editor of Wellington's dispatches, received the sword of the Governor in the castle. The loss incurred by the battalion in manning the trenches during the twelve days of the siege was 2 killed and 18 wounded—viz. on the 11th of January, 4 wounded; on the 15th, 1 killed, 7 wounded; on the 19th, 1 killed, 7 wounded.

After the capture of the fortress the battalion, whose effective strength was now 644, moved to San Felices de Chico, where it was detained for several days owing to constant heavy rain which caused the River Agueda to rise to an alarming extent. On the weather conditions improving, the battalion marched to Gallegos.

Towards the end of January Wellington decided to lay siege to Badajoz. His preparations were carried on with great secrecy, and various ruses were resorted to for the purpose of deceiving the French.

Although all the stores required for siege purposes had not accumulated by the 9th of March, Wellington decided on that day to set out for Badajoz, leaving only some cavalry behind to watch Ciudad Rodrigo. By the following day the army had crossed the Tagus by a bridge of boats at Villa Velha, and on the night of the 16th of March the 4th Division bivouacked on the heights to the south of Badajoz. The following day the fortress was invested by the 3rd, 4th, and Light Divisions, numbering in all about 11,000 men. Badajoz is situated on the left bank of the River Guadiana, and was protected by eight bastions. It had been considerably strengthened since its last siege by the British.

From the 17th of March until the 6th of April the siege was carried on with the utmost vigour. The casualties during this period were as follows: from the 18th to 22nd of March, 2 rank and file killed, Brevet Major W. M. Potter wounded (died of wounds), 17 rank and file wounded; from the 22nd to the 26th of March, 4 rank and file killed, 7 wounded; from the 31st of March to the 2nd of April, 1 rank and file wounded. The engineers having reported on the afternoon of the 6th of April that a practicable breach had been made in the La Trinidad bastion, Wellington, who knew that Soult was advancing from Seville with the object of raising the siege, determined to lose no time in storming the place. Accordingly orders were issued for the assault to be made at 10 p.m. that night.

The task assigned to the 4th Division under General Colville was to assault the breach in the bastion of La Trinidad, the Light Division on the left at the same time advancing against the bastion of Santa Maria. Each division was furnished with ladders and axes, and was preceded by a storming party of 500 men.

At a given signal the division moved to the assault without firing a shot. On reaching the glacis it was discovered by the enemy, who poured in a murderous fire. Nothing daunted, the men flew down the ladders or recklessly jumped into the ditch, which, being full of water, caused many deaths by drowning.

At this stage the Light Division unfortunately inclined somewhat to its right and the 4th Division to its left, the consequence being that the men became intermingled and all formation was lost.

The sharpshooters, who had been posted on the glacis to keep down the fire of the defenders, being shot down almost to a man by a withering fire from the bastions, enabled the French to mow down with the greatest ease the confused and huddled-together mass of stormers, who, despite the inferno of bursting shells, grenades, and powder barrels, with desperate courage made several rushes at the breaches, endeavouring over and over again to achieve the impossible.

Many officers and men reached the summit but could progress no farther, as they found themselves confronted by sword-blades set deeply in trunks of trees, and fell, riddled by bullets. The Light Division also could make no headway at the Santa Maria bastion, where the carnage was dreadful. In the words of Mr. Fortescue, " all that impetuous valour could do was done."

Wellington, on learning that nearly all the officers and prodigious numbers of the men had fallen, gave orders for the remnants of the two divisions to be withdrawn, preparatory to a fresh assault being made before daylight, it being now nearly midnight. Happily, the necessity for it never arose, as the 3rd Division under General Picton, and the 5th Division under General Leith, accomplished the extraordinary feat of escalading the castle and the bastion of St. Vincente. Presently the remnants of the 4th and Light Divisions entered the fortress unopposed. The British were now masters of Badajoz.

During the siege and assault of the 6th of April the battalion lost the following :

Killed.—Captain Maw and Lieutenant Collins, 1 ensign, 4 sergeants, and 29 rank and file.

Wounded.—Lieutenant Colonel Ellis, Brevet Major Potter, Captains Leahy, Stainforth, and Hawtyn, Lieutenants Farmer, Johnston, Harrison, G. Browne, Brownson, Whalley, Walker, Tuckey, and Fielding, 2nd Lieutenants Holmes, Llewelyn, and Wingate, 7 sergeants, 1 drummer, 84 rank and file.

Missing.—1 sergeant and 19 rank and file. Brevet Major Potter and 2nd Lieutenant Llewelyn died soon after of their wounds.

It is recorded in Major Broughton-Mainwaring's *History of the 23rd Regiment* that " Major-General the Honourable Charles Colville was severely wounded, and carried from the breach by Serjeant James Ingram, of the Royal Welsh Fusiliers."

On the 15th of May 1821, " In commemoration of the distinguished services of the regiment at the siege of Badajoz on the 16th of March 1812," it was permitted to bear on its colour and appointments the word "BADAJOZ" in addition to any badges or devices already granted.

After the fall of Badajoz Soult cantoned his army in the neighbourhood of Seville; thereupon Wellington decided to follow his example, as his troops required rest, and the green crops were not sufficiently advanced to supply forage for the horses. He therefore cantoned them over a wide area extending from the Douro in the north to the Sierra Morena in the south. The battalion marched northward and cantoned at Sabugal, where it was joined by 3 sergeants, 1 drummer, and 70 privates from the 2nd battalion.

Towards the end of May it was at Traves, the present fit at headquarters being 10 officers, 19 sergeants, 13 drummers, and 289 rank and file. During that month 1 sergeant and 23 rank and file died. On the 25th of May it was inspected there by Major-General Wm. Anson.

Wellington, who had been making since the fall of Badajoz strenuous efforts to accumulate supplies for a meditated advance into Spain, being assured that all things were in readiness, on the 13th of June crossed the Agueda into that country, and arrived on the 16th within six miles of Salamanca. On the following day the British Army crossed the Tormes, by fords both above and below Salamanca: the 6th Division proceeded to invest the three forts of Salamanca which Marmont had erected, the main army taking up its position on the heights of San Christobal a few miles to the north of the town.

On the 20th of June Marmont appeared before the British position, when a slight skirmish between the cavalry of both armies took place on the plain. Lieutenant Leonard of the battalion, while witnessing this skirmish, was killed by a chance shot fired from a considerable distance.

On the 22nd, after carefully reconnoitring Wellington's position, Marmont withdrew to a position behind the Douro, and left the forts to their fate. On the 27th of June the forts were captured and promptly blown up.

Marmont then fell back upon the northern bank of the Douro, and took up a position between Toro and Tordesillas, a distance of nearly fourteen miles. He was followed by Wellington, who hoped to be able to force the passage of the river, but was disappointed as the recent rains had swelled the waters to such an extent as to render the fords impassable for the time being. He therefore contented himself with drawing up his army facing the French.

From the 3rd to the 16th of July the two armies remained

impassive in sight of each other, the soldiers of both often exchanging rations and never firing a shot. The suspense was put an end to on the 16th by Marmont suddenly moving his army towards Toro, and with part of it crossing the Douro as if to march upon Salamanca. This movement was merely a blind to draw the Allied army from Tordesillas and Pollos, so that the passages over the Douro at those points might be left open.

On the following day Marmont doubled back rapidly along the right bank of the river, crossed it at Pollos and Tordesillas, and concentrated his whole army at Nava del Rey, thus accomplishing his object of crossing the Douro unopposed.

This movement of Marmont's necessitated the concentration of Wellington's whole army behind the River Guarena. An attempt of Marmont to force a passage of that river was defeated, and on the 19th both armies faced each other along its banks; in this affair the regiment lost 2 rank and file killed, 2 missing, and 9 wounded.

On the morning of the 20th Marmont was again on the move, marching so rapidly that he outflanked the British, and by nightfall held the ford of Huerta on the Tormes. On the following day he crossed the river there; Wellington also passed it by the ford of Santa Marta.

At this stage, an intercepted letter in which Wellington intimated his intention to fall back to the frontier of Portugal having fallen into the hands of Marmont, the latter decided to prevent his doing so, which brought about the battle of Salamanca.

On the morning of the 22nd of July the Allied right occupied a position extending along a ridge of heights terminating in low ground near the village of Arapiles, their left resting on low ground, adjoining the River Tormes, near Santa Marta. The French occupied the wooded ridge of Calvarisa de Ariba. On their left and to the British right were two "steep and savagely rugged" hills of no great height, but the possession of which would be most useful to the French Marshal, as it would enable him to bring on an engagement with great disadvantage to the Allies.

At daylight a race was made by both armies to gain possession of these heights: the Allies secured the one nearest to their position known as the Lesser Arapile, but the French outstripped them in the race for the other. On gaining possession of the height, Wellington extended his right into the low ground near the village of Arapiles, placing the light companies of the Guards there, and the 4th Division with the exception of the 27th Regiment, which he posted on the rocky summit of the height, on a gentle ridge behind them.

Marmont, being under the impression that it was Wellington's intention to retreat by the Ciudad Rodrigo road, made arrangements to prevent his escape, which occupied him several hours.

At 3 p.m. word was brought to Wellington that the French left, under General Thomières, was in motion marching towards the Ciudad Rodrigo road, and that an appreciable gap then existed between it and their centre. Wellington proceeded at once to some high ground and intently watched Thomières's movements for some minutes. In the words of Napier, " The fault was flagrant, and he fixed it with the stroke of a thunderbolt."

Riding up to Pakenham, his brother-in-law, who temporarily commanded the 3rd Division in the absence of Picton on the sick-list, he ordered him to launch it against the head of Thomières's division which formed the left of the French army. Brigadier-General Pack's Portuguese Brigade, 2,000 strong, was directed to assault the Greater Arapile. At the same time the 4th and 5th Divisions, together with Brigadier-General Bradford's Portuguese, supported by the 6th and 7th Divisions, were hurled against the enemy's centre.

Although Pack made a gallant attack upon the Greater Arapile, it was not successful, but it served a most useful purpose, as it diverted the attention of the enemy corps posted upon it for some time from the troops advancing under Sir Lowry Cole, thus relieving them of a flanking fire.

The 4th Division, marching in line, met with a desperate resistance, and was exposed to a destructive fire of grape and round shot. The first line, consisting of the Fusilier Brigade, under the command of Lieutenant-Colonel Ellis, of the 1st battalion of the 23rd Regiment, on the right, and Colonel Stubb's brigade of Portuguese Infantry on the left, seven battalions in all, worked its way, despite a terrific cannonade, through the village of Arapiles, then, reforming, it drove the enemy from their first position. Despite the fact that the French were now pouring in a withering, enfilading fire from the Greater Arapile, the 4th Division bore down upon the second position taken up by the enemy, and again dislodged them, capturing eighteen guns.

The British were now in possession of the crest of the ridge, but, unfortunately, Cole was wounded just as it was gained, his troops were out of breath and somewhat disordered after their victorious progress, and to render matters worse the 6th Division, which should have actively supported the 4th Division, was slowly advancing in column. The situation suddenly became very critical, as a reinforcement of three French regiments sallied out from behind the Greater Arapile, and joined the five battalions under Clausel which had hitherto striven in vain to check Cole's progress.

Clausel now became the assailant. Advancing briskly, he charged the 4th Division, which, "thinned and exhausted by its effort," was not in a position at the moment to withstand such an onset. The Portuguese were the first to give way, the Fusilier Brigade was compelled to follow suit, with the result that the victorious French recaptured their guns.

At this point their success terminated, as Marshal Beresford, who happened to be on the spot, detached Brigadier-General Spry's Portuguese brigade, which was in the second line of the 5th Division, with directions to change front and bring its fire to bear upon Clausel's left flank, which had the effect of causing the French counter-attack to terminate abruptly.

The opportunity being now afforded the 4th Division of reforming, and being joined by the 6th Division, both renewed the attack with the greatest vigour, and compelled the enemy to retire from hill to hill for the greater part of half a mile.

While the contest in the centre was being waged with desperate valour on both sides, Pakenham's division, "bearing onward with a conquering violence," bore down upon the French left wing, and almost annihilated it, taking over 2,000 prisoners. Marmont made desperate efforts to retrieve the fortunes of the day, but the destruction of his leading divisions removed all hope of his doing so.

Clausel, who succeeded to the command of the French—Marmont being wounded—as evening approached, skilfully drew off his beaten army through the forest towards the ford of Alba on the Tormes, and by 10 p.m. " the whole French Army vanished as it were into darkness."

This brilliant victory obtained on the 22nd of July cost the battalion the following casualties:

Killed.—Major Offley, and 10 rank and file.

Wounded.—Lieutenant-Colonel Ellis, Major T. Dalmer, Lieutenants Enoch, Macdonald, Fryer, Clyde, 6 sergeants, and 84 rank and file.

The present fit now numbered 13 officers, 27 sergeants, 15 drummers, 337 rank and file.

For its gallant conduct in this battle the regiment was permitted on the 15th of May 1821 to bear the word "SALAMANCA" upon its colour and appointments.

The following is a copy of a letter from Captain George Browne to Colonel Torrens, dated Dublin Castle, the 3rd of October 1850:

"MY DEAR COLONEL,

"I have just been reading the records of the Royal Welch, the book is very well got up particularly the early campaign of Marlborough, and the old American War. I think, however, the services of the Regiment in the Peninsula are not well detailed and I feel myself a little aggrieved in this particular, for instance at the Battle of Salamanca, the left company of the 23rd was engaged at a very early hour in the morning with the Brunswick Oels Rifle Company and the left company of the 7th Fusiliers and Light Company of the 48th, the 4 companies went into action commanded by Dalmer who was wounded at the commencement of the skirmish. Captain Thwaites of the 48th next in command was also wounded and I remained the senior officer of the four companies which did very good service, and defended for some hours the lesser Arapiles. Poor Ellis was anxious to have done something for me on this occasion, unfortunately being only a Lieutenant at the time I got nothing, had I been a Captain I must have obtained a Brevet Majority. The left company had 4 men killed and 14 wounded at Salamanca before the Regiment fired a shot. Again you will observe on page 145 it is said ' on this occasion, Vittoria, the regiment did not come into immediate collision with the enemy but Lieut. Sydney [? Sidley] was wounded and 4 men killed in driving the French across the Zadossa on the 19th July.' Now I beg to mention that the left company which I commanded was engaged on the 18th July and on the 19th July at La Bogarna [?] de Morilles and on these two occasions lost 4 men killed and 9 wounded. Lieutenant Sedley [? Sidley] was severely wounded with this company on the 19th. At the Battle of Vittoria the left company where I commanded was sent to the front where we secured 73 prisoners and a great number of waggons and mules which I delivered up to Colonel B. appointed Commandant of Vittoria.

"On the 25th July at Roncesvalles I again commanded the left company which was detached to support the 28th regiment. I was very severely wounded, receiving at the present moment a pension for the wound. Lieutenant O'Flaherty sent to succeed me was severely wounded also, and the company had 7 men killed and 15 wounded. Neither O'Flaherty's name or mine are mentioned in this severe skirmish and I should feel much obliged if you would have both placed in the Record Book in your orderly room. I could say a great deal more upon the Peninsular Campaign but will not take up your time any further. Knowing you to have all the true feelings of a soldier you will excuse what might be deemed egotism and I hope you will kindly order the names of Lieutenant George Browne and Lieutenant O'Flaherty to be entered in your Regimental Records as having been severely wounded on 25th July 1813 in the pass of Roncesvalles. My sister the late Mrs. Hemans wrote for me a beautiful song which is set to air 'Am Bhein' and as I have heard you and Mrs. Torrens are very musical, I enclose a copy, etc., etc.

"GEO. BROWNE."

The following day the pursuit of Clausel began and was continued until Valladolid was reached on the 31st of July, where seventeen guns and considerable stores were captured. Wellington entered Madrid on the 12th of August, and was received with every sign of the deepest emotion by the multitude, whose spirits had become depressed by long-continued misery. The battalion was posted at the Escurial.

In consequence of French armies beginning to collect from north and south, Wellington deemed it advisable to leave Madrid on the 1st of September. He then marched towards Valladolid, against the Army of the North under Clausel, which was assembling on the Douro.

On his approach Clausel retired before him, whereupon Wellington made for Burgos, which he entered, and at once laid siege to the castle, in which, however, he was not successful, owing mainly to the material for its reduction at his disposal being too limited. No less than five assaults were made and repulsed. After persevering for thirty days, Wellington decided to raise the siege.

On the 21st of October he retired towards Salamanca, blowing up the bridges across the Douro in his retreat. On the 18th of November he reached Ciudad Rodrigo, and subsequently went into cantonments about the Coa and the Agueda.

On the 5th of December the battalion reached Soutilla in Portugal, where it rested for several weeks. On the 25th of that month the present fit at headquarters were as follows: 26 officers, 30 sergeants, 14 drummers, 294 rank and file. The following draft from the 2nd battalion was then on the march from Lisbon: Captains F. Dalmer and Strangeways, Lieutenants Harris, Jocelyn, and Cowell, 2nd Lieutenants Wingate, Griffiths, Gledstanes, Assistant Surgeon Smith, 2 sergeants, and 72 privates.

1812.

2ND BATTALION.

During the whole of this year the battalion remained at Haverford West. Owing to the numerous drafts it was called upon to furnish to the 1st battalion, the effective strength of the rank and file present never exceeded 150 men. It was inspected there by Major-General Robert Browne on the 27th and 28th of July, when the following were returned as "Welch": 6 sergeants, 4 corporals, 8 drummers, 80 privates. In this report he states that the number of musicians was "five fifers," and as regards the regimental school that "this is in its infancy but a good system seems adopted, the schoolmaster appears a correct and proper man."

1813.

1ST BATTALION.

The favourable result of the campaign of 1812 influenced the home authorities in deciding to make a great effort in the following year for the complete expulsion of the French from the Peninsula. While the army was cantoned during the winter of 1812–13, preparations were made on an extensive scale to render it thoroughly fit for active service in the field.

Large reinforcements mainly of cavalry arrived from England. Numbers of skulkers at general hospitals and depôts were rounded up, and ordered to rejoin their units without delay. So thoroughly was the army reorganised by Wellington that when the time came for resuming operations, the Anglo-Portuguese force amounted to 75,000 men, of whom 50,000 were British, with 90 guns.

On the 25th of January Sergeant-Major Gordon was promoted to an ensigncy in the 13th Veteran Battalion.

In March the battalion left Soutilla, and moved to Algodras, also in Portugal. Nine rank and file died during that month.

On the 12th of April it was inspected at Almendra by Colonel Skerritt. In his remarks he observes:

> "*Officers.*—All are equal to, and have performed, their duty with perfect zeal, a great many have been wounded, and with the exception of a few lately joined, have seen much active service, perfect unanimity prevails among them.
>
> "*Non-Commissioned Officers.*—Very good, most of them very old soldiers, who have seen much severe service and been wounded.
>
> "*Privates.*—A fine body of men, very stout, cleanly, and at the moment very healthy, lately they have suffered from sickness from unavoidable circumstances.
>
> "*Messing.*—The men are provided with a breakfast, and vegetables, altho' extremely difficult to procure. The battalion as a whole is highly fit for service although weak in numbers.
>
> "*Courts Martial.*—Punishments appear to have been avoided as much as possible."

In connection with courts-martial, from a list appended to the Report, it appears as if the desire for "pork" was the cause of the downfall of some of the regiment: on the 11th of December 1812, Privates Batt, Edwards, and Cotter were sentenced to receive 200 lashes each, actually receiving 170 each, for "destroying a pig"; and on the 8th of March 1813, Private McLaughlin was sentenced to 300 lashes, actually receiving 75, "on suspicion of killing a pig."

In April 3 sergeants and 22 privates were transferred to the 13th Veteran Battalion.

Wellington's plan for the ensuing campaign, which may be said to have been "the crowning one of the war," was to cross the Douro, ascend the right bank of it to the neighbourhood of Zamora, and there effect a juncture with the Spanish army in Galicia, which would have the effect of turning the French line of defence on the Douro.

With this object in view the Allied army moved from its cantonments about the middle of May in three columns. The left, commanded by Sir Thomas Graham, crossed the Douro, advanced northward to Braganza, joined up with the Galicians, and marched towards Zamora. Wellington, commanding the centre in person, advanced upon the direct road to Salamanca. The right, under General Hill, crossed the Tormes and also made for Salamanca.

The effective strength of the battalion at headquarters on leaving its cantonment was as follows: 34 officers, 38 sergeants, 15 drummers, 394 rank and file. One officer (Lieutenant Farmer) was a prisoner of war at Valladolid. Twenty-five men died during the last month of its stay at Algodras.

On the 3rd of June all three of the Allied columns united at Toro. The first great object of the Allies, which, as already stated, was the turning of the French line of defence upon the Douro, was now accomplished.

This strategic movement necessitated the falling back of the enemy troops under Joseph Bonaparte to a strong position at Vittoria behind the Ebro. Burgos, being threatened by the left of the Allied army, was evacuated by the French troops that remained there, and the castle blown up.

On the 19th of June Wellington came up with the rearguard of the enemy, which had taken up a strong position on the left of the River Bayas at Subijana de Moullos. While the Light Division turned the enemy's left, the 4th attacked it in front, with the result that it was driven back upon the main body of the army, which was marching from Pancorbo to Vittoria. The regiment lost in this engagement 1 officer (Lieutenant Sidley), 1 sergeant, 3 rank and file wounded.

As Joseph Bonaparte's position was too strong for a direct attack, Wellington determined to turn it if possible. With this object in view he decided to cross the Ebro near its source, and traversing the left bank, descend upon the French near Vittoria.

On the 20th of June Wellington halted to close up his columns, which had become extended owing to the nature of the country, and having done so, advanced to the Ebro, which was successfully crossed by the Allies, who then encamped along the River Bayas.

The following day Wellington attacked Joseph in the position he had taken up, his main object being to force the enemy's right, and so cut him off from the "royal road" leading from Madrid to the Bayonne road—his only line of retreat. Wellington had now 80,000 men in the field, of whom 20,000 were Spaniards. Joseph Bonaparte's army numbered between 60,000 and 70,000 combatants.

Wellington formed his army in four columns, viz. the right, right centre, left centre, and left. The right centre was composed of the Light and 4th Divisions, the reserve artillery and some cavalry. It was directed to move to Nanclares, upon the River Zadora, to the west of Vittoria, and there await instructions.

On the morning of the 21st of June, in thick mist, the operations of the day began. By 10 a.m. Sir Rowland Hill had succeeded in seizing the heights of La Puebla, upon which the enemy's left rested, and pushing through the Puebla Pass, attacked and gained possession of the village of Subijana de Alava in front of the enemy's line, which he made repeated attempts to regain.

While Hill was traversing the Puebla Pass, the left column under Sir Thomas Graham moved forward to assail the enemy's right. By 12 o'clock his attack seriously developed, with the result that position after position was gained, the Portuguese and Spanish troops forming part of his column behaving admirably on this occasion. He then proceeded to attack the village of Abechuco, which was carried, with the result that the enemy's retreat by the high-road to France was intercepted.

While the right and left columns were hotly engaged, the centre columns, which were posted on rugged ground between Nanclares and Villodas, proceeded to attack the heights upon which the right of the enemy's centre was placed. The troops advanced in admirable order, despite the difficulty of the ground. The French made desperate efforts to maintain their position, which covered Vittoria; but on the 4th Division seizing a summit on their left, they abandoned the heights and fled along the Pampeluna road. The pursuit was kept up until after darkness had set in.

The loss sustained by the battalion in this action, fought on the 21st of June, was fortunately very light. It amounted to no more than 1 rank and file killed, 1 sergeant and 2 rank and file wounded.

Lieutenant Farmer, who had been a prisoner at Valladolid, was retaken on the advance of the Allied army against Joseph Bonaparte.

For its services in this battle the regiment was permitted on the 15th of May 1821 to add the word "VITTORIA" to those already emblazoned on its colour.

The present fit at headquarters four days after the battle were as follows: 27 officers, 33 sergeants, 14 drummers, 223 privates. One sergeant and 43 privates were taken prisoners of war, and 5 sergeants and 72 privates had been invalided, and sent home during the previous four weeks.

Great were the rejoicings in England on tidings of this important victory being received. Throughout the length and breadth of the country every town and village was illuminated in honour of Wellington and his victorious army.

Joseph Bonaparte, with the main portion of the retreating French, reached Pampeluna in great disorder on the 24th of June. Leaving a garrison there, he retired in hot haste across the Pyrenees, closely followed by the light troops.

Although the French were practically expelled from Spanish soil, Wellington decided to carry the war into France with the object of completely crushing the power of Napoleon. Before doing so, he considered it necessary to reduce the fortresses of Pampeluna and San Sebastian, for fear that his lines of communication might be endangered. The former was blockaded on the 26th of June.

On Wellington ascertaining that General Clausel had remained in the neighbourhood of Logroño for some days after the battle was fought, he moved the 3rd, 4th, 7th, and Light Divisions towards that place, in the hope of intercepting him on his line of retreat to France. Clausel, however, getting wind of this movement, by some "extraordinary forced marches" reached Tudela on the 27th, and crossing the Ebro there, continued his march towards Saragossa, pursued by General Mina with a force of Allied cavalry.

Clausel succeeded in eluding the pursuit, and got in touch, about the middle of July, with Marshal Soult, who had been sent post-haste from Germany by Napoleon to supersede Joseph Bonaparte after the battle of Vittoria.

Soult had now about 80,000 men under his command at the foot of the mountains near the Bidassoa River, and talked grandiloquently of forcing the passes of Roncesvalles and Maya, and then chasing Wellington beyond the Ebro.

The Allied army, about 82,000 strong, was posted in the passes of the mountains, the 4th Division being at Viscarret as a support to Major-General Byng's Brigade, and General Morillo's division of infantry, which were on the right at Altobiscar, near Roncesvalles.

On the 25th of July Soult attacked Byng's post, whereupon the 4th Division, under General Sir Lowry Cole, moved up to his support. The post was maintained until late in the afternoon, when it was turned by the enemy. Cole considered it advisable to withdraw, and that night moved his troops to the neighbourhood of Zubiri.

The battalion suffered the following loss in this engagement: Captain Booker, Lieutenants G. Browne, O'Flaherty, and Ledwith slightly wounded; 1 sergeant and five rank and file killed, and 15 wounded.

The same afternoon Sir Rowland Hill's position in the Puerto de Maya was heavily attacked by General d'Erlon. Part of the post which was the key of the whole was taken, but subsequently regained. A day of inactivity on the part of d'Erlon followed, which enabled Hill to concentrate his troops.

On the 27th of July Hill was about to attack him when he received word that Cole was retiring. He thereupon withdrew his troops by a night march of fifteen miles to Irueta. Cole, considering that his position at Zubiri would not be tenable for the length of time required to hold it, also retired on the 27th and took up a position on the heights near Villalba along with the 3rd Division to cover the blockade of Pampeluna.

The two divisions had hardly taken up their ground before the French formed their army on a mountain, and soon afterwards attacked a hill on the right of the 4th Division, from which they were driven at the point of the bayonet. Repeated efforts were made by them that afternoon and evening to gain the hill in question, but all to no purpose.

On the morning of the 28th the 6th Division appeared upon the scene, and was almost immediately attacked by a much superior force of the enemy which had assembled in the village of Sorauren. Aided by a well-sustained fire from the light troops of the division, who occupied some heights to the left, and also by the fire from heights on its right held by the 4th Division and Brigadier-General Campbell's Portuguese brigade, the 6th Division drove the enemy back with immense loss.

The French then turned their attention to the heights on which the left of the 4th Division stood. They were occupied by the 7th

Caçadores, who were fiercely assailed, but being supported by Major-General Ross's brigade of the 4th Division, of which the 23rd formed part, drove the enemy back, inflicting considerable loss, despite the fact that the assailants obtained temporary possession of the heights where this Portuguese regiment was posted.

The battle now became general along the whole front of the heights occupied by the 4th Division, and went greatly in favour of the Allies, except at one point where a Portuguese regiment was overpowered. The balance, however, was quickly restored by dashing charges of the 27th and 48th Regiments, with the result that the enemy was driven pell-mell from the heights with huge loss. The attack upon this front then ceased entirely, and languished on other points of the line, eventually dying out soon after sunset.

Wellington, in his account of the operations during the preceding week, in referring to the battle fought on the 28th of July, remarks as follows :

" In the course of this contest, the gallant fourth division which has so frequently been distinguished in this army, surpassed their former good conduct. Every regiment charged with the bayonet, and the 40th, the 7th, 20th, and 23rd, four different times. Their officers set them the Example, and Major General Robert Ross had two horses shot under him."

Lieutenant-Colonel Henry Walton Ellis, commanding the battalion, writing to Captain Harrison a few days after this battle was fought and won, narrates how gallantly it withstood the onslaught of the French, and feelingly alludes to its depleted condition both before and after the 28th of July.

The following is an extract from his letter :

" The battle of the 28th of July was a beautiful display of military manœuvres : the enemy formed his columns in the most perfect order, and advanced to the attack with a rapidity and impetus apparently irresistible. I was in immediate support of the seventh Caçadores (Portuguese), who were the advanced piquet, and consequently received the first shock of the enemy's column. My people only thought of fighting, and at once checked their progress. Our supports on both sides were brought up, and the contest continued with varying success till four o'clock, when the enemy withdrew, only leaving his voltigeurs in our front. We had three divisions upon us,—the fourth, fifth and seventh: the two former were chiefly opposed to the fortieth, who made two unheard of charges: indeed, the whole day was a succession of charges.

"The battalion has only the semblance of one. I commenced the action of the 25th, with only two hundred and fifty-four: so with the loss of one hundred and five in action, sick, and attendants on the wounded, I am reduced to one hundred and sixty bayonets. On the morning of the 30th, when formed for the pursuit of Marshal Soult, I only stood one hundred and twenty-one: and by the 2nd of August, I was reduced to one hundred and eight."

On the 28th of July Captains Stainforth, Walker, and Volunteer John Basset, 1 sergeant, 1 corporal, 1 drummer, and 13 rank and file were killed; Lieutenant-Colonel Ellis, Lieutenants Nevill, Brice, Harris, and Adjutant McLellan were wounded, Nevill and McLellan severely.

On the 29th both armies remained facing each other. On the following morning Soult drew off his army to the right, with a view to concentrating his forces for the relief of San Sebastian. He took up a strong position on the crest of a mountain on the British left of the River Lanz. Wellington, who had now nearly 50,000 men under him, determined to drive Soult from his position.

For this purpose he ordered the 3rd Division under Picton to turn the French left by the Zubiri Valley, and the 7th Division to attack their right, which was posted on the hills beyond the Lanz. The 6th Division was launched against the village of Sorauren. To the 4th Division was allotted the task of attacking the front of the enemy's main position. All these operations were successfully carried out, and in the words of Wellington "obliged the enemy to abandon a position which is one of the strongest and most difficult of access that I have yet seen occupied by troops."

Soult had now no alternative but to retreat as fast as possible and endeavour to escape into France by the mountain passes, which he successfully accomplished by the 3rd of August.

As a distinction commemorative of the three days' hard fighting in the Pyrenees between the 28th of July and the 3rd of August, the regiment was permitted on the 15th of May 1821 to bear the word "PYRENEES" on its colour.

The siege of San Sebastian, which had been turned into a blockade on the 25th of July, owing to the approach of Soult to relieve Pampeluna, was now resumed.

During the siege operations the regiment was encamped near Lesaca, about fifteen miles to the north-east of San Sebastian. While there it received a draft from the 2nd battalion consisting of 5 sergeants, 1 drummer, and 175 privates.

On the 26th of August several heavy guns and a quantity of war material reached Wellington, which enabled him to keep up for four days an incessant fire from sixty-three guns upon the walls of the town; by which time practicable breaches had been made and the artillery of the fortress almost entirely silenced.

At 11 a.m. on the 31st of August the attempt to effect a lodgment in the breaches was made by the 2nd Brigade of the 5th Division, supported by volunteers supplied by the other divisions on the spot, 200 being drawn from the 4th Division under Major Rose of the 20th Regiment. After a desperate conflict the British troops succeeded in entering the works. In this assault Lieutenant Griffiths, who commanded the detachment of the battalion, was slightly wounded, 4 rank and file were killed and 4 rank and file wounded. The garrison withdrew to the castle, which, however, surrendered on the 9th of September.

During the following four weeks Wellington remained at Lesaca, being busily occupied in reorganising the Allied army and making the necessary arrangements for his contemplated invasion of France.

After the capture of San Sebastian the battalion moved to Yansi, being encamped about two miles from Wellington's headquarters. On the 3rd of September Lieutenant Ledwith died of wounds. Volunteer Fitzgibbon was appointed 2nd Lieutenant in the regiment. Lieutenant Walker was promoted Captain, and transferred to the 67th Regiment. Lieutenant Brice was appointed A.D.C. to Major-General O'Laughlin. The present fit on the 25th of September were as follows: 25 officers, 31 sergeants, 10 drummers, and 333 privates. Forty-two privates were prisoners of war, and 2 sergeants and 23 privates had died since the 25th of August.

On the 7th of October the Bidassoa was crossed by the left of the Allied army. Wellington's preparations for this movement were conducted with such secrecy that the passage was completed and the Allies firmly established on the right bank of the river before a single French gun was fired. The passage of the Bidassoa compelled Soult to retire behind the River Nivelle, where he occupied himself in strengthening his position. No forward move was made by Wellington in anticipation of the fall of Pampeluna, which took place on the 31st of October.

Volunteer David Satchwell was appointed 2nd Lieutenant in the battalion on the 21st of October.

As several volunteers attached to the regiment were successful in gaining commissions, it may be interesting to note that at this period a volunteer was required to procure a letter of recommendation from the colonel of the regiment in which he was desirous of serving to the commanding officer of it on active service. He was dressed at his own expense in the uniform of a private of that regiment and was required to perform the duties of the rank.

After the affair of the 7th of October Wellington moved his headquarters to Vera (in Spanish territory), to which place the battalion marched, and there encamped until the next forward move was made.

For the advance Wellington organised his army in three columns of divisions. The right was commanded by Sir Rowland Hill, the centre—to which the 4th Division was attached—was under the direction of Marshal Beresford, and the left under that of Lieutenant-General Sir John Hope, who had arrived from Ireland on the 7th of October to take over command from Sir Thomas Graham on his departure for England. Heavy rain prevented the columns advancing to force Soult's entrenched position on the Nivelle until the 10th of November.

On the morning of that day 90,000 Allied troops with 95 guns, when the signal guns were fired from the Atchubia Mountain, advanced to the attack. The 4th Division stormed the redoubts of St. Barbe, and Grenada in front of Sarre, and together with the 7th Division captured that village and the heights behind it. It then, supported on the left by the reserve of Andalusia, attacked the centre of the enemy's main position, while the 3rd and 7th Divisions were launched against the redoubts on the left of the enemy's centre, and the Light Division against those on the right of it.

All these attacks were successful, with the result that the enemy was obliged to abandon strong positions, which they had fortified with much labour. While these operations were taking place in the centre, the 2nd and 6th Divisions attacked three very strong redoubts perched upon the crest of a wooded ridge. All three were soon carried, with the result that communication between Clausel and d'Erlon was cut off.

The Allies were now well established in the rear of the enemy's right, but darkness setting in prevented them from making any further movement. During the night the enemy retreated across the Nivelle, and destroyed all the bridges over the lower portion of it. Sir John Hope followed the retreating French as soon as he could cross the river. On the night of the 11th of November they succeeded in reaching an entrenched camp on both banks of the Nive in front of Bayonne.

On the 15th of May 1821 the regiment was permitted to bear the word "NIVELLE" on its colour.

The battalion was very fortunate in not suffering any loss in this battle. After this engagement the battalion was encamped on the heights of Ascain. During the month of November it received a draft from the 2nd battalion consisting of 2 sergeants and 46 privates.

Wellington had intended to pass the Nive directly after effecting the crossing of the Nivelle, but the very bad condition of the roads, coupled with the fact that the rivulets continued to be abnormally swollen, prevented him from commencing his advance until the 8th of December, when he moved the troops out of their encampments. The 23rd, forming part of the 4th Division, marched from Ascain to St. Barbe.

On the following day Sir Rowland Hill with the 2nd Portuguese Division, supported by the 6th Division under the command of Marshal Beresford, effected the passage of the Nive near Ustaritz and Cambo. On the 10th Soult, having under his command 60,000 men and 40 guns, attacked Sir John Hope with 30,000 men and 24 guns in a position which the latter had taken up about three miles south of Bayonne. As Soult could only advance slowly, Beresford was enabled to afford timely assistance to Hope. After a keen struggle the French retired, baffled.

On the 11th Soult, on ascertaining that the defenders of the ridge of Barrouilhet had scattered somewhat in order to collect fuel, attacked it, and a hand-to-hand encounter followed in which the French were worsted and compelled to retire.

On the 12th an artillery duel was carried on for several hours, during which Soult was preparing to overpower Hill, whose force of 14,000 men and 14 guns was posted upon the right bank of the Nive. This attack was anticipated by Wellington, who directed the 6th Division to march at once to the support of Hill. Unfortunately, this reinforcement was unable to reach the latter, owing to very heavy rain that night, which swelled the Nive to such an extent as to carry away the bridge near Villefranque.

The following day Soult with 35,000 men made a "most desperate attack" upon Hill. "One of the most bloody contests of the war ensued." Soon after noon the 6th Division, followed by the 4th Division and two brigades of the 3rd, arrived upon the scene, having crossed the bridge at Villefranque which Wellington by great efforts had repaired. The battle had, however, been won before their arrival. A general advance of the Allied army then took place, Soult falling back upon Bayonne. The 4th Division was not actively engaged in any of this series of battles, its rôle being to support either flank as required.

On the 10th of December two battalions of the regiment of Nassau and one of Frankfurt, the whole under the command of Colonel Kruse, of the former, came over to the posts of Major-General Ross's brigade of the 4th Division, on the condition of being sent immediately to Germany, which stipulation was agreed to. They were taken over by Lieutenant-Colonel H. W. Ellis, who then commanded the Fusilier Brigade.

The recent torrential rains had made the surrounding country a vast quagmire, which rendered the task of driving Soult from Bayonne an impossible one for Wellington to undertake until such time as the roads hardened. The Allies, therefore, went into winter quarters, the battalion being at first cantoned near St. Pé.

The Monthly Return of the battalion dated the 25th of December furnishes the following information respecting its condition on that date. Present fit, 26 officers, 33 sergeants, 9 drummers, 409 privates; sick absent, 1 officer, 10 sergeants, 3 drummers, 216 privates; sick present, 6 privates; prisoners of war, 40 privates. Wanting to complete, 3 sergeants, 9 drummers, 210 privates.

1813.

2nd Battalion.

In April the battalion moved to Honiton, where 116 privates joined from the Militia. In May it moved to Ottery Barracks, and there received 85 additional men from the Militia. In June it moved to Kingsbridge Barracks, where it again received a further 62 men from the Militia.

In the return for that month the following were denominated "Welsh": 7 officers, 7 sergeants, 6 corporals, 7 drummers, 88 privates.

In August the battalion moved to Berry Head, where it remained until January in the following year. On the 18th of September it was inspected there by Major-General T. Seward. In his "General Remarks" he states that "the recruits are a very fine body of men, with a general appearance of health and cleanliness." The clothing and arms were in "remarkable good condition, every man was in possession of a great coat" . . . "this battalion till lately has been permitted to attend Divine Service on Sunday at the Parish Church at Brixham, but is now prevented for want of room. It was impossible not to be highly gratified with the appearance of this little battalion in the field, and the excellent regulations for its interior economy."

1814.

1st Battalion.

In January the battalion was cantoned at Ustaritz. On the 3rd of that month the enemy drove in the cavalry pickets between the Joyeuse and Bidouse Rivers, and attacked posts occupied by the 3rd Division and a Portuguese brigade, compelling the latter to retire towards Briscous. The ground vacated by the Portuguese was immediately occupied by two divisions of the enemy. On the 6th these were attacked by the 3rd and 4th Divisions, and dislodged without loss on the side of the British, the posts being "replaced where they had been." The troops were then ordered to return to their cantonments, owing to the weather rendering further operations at the moment impossible.

On the 18th of January 1 sergeant and 4 rank and file were taken prisoners of war "when on a foraging party."

During the month of January 3 sergeants and 33 rank and file were discharged as unfit for further service.

On the 14th of February hostilities were resumed. Early the following morning the 4th Division took possession of the heights of La Bastide, and remained in observation of the Lower Bidouse until the 23rd, when, together with the 7th Division, it attacked the fortified posts of Hartingues and Oeyregave, on the left bank of the Gave de Pau, and compelled the enemy to retire at first within the *tête de pont* at Peyrehorade, and later to a strong position near Orthes on the Gave de Pau.

On the 25th of February the battalion was encamped at Sordes.

The present fit were then : 26 officers, 35 sergeants, 11 drummers, and 465 rank and file. The sick absent consisted of 1 officer, 10 sergeants, 1 drummer, and 168 rank and file.

On the morning of the 26th of February the Gave de Pau was crossed by the 4th and 7th Divisions near its junction with the Gave d'Oleron. The same evening the left of the Allied army also crossed the Gave de Pau without encountering any opposition.

On the morning of the 27th Wellington ascertained by observation that Soult had placed his army in such a position as to give extraordinary advantages to his flanks. His right was posted on a height on the high-road to Dax, and occupying the village of St. Boës, and his left on the heights above Orthes. At 9 a.m. that day the general movement began. On the left, where the principal attack was to be delivered, the 4th and 7th Divisions were ordered to turn and attack the enemy's right. After a fierce struggle the 4th Division carried the village of St. Boës, but owing to the narrowness of the ridge, which formed the only approach to the enemy's position, the troops could not deploy to attack the heights, although they made five attempts to do so, experiencing all the time a concentric fire of round shot and grape.

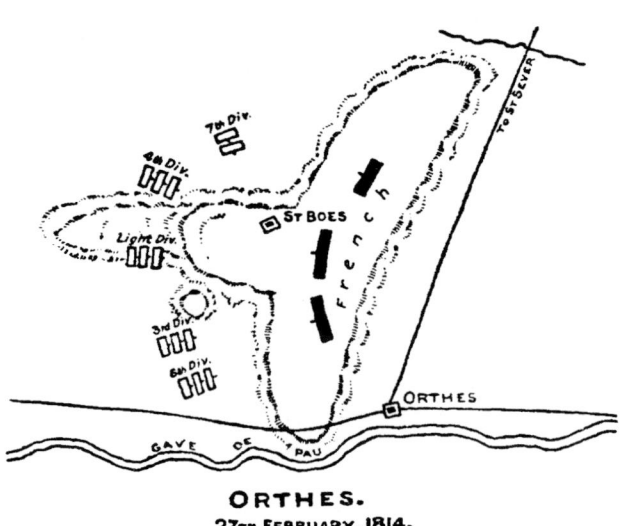

ORTHES.
27th FEBRUARY, 1814.

Wellington thereupon directed the 3rd and 6th Divisions, together with Colonel Barnard's brigade of the Light Division, to attack the left of the heights upon which the enemy's right stood, with the happy result that the French were dislodged from the heights and the narrow pass behind St. Boës opened, through which the 4th and 7th Divisions quickly poured.

The passage of the Gave above Orthes having been forced by Sir Rowland Hill completed the discomfiture of the enemy, who at first retired in admirable order, but being later on overtaken by the

7th Hussars, part of Hill's cavalry, his retreat developed into a rout, in which scores of the soldiers threw away their arms and knapsacks, and the desertions ran into thousands. The 4th Division was highly commended by Wellington in his dispatch for its distinguished conduct in the attack of St. Boës, and its subsequent endeavours to carry the right of the heights.

The casualties of the battalion in the battle of Orthes fought on the 27th of February were: 1 sergeant, 15 rank and file killed; Captains Henry Wynne, Charles Jolliffe, and Lieutenant Isaac Harris severely wounded; and 6 sergeants and 69 rank and file wounded.

On the 15th of May 1821 the regiment was permitted to bear the word "ORTHES" on its colour.

Soult continued his retreat during the night, and on reaching the Adour at St. Sever, crossed it and destroyed the bridge. He then halted to reorganise his army.

On the 1st of March the Allied army crossed the Adour, and had hardly done so before a violent storm came on, which filled the rivers and torrents, carrying away the bridges of pontoons and so cutting off all communications for the movements of troops, supplies, etc.

To repair the evil Wellington was obliged to halt. During this pause, he was informed through a reliable channel that if he approached Bordeaux with 3,000 men the city would declare for the Bourbons. The advantage of having it on his side was that his left flank would then be in no danger of attack from the line of the Garonne.

On the 8th of March Beresford set out for Bordeaux with the 4th and 7th Divisions and Vivian's cavalry; on reaching there on the 12th the French garrison withdrew. The inhabitants received him with acclamation. The flag of the House of Bourbon was unfurled and Louis XVIII proclaimed.

Leaving the 7th Division there and three squadrons of cavalry, Beresford set out on the 16th of March with the 4th Division and the remainder of the cavalry to rejoin Wellington, whose headquarters was reached on the 18th. The same day the Allied force moved forward, and coming up with the enemy under Clausel at Tarbes on the 20th of March, drove him from that town, with the result that the main French army under Soult, which had taken up a position at Oleac, a short distance behind Tarbes, retired precipitately under cover of darkness, and continued its retreat until Toulouse was reached on the 24th of March.

On the following day the 4th Division reached St. Foix. During the month ending the 25th of February, 1 sergeant and 23 rank and file of the battalion had died.

On the 26th the 4th Division entered St. Lys and took post on the Auch road facing the French army covering Toulouse. On the 28th the enemy retired into Toulouse.

The River Garonne, which had been very full and rapid, subsided sufficiently on the 3rd of April to enable a bridge to be laid over it near Grenade next day, when the 3rd, 4th, and 6th Divisions, together with three brigades of cavalry, crossed it.

Wellington, having reconnoitred the ground, decided to attack the Mont Rave ridge on the 10th of April, the 4th and 6th Divisions being directed to attack St. Sypière, which was the southern summit of that range, and on which a strong redoubt had been constructed, which covered and protected the enemy's right flank. To achieve its object the division had in the first place to carry the village of Mont Blanc, and march in column parallel to and within range of the Mont Rave redoubt. The attack was driven home and the enemy ejected from the height, "where directed rockets, whose noise and dreadful aspect were unknown before, spread dismay among them."

The two divisions under Beresford then continued their movement along the ridge, and, together with General Pack's brigade of the 6th Division, carried two principal redoubts and fortified houses in the enemy's centre. Desperate but unsuccessful efforts were made to regain these redoubts, but were repulsed with considerable loss, and soon the whole range of heights was in possession of the Allies.

Marshal Beresford, in reporting to Wellington on the conduct of the 4th Division in this battle, observes as follows: "Their formation for the attack under the fire of the enemy was most regular, and their advance most gallant, and consequently successful."

Wellington in turn makes the following reference to the division in question in his dispatch of the 12th of April 1814: "The 4th Division, although exposed on their march along the enemy's front to a galling fire, were not so much engaged as the 6th, and did not suffer so much: but they conducted themselves with their usual gallantry."

The battalion's loss at Toulouse on the 10th of April was insignificant, being only 1 private killed and 7 wounded.

The regiment was permitted on the 15th of May 1821 to add the word "TOULOUSE" to its battle honours.

On the night of the 11th of April Soult abandoned Toulouse, cutting the bridges over the canal and the Upper Ers. On the following morning Wellington entered the town, and found the white flag flying, the statues of Bonaparte overturned, and a large proportion of the inhabitants wearing white cockades and scarves. The same afternoon he received intelligence that the Allies had entered Paris on the 31st of March, and that a Provisional Government had been set up which declared that Napoleon had forfeited the throne.

No time was lost by Wellington in communicating to Soult the trend of events, which at first he refused to credit. On the 19th a convention was signed for the suspension of hostilities.

"Thus was the war concluded. . . . It was by the persevering efforts of Great Britain in the Peninsular War, the courage of her troops, and the skill of her great commander that Bonaparte's fortune had been checked at its height, and successfully resisted."

On the 25th of April the battalion was encamped at Castera. During the previous month Captain Thomas Farmer, Lieutenants Charles Fryer and John Clyde, 2nd Lieutenants George Dunn, George Allan, George Stainforth, 2 sergeants, 3 drummers, and 87 privates joined from the 2nd battalion. Lieutenant-Colonel H. W. Ellis, commanding the 1st battalion of the regiment, was, some days later, employed as president of a General Court-martial which sat upon a deputy assistant commissary-general. The verdict was not at all to Wellington's liking, as he wrote to Lieutenant-Colonel Ellis in the following terms:

"If conduct such as that of which Mr. . . . has been upon clear evidence found guilty be passed over, it will be impossible to maintain the necessary discipline of the army, which mainly depends upon Courts Martial performing their duty, and not being misled by false principles of lenity. I beg, therefore, to submit to the Court the propriety of withdrawing that recommendation."

On the 25th of May the battalion was at Condom, about midway between Toulouse and Bordeaux.

From Condom it proceeded to Blancfort, in the neighbourhood of Bordeaux, which was reached on the 6th of June, and on the 14th it embarked at Pauillac for Plymouth in H.M.S. *Egmont*, then lying off Verdon Roads in the Gironde, and reached Plymouth Sound on the 25th of June. The captain's log tersely records: "Moored ship, boats employed disembarking the troops, came alongside lighter for the troops." On landing, the regiment mustered 4 captains, 15 lieutenants, 7 2nd lieutenants, 3 staff, 36 sergeants, 39 corporals, 13 drummers, 437 privates, having left in the Peninsula, either sick or on command, 9 sergeants, 5 corporals, 167 privates, prisoners of war 40. Lieutenant-Colonel Ellis, 2 captains, 1 lieutenant, and 10 privates did not accompany the battalion, as they were attending a court-martial at Pauillac in France.

It proceeded on the 5th of July to Ivybridge, on the 12th to Dorchester, and on the 16th to the "New Military Barracks" at Gosport, where it remained until March in the following year.

The battalion was inspected on the 18th of October by Major-General Howard. He reported that on the reduction of the 2nd battalion a regimental school would be established in the regiment, and that the schoolmaster of the 2nd battalion would be appointed to it.

In October it received from the 2nd battalion 26 sergeants, 21 corporals, 23 drummers, and 377 privates. This brought the strength of the battalion up to 1,197 non-commissioned officers and men, the establishment being 1,176.

Lieutenant-Colonel Ellis, who had been promoted (4th of June 1814) to the rank of colonel by brevet, was appointed a Knight Commander of the Bath, and received the honorary distinction of a cross and one clasp; Lieutenant-Colonel Sutton, also colonel by brevet, and Knight Commander of the Bath, a cross and three clasps for his services in the Portuguese army; Lieutenant-Colonel Pearson, a medal; Brevet Lieutenant-Colonel T. Dalmer, a medal and one clasp; Brevet Lieutenant-Colonel Hill, attached to the Portuguese army, a cross; Brevet Lieutenant-Colonel Hurford, a medal and one clasp; Captain J. T. Leahy, who commanded the regiment at the storming of Badajoz, a medal.

In addition to the official recognition of Colonel Ellis's great services to the State, the inhabitants of the county and city of Worcester presented him with a gold vase and the freedom of the city. The following is a description of the proceedings extracted from contemporary newspaper accounts:

"WELCH FUSILEERS.

"Tribute to Valour.

"Presentation of a Vase to Colonel Ellis, of the 23rd Welsh Fusiliers.

"Worcester, Dec. 29. A liberal subscription having been entered into by the county and city of Worcester, for the above purpose, the ceremony of presenting this honorable memorial took place on Monday, 26th December, in the Guildhall, the Earl of Coventry attending about one o'clock for that purpose, when his Lordship addressed the Colonel as follows :

" ' Colonel Ellis—I feel proud to have the honour of presenting to you this tribute of respect from the county, and your native city of Worcester, in testimony of the high sense they entertain of your meritorious services, so repeatedly displayed in the defence of your country : and I rejoice in this opportunity of expressing our anxious wish that Providence may long preserve the valuable life of a deserving and distinguished officer, who, at so early a period, is justly esteemed an ornament to his country.'

" The Colonel replied as follows :

" ' Amidst the variety of feelings which the partiality of this honourable Assembly has given rise to, none predominates more forcibly than that of gratitude, and, for the first time, I confess renders me susceptible of vanity.

" Unaccustomed to receive public applause, I feel incompetent adequately to convey to you, my Lord, and this respectable Meeting, my acknowledgements for this distinguished mark of your approbation.

" ' The flattering manner with which you have been pleased to receive my services is peculiarly gratifying to me : as it enables me publicly to acknowledge, that I am more indebted to the assistance of my officers and men, than to those personal merits you have been kind enough to attribute to me.

" ' Happily placed at the head of a most distinguished corps, I had only to attach myself to their fate, assured that their enthusiastic bravery would lead to an honourable result. To their exertions I shall ever attribute the distinctions you have this day conferred upon me.

" ' To the memory of my father, however, (whose loss I sustained at an early period of my life) I must, in addition, also attribute this recollection of me : and amidst this assembly I witness those friends, respectable for their years and abilities : and proud indeed am I, amongst that number, to recognise the Noble Lord who heads, in his official capacity, this numerous and flattering assembly of my country, who, this day, by rewarding the exertions of the Sons, pay a tribute of respect to the memory of the father. His talents and urbanity of manners endeared him to an amiable and intelligent society : with less ability, but an equal warmth of heart, I hope, some future day, to solicit a transfer of those bonds of affection, and to live in the same social habits which my Father enjoyed in this city and neighbourhood.

"'I now beg to offer my most sincere thanks for a present, which, in itself, conveys every thing gratifying to me as an officer. Feeling as I do upon the present occasion, I shall make no further comment, than that to the latest period of my life I shall treasure up a present which, while it obliterates every hardship undergone in the cause of my country, acts as an unbounded stimulus to my future exertions, whenever the duties of a soldier may again call me into more active service.'

"This speech excited much applause, and at the conclusion of it Lord Deerhurst proposed three cheers which were heartily acceded to by the Company, who then adjourned to another table, which, through the polite attention of the Mayor, was covered with cake and wine of various descriptions. After partaking of this refreshment, the spectators were again drawn to the former spot, to witness another imposing ceremony. Benjamin Johnson Esq., the Town Clerk, then proceeded to present the Colonel with the freedom of the city, addressing him as follows:

"'Colonel Ellis—In addressing you upon this occasion, it is with great satisfaction I observe, that your great courage, your signal military talents, (the admiration of all around you) so eminently displayed on every part of the Continent, entitle you not only to the highest praise, but to every mark of distinction. Sir, I beg leave to assure you that the Corporation of Worcester, impressed with these sentiments, present you with the Freedom of your City, a City proud of your nativity, in testimony of their approbation for your valorous conduct: wishing you Happiness and long Life, and that Government may advance you to a high command in your profession, the reward so justly due to your long and meritorious services in defence of your King and Country.'

"The Colonel made a suitable reply.

"Besides the Earl of Coventry, the Countess, Lord Deerhurst, the Hon. J. Coventry, and other branches of the family were present. The company would have been more numerous, had not the weather been so unfavourable. The Colonel and a large party dined afterwards at Lord Coventry's seat.

"The Vase which has been presented is completed with singular taste and elegance: it stands on a handsome pedestal, contains many military devices, the arms of the Colonel and the City of Worcester, and does honour to the liberality of the subscribers.

"On one side is the following inscription:

" ' TO

Col. HENRY WALTON ELLIS

OF THE 23RD ROYAL FUSILIERS
THIS TRIBUTE TO HIS MERITORIOUS AND DISTINGUISHED
CONDUCT, DURING FIFTEEN YEARS OF ACTIVE SERVICE
IN HOLLAND, EGYPT, AMERICA, THE WEST INDIES
SPAIN, PORTUGAL AND FRANCE
IS RESPECTFULLY OFFERED BY THE COUNTY,
AND HIS NATIVE CITY OF WORCESTER,
AND PRESENTED AT THEIR DESIRE,
BY THE EARL OF COVENTRY
LORD LIEUTENANT AND RECORDER.

1814.' "

For its services during this war the regiment was permitted on the 29th of March 1815 to add the word "PENINSULA" to those already emblazoned on its colour.

In addition to this honour the 1st battalion received the Royal Authority to bear on the regimental colour and appointments the words "ALBUHERA," "BADAJOZ," "SALAMANCA," "VITTORIA," "PYRENEES," "NIVELLE," "ORTHES," "TOULOUSE," as already narrated in the account of each of these actions.

1814.

2ND BATTALION.

In February the battalion moved to Winchester, the "Welch" in it being 6 officers, 5 sergeants, 6 corporals, 7 drummers, 105 privates. In March it received 68 men from the Militia, and supplied a draft of 2 sergeants, 1 drummer, 90 privates to the 1st battalion. On the 23rd of May it was inspected at Winchester by Major-General William Houston, who in his report states that 75 recruits had joined, and 131 had been received from the Militia. In July it moved to Gosport. On the 24th of October it was disbanded, as will be seen by the following letter addressed to General Richard Grenville, the Colonel of the regiment, viz. :

"Horse Guards, 30th September, 1814.

"Sir,
"His Royal Highness The Prince Regent having been pleased to order, that the 2nd Battalion of the 23rd shall be disbanded on the 24th October next, and it being considered expedient, preparatory to that measure being carried into effect, to relieve it from such men as may not be considered fit for service, or to be transferred to the First Battalion, I have the honor to signify the Commander in Chief's commands, that you will be pleased to cause such men as may be deemed fit subjects to be discharged, to proceed to York Hospital, with the view to their cases being finally decided upon.

"I have the honor to be, etc.,
"R. A. Darling,
"Dep. Adjt. General.

"P.S. You will be pleased to transmit to this Department, the usual report of such men as being unfit for service, you have caused to proceed to York Hospital.
"R. A. D."

In consequence the whole of the officers were placed on half-pay, and 26 sergeants, 21 corporals, 23 drummers, and 377 men were taken on the strength of the 1st battalion.

1815.

The "wonderful and unexpected" events that occurred in France, arising out of the first abdication of Napoleon, and his escape from Elba on the 26th of February this year, again placed the fate of Europe "under the guardianship" of the Duke of Wellington, who was appointed to the command of His Majesty's forces serving on the continent of Europe on the 28th of March.

Consequent upon the military authorities deciding at the last moment to send an additional brigade, consisting of the 3rd battalion of the 14th, the 23rd, and 51st Regiments to France, under the command of Lieutenant-Colonel (Brevet Colonel) H. H. Mitchell of the 51st Foot, ten companies of the regiment, under Lieutenant-Colonel (Brevet Colonel) Sir H. W. Ellis, K.C.B., embarked at Gosport on the 23rd, on board the transports *Ariel*, *Percival*, and *Poniana*, which sailed on the 25th and arrived in the Downs next day. On the 29th the battalion transhipped, and landed at Ostend on the 30th of March.

On embarking the regiment numbered 42 officers, 31 sergeants, 24 drummers, 36 corporals, 611 privates. The following were left at the depôt, Gosport: 1 captain, 2 lieutenants, 1 2nd lieutenant, 14 sergeants, 11 drummers, 15 corporals, 190 privates.

On the 31st of March the regiment proceeded by canal boats to Bruges, and thence to Ghent, which was reached on the 2nd of April. It arrived at Oudenarde on the 7th, was reviewed on the 20th, with the rest of the brigade, by the Duke of Wellington, and moved thence into cantonments at Grammont on the 24th of April.

The army was then organised in divisions and brigades. Colonel Mitchell's brigade, designated the 4th British Brigade, constituted part of the 4th Division (British and Hanoverians) under the command of Lieutenant-General the Hon. Sir Charles Colville.

At the beginning of May Lieutenant-General Lord Hill moved Mitchell's brigade to Renaix, " in order to give Sir Charles Colville an opportunity of attending to it before active operations commenced." In accordance with Wellington's order of the 9th of that month, the brigade returned to Grammont with the object of being within easy access of Enghien or Hal, should the enemy move forward. It remained at Grammont until early on the morning of the 16th of June, when it set out for Enghien, and on reaching there received a fresh route for Braine-le-Compte, which, after a trying march, was reached late that night, the weary soldiers, bivouacking in a wheat-field, being " persecuted " by torrents of rain.

Next morning, by good luck, it was the first brigade of the 4th Division to leave there, as on reaching Nivelles it learned that by Wellington's order such troops of the 4th Division as were either at Braine-le-Compte or marching to Nivelles were to assemble at the former place and await orders, while all the other troops were to retire without delay to Waterloo.

Had not Mitchell's brigade outstripped this order, its fate would have been to be posted on the memorable 18th of June on the flank of the army at Hal, about seven miles from Waterloo, seeing nothing, and hearing only the first reverberation of the guns.

Mitchell's brigade, on reaching Nivelles, joined the 2nd Division under Lieutenant-General Sir H. Clinton, and both proceeded north by the Brussels road, threading their way through men, guns, wagons, etc., withdrawing from Quatre Bras, which had been fought the day before. Braine-la-Leud was reached on the evening of the 17th of June, and there the battalion and the other regiments composing Mitchell's brigade bivouacked for the night in torrents of rain, which drenched the unfortunate soldiers, who were lying out in the open, to the skin.

Early on the morning of the 18th the remainder of the 4th Division which was at Braine-le-Compte marched to Hal, as Wellington was of opinion that Napoleon would make an effort to turn his right flank and press forward to Brussels by the road that ran through Hal. To Mitchell was allotted the task of holding in check any pronounced movement of the enemy in that direction.

Wellington's army, numbering some 67,000 men, of whom about one-third were British, was established on both sides of the high-road running from Charleroi to Brussels, on a ridge in front of the forest of Soignies, with his reserves concealed by the folds of the ground. Napoleon's army, consisting of about 61,000 troops, was posted on an opposite ridge barely, if at all, concealed.

Shortly before noon the battle commenced, by Napoleon sending forward a column under his brother Prince Jerome, supported by General Foy's division, against the château and enclosures of Hougoumont, that stood about 300 yards in front of the right centre of the Allied line.

After several desperate onsets the French succeeded in gaining the open wood, covering an area of about four acres, that encircled the château, part of the orchard, and a short avenue leading to the Nivelles-Waterloo Road. Although repeated attacks were made during the day, and even as late as 8 p.m., the enemy could not carry the château itself, or the walled garden belonging to it.

While the first attack upon the château was at its height, Marshal Ney had been occupied in massing 20,000 men in four columns under d'Erlon for an attack upon the British centre and left. On Napoleon giving the signal to advance about 1.30 p.m., three of d'Erlon's columns moved forward in echelon of divisions, the left leading, towards the Allies' centre, while the remaining column advanced against the left flank. One of the three columns referred to gained possession of the orchard and garden of La Haie Sainte, and twice succeeded in setting on fire the farmhouse, which, however, was not captured until about 6 p.m.

Another French column succeeded in driving back Major-General Count de Bylandt's Dutch-Belgian division. Luckily, in rear of the Dutch-Belgians stood Kempt's and Pack's brigades of Picton's (5th) division. Taking advantage of the French columns deploying into line, these two brigades poured in a withering fire, and then charged with the bayonet, which caused the enemy's ranks to reel. Their discomfiture was completed by Major-General Sir W. Ponsonby's "Union Brigade," consisting of the 1st Royal Dragoons, the Scots Greys, and the Inniskillings, which, passing through spaces offered for them by the infantry, "swept down upon the shaken troops in one of the most brilliant and successful charges in the annals of cavalry." The panic-stricken French were mown down with fearful carnage.

About 4 p.m. another phase of the battle began, when Ney launched forty squadrons of cavalry against that portion of the right centre which was posted to the west of the Charleroi road. The squares into which Wellington rapidly formed his infantry to meet this charge resisted all efforts to break them. Four times the French cavalry advanced with loud shouts, but instead of charging the squares in front, they rode around, and between them, in the hope of enveloping the infantry. The rattling musketry fire which they encountered in all directions threw the squadrons into disorder, and compelled them, exhausted and greatly diminished, to draw off with heavy losses in killed, wounded, and prisoners.

The only success that attended Napoleon's efforts during the day was when at 6 p.m. La Haie Sainte, which was stubbornly defended by 380 men of the King's German Legion under Major Baring, was captured by the enemy, mainly owing to the supply of ammunition becoming exhausted. Napoleon now determined to make one last effort for victory before the Prussians, who were pushing in his detachments upon Planchenoit, arrived upon the scene. He ordered Ney with the reserve, consisting of the veterans of the Old Guard supported by cavalry and artillery, to attack the Allied line between La Haie Sainte and Hougoumont. Advancing in two bodies, one of them moved in the direction of Maitland's Brigade of Guards, which was lying in four-deep formation concealed along the ridge.

When the enemy had reached within about twenty paces of the brigade, up sprang the men at Wellington's order, and poured in a volley which laid low about 300 of the enemy. The combined fire of the field batteries and infantry effectually prevented the column from deploying. Advantage of the situation was taken by Maitland to charge with the bayonet, which caused Napoleon's veterans to retreat in confusion. A similar fate befell the second column, due in great measure to the energy and resource of Colonel Colborne of the 52nd Regiment, in Major-General Adam's brigade of the 2nd Division.

What followed is graphically described by Colonel Samuel Rice of the 51st Regiment, in *The Life of a Regimental Officer during the Great War* 1793-1815:

"Barely four hundred yards separated the head of the leading French column from the British position, when Sir John Colborne, commanding the 52nd, of Adam's Brigade, swiftly realised the situation. Acting on his own initiative, he gave the order to his regiment to advance in quick time towards the flank of the attacking columns, and the long red line moved forward in perfect order. Then suddenly he wheeled his whole line up, so as to face the flank of the columns, and threw out a company of skirmishers with orders to open fire on the Imperial Guard. The Frenchmen, thus challenged, halted and replied, and by so doing brought destruction upon themselves, for Colborne's line was ready for them. The ranks closed up: the bugles rang out: and with one mighty roar from the regiment, eight hundred British bayonets bore down on the veterans of France. But the latter did not stand to receive the charge: the sudden onslaught appalled them: the leading battalions broke and fled to the rear, and in their flight carried with them the whole of the Imperial Guard—the flower of the French army, and Napoleon's last hope. No time was given to them to re-form, for the remainder of Adam's brigade and Maitland's Guards opened fire upon them from the higher ground as they fled: and Wellington, with the light of victory in his eyes, ordered a general advance towards La Belle Alliance, where Napoleon and Ney could be seen rallying their men for a last stand."

Before, however, dealing with the advance of the British after Napoleon's final attack, the part played by the 23rd up to this point in the great battle will now be narrated.

At the time when Waterloo was fought, an avenue of fine trees extended from the Château of Hougoumont to the Nivelles road. In the part of this avenue that abutted on to the road the light company of the regiment was posted. The remaining companies were stationed to the left of the Nivelles road on the reverse slope immediately under the crest of the main ridge in rear of the 2nd Brigade of Guards. On the latter being moved as reinforcements to Hougoumont, their ground was occupied by the 23rd and some Brunswick troops. The regiment remained in square all day, owing to the numerous attacks of cavalry from time to time.

The heavy repulse of the enemy's final attack enabled Wellington to attack in turn. In this forward movement the regiment, under the command of Major (Brevet Lieutenant-Colonel) T. Dalmer, in consequence of Lieutenant-Colonel (Brevet Colonel) Sir H. W. Ellis being wounded, advanced as a support to the right of the attack. Comte de Lobau holding out gallantly for some time at Planchenoit enabled the French to retire, though in great disorder. The pursuit of the French was then taken up by the Prussians, " the British soldiers being tired to death."

Lieutenant-General Sir H. Clinton, under whose orders Mitchell's brigade acted throughout the 18th of June, in writing to Lieutenant-General Lord Hill the next day, refers to it in the following terms: "The brigade of the 4th Division commanded by Colonel Mitchell having been placed for the moment under my orders, I am happy in having to make the same favourable report of the conduct of every corps composing the brigade." The battalion bivouacked for the night close to La Belle Alliance.

The following letter from Major R. P. Holmes of the regiment, who as a subaltern fought at Waterloo, which is contained in the *Waterloo Letters* edited by Major-General H. T. Siborne, will be read with interest:

"Major R. P. Holmes, 23rd Fusiliers.
"[Lieutenant, 23rd Fusiliers.]

"WINCHESTER, *April 29th*, 1835.

"To the best of my recollection the 23rd Fusiliers was the only Regiment of the Division to which they were attached absolutely engaged. Our Brigade was stationed somewhere about Hal watching the road leading from Lille to Brussels. The two Regiments brigaded with the 23rd, viz. 51st and 3rd battalion 14th, remained during the day in the second line, I think on the right of the road leading to Nivelles.

"During the night of the 17th June the 23rd bivouacked in a rye-field near the village of Merbe Braine, but early the following morning moved into the second line on the left of the Nivelles road, in rear of a Battalion of Guards, where the Regiment deployed into line and lay on the ground, in consequence of the French having placed some Guns on the Nivelles road which killed one of our Captains and wounded some men.

"The Guards in the front line having been withdrawn to the support of Hougoumont, the 23rd formed square and moved up into that line. In consequence of the numerous attacks of Cavalry we remained in square the whole day. I only recollect one attack of Infantry (in column) during the day, which did not alter our formation. Some Regiment in our rear, I think the 71st, deployed into line and advanced with the 23rd Square (a wing on each flank) some distance down the slope of the hill. The Infantry having given way, a charge of Cavalry immediately followed. The Regiment in line ran into square to our right, a little in advance and nearer to the garden of Hougoumont.

"I believe the Cavalry that attacked these two Squares were nearly annihilated. Having suffered much from the Squares they attempted to retreat by the Nivelles road, which was thickly lined with skirmishers, and the Officer who commanded the left company of the Regiment stationed on that road assured me at the time [that] scarcely a man succeeded in making his escape.

"After this charge, finding that we were suffering both from the French Guns and the fire from the garden of Hougoumont, we again retired to our former position, where we remained until the attack on the centre by the French Guards, when we again advanced some short distance in square, then deployed and advanced in line; but finding nothing to oppose us, we wheeled by Companies to the right and moved in column on the right of the Charleroi road to about ——

where we bivouacked for the night, and on the following morning retraced our steps and rejoined the two other Regiments of the Brigade, and marched upon Cambray by the Nivelles road.

"Yours, &c.,
R. P. HOLMES,
"*Major, 23rd Fusiliers.*"

For some reason or other Mitchell's brigade was singled out as a target for artillery fire on the 18th of June, which is evident by the following extract from *Fifty Years of my Life*, by the Earl of Albemarle:

"Fifteen years after the battle I was present at Paris at the Grands Couverts, the annual dinner which the older Bourbon Princes were in the habit of eating in public. A French officer on duty entered upon a subject of his own choosing, but one generally avoided by his countrymen—'Waterloo.' He told me that he was an artillery officer posted in that action on the extreme left of the French line, and that his orders were to fire upon three British regiments, the colours of which were respectively blue, buff, and green, thus proving, beyond all doubt, that it was against our brigade [Mitchell's] that his practice had been directed."

The strength of the regiment on the morning of the battle of Waterloo was as follows: 3 field officers, 10 captains, 25 subalterns, 6 staff, 35 sergeants, 23 drummers, 639 rank and file; on command, 3 sergeants and 3 rank and file; sick, 3 rank and file.

The loss suffered by the regiment at Waterloo was as follows:

Killed.—Brevet Major Joseph Hawtyn, Captains Charles Jolliffe and Thomas Farmer, Lieutenant G. Fensham, 2 sergeants and 9 rank and file.

Wounded.—Brevet Colonel Sir H. W. Ellis (died on the 20th of June), Brevet Lieutenant-Colonel J. Humphrey Edward Hill, Captain Henry Cavendish Johnson, Lieutenants George Fielding, W. A. Griffiths, John Clyde (died of his wounds on the 3rd of July), Anthony G. Sidley, 7 sergeants, and 71 rank and file.

In the afternoon, when the regiment was formed in square to meet the repeated charges of the French cuirassiers, Colonel Ellis, while on horseback in the centre of the square, was struck by a musket ball in the right breast.

"Feeling himself faint from loss of blood, he calmly desired an opening might be made in the square, and rode to the rear. At a short distance from the field he was thrown from his horse while in the act of leaping a ditch : here he was found soon afterwards, much exhausted, and conveyed to a neighbouring out-house, where his wound was dressed. In the course of the night of the 19th, the hovel in which he was lodged unfortunately caught fire, and he was with difficulty rescued from the flames by Assistant Surgeon Munro, of the regiment, but exhausted by so many shocks, he soon after expired."

A monument to his memory was erected at a cost of £1,200 by the officers and men of the regiment in the cathedral of Worcester, which was his native city, although he was actually born at Cambray. The following is the inscription on it :

" IN MEMORY OF
COLONEL SIR HENRY WALTON ELLIS, K.C.B.
A NATIVE OF THIS CITY,
WHO, AT AN EARLY AGE, ENTERED THE TWENTY-THIRD REGIMENT,
OR, ROYAL WELSH FUSILIERS,
THEN COMMANDED BY HIS FATHER, MAJOR-GENERAL JOHN JOYNER ELLIS,
AND AFTERWARDS LED ON TO HONOURABLE DISTINCTION BY HIMSELF,
DURING SEVEN YEARS OF UNEXAMPLED MILITARY RENOWN :
HAVING RECEIVED EIGHT WOUNDS, AND RENDERED SERVICES AS IMPORTANT
AS THEY WERE BRILLIANT,
IN HOLLAND, EGYPT, THE WEST INDIES, AMERICA, SPAIN, PORTUGAL, AND
FRANCE,
HE FELL BY A MUSKET-SHOT AT THE HEAD OF HIS REGIMENT,
ALMOST IN THE GLORIOUS MOMENT WHICH ANNOUNCED VICTORY TO
GREAT BRITAIN, AND PEACE TO EUROPE, ON THE MEMORABLE
PLAINS OF WATERLOO.
HE DIED OF HIS WOUNDS ON THE 20TH OF JUNE, 1815, AGED 32 YEARS.
HIS LOSS WAS LAMENTED, AND HIS WORTH RECORDED, BY HIS
ILLUSTRIOUS COMMANDER, WELLINGTON,
IN WORDS THAT WILL PERISH ONLY WITH HISTORY ITSELF.
THIS MONUMENT WAS ERECTED
BY THE OFFICERS, NON-COMMISSIONED OFFICERS, AND PRIVATES
OF THE ROYAL WELSH FUSILIERS,
AS A TRIBUTE OF THEIR RESPECT AND AFFECTION TO THE MEMORY OF A
LEADER, NOT MORE DISTINGUISHED FOR VALOUR AND CONDUCT IN THE
FIELD, THAN BELOVED FOR EVERY GENEROUS AND SOCIAL VIRTUE."

COLONEL SIR HENRY WALTON ELLIS, K.C.B.
From a miniature at Wrexham Barracks. Block supplied by "Country Life."

The following extract from the Duke of Wellington's dispatch of the 29th of June 1815 shows the high opinion he entertained of him:

"Your Lordship will see in the enclosed lists, the names of some valuable officers lost to His Majesty's service. Among those I cannot avoid to mention Colonel Cameron, of the Ninety-second, and Colonel Sir Henry Ellis, of the Twenty-third regiment, to whose conduct I have frequently drawn your Lordship's attention, and who at last fell, distinguishing themselves at the head of the brave troops which they commanded.

"Notwithstanding the glory of the occasion, it is impossible not to lament such men, both on account of the public and as friends."

In a letter written by " a British officer of the 23rd Regiment, dated June 20th 1816, to his friends in Dumfries " with reference to his late lamented Colonel, occurs the following:

"Almost his last words to me were—I am happy—I am content—I have done my duty. I buried him, on the evening of the 23rd of June, with honours of war, on the mound of the only windmill at Braine-la-Leud, about one mile and a half to the rear of the right of the position. To show how much he was beloved by his men and officers, I may give the following anecdote: Among several of the soldiers of his regiment, who were at the same farm-house with him, mortally wounded, and inquiring anxiously after their Colonel, there was one who supported a very bad character, and he had been frequently punished. To this man I said, to learn his attachment,—'He is just dead; but why should you care? You cannot forget how oft he caused your back to be bared?' 'Sir,' replied he, his eyes assuming a momentary flash and his cheek a passing glow, 'I deserved the punishment, else he would never have punished me.' With these words, he turned his head a little from me, and burst into tears."

The regiment was on the 23rd of November in this year permitted to bear the word "WATERLOO" on its colour and appointments. A medal was conferred on each officer and soldier, and the privilege in the case of subalterns of being allowed two years towards the attainment of the additional shilling per day which they received after seven years' service, and in that of the men of reckoning two years' service towards additional pay and pension on discharge; they were thenceforth known as "Waterloo men."

On the morning after the battle, when all was as still as the grave, the regiment, which had bivouacked at La Belle Alliance, marched back and rejoined its brigade, which then advanced to Nivelles. Mons was reached on the 20th, where the following 2nd Corps General Order was issued:

"NIVELLES,
"20th June, 1815.

"Lieut.-General Lord Hill has great satisfaction in congratulating the Troops on the brilliant success attending their gallant exertions in the action with the enemy on the 18th inst. The highly distinguished conduct of the 2nd Division and Colonel Mitchell's Brigade of the 4th Division, who had the good fortune to be employed in this memorable action, meet His Lordship's fullest approbation, and he begs that Lieut.-General Sir Henry Clinton, commanding the 2nd Division, Colonel Gold, commanding the artillery of the 2nd Corps, Major-General Adam, Colonels Du Platt, Mitchell and Halkett, commanding Brigades, Major Sympler, commanding troops of Horse Artillery, K.G.L., Captain Napier, to whose lot it fell to command the nine pounder Brigade in the 2nd Division, on the death of Captain Bolton, will accept his best thanks for their exemplary conduct, and they will be pleased to convey his sentiments to the Officers, Non-Commissioned Officers and men of their respective commands.

"Amongst the deaths His Lordship has sincerely to lament that of Lieutenant-Colonel Currie, Assistant Adjutant General, and Captain Bolton, Royal Artillery, and he trusts that the wounds received by Major-General Adam, Colonels Du Platt, Sir H. W. Ellis, and Reynolds and the other officers who were wounded will not long deprive him of their services.

"NOEL HILL, *Lieut.-Colonel,*
"*Assistant Adjutant General.*"

The regiment arrived at Valenciennes on the 21st, and Cateau-Cambrésis next day. While there the following order from Lieutenant-General Sir Charles Colville was read at the head of each regiment composing the 4th (Mitchell's) Brigade:

"Lieutenant-General Sir Charles Colville cannot deny himself the satisfaction of adding to those of Lord Hill, his most hearty congratulations to Colonel Mitchell and the 4th Brigade, on the share they so fortunately had on the glorious and ever memorable battle of the 18th instant.

"From every statement it appears that the 23rd and 51st Regiments acted fully up to their former high character, while the very young battalion of the 14th displayed a gallantry and steadiness becoming veteran troops.

"An acquaintance of many years with Colonel Sir H. W. Ellis has fully impressed the Lieutenant-General with the loss to His Majesty's service, and to society which his death from wounds has occasioned.

"The loss of his brother officers who have shared his fate is also such as he cannot pass over, without offering his condolence to the 23rd Regiment on their loss the sense of the occasion alone can reconcile.

"W. L. DARLING, *Assistant Adjutant General.*"

On the 24th the 4th Division proceeded to Cambray, which was occupied by the same day. The regiment entered the town by an old breach adjoining the Paris gate, with the loss of 2nd Lieutenant William Leebody and one private killed, two privates wounded. The following day the citadel surrendered. There were then present 1 major, 3 captains, 14 lieutenants, 4 2nd lieutenants, 6 staff, 26 sergeants, 22 drummers, 37 corporals, and 504 rank and file. Two sergeants and 54 privates joined from the depôt.

On the 25th of June Colonel Mitchell issued the following Brigade Order:

"PROVILLE, 25*th June*, 1815.

"Colonel Mitchell requests that commanding officers of regiments will return his thanks to the officers, non-commissioned officers, and men of the 14th, 23rd, and 51st regiments for their gallant conduct in the attack of the town of Cambrai yesterday evening, and their steady behaviour after carrying the walls equally merits his approbation.

"(signed) G. BLACK, M.B."

The 4th Division left Cambray on the 26th of June, and marching via Douay, Puzeaux, Petit Crève-Cœur, Clermont, Chantilly, Aubervilliers, reached the Bois de Boulogne on the 4th of July. On the 3rd the following Division Order was issued:

"Sergeant Smith, 23rd Regiment, or R. W. Fusiliers, is appointed Assistant Baggage Master to the 4th Division of Infantry, vice Sergeant-Major Morrissey, killed in action.

"(signed) W. L. DARLING, *Assistant Adjutant General.*"

On the 5th of July Lieutenant W. P. Lloyd, 2nd Lieutenants H. P. Pemberton and J. Drury, 2 sergeants, 1 drummer, and 52 rank and file joined the regiment from the depôt, Albany Barracks, Isle of Wight. From the Bois de Boulogne the regiment marched to Neuilly, in the neighbourhood of which it was encamped until the 30th of October, when it went into cantonments. On the 20th of July Lieutenant-Colonel Thomas Dalmer succeeded to the command of the battalion, vice Colonel Sir H. W. Ellis, died of wounds.

The distribution of prize-money for the battle of Waterloo and the capture of Paris was for the regimental ranks in the following proportion, avoiding fractions of a penny:

	£	s.	d.
Each Field Officer	433	2	4
„ Captain	90	7	3
„ subaltern	34	14	9
„ sergeant	19	4	4
The rank and file, each	2	11	4

Lieutenant-General the Hon. Sir Lowry Cole having now joined the army, the Royal Welch Fusiliers were, at his request, transferred to the 6th Division, in which they were again brigaded with the 7th Royal Fusiliers, their associates in so many victories. This was the outcome of a correspondence between Lieutenant-General Sir Lowry Cole and the Duke of Wellington, as will be seen from the following:

On the 28th of May 1815 Lieutenant-General Sir Lowry Cole, on his appointment to command the 6th Division, addressed the following request to the Duke of Wellington that his division might resume its old Peninsula number as the Fourth: and also that he might have as many of his old regiments as possible, especially the 23rd Fusiliers, which was then attached to Colville's 4th Division.

"MY DEAR LORD,

"Having at length received orders to join your Grace's Army, may I request to be appointed to the 6th Division in preference to the 5th as I cannot help feeling a very strong partiality for those regiments which composed the 6th in Spain, and I understand that General Lambert's Brigade of which the 20th and 40th form a part are already attached to the 6th Division: and that the Brigade daily expected from America among which are the 7th Fusiliers, are likewise to be attached to the 6th Division, and if, without inconvenience to the service, the 23rd Fusiliers which have been for some time in Flanders could be added to it I should have 4 of my old regiments with me, a circumstance by which I should feel much gratified and obliged. I trust my Lord you will not think this a ridiculous feeling on my part, as I am convinced I am more likely to meet your future approbation with officers who are well acquainted with me and whose merits I can appreciate than with entire strangers.

"I could add another wish which perhaps your Grace may not think quite so reasonable, namely, that the Division might, if possible, resume its old name of the 4th Division, one so often sanctioned by your approbation and both Sir T. Picton and myself are considerably senior to all the Lieut.-Generals in command of Divisions.

"I remain, etc.,
"LOWRY COLE."

The reply of the Duke is so laudatory of the Royal Welch that it is here quoted in full.

"BRUSSELS,
"June 2nd, 1815.

"MY DEAR COLE,
"I wish I could bring everything together as I had it when I took leave of the Army at Bordeaux, I would engage that we should not be the last in the race: but as it is I must manage matters as well as I can and you may depend upon it, I will give you as many of your old troops as I can lay my hands upon.

"I saw the 23rd the other day and I never saw any regiment in such order. They were not strong but it was the most complete and handsome military body I ever looked at. I shall find it very difficult to get General Colville to part with it, however I will do what I can: in the mean time I will settle nothing about the command of the two Divisions till you or Sir T. Picton will arrive.

"I feel your partiality for your old number, which also shall be gratified if I can do it without hurting the feelings of others who have already got your number. It is a symptom of the old spirit we had amongst us: than which we cannot have a better.

"Ever my dear Cole,
"Yours most sincerely,
"WELLINGTON."

I—19

"Neuilly,
"10th July, 1815.

"His Grace the Field Marshal has been pleased to refer to the Lieut.-General the wish of Lieut.-General Sir Lowry Cole that the 23rd Royal Welch Fusiliers may be reunited to the 7th Royal Fusiliers under his command in the 6th Division of the Army.

"Sir Charles Colville unwilling as he is to part with that corps, with which he himself has served so much in the course of the last one and twenty years, could not decline a proposal which brings it again under the same Chief Commanders who have acted so long together to their own honour and the good of the service.

"Having reason to believe therefore that the Royal Welch Fusiliers will be removed from the 4th Division of the Army, the Lieut.-General has only to assure them of his continued good wishes.

"W. L. Darling,
"*Assistant Adjutant General.*"

The following General After Order of the Commander of the 2nd Corps records the high opinion he entertained of the regiment:

"Paris,
"19th July, 1815.

"Lieut.-General Lord Hill cannot allow the 23rd Royal Welch Fusiliers to leave the 2nd Corps without expressing his regret on the occasion, and requesting Lieut.-Colonel Dalmer and the whole Regiment will accept his best thanks for their conduct and services during the period they have been in Sir Charles Colville's Division."

On the 16th of August Volunteer E. T. Ellis was appointed a 2nd lieutenant in the regiment.

On the 24th of July the Allied army of occupation was reviewed by the Emperor of Russia. In Wellington's General Order respecting the disposition of the troops on this occasion he begs that officers may be dressed uniformly and, if possible, according to the King's orders.

In October it was the intention of the Government to leave 20,000 British troops in France. Thereupon the Duke of York, the then Commander-in-Chief, included the 23rd Regiment in a list of those regiments which it was intended should return from France. On this number being increased to 30,000, the Prince Regent decided that the regiment should be one of those to remain in that country.

The regiment was inspected by Major-General Sir M. Power, K.C.B., on the 20th of October at the camp at Neuilly. From his remarks it appears that thirteen additional drummers had been transferred from the 2nd battalion on disbandment; that the officers did not mess together; and that the general health of the regiment was not as satisfactory as he would have wished.

On the 9th of November—the date of the Prince Regent's decision —the strength of the regiment was 671, exclusive of 29 recruits about to join from England.

On the 24th Captain Harrison with Lieutenants Towers, Baillie, and Bouchier arrived at Priel from the regimental depôt with a new set of regimental colours.

The formation of the troops to remain in France was announced in Wellington's General Order of the 30th of November. The 1st battalion of the 7th, the 23rd, and the 1st battalion of the 43rd Regiments were brigaded and numbered the 7th Brigade of Infantry under the command of Major-General Sir J. Kempt. The 1st, 7th, and 8th Brigades composed the 1st Division, which was placed under the command of Major-General the Hon. Sir Lowry Cole. The 3rd battalion of the 14th and 51st Regiments, with whom the 23rd had been recently so intimately associated, returned to England. On the 24th of November the death of Lieutenant F. L. G. Cowell of the regiment took place.

Depôt Company

When on the 23rd of March the regiment embarked for foreign service it left behind it a "depôt company" under Captain J. C. Harrison, with Lieutenants F. Cowell, R. Trotter, H. Pemberton, 14 sergeants, 11 drummers, 15 corporals, and 190 privates. This company was used as a headquarters for the recruiting parties at Dudley, Wrexham, Liverpool, etc. In April the depôt company moved to Newport, Isle of Wight. In July a draft of 1 sergeant and 21 privates was sent to the regiment.

On the 18th of October the company was inspected by Colonel Mainwaring, the effectives being returned as 17 sergeants, 1 drummer, 119 rank and file: total, 137.

APPENDIX I

SUCCESSION OF COLONELS OF THE ROYAL WELCH FUSILIERS

HENRY, [FOURTH] LORD HERBERT OF CHERBURY.
Appointed 16th March 1689.

Son of Richard, second Lord Herbert of Cherbury, and brother of Edward, third Lord. He had been associated with Booth's rising in 1659; was appointed a lieutenant in a company in the Ludlow Garrison, under Richard, Earl of Carbery, 19th May 1665, and Captain 15th January 1667 in the Lord High Admiral's Regiment (afterwards styled " The Duke of York's Maritime Regiment "), then commanded by Sir Chichester Wrey. He served under the Duke of Monmouth as captain of a troop of horse, engaged in the service of France, 1672, but withdrew from the army on succeeding to the peerage in 1678, and was made Custos Rotulorum of Montgomeryshire 20th December 1679. He afterwards joined his cousin Henry Herbert in promoting the Revolution, and was made Cofferer to the Household of King William and Queen Mary. He married Lady Catherine, daughter of Francis Newport, Earl of Bradford. He was authorised by King William III, by a letter dated 16th March 1689, to raise a regiment of foot, afterwards the 23rd, or Royal Welch Fusiliers, for service in Ireland, and appointed its Colonel; he retired, however, from the command, probably on account of ill-health, on 10th April 1689, being succeeded in the colonelcy of the regiment by his cousin Charles Herbert. He died without issue 21st April 1691, and the titles became extinct. A portrait in armour (the hair is red) is now at Powis Castle.

CHARLES HERBERT.
Appointed 10th April 1689.

Younger brother of Arthur Herbert (son of Sir Edward Herbert), created Earl of Torrington by King William III. He was M.P. for Montgomeryshire, and next in succession to the Earldom of Torrington. He appears to have been a captain 15th January 1678 in the Duke of York's Regiment; but the company was reduced in 1679, and we find his name appearing 31st January 1680 as a lieutenant in the same regiment, and as captain 31st August 1683. The title of the regiment was changed in October 1684 to " Duke of York and Albany's Maritime Regiment of Foot," and in February 1685 to " Prince George of Denmark's Regiment of Foot "; it was reduced in 1689.

He was summoned, with his cousin Henry, Lord Herbert of Cherbury, amongst other Lords and commoners, to meet the Prince of Orange (King William III) at Westminster 22nd January 1689.

On 10th April 1689 he was appointed to the colonelcy of the 23rd in succession to his cousin Henry, Lord Herbert of Cherbury, and went with his regiment to Ireland in August 1689; was present at the battle of the Boyne, 1st July 1690. At the battle of Aughrim, 12th July 1691, after leading his regiment twice across a bog to the attack, he was unfortunately taken prisoner, and the enemy, seeing a probability of his being rescued, inhumanely put him to death. The honours of his brother, the Earl of Torrington, were entailed on him, so that his dying unmarried made his loss all the more to be regretted.

TOBY PURCELL.
Appointed 13th July 1691.

He was a son of William Purcell, fifth in descent from Sir Hugh Purcell, of Rossestown, co. Tipperary, second son of the Baron of Loughonoe. The first appearance of his name in the Army Lists is as a cornet to Captain Chambre Brabazon in " the Troops of Horse in Ireland," 10th July 1680. In 1702 he stated that he " had served the Crown thirty-three years "; it is therefore evident that his first acquaintance with the army must have been previous to this, probably in 1670. His name then appears as captain in a company of foot, 25th June 1682, as major in Sir Thomas Newcomen's Regiment of Foot 1686, and as lieutenant-colonel in the same in 1687. The name then appears in " A List of such Protestant officers as have been lately in the Army in Ireland and are now out of employment in and about London and desire to be entertained in his Majestys Service," 22nd March 1689. His name is included in a warrant, dated 17th July 1689, for pay at 7s. 6d. a day as " Lieutenant-Colonel and Captain of Foot " on the Irish Establishment. He also presented a petition, dated 10th September 1689, for " such a sum of money as may enable him to go as a volunteer to Ireland as he had been bred a soldier but quitted his post " when the Irish Army sided with King James.

On 14th November 1689 Duke Schomberg writes to King William that he has appointed Toby Purcell lieutenant-colonel to Sir Henry Ingoldsby's regiment; and at the battle of the " Newery," 24th November 1689, he distinguished himself when the English camp was attacked by the Irish in force. He was appointed major in the 23rd Royal Welch Fusiliers in 1689, presumably after this last date. His commission as lieutenant-colonel in the 23rd (Colonel Charles Herbert's regiment) Royal Welch Fusiliers is dated 20th June 1690. He served as second-in-command of the 23rd at the battle of the Boyne, 1st July 1690, where he again distinguished himself. The spurs he wore at this battle were the property of the senior major of the regiment for the time being, and Colonel Purcell's name is always honoured at the regimental dinner on St. David's Day. The spurs were lost when Major Holmes's house in Montreal was burnt to the ground in 1842.

In March 1691 he on several occasions accounted for large numbers of " Rapparees " in co. Longford. On 18th June 1691 he was appointed to the command of four companies of General Douglas's regiment, who were placed as a garrison in charge of the fort at Ballymore. He was given command of the 23rd on the death of Colonel Charles Herbert at the battle of Aughrim, 12th July 1691. In July he was one of the three hostages exchanged for three others of King James's army, pending the negotiations for the capitulation of Galway. He remained in command of the regiment till 20th April 1692, when he retired on account of ill-health, being succeeded by Sir John Morgan. On 18th April 1692 a letter was dispatched from the Secretary-at-War to Colonel Purcell to repair to Cork immediately, " taking upon you the charge of our said Citty and Garrison whereof we have constituted and appointed you Governor "; and on 20th July 1694 a warrant was prepared putting him on the Irish Establishment for an allowance of 9s. 6d. a day in lieu of a company of foot which the King had promised him on quitting the 23rd, the allowance to commence from 20th April 1692. From 1695 to 1699 Colonel Purcell was M.P. for Ardfert.

In April 1698 he was appointed Governor of Duncannon Fort, co. Wexford, in place of Captain George Weightson, at 20s. a day, and was ordered to send forces from Duncannon Fort on 16th June to suppress Tories and Rapparees in co. Wexford.

On 11th February 1699 he recommended Mr. Toby Purcell, his second son, as fort major at Duncannon Fort at 4s. per day, and the appointment was made on 15th May, and he still held it in October 1703. On 24th February 1699 a letter was sent from the Lords Justices of Ireland to the Lords of the Treasury, recommending Colonel Purcell for the grant of the estate of Thady Quin, of Adare, co. Limerick, or such other forfeited lands as were worth £400 per annum, in reward for his services. On 13th April 1702 Colonel Purcell obtained leave to go to England for his health for three months.

On 17th July 1702 he petitioned for a grant of the Crown's title to certain lands which he had purchased in co. Tipperary from John Butler. In this he states he " has served the Crown thirty-three years," and that he " had incurred many expenses at Newry for drums, trumpets, memorials and exchange of prisoners, and these were never repaid." He received a warrant dated 9th December 1709 authorising him to hold courts-martial, and on 12th June 1711 he was ordered to send a guard to Waterford for French prisoners.

Colonel Purcell was living in Dublin in July 1715, and was then " of a great age," and apparently died in 1717 or 1718 (in any case before May 1718). He had married Elizabeth, daughter of Lancelot Sandes, of Carrigafoyle, co. Kerry : had two sons, Richard (died 1715) and Major Toby (died 1752), and one daughter, Ann, who married Michael Cox, Archbishop of Cashel.

SIR JOHN MORGAN, BART.
Appointed 20th April 1692.

He was a son of Sir Thomas Morgan, of Llangattock, first Baronet, M.P. for Hereford in the time of Charles II. He was a D.L. for Herefordshire ; lieutenant-colonel of Colonel Henry Cornwall's regiment of foot, just newly raised (now 9th Regiment), 19th June 1685. He must then have retired from the regiment, as in November 1687 his name is no longer in it, appearing, however, as a captain in Colonel John Carne's regiment of foot, 13th October 1688, newly raised. This regiment, which was exclusively Welsh, was disbanded in January 1689. He succeeded Captain Peter Shackerley as Governor of the Castle and City of Chester, 28th May 1689, his pay being £182 10s. per annum, with one master-gunner and three other gunners.

On being appointed colonel of the 23rd on 20th April 1692, in succession to Colonel Toby Purcell, he was specially permitted to continue as Governor of Chester and to continue drawing the pay of 10s. per diem.

Luttrell, in his *Narrative*, states, under date " 10th January 1693," " Sir John Morgan coll. of a regiment and governor of Chester is dead "; and again, " 14th January 1693," " The corpse of Sir John Morgan, late governor of Chester was carried in a herse thro' the citty to goe into the country "; and again on " 14th February 1693," " Charles Villiers of the guards is made coll. of Sir John Morgan's Regiment," but corrects this under date of 11th March by saying, and correctly, that the regiment has been given to Colonel Richard Ingoldsby.

RICHARD INGOLDSBY.
Appointed 28th February 1693.

A son of Sir George Ingoldsby, younger brother of the regicide Sir Richard Ingoldsby, and a nephew of Sir Henry Ingoldsby (in whose will, dated 19th March 1700, he is mentioned as executor). He was appointed major, 8th March 1689, in Sir Henry Ingoldsby's regiment of foot, raised in Staffordshire on that date; on Sir Henry resigning the command, owing to ill-health and old age, he was appointed colonel, 8th November 1689. He served at the sanguinary action at Newry, co. Down, on 24th November 1689, but owing to losses, etc., the regiment was disbanded on 9th January 1690. From a petition to the House of Lords, dated 3rd January 1691, it appears that he had lost £11,000 by forfeiture of his Irish estate in the late reign. He was appointed Adjutant-General of the Forces, 30th June 1692, to the expedition to the French coast that year, under the Duke of Leicester. On 28th February 1693 he was appointed colonel of the 23rd vice Sir John Morgan, Bart., deceased; and commanded the 23rd at the siege of Namur, June 1695. Was promoted Brigadier-General 1st June 1696. On 1st January 1698 he was committed to the Tower, with Lord Kerry, for carrying a challenge from his lordship to the Irish Lord Chancellor, but both were released on 5th January. Early in 1699 he had charge of the disbanding of the regiments of the Marquis de Mirecourt, Lord Lilford, and three others in Ireland; and on 6th June 1701 was sent to Cork to superintend the embarkation of ten regiments for Flanders, in concert with Admiral Hopson. Promoted major-general 9th March 1702; the same year he was offered and declined the governorship of Jamaica; in 1703 was elected M.P. for Limerick; was promoted lieutenant-general 1st January 1704; commanded a division under Marlborough 1702–1706; was present at the battles of Schellenberg and Blenheim in 1704, at the latter battle was second-in-command of the 1st Line under Lieutenant-General Charles Churchill; on 1st April 1705 was transferred to the colonelcy of the 18th Foot, Royal Irish Regiment.

He was appointed Master-General of the Ordnance in Ireland by warrant dated 20th February 1706, vice Lord Mount Alexander, with an allowance of £500 a year. He commanded the English troops at the capture of Aeth on 3rd October 1706. In

1707 was appointed one of the Comptrollers of Army Clothing. In 1708 he inspected the regiments stationed in Ireland, visiting Crookhaven and Beerhaven with a view to the erection of a fort for the security of ships coming from the West Indies. In September 1709 he was nominated one of the Lords Justices for Ireland during the absence of the Lord-Lieutenant.

He died in Dublin, 11th (? 27th) January 1712, and was buried in Christ Church. By his will, dated 29th January 1711/12, he left a house in Golden Square, London, to his wife Frances, £1,000, and £500 a year; all else and remainder in England and Ireland to his son Henry and his heirs male.

JOSEPH SABINE.

Appointed 1st April 1705.

Born about 1662; descended from a family settled at Patricksbourne, in Kent. His grandfather was Avery Sabine, an alderman of Canterbury. He was appointed captain-lieutenant in Sir Henry Ingoldsby's regiment of foot when it was raised 8th March 1689, and became captain of the grenadier company some time before 18th October 1689; appointed brevet major in the 23rd, 13th July 1691, and lieutenant-colonel 6th June 1695. Served with his regiment at siege of Namur, July 1695. On 1st January 1703 was appointed brevet colonel. He was wounded at the battle of Schellenberg, 2nd July 1704, when in command of the regiment. He was appointed colonel of the 23rd on 1st April 1705, on the transfer of Lieutenant-General Ingoldsby from the 23rd Regiment to the 18th Regiment. He was present with the regiment at the battle of Ramillies, 23rd May 1706, and was appointed brigadier-general on 1st January 1707; was present at the battle of Oudenarde, 11th July 1708, and also at the siege of Lille. On 1st January 1710 promoted major-general, and made Governor of Berwick-on-Tweed and Holy Island in succession to Lieutenant-General George Macartney, appointed Governor of Portsmouth.

Returned with the regiment in 1713 on signing of the Treaty of Utrecht; and on 25th March 1715 he was placed on the Irish establishment as brigadier. In the same year he purchased the estate of Tewin, Hertfordshire, and rebuilt the house there in 1716. In 1722, with Brigadier Stanwix, he was appointed to examine the reduced officers and out-pensioners of Chelsea Hospital. In 1727 he represented the borough of Berwick in Parliament, and on 4th March 1727 was promoted lieutenant-general. Nominated Governor and Commander-in-Chief of Gibraltar 3rd April 1730, and promoted to general on 2nd July 1730. He died at Gibraltar on 24th October 1739, and was buried in Tewin Church, his nephew Lieutenant-Colonel Newsham Peers succeeding him in the colonelcy.

He was twice married: (1) Hester, daughter of Henry Whitfield, of Bishops Stortford; (2) Margaretta, youngest daughter of Charles Newsham, of Chadshurst in Warwickshire, and by her he had five children, of whom Joseph, a captain in the 23rd, was killed at Fontenoy. His portrait by Kneller, painted in 1711, was engraved in 1742 by Faber. In his will, dated 4th November 1738, he mentions an estate in co. Kildare, and " my silver bason and ewer which the Magistrates of Ghent presented to me when

I commanded them as Governor of that City "; also " my good friend and nephew Lieutenant-Colonel Newsham Peers."

Lewis Melville, in his *First George in England and Hanover*, says, " George I twice visited Tewin House, near Hertford, the property of General Sabine, who had spent £40,000 on building and furnishing it, inspecting the fine marble hall and staircase, the collection of pictures, and fine frescoes."

NEWSHAM PEERS.
Appointed 23rd November 1739.

His first commission is dated as second lieutenant in the 23rd 25th April 1706, lieutenant 24th June 1707; wounded at the battle of Malplaquet on 31st August 1709; captain-lieutenant 1st May 1710; captain 24th December 1710; major 25th May 1720; lieutenant-colonel 22nd December 1722; and colonel of the 23rd on 23rd November 1739, on the death of his uncle, General Joseph Sabine, at Gibraltar (he is mentioned as executor in the General's will). In 1742 he went abroad with the regiment and was mortally wounded at the battle of Dettingen, 16th June 1743, dying the same day.

JOHN HUSKE.
Appointed 28th July 1743.

He was appointed ensign 7th April 1708 in Colonel Toby Caulfield's (afterwards Creighton's) regiment of foot, then in Spain and afterwards disbanded; was appointed captain 11th January 1715 in Colonel Harrison's regiment of foot (15th Regiment); on 22nd July 1715 was made captain and lieutenant-colonel in one of the four newly raised companies of the 2nd Foot Guards (Coldstreams); he also acted as A.D.C. to Lord Cadogan. In the Ninth Report of the Hist. MSS. Commission, dated 1st November 1716, he is stated to have acted as confidential envoy for Lord Cadogan, who was endeavouring to obtain information as regards Jacobite plots; and in Treasury Papers CXCI, 68, it is mentioned that he received £100 for a journey to Paris on particular service; and again in Treasury Papers CCXXVII, 4, it is stated that he and the British plenipotentiary at the Hague, Whitworth, arranged measures for collecting at Williamstadt three Dutch and two Swiss battalions in the pay of Holland, and bringing them to the Thames. On 8th July 1721 he was appointed Captain or Keeper of Hurst Castle, and on 30th October 1734 second Major in the Coldstreams, becoming first Major on 5th July 1739. On 25th December 1740 he was promoted to the colonelcy of the 32nd Regiment of Foot, and was in command of a brigade at Dettingen 1743, when he " behaved gloriously," according to a narrative of the day, and was very severely wounded. On 28th July 1743 he was, in recognition of his distinguished services, promoted major-general, and appointed colonel of the 23rd, in succession to Colonel Newsham Peers.

He was made Governor of Sheerness in 1745, and on the outbreak of the rebellion was appointed to serve under General Wade at Newcastle; and on 25th December was given a command in Scotland. When second-in-command to Hawley, at the battle of Falkirk, 17th January 1746, he was able to secure the retreat of the loyal army to Linlithgow; at the battle of Culloden, 16th April 1746, he again distinguished himself, when in command of the second line of the Duke of Cumberland's Army, composed of the 8th, 13th, 20th, 25th, and 48th Regiments. He was promoted to lieutenant-general on 11th August 1747, general 5th December 1756, and Governor and Captain of the Island of Jersey in 1760. He died at Ealing, Middlesex, on 18th January 1761.

He has been described as " a brave, blunt veteran, whose solicitude for his soldiers earned him the nickname of ' Daddy Huske.' " His will, which appears in the *Gentleman's Magazine* for 1761, also shows his care and thought for those under him. Dying worth nearly £42,000, he left legacies to his postilion £500, undergroom £500, town housekeeper £300, footman £1,200, valet £3,000, groom of stables £5,000 and all his horses, carriages, etc., and to the poor of Newmarket £100.

THE HON. GEORGE BOSCAWEN.
Appointed 16th January 1761.

Brother of Viscount Falmouth; entered the army as an ensign in the Foot Guards 1728; served at Dettingen 16th June 1743, and at Fontenoy 30th April 1745. He was appointed Deputy-Governor of Scilly and Colonel in the Army 18th August 1749; and on 14th October 1749 was appointed Aide-de-Camp to the King. On 4th March 1752 he was made Colonel of the 29th Regiment (late Hopson's); promoted major-general 14th January 1758, and lieutenant-general on 22nd February 1760. He was appointed Colonel of the 23rd Regiment on 16th January 1761, on the death of General John Huske. He died on 3rd May 1775 in York Street, St. James's, London.

WILLIAM, VISCOUNT HOWE, K.B.
Appointed 11th May 1775.

Born 1729, he was appointed a cornet in the Duke of Cumberland's Regiment of Light Dragoons, being appointed to a lieutenancy on 21st September 1747. The regiment was disbanded in 1749. On 1st June 1750 he was appointed to a captaincy in the 20th Regiment, and major in the 60th (afterwards 58th) Regiment on 4th January 1756. On 17th December 1757 he was promoted lieutenant-colonel of the 58th Regiment. During the " Seven Years' War " he served under Major-General Wolfe in America, and was made brevet colonel 19th February 1762. On 21st November 1764 he was promoted to the colonelcy of the 46th Regiment, and advanced to the rank of major-general 25th May 1772. Appointed Commander-in-Chief in North America 1775, in succession to General Gage, being made Colonel of the 23rd on 11th May 1775, in succession to Lieutenant-General the Hon. George Boscawen, deceased. On 29th August 1776 he was promoted lieutenant-general, and in the spring of 1778 returned to England, having resigned the command of the army to Lieutenant-General Sir Henry Clinton. On 21st April 1786 Sir William Howe was removed to the colonelcy of the 19th (late 23rd) Light Dragoons, which he retained until his decease. On the 12th October 1793 he was promoted to the rank of general.

In 1799 he succeeded to the Irish peerage held by his brother Richard, Earl Howe, the celebrated admiral, and in 1805 was appointed Governor of Plymouth. General Viscount Howe died on 12th July 1814, in the 85th year of his age.

RICHARD GRENVILLE.
Appointed 21st April 1786.

Entered the Army in 1759 as ensign in the 1st Foot Guards; obtained the rank of captain 1760 by raising an independent company; on 7th May 1761 he was removed to a company in the 24th Foot. He served in 1761 and 1762 in Germany as aide-de-camp to the Marquis of Granby. In 1772 purchased a company in the Coldstream Guards, and in 1776 accompanied the Brigade of Guards to America. On 19th February 1779 became colonel; 20th November 1782, major-general; and on 21st April 1786 he was made Colonel of the 23rd, in succession to Lieutenant-General Sir William Howe (afterwards Viscount Howe), who had been tranferred to the colonelcy of the 19th (late 23rd) Light Dragoons. On 3rd May he was advanced to the rank of lieutenant-general, and on 1st January 1801 to that of general. General Grenville died in London 22nd April 1823.

APPENDIX II

EXTRACTS FROM THE REGIMENTAL MESS RECORDS

The following interesting " Rules of the Mess " and extracts from the Minutes up to 1888 are preserved in three manuscript books now in possession of the regiment, viz.:

"Berwick, 7th May, 1787.

"Mr. Hall at the Red Lion will furnish the officers of the Regiment during their stay here with dinner and small beer at 1s. 2d. each per day: they paying for other malt liquor at the usual prices, viz., Ale 4d. and Porter 5d. per quart.

The Rules of the Mess are:

1. A President and Vice-President shall be appointed daily in rotation: each of whom is to bring his servant to assist in attending at dinner.

2. The President is to order dinner for the number the Mess consists of: each of whom is to pay 1s. 2d. for dinner and beer, whether he comes or not.

3. Any officer going away for more than two days, is to give notice to the landlord, that dinner may be ordered accordingly. If he neglects to give notice, he is to be charged as usual.

4. The President to order in a bottle of wine for every three persons present, and a bottle for any over. When that allowance is drank, the bill to be called and paid, if no stranger is present.

5. When a stranger is asked, the same allowance of wine to be ordered in, and when that is used, the President will call for more, at which time those who do not choose to sit longer are at liberty to go away without being liable to pay for more than the allowance.

6. Any wine drank after the allowance is to be paid for by those who remain, in equal proportions, the person who invites a stranger paying for him.

7. No wine is to be called for but port, unless by those who invite strangers: and in that case the persons inviting, and those who partake of white wine, are to pay the proportion of the difference.

8. All bills to be settled and paid every Sunday, on which day no stranger is to be invited, unless in case of necessity.

9. It is expected that no member of the Mess drinks more than one glass of wine during dinner.

10. The President to be answerable for the bill of the day.

11. Each member of the Mess to pay 1s. every Sunday, out of which 14s. per week

is to be paid to the waiter of the house for attendance: the remainder to be paid into the hands of an officer, to be disposed of as the Mess may determine.

12. No dogs to be admitted into the Mess Room at any time.

The above Rules having been agreed upon in a very full Mess, consisting of twenty two persons, It is Resolved that no alteration shall be made in them, but by the unanimous concurrence of those members present at quarters, and should any temporary alteration be made for the convenience of those present, the original Rules must be adhered to, should any member join and desire it.

A book to be bought by the Mess in which these rules are to be entered and signed by each member."

The regiment having moved to Chatham from Berwick, these second set of Mess Rules drawn up there are likewise reproduced from the original " Mess Books ":

"CHATHAM BARRACKS, 25TH NOVEMBER, 1787.

"No. 1. That it is the unanimous opinion of the officers of the 23rd Regiment now present, that a general mess is absolutely necessary for the convenience and benefit of the Officers of the Corps.

2nd. That to establish the same, every Officer belonging to it shall pay on joining the mess three guineas, in order to buy utensils and things necessary for it. Married men excepted, who must pay one guinea and an half should they wish to belong to the mess.

3rd. And to support a fund for hereafter providing such utensils as may be wanted it is resolved that any Officer who may after the date hereof gett promotion in or be appointed to the Regiment shall pay according to the rank he gets or comes in with.

Officers on promotion in the Regiment to pay in the following proportions, viz.:

	£	s.	d.
A Lieut.-Colonel getting the Regiment	20	0	0
A Major appointed to the Lieut.-Colonelcy without purchase	16	16	0
A Major appointed to the Lieut.-Colonelcy with purchase	8	8	0
A Captain getting the Majority without purchase	12	12	0
A Captain getting the Majority with purchase	6	6	0
A Capt.-Lieut. getting a Company without purchase	8	8	0
A Capt.-Lieut. getting a Company with purchase	4	4	0
A Lieut. getting the Capt.-Lieutenancy without purchase	6	6	0
A Lieut. getting the Capt.-Lieutenancy with purchase	3	3	0
A 2nd Lieut. getting a 1st Lieutenancy without purchase	4	4	0
A 2nd Lieut. getting a 1st Lieutenancy with purchase	2	2	0
An Officer of the Regiment appointed Quarter-Master without purchase	4	4	0
An Officer of the Regiment appointed Quarter-Master with purchase	2	2	0
An Officer of the Regiment appointed Adjutant without purchase	2	2	0
An Officer of the Regiment appointed Adjutant with purchase	1	1	0
A Mate appointed Surgeon without purchase	4	4	0
A Mate appointed Surgeon with purchase	2	2	0

EXTRACTS FROM THE REGIMENTAL MESS RECORDS

Officers coming from other Regiments to pay in the following proportions, viz.:

	£	s.	d.
A Colonel appointed from another Regiment	23	0	0
A Lieut.-Colonel without purchase	19	19	0
A Lieut.-Colonel with purchase	11	11	0
A Major without purchase	15	15	0
A Major with purchase	9	9	0
A Captain without purchase	11	11	0
A Captain with purchase	7	7	0
A Capt.-Lieutenant without purchase	9	9	0
A Capt.-Lieutenant with purchase	6	6	0
A 1st Lieutenant without purchase	7	7	0
A 1st Lieutenant with purchase	5	5	0
A 2nd Lieutenant without purchase	4	4	0
A 2nd Lieutenant with purchase	3	3	0
A Chaplain without purchase	6	6	0
A Chaplain with purchase	3	3	0
A Surgeon without purchase	7	7	0
A Surgeon with purchase	5	5	0
A Quarter-Master without purchase	7	7	0
A Quarter-Master with purchase	5	5	0
An Adjutant without purchase	4	4	0
An Adjutant with purchase	3	3	0
A Surgeon's Mate without purchase	4	4	0
A Surgeon's Mate with purchase	3	3	0

4th. And as a further support to this fund it is resolved that Twenty pounds per annum be raised by the members of the mess, to be paid in the following proportions, viz.: Two days full pay of each member of the Mess, the married Officers only excepted, who are to pay only one day's full pay. And moreover resolved that the above sums be immediately paid into the hands of the treasurer up to the 15th April 1789 and in future upon every 15th of April for the insueing year.

5th. That a treasurer be chosen he being one of the Mess, to receive each person's subscription, and all other money collected on account of utensils, and that he shall enter all money received or disbursed on account of the Mess in a book regularly kept for that purpose.

6th. That in case the treasurer should be absent for a fortnight or more, another shall be appointed to act with equal power, the treasurer giving over to him his books, and any cash he may have in hand.

7th. Resolved that five members of the Mess shall be appointed as a Committee to have the entire management of the same with full power to make any alterations that may appear to them necessary—that the said Committee shall remain in office till the 15th April following the appointment when a new Committee may be chosen—and moreover resolved that should two or more of said Committee leave the Regiment for a fortnight or more that there shall be an equal number chose from the Body of the Regiment then present to act till their return—resolved in consequence of the foregoing resolution that the following five gentlemen shall compose the Committee till the 15th April 1789, viz.:

> CAPTAIN PETER
> ,,   CHAMPAGNE
> LIEUTENANT BAYNTUN
> ,,   SKINNER
> SURGEON WILLIAMSON

8th. That a treasurer be appointed to collect the money arising from the consumption of wine, which treasurer may or may not be one of those who compose the above-mentioned Committee but he must be a member of the Mess.

9th. Resolved that Captain Peter is appointed treasurer for the money collected on account of utensils and Lieutenant Skinner for the wine department.

10th. Resolved that any member of the Mess who shall neglect to pay for his messing (provided the Mess-man demands it) the space of three days after the usual time of collecting the same shall forfiet two bottles of port for each offence.

11th. Resolved that any officer who shall disobey the 8th article of the rules made at Berwick shall pay two bottles of port wine to the Mess.

12th. Resolved that any member of the Mess breaking or rendering useless any part of the utensils belonging to it, shall pay in the hands of any one of the Committee on the spot, or when called upon by them, the value in cash, double what the said utensil originally cost, a cork screw, only in this case excepted, when he is actually endeavouring to draw a bottle of wine at least two of the Mess being present, but should any stranger break or render useless any part of the utensils the Person inviting them shall only be liable to replace what was broke or rendered useless.

13th. Resolved that when any strangers dine at the Mess no wine can be called for or cork drawn after they go away without whipping.

14th. That none but port be the wine in general use of the Mess except where the whole body then present, chuse to drink any other, or where it cannot be got so good, and cheap as other wines.

15th. That no member of the Mess at dinner, or during the time that the Mess wine is drinking, can call for any quantity under a bottle, of white or other wine.

16th. That no Person shall remain in the Messroom after the allowance of wine is out, (while any party are drinking) unless he whips.

17th. That no whip shall be under sixpence at a time each person.

18th. That if a member of the Mess, from sickness, or any other cause, shall find it improper to drink port wine, he shall in that case pay for whatever liquor he may call for, as well as his proportion of the allowance.

19th. That the treasurer of the wine department shall pay off the Wine Merchants bill at least once a month, at which time he shall settle with the Mess-man for his profit on the same.

20th. That the person who undertakes to mess the Regiment shall receive at the

EXTRACTS FROM THE REGIMENTAL MESS RECORDS

rate of ten shillings and sixpence a week from each member of the Mess, for a good dinner and small beer, one good fire in the Mess Room, and as many candles as may at times be thought necessary.

21st. That he shall likewise receive three pence profit on each bottle of port wine consumed in the Mess house by the Mess.

22nd. That should there be any other kind of wine called for beside port, the Mess-man may provide it having a reasonable [? profit] on the same.

23rd. That the Man who undertakes to mess the Officers of the Regiment, shall provide a Cook, and other necessary People at his own expence, likewise pay all charges of washing and such like.

24th. That any member of the Mess ordering cold meat for supper, shall pay sixpence ; if oysters or any hot dish a reasonable price, in proportion, to the expence and trouble the Mess-man may be at.

25th. That the above-mentioned allowance to the Mess-man is only intended during the stay of the Regiment in Chatham Barracks.

26th. That the utensils purchased for the use of the Mess be given regularly over to the man who undertakes to mess the Regiment, both the treasurer and Mess-man keeping an invoice of the same.

27th. That the Mess-man be answerable to the Mess for all utensils and every other article give to his care, and that he be obliged to make good all deficiencies in case there are any : that is provided it appears to the Committee that such defficiency did arrise from neglect, or inattention of the Mess-man.

28th. That every utensil wore out in the service of the Mess be replaced at its expence.

29th. That the Mess-man be permitted to sell spirits of all sorts, likewise porter, and strong malt liqour, and every article of that kind for the use of the Mess, he charging a reasonable price for the same likewise tea and such like, so as to be able to provide any of the Mess with a breakfast.

30th. That no article of the Mess utensils be permitted to be sent away from the Mess house on any pretence whatever, in case of sickness only excepted, when any Member of the Mess so circumstanced may be allowed to have what is necessary : but to be answerable that they are returned after the meal is over, and in case any of the utensils are broken or lost, they must be made good by the person who sent for them, and the cash lodged in the hands of the treasurer appointed to superintend that department.

31st. That should the Mess-man neglect to report to the Mess any difficiency that may come within his knowledge arrising from the above-mentioned regulation that is in number 30 he becomes answerable to make good the loss.

32nd. That no division of the mess utensils can take place except that in case the Regiment goes abroad, and then one third of the Officers who compose the Mess, and duty of the Regiment, in case of being detached for a month or more, may have their proportion of the Mess utensils, observing the general rules of the Mess on joining the Headquarters of the Regiment.

33rd. That the above rules are to govern all Detachments who may take part of the Mess utensils with them, in the same manner as when the Regiment is assembled.

34th. That no utensil whatever belonging to the Regimental Mess be used on board ship on any account.

35th. That no person whatever can become a member of the Mess unless he either is, or has been an Officer of the Regiment.

36th. That to make these rules and regulations more binding, every member of the Mess shall subscribe his name to them, with an assurance that he will do all in his power, consistant with the situation, to keep up the spirit and true meaning of them, as well for the good of the Mess, as to promote harmony and unanimity in the Regiment.

37th. Resolved that no alteration shall be made in the above rules except at the time the Officers have joined for the spring review and the Regiment together, then there must be notice given of a meeting two days prior to its taking place which all Officers are bound to attend according to the meaning of Number 36."

Nine additional Rules were added subsequent to November 1787 and previous to 1st June 1795, No. 45 being worded as follows : " Great inconvenience having arisen to the Mess from the custom of officers, when sick, sending for their dinners from the mess table : Resolved that no part of the dinner intended for the Mess shall be taken from the table for that purpose " ; and No. 46 : " Each member is to make his servant attend three days at the Mess in turn, viz. the day he is Vice, the day he is President, and the day following."

At Port au Prince, 1st June 1795, it was resolved that " no person be permitted to ask more than one stranger to dine at the Mess without giving notice to the Messman on the evening before. The forfeit one bottle of wine for each offence."

Annual meetings for the election of a Committee were held at Chelmsford, 16th April 1797 ; at Norwich, 15th April 1798 ; at Eling, Hants, 15th April 1799 ; Plymouth, 20th June 1800 ; and at Gibraltar, 2nd December 1801. At the latter meeting the following resolutions were passed : "Each member to pay four current dollars per week to the Mess-man for dinner : the allowance of wine to be one pint when there are not any strangers, and one bottle when there are strangers, a proportion of wich to be sherry : it is expected that officers will drink only two glasses of wine at dinner when a pint is the allowance, but are under no restrictions as to the number of glasses during dinner, when there are strangers : members having strangers to dine will pay one current dollar for the dinner of each : members calling for claret or other wines not usually drank in the Mess (or porter, ale, spruce, fruit etc.) to be charged separately : fines limited to 2 bottles of wine to be increased to 4 bottles whilst in this garrison, in consequence of the difference in the price of wines in England and on this Rock : every member inviting a stranger must have his servant to attend in the Mess Room during dinner."

At the meeting held at Portsmouth on 20th August 1803 it was resolved that owing to the increased price of wine, when no strangers were at Mess it was not necessary that any member should drink wine, but the Mess-man was to have one penny, being his profit on one-third of a bottle.

Further meetings were held at Freshwater Camp, 24th October 1803 ; Hailsham, Sussex, 16th April 1804 ; and at Bletchington Barracks, Sussex, 3rd February 1805 : when the Rules. and contributions of members going, were revised, the latter varying from 24 days' full pay for a colonel going from another regiment to 8 days' full pay for a quartermaster from another regiment.

Rule 3 states that " It being the established custom of the Regiment to commemorate the first of March in honour of St. David (the tutelar Saint of Wales) It is Resolved that one days pay shall be subscribed by every member of the Mess, whether present or absent on that day, for the purpose of defraying the extra expense incurred on the occasion. And in case such sum shall not be sufficient, the deficiency is to be paid by such officers of the Mess as are present on that day in equal proportions."

Rule 19 : " During the time that members are drinking wine, no other party can be permitted in the Mess Room, nor can any smoking party at any time be allowed."

Rule 20 states it has been the custom to prohibit the drinking of spirits at the mess-table, no deviation to be allowed " from such old Regulation " except under the surgeon's certificate. At the meeting held at Woodbridge, Suffolk, 15th April 1806, it was resolved that Sunday and Thursday " should be the public days at which strangers are to be invited to dine at the Mess and that all servants attend at the mess."

In " the Standing Rules " of 15th April 1819 it appears that an allowance of £250 per annum in aid of the Regimental Mess was granted while the corps was in England.

At a General Meeting of the Mess held on 24th February 1825 at Gibraltar, it was settled that a Ball should be given on the approaching 1st of March, for the purpose of marking and commemorating that day instead of the dinner that had hitherto been the annual custom, but it was to be expressly understood that this substitution should not be considered as superseding the established rules of the Corps with regard to St. David's Day. Of 63 ladies invited 42 came, and of 108 gentlemen 88 came.

At a meeting held on 5th February 1829 at Gibraltar, it was resolved that a snuffbox, value 50 guineas, should be presented to Captain E. M. Brown, late Paymaster, as a testimony of the esteem of his brother officers, and the high sense entertained by them of his private character, and public services to the Corps.

In an official memorandum dated Horse Guards, 15th February 1829, it was commanded that 30 days' pay was to be paid by each officer on appointment, and an annual subscription of not more than eight days' pay in support of the Mess contingencies, and in cases of promotion the difference on 30 days' pay between the rank obtained and that previously held.

The Standing Rules and Regulations were again revised on 3rd January 1833 at Gibraltar. Early in March 1840 a silver breakfast service was presented to T. Smith, late Surgeon of the Regiment, who had been appointed in 1826. On 8th July 1840 it appears that a four-oared gig was presented to the officers of the 36th Regiment (Lieutenant-Colonel Maxwell ?).

At a meeting held in " the camp before Sebastopol, November 25th 1854," it was resolved unanimously " that Lieutenants Browne, Beresford, and Radcliffe of the 88th Connaught Rangers who have been doing duty with the Regiment for a considerable time, shall be requested to become Permanent Honorary Members." In connection with the making of these officers as Permanent Honorary Members of the Mess, it is of interest to note the names of others similarly made. The officers of the 7th Regiment,

Royal Fusiliers; Sir Thomas Tobin, on presenting a piece of plate as a memorial of his son the late Lieutenant Arthur Lionel Tobin; Mr. H. N. Smith, as the donor of the twelve silver goblets; Major H. W. L. Hime, R.A., as a token of gratitude for his trouble with regard to the field-gun captured by the late Major-General E. W. Bell, V.C., C.B., at the battle of the Alma; Surgeon-Major James Hector, on his retiring from the regiment; and Major W. T. Walker, 1st Volunteer Battalion Middlesex Regiment, for his care and attention in the removal to England of the original tombstone which was erected over the grave of the officers who fell at the battle of the Alma.

At a meeting held at Portsmouth 10th March 1857, it was resolved that " a committee be appointed for carrying out the erecting of the monument to those officers and men of the Regiment who fell in the Crimea, and that it do consist of the Captain commanding Depot—Colonel Lysons 25th King's Own Borderers, H. A. Campbell Esq. (late 23rd R.W.F.), and Dr. Watt."

During the Jubbulpore Exhibition of December 1867, a ball was given by the regiment on 31st December. When at the Raglan Barracks, Devonport, in November 1869, it was decided to spend about £200 in the purchase of two pieces of plate, one to commemorate the officers who fell in the Crimea, and the other to those who fell in India.

Whilst at Pembroke Dock in January 1872 the following appears: " That application be made for a goat in place of that which died at Newport in May 1871."

Whilst stationed at Chakrata, N.W. Province, India, in August 1881, it was decided that, as hounds were being brought from England, a Hunt Committee should be appointed, consisting of Captain R. F. Williamson, President; Lieutenants Lyle and Chapman as whips; and Lieutenant Dunn, kennel huntsman: the hounds were still being kept up in July 1887 at Lucknow, under Lieutenant-Colonel Creek as master.

On October 8th 1887 it was decided that subscriptions should be collected for the purpose of erecting a monument in Wrexham Church in memory of the officers, non-commissioned officers, and men who died during the Burma Campaign of 1885-7.

In May 1888 it was decided to sell the hounds, with the exception of those considered as sufficient to start a bobbery pack, with Captain Lyle as master.

A LIST OF THE PRINCIPAL WORKS CONSULTED IN THE COMPILATION OF THIS VOLUME

ALBEMARLE, EARL OF: "Fifty Years of My Life." London, 1876.
CANNON, RICHARD: "Historical Record of the Twenty-third Regiment or the Royal Welsh Fusiliers." London, 1850.
CARLETON, CAPTAIN GEORGE: "Memoirs, including Anecdotes of the War in Spain under the Earl of Peterborough." 4th edition; Edinburgh, 1809.
CLINTON, N. R.: "The War in the Peninsula and Wellington's Campaigns in France and Belgium." 3rd edition; London, 1881.
DALTON, CHARLES: "English Army Lists and Commission Registers, 1661–1714." Six vols.; London, 1892–1904.
D'AUVERGNE, REV. EDWARD: "History of the Last Campaign in the Spanish Netherlands, 1692–1696," etc. London, 1693–1697.
FORTESCUE, HON. J. W.: "A History of the British Army," Vols. I to VIII. London, 1899–1917.
HOWE, GENERAL SIR WILLIAM: "General Sir William Howe's Orderly Book at Charlestown, Boston, and Halifax, 1775–1776." London, 1890.
KANE, BRIGADIER-GENERAL RICHARD: "Campaigns of William and the Duke of Marlborough." London, 1747.
LAMB, R. (Sergeant, Royal Welsh Fuziliers): "An Historical and Authentic Journal of Occurrences during the Late American War from its Commencement to the year 1785." Dublin, 1809.
MAINWARING, MAJOR R. BROUGHTON: "Historical Record of the Royal Welch Fusiliers, late the 23rd Regiment." London, 1889.
MOCKLER-FERRYMAN, LIEUTENANT-COLONEL A. F.: "The Life of a Regimental Officer during the Great War, 1793–1815." Compiled from the correspondence of Colonel Samuel Rice, C.B., K.H., 51st Light Infantry, and from other sources. Edinburgh, 1913.
MURRAY, GENERAL RT. HON. SIR GEORGE: "Letters and Despatches of John Churchill, First Duke of Marlborough, from 1702 to 1712." Edited by Sir G. M.; London, 1845.
NAPIER, COLONEL W. F. P.: "History of the War in the Peninsula and in the South of France, 1807–1814." Six vols.; London, 1828–1840.
OMAN, CHARLES W. C.: "A History of the Peninsular War." Five vols.; London, 1902–1914.

LIST OF WORKS CONSULTED

PARKER, CAPTAIN ROBERT: "Memories of the Most Remarkable Military Transactions from 1683 to 1718." London, 1747.

ROBINSON, MAJOR-GENERAL C. W.: "Wellington's Campaigns, 1808–1815." Parts I, II, and III; London, 1905.

SIBORNE, MAJOR-GENERAL H. T.: "Waterloo Letters." A selection from original and hitherto unpublished letters, edited by Major-General H. T. S. London, 1891.

SKRINE, F. H.: "Fontenoy and Great Britain's Share in the War of the Austrian Succession, 1741–1748." Edinburgh, 1906.

STEDMAN, C.: "History of the American War." Two vols.; London, 1794.

STORY, REV. GEORGE: "Impartial History of the Wars in Ireland." London, 1693.

TARLETON, LIEUTENANT-COLONEL BANASTRE: "History of the Campaign, 1780–1781, in the Southern Provinces of North America." Two vols.; London, 1787.

WALTON, COLONEL CLIFFORD: "History of the British Standing Army, A.D. 1660 to 1700." London, 1894.

WILSON, COLONEL R. T.: "History of the British Expedition to Egypt." Two vols.; London, 1803.

WITHEROW, REV. THOMAS, D.D.: "The Boyne and Aghrim." Belfast, 1879.

YOUNG, R. M.: "Old Belfast." Belfast, 1896.

"Gentleman's Magazine," 1731–1815.
London Gazettes.
Military Manuscripts, preserved at the Royal United Service Institution, Whitehall.
"Ulster Journal of Archæology." Belfast, 1853–1862.

INDEX

Abechuco, 258
Abercrombie, Lieut.-Colonel, 183
Abercromby, Sir Ralph, in Helder Expedition, 198-9; in expedition against Spain, 202-3; at Aboukir and before Alexandria, 204-5; death from wound, 206
Aberdeen, 118, 146, 148
Abergavenny, 3, 195
Aberystwyth, 99, 120
Abington, 51
Aboukir, 204-6
Adam, Major-General, 280, 286
Adderley, Captain G., 193
Addington Ministry, 209, 210
Adey, William, Lieut., 117; Captain, 120
Adour River, 269
Aerschot, 60, 61
Agnew, Brigadier-General, 159, 162, 163
Agueda River, 244, 246, 249, 255
Aire, 87
Aix-la-Chapelle, Treaty of, 117, 118
Alba Ford, 252
Albany Barracks, Isle of Wight, 288
Albemarle, Earl of, *Fifty Years of my Life*, 283, 309
Albuera, battle of, 228, 239-43, 275
Aldea da Ponte, engagement, 244, 245
Alderney, 246
Alderton, 2nd Lieut., 123
Aldy, Lieut. William, 64
Alexandria, surrender of, 206
Alfaiates, 244
Algodras, 256, 257
Alkmaar, 199
Allan, 2nd Lieut. George, 271
Allanson, Lieut. George, 171
Allegre, Marquis d', 70
Almanza, battle of, 75
Almendra, 256
Almendralejo, 242
Alost, 77, 112
Alresford, 102
Alten, Major-General Charles von, 239
Altobiscar, 260
Alton, 31
Ameland, 201
America, North, 120, 125, 151, 288
American Independence, War of, 153-85
Amesbury, 3
Amherst Barracks, Guernsey, 197
Ancram, Major-General the Earl of, 124, 150

Andalusia, reserve of, 264
Anderlecht, 35, 50, 74, 109
Anglesea, 210
Anhalt, Prince of, 131, 132, 140
Annapolis Royal, 218
Anne, Queen, 57, 73
Anson, Major-General William, 249
Antrim, 7, 53
Antwerp, 60, 61, 69, 116, 231
Apthorpe, C., Lieut., 171; Captain, 184, 186, 190, 193
Arapile, Greater, 250-2
Arapile, Lesser, 250-3
Arapiles, village, 250-2
Arbroath, 146
Arbuthnot, Admiral, 174
Ardagh, 22
Ardee, 5, 10
Ardersier Point, 119
Ardfert, 51
Aremberg, Count d', 105, 108
Argyll, Duke of, 78, 100
Arklow, 189
Arleux, 88
Armagh, 7, 10, 53, 190
Arnold, General, 163, 182
Aronches, 238
Arras, 86
Arseele, 40
Arundel, 102
Ascain, 265
Aschaffenburg, 105
Ase River, 139, 140
Ashby, Lieut. Richard, 85
Ashford, 217
Ashley River, 174
Asia Minor, 204
Askeaton, 51
Asper, 77
Assche, 77, 108
Astorga, 219-21, 225, 228, 229
Atchubia Mountain, 264
Ath, 48, 49, 77, 112
Athboy, 91
Athenry, 30
Athlone, 15, 16, 22-26 (siege), 30, 91
Athlone, Earl of (Lieut.-General de Ginckle), in command in Ireland, 21-31; in Low Countries, 44, 56, 57; death, 60
Athy, 52
Aubervilliers, 287
Auch, 270
Aughrim, battle of, 26-30
Augsburg, 64
Aumore (?), 96
Austria, Emperor of, 54, 69, 74, 86
Austria as an Ally, 69, 105-12, 116, 117; as an enemy in Seven Years' War, 128; against Napoleon, 225
Austrian succession, 103
Autre-Eglise, 71
Auvergne, d', cavalry, 84
Aveiras de Cima, 235, 236, 239
Awbry, Lieut. William, 111
Azambuja, 234, 235

Badajoz, 236, 238-40, 242, 247-9 (siege), 272, 275
Baggott, 2nd Lieut. P., death, 192
Bailey, Lieut. Richard, 157
Baillie, Lieut., 291
Baird, Lieut.-General Sir David, 214, 215, 219, 220, 226, 229
Baker rifle, 218
Bakkum, 199
Bala, 212
Balart bastion (Namur), 42, 43
Balbriggan, 15
Baldock, 97
Baldwin, 2nd Lieut. Richard, 97
Baldwin, Captain Thomas, 117, 120
Balfour, Lieut.-Colonel Nesbit, 118, 171, 186
Balliboy, 16
Ballinahinch, 8, 19
Ballinasloe, 26
Ballyburn Pass, 23
Ballymoney, 53, 54
Ballymore, 22
Ballyneedy Castle, 17
Balrothery, 52, 53
Baltic, the, 214
Banagher, 16, 17, 30
Banff, 119, 149
Bangor, Co. Down, 4
Bantry, 51
Barbadoes, 192, 218
Barber, Lieut. Arthur, 123, 133
Barham Down Camp, 198
Baring, Major, 279
Barnard, Colonel, 268
Barnstaple, 31
Barr, Assistant-Surgeon, 239
Barrouilhet, ridge of, 265
Bartley, Lieut. Joseph, killed, 85
Basingstoke, 31
Basset, Volunteer John, killed, 262
Bassieux, 89
Bastau River, 131
Bastide, La, 267
Batancos, 229
Bath, 51, 114, 115
Batt, Private, 256
Batthyani, Austrian commander, 116
Battle, 102, 201, 202

311

INDEX

Battles:
Aboukir, 204
Albuera, 239-41
Aldea da Ponte, 244
Alexandria, 205-6
Athlone (siege), 22-26
Aughrim, 26-29
Badajoz (siege), 247-8
Bergen, 130
Blenheim, 64-67
Bouchain (siege), 88
Boyne, the, 10-15
Brandywine, 166
Bunker's Hill, 155-6
Campen, 137
Ciudad Rodrigo (siege), 246
Corunna, 226-8
Dettingen, 106-8
Douay (siege), 86
Egmont-aan-Zee, 199
Fontenoy, 110-11
Guildford, 180-1
Kirch Dünckern, 140-1
La Hogue, Cape (naval), 32
Lauffeld, 116-17
Lexington, 153-5
Lille (siege), 79-81
Malplaquet, 83-85
Martinique, 221-4
Minden, 130-4
Minorca (siege), 121-2, 125
Namur (siege), 39-47
Nivelle, 263-5
Orthes, 267-9
Ostend, 196-7
Oudenarde, 77-79
Pyrenees, 262
Ramillies, 71-73
Salamanca, 250-3
San Sebastian (siege), 262-3
Schellenberg, 62-64
Toulouse, 270
Tournay (siege), 82-83
Vittoria, 257-9
Waterloo, 278-83
Yorktown (siege), 182-4
Bavaria, invasion of, 64-67
Bavaria, Elector of, as an Ally against Louis XIV, 38-49; as an enemy, 61-67, 76
Bavaria, Electress of, 67
Bavay, 85
Bayas River, 257, 258
Bayly, 2nd Lieut. Edm., 67
Bayntun, Lieut. W. G., 171, 304
Bayonne, 258, 265, 266
Bay Robert, Martinique, 221
Beatty's Ford, 178, 179
Beaumaris, 211
Beccalaer, 40, 41
Beccles, 231
Beckwith, Lieut.-General George, commands Martinique Expedition, 221-4
Beckwith, Lieut. Onslow, 156
Bedburg, 62
Bedford, 149
Bedford (America), 160, 174
Bedminster, 51
Belem, 143, 235, 239
Belfast, 47-49, 55, 231
Bellasis, General Sir Henry, 27, 28, 31, 38
Belle Alliance, La, 280, 281, 286

Bellem, 48
Bellew, Lieut. Lewis, 123
Belturbet, 9
Benavente, 229
Bennett, Captain, 37
Bent, Private Charles, death from wounds, 215
Beresford, Colonel William, 220, 227; Portuguese Marshal, 235-43, 252, 264-70
Bergen, 130
Bermuda, 195
Bernard, Lieut., 124
Bernard, Lieut.-Colonel Benjamin, 118, 150, 151, 155
Bernard, John, 2nd Lieut., 95; Captain, 111, 118
Bernard, Lieut. and Adjutant W., 95
Berners, Lieut. Gregory, 111
Berry Head, 267
Berwick, 94-102, 146, 149, 187; "Rules of the Mess," 301-2
Berwick, Duke of, 5, 17, 76, 80, 86
Bethlehem, near Louvain, 38
Bethnal Green, 92
Béthune, 82, 86
Beverwyk, 199
Bidassoa River, 259, 263
Bidouse River, 267
Bielevelt, 142
Bilboa, Co. Limerick, 51
Bilsen, 71
Bingham, Captain George, 123
Bird, Lieut.-Colonel, 163
Birmingham, 92, 99, 187, 212
Biron, Marquis de, 77
Birr, 52
Bissell, Captain, 95
Bissell, 2nd Lieut., 95
Black, G., 287
Blackburn, 186
Black Forest, 61
Blackheath, 150
Blackwater River, 9, 20
Blacquire, Captain John, 123
Blair, Captain C., 192, 193
Blake, General, 229
Blakeney, Colonel, at Albuera, 241
Blakeney, General, 121, 122, 124
Blakeney, William, Lieut., 123, 124, 137; Captain, 145, 156
Blancfort, 271
Blenheim, battle of, 64-67; honours, 85
Blomberg, 142
Blucke, Lieut. John, 171
Boffin, 31
Bois de Boulogne (Paris), 287, 288
Bois Seigneur Issaau, 49
Boisseleau, French officer in Ireland, 17
Bolton, 94, 195
Bolton, Captain, killed, 286
Bolton, Duke of, 115
Bolton, Lieut. Francis, 96
Bolton, Captain Richard, 133
Bonaparte, Prince Jerome, 278
Bonaparte, Joseph, King of Spain, 257-9
Bonn, 60, 62
Booker, Lieut., 241; Captain, 260
Booker, Abraham, Ensign, 39; Lieut., killed, 43

Borchleon, 71
Bordeaux, 269, 271, 289
Boscawen, Lieut.-General the Hon. George, 138; death, 155; career, 299
Bose, Hessian Regiment of, 178
Boston, 152-8
Boucafarinha, 245
Bouchain, 87; siege, 88
Bouchier, Lieut., 291
Boufflers, Marshal, outmarches Elector of Bavaria, 39; enters Namur, 41; surrenders citadel, 46; in campaigns of 1696 and 1697, 48-49; in campaign of 1702, 58; defeats General Opdam, 60-61; at Lille, 80; surrenders citadel, 81; retreats from Malplaquet, 85
Bouge Hill (Namur), 42, 43
Bourbons, 269, 283
Bourke, Lieut.-Colonel Miles, 22, 23
Boyne, the, 6; battle of, 10-15
Bradford, 187
Bradford, Brigadier-General, 251
Bradford, John G., Lieut. at St. Domingo, 192-4; Captain, 197, 203
Braemar Castle, 149
Braganza, 257
Braine-la-Leud, 278, 285
Braine-le-Compte, 277, 278
Brakel, 142
Brandenburgers, 13, 41, 45
Brandywine Creek, 165
Brandywine River, battle of, 166
Brecknock, 3
Breda, 56, 57, 60-62, 115
Bredene, 197
Breed's Hill, 155
Bree-Zand, 199
Bremen, 141, 143, 212
Brentford, 98
Brest, 34
Brett, Captain Arthur, 85
Brice, Lieut., 262, 263
Bridgenorth, 92, 98
Bridges, Sir Matthew, 52
Briscous, 267
Brissoel, 110
Bristol, 18, 51, 93, 97, 114, 115, 120, 144
British Museum, 16, 59
Brixham, 267
Broglie, Marshal de, at Minden, 130; against Ferdinand of Brunswick, 134-41
Bromley, 120
Bromyard, 93
Brooklyn Heights, 159
Brown, Captain, 212
Browne, George, Lieut., 239, 248; Captain, 253-4 (letter), 260
Browne, Lieut. John, 171
Browne, Major-General Robert, 231, 255
Browne, Lieut. T., 235
Brownson, Lieut., 248
Bruges, 38-41, 47-49, 76-81, 89, 277
Brune, General, 199
Brunswick, Hereditary Prince of, 134-7, 141
Brunswick troops, 281

INDEX

Brunswick-Oels Corps, 234, 253
Brussels, 39, 40, 44, 49, 50, 76, 77, 80, 108, 109, 278
Buckley, Captain William, 213
Bunker's Hill, 155-6
Buonaparte. See NAPOLEON BONAPARTE
Büren, 141
Burgos, 220, 254, 257
Burgundy, Duke of, 57, 76-79
Burke, Colonel Walter, 29
Bury, Captain Thomas, 195, 197, 198
Butler, 2nd Lieut. R., 244, 246
Bylandt, Count de, 279
Byrnes, Ensign Arthur, 242
Byng, Admiral, 121
Byng, Major-General, 260

Caçadores, 7th, 261
Cadiz, 202, 203
Cadogan, Earl of, 115
Cadogan, Major-General, 77, 78, 86-88
Cadroy, Lieut. Stephen, 64
Cæsar, French navy, 170
Caesar, Major-General, 139
Cahercoulish, 16
Caillemotte, Huguenot leader, 13
Cairo, 206
Caithness, 119
Calvarisa de Ariba, 250
Calvert, 2nd Lieut. Harry, 172
Camberwell, 112
Cambo, 265
Cambray, 195, 283, 284, 287
Cambridge, 109
Cambron, 110
Camden, 175-7, 181
Cameron, Colonel, 285
Campbell, Brigadier-General, 260
Campbell, Lieut.-General, 120
Campbell, Major, 222, 223
Campbell, Colonel Colin, 192
Campbell, James, of Ardkinglas, *Memoirs*, 139
Campbell, John H., Lieut., 171; Captain, 190, 193
Campe, 199
Campen, 137
Campo-Mayor, 238
Camps Point, 163
Cancale, 126, 127
Cane, Captain James, 245
Cannon, Richard, *Historical Record of the Twenty-third Regiment* (1850), 3, 33, 42, 81, 88, 200, 205, 309
Canterbury, 102, 120, 196, 216
Carey, James, Lieut., 95; Captain, 101, 111, 114
Carisbrook Castle, 144
Carleton, Captain George, *Memoirs*, 309
Carlingford, 4, 5, 52, 53
Carlingford, Lord, 15
Carlisle, 114, 119
Carlisle Bay, Barbadoes, 218, 221
Carlow, 219
Carmarthen, 234, 246
Carnarvon, 195, 210, 212
Caroline, Princess, 115
Carrickfergus, 4, 9, 55

Carrick-on-Suir, 15
Cartaxo, 234, 235
Cashel, 16, 20, 85
Cassel, 130, 135, 138, 142, 143
Castello Branco, 244
Castera, 271
Castle, Lieut., 241; death from wounds, 242
Castledermot, 15
Castleforbes, 20
Castricum, 199
Castries, M. de, 137
Catanat, Marshal, 49
Catawba River, 178
Cateau-Cambrésis, 89, 286
Cathcart, Lord, 212, 214
Cavallo Torto, 229
Cavan, 9
Cavendish, Major-General Lord Frederick, 139, 140
Celle, 135
Cesternes, French writer, 122
Chad's Ford, 165
Chambre, Lieut., 95
Champagné, Captain Forbes, 182, 304
Chandos, Lord, 77
Chantilly, 287
Chapman, Thomas, Lieut., 171, 180; Captain, 192 (death), 193
Chard, 202
Charlemont, 9, 190
Charleroi, 48, 278, 279, 282
Charles, Archduke, 54
Charles II, warrant of, 93
Charles II of Spain, 54
Charles VI, Emperor of Germany, 103
Charles Albert, Elector of Bavaria, 103
Charles River, 155
Charleston, 154-9, 174-7
Charlottenlund, 215
Charlottetown, 177
Charlotteville, 182
Charlton, 115
Chatham, 92, 93, 113, 125, 149, 150, 172, 187, 188, 195; "Rules of the Mess," 302-6
Chatham, Lieut.-General the Earl of, 231, 232
Cheap, Lieut., 7
Chelmsford, 126, 195
Chelsea, 92
Chelsea Hospital, 124, 234
Cherbourg, 127
Cherokee Indians, 178
Chertsey, 143, 144
Chesapeake River, 165, 166
Cheshire, 3
Chester, 4, 91, 94, 97-99, 212, 213, 217
Chester (America), 167
Cheyney, Colonel, 228
Chipping Norton, 31
Cholmondley, Major-General, 109
Churchill, General Charles, 40, 60, 61, 66
Cirencester, 146
Ciudad Rodrigo, blockaded, 244; captured, 246; mentioned, 247, 251, 255
Clare, Co., 17
Clarke, Lieut. Esme, 111

Clausel, General, 252-5, 259, 264, 269
Clermont, 287
Clinton, Lieut.-General Sir Henry, in War of American Independence, 156-84; at Waterloo, 278, 281, 286
Clinton, N. R., *The War in the Peninsula*, 309
Clogher, 55
Clonakilty, 51
Clonmel, 15, 16, 51
Clyde, Lieut. John, 253, 271; death from wounds, 283
Coa River, 245, 255
Coblentz, 62
Cochrane, Lieut. Thomas, 145, 156
Cockle, Lieut., 45
Cocklé (Namur), 42
Cohorn, General, 60
Cohorn (Namur), 40, 45
Coimbra, 238
Colborne, Colonel Sir John, 280
Colchester, 104, 109, 212, 213, 216
Cole, General Sir Lowry, commands 4th Division in Peninsular War, 234-71; correspondence with Duke of Wellington, etc., 288-91
Colehampton, 120
Coleraine, 53-55
Collier, Brigadier-General Sir David, 36, 38
Collins, Lieut., killed, 248
Collot, General, 193
Colon, 192
Colonels of the Royal Welch Fusiliers, succession of, 293-300
Colville, General Sir Charles, at Badajoz, 247-8; commands 4th Division in Waterloo campaign, 277, 286-90
Colyear, Colonel Walter, 49
Combe, Captain, 95
Concord, 153, 154
Condé, Prince de, 3
Condeixa, 237
Condom, 271
Connaught, 22
Connecticut, 155, 161, 163, 173, 182
Consaarbrück, 69
Contades, Marshal, 130-3
Conway, General, 139, 140
Conyngham, Sir Albert, 27
Cook, Lieut., 7
Cooke, Lieut. Samuel, 206
Cookman, Captain Henry, 67
Cooper River, 175
Coote, Colonel, 30
Coote, General, 197
Coote, General Sir Eyre, 231-3
Cootehill, 190
Copenhagen, 214-6
Cops Hill, 156
Corbach, 135
Corgarff Barracks, 149
Cork, 19, 20, 31, 55, 90, 93, 189, 190, 191, 217, 219
Cornwallis, General Lord, in War of American Independence, 165-8, 176-84
Corran Ardgour, 96
Cortland, Lieut. J. V., 197, 198

INDEX

Corunna, 164, 219, 220, 225-8 (battle), 229, 230
Cotter, Private, 256
Cotterell, Colonel, 109
Cotton, Lieut. L., 197
Coulthurst, Captain, 212
Courtland, Captain John Van, 218; killed, 245
Courtray, 87, 108
Coventry, Earl of, 273-5
Coventry, Hon. J., 274
Cowell, Lieut. F. L. G., 255; death, 291
Cowes, 208
Cowpens, 178
Coy, Colonel John, 19
Craddock, General, 205
Cranbrook, 102, 120
Cranenburg, 57
Craufurd, Brigadier-General, 219, 220, 228
Crayford, 50
Crescent, Order of the, 207-8
Cresfeld, 130
Crewkerne, 202
Crookhaven, 51
Crotton River, 162
Culmore Fort, 54, 55
Cumberland, Duke of, 109, 115, 188
Curragh, the, 219
Currie, Lieut.-Colonel, killed, 286
Curties, 2nd Lieut. W., 244, 246
Cutts, Lord, at Namur, 41, 45; at Blenheim, 64-65
Cuxhaven, 211, 212

Dagieu, M., Commandant of Minden, 134
Daily Courant, 59
Daily Post, 105
Dalhousie, General the Earl of, 231
Dalmer, Captain F., 255
Dalmer, Lieut.-Colonel Thomas, 244, 246, 253, 272; at Waterloo, 281; in command of battalion, 288, 290
Dalrymple, General Sir Hew, 197
Dalton, Charles, *English Army Lists*, 309
Dan River, 179
Danbury, 163
Danish troops in Ireland, 9, 13, 20, 23; three soldiers at siege of Athlone, 24; at Aughrim, 29; cross Danube, 64, 67; at Oudenarde, 79
Danube, 61-66
Darling, R. A., Deputy Adjutant-General, 276
Darling, W. L., Assistant-Adjutant-General, 287, 290
Darlington, 187, 217
Dartford, 50, 229
Datchet, 188
D'Auvergne, Rev. Edward, *Last Campaign in the Spanish Netherlands*, 309
David, St., 157
Davidson, Colonel, 179
Davison, Lieut., 145
Dawson, Captain George, 169
Dax, 268
Deal, 93, 120, 123, 195, 211, 216
De Bork's estate (Martinique), 222

Deerhurst, Lord, 274
Delaware Regiment, 176
Delaware River, 162, 165-8
Deloraine, Earl of, 99
De Manceaux's estate (Martinique), 222
Demar River, 69
Denbigh, 210, 234
Denbigh and Glamorgan Militia, 246
Dender River, 77
Denmark, 214
Deptford, 50, 105, 150, 195
Dettingen, battle of, 106-8
Deule River, 80
Devereux, Lieut., 7
Devil's House (Namur), 45
Devizes, 103
Deynze, 40, 48, 49
Dickens, Ensign, 7
Dickens, Lieut. John, 39
Dieghem, 105
Diemel River, 136-9
Digby, 218
Dillon, Lord Henry, 30
Dilworth, 166
Dinant, 46
Dingle, 51
Disney, Lieut. Thomas, 7, 43
Dixmude, 35, 40
Don, General, 211, 212, 233
Donauwörth, 62, 64
Doncaster, 3, 185-7
Donkin, Major, *Military Recollections*, 157, 197
Donore Hill, 12, 14
Dorchester, 3, 272
Dorchester Hill (America), 158
Dormer, 2nd Lieut. Fleetwood, 67
Dornoch Firth, 119
Dorsenne, General, 244, 245
Douay, 82, 86 (siege), 87, 287
Douglass, General, in Ireland, 10-23
Douro River, 220, 249, 250, 254, 255, 257
Dover, 92, 93, 102, 120, 125, 126
Down, Co., 11
Downpatrick, 234
Downs, 214, 231, 277
Doyle, General Sir John, 206, 234, 235
Draper, Colonel, 126
Dresden, 128
Drogheda, 5, 11, 14-16, 20, 52, 53, 91
Drogheda, Earl of, 3
Dromin, 20
Drumlane, 10
Dry Bridge, 14
Drury, Captain James, 177
Drury, 2nd Lieut. J., 288
Drysdale, Captain James, 111
Dublin, 6, 11, 12, 15, 16, 19, 21, 24, 52, 53, 91, 189; Public Record Office, 18, 19; Custom House Records, 31
Dudley, 291
Dudley, Quartermaster, 95
Duelling, 33
Duleek, 10-12
Dülman, 129
Du May, Monsieur, 81
Dumbarton, 149
Dumfries, 285
Dunbar, Lieut., 95

Duncannon, 18, 189
Dundalk, 4-10, 52, 53
Dundas, Henry (Viscount Melville), 191, 202, 204
Dundas, Captain William, 123
Dundee, 146, 231
Dungan, Lord, 14, 15
Dunleer, 52, 53
Dunn, 2nd Lieut. George, 271
Dunstable, 92, 97, 98
Du Platt, Colonel, 286
Durham, 99
Dutch troops in Ireland, 13-23; in Low Countries, 42-50, 56-89, 105-18; in Seven Years' War, 129-43; at the Helder, 198-200; in Waterloo campaign, 277-9
Dyle River, 76

Eastbourne, 209-11
East River, 163
Ebro River, 257-9
Eckeren, 60
Edinburgh, 100, 102, 146, 147
Edisto River, 174
Edmonton, 185
Edwards, Private, 256
Edwards, Sir Francis, 6, 7
Edwards, Captain H., 196, 198, 207
Egan, Lieut. Constantine, killed, 63
Egham Common, 189
Egmont-aan-Zee, 199
Egypt, 204-7
Elba, 276
Elbe River, 211
El Burgo, 226
Elgin, 95, 119
Eling Barracks, 198
Eliott, George Augustus (Lord Heathfield), 100
Elk River, 165, 183
Ellenberg, General, 40
Ellesmere, 228
Elliott, Brigadier, 127
Ellis, 2nd Lieut. E. T., 290
Ellis, Colonel Sir Henry Walton, commissioned in infancy, 195-6; Captain, 196, 198, 205; Lieutenant-Colonel, 218-88; death from wounds, 283; inscription on monument, 284
Ellis, Colonel John Joyner, 193, 195, 284
Elsinore, 214, 215
Elvas, 239, 242, 243
Elvina, 226
Elwes, Mrs., 228
Emden, 128
Ems River, 128
Enghien, 277
Enniscorthy, 189
Enniskillen, 1
Enoch, Lieut. John, 234, 239, 253
Enos, Lieut. Archibald, 97
Eppinger, Brigadier, 27, 30
Erith, 50
Erle, Colonel, 3, 11
Erlon, General d', 260, 264, 278
Erne, Lough, 8
Ers, Upper, 270
Erskine, Lieut. Francis, 170, 171
Erskine, General Sir William, 163, 164, 187

INDEX

Escurial (Madrid), 254
Espinhel, 237
Estaing, Count d', 169
Estrées, Marshal d', 142
Estremoz, 244
Eu, Redoubt d', 110, 111
Eugene of Savoy, Prince, an Ally of Marlborough (1704-1709), 62-83; in supreme command, 89
Evans, Lieut. Edward, 123
Evesham, 218
Exeter, 114, 120, 144, 146
Eyme, Captain Isaac, 64
Eyndhoven, 117
Eyne, 77, 78
Eyre, Lieut. Henry, 111, 117
Eyres, Lieut. Thomas, 171

Fairfield, 173
Falmouth, 151, 219
Fane, Brigadier-General John, 220
Faringdon, 31
Farmer, Lieut. George, 234, 248, 257, 259
Farmer, Captain Thomas, 271; killed, 283
Farnham, 102
Farquison, Lieut., 124
Farrel, Ensign, 7
Faversham, 218
Fensham, Lieut. G., killed, 283
Ferdinand of Brunswick, Prince, in Seven Years' War, 128-43, 146
Ferguson, Brigadier, 62, 65, 70
Ferguson, 2nd Lieut. David, 133
Ferguson, Lieut. Joseph, 123, 137
Ferrol, 202
Fielding, Brigadier-General, 99
Fielding, Lieut. George, 244, 246, 248, 283
Finglas, 15
Fisher, Major-General G., 213
Fitzgerald, Lord Ed., 186
Fitzgerald, Colonel Nicholas, 24
Fitzgibbon, Volunteer, 263
Fitzpatrick, Brigadier, 40
Finea, 91
Flanders, 1, 32, 34, 55, 90, 105, 289
Flat Bush, 159
Fletcher, Miss, letter, 227
Fletcher, Captain Thomas Lloyd, 227
Fletcher, Mr. Phillips Lloyd, 227
Flint, 210, 227
Floyde, Ensign, 7
Flushing, 231-3
Folkestone, 125
Fontainebleau, Peace of, 143
Fontenoy, battle of, 110-3
Foot, Major S., 193
Forres, 95, 119
Forster, Lieut. Arthur, killed, 111
Fort Augustus, 149
Fort Bizothon, 191-3
Fort Bourbon, 192, 223, 224
Fort Clarence, 225
Fort de France, 223
Fort-den-Haake, 232
Fort George, 119, 148
Fort George, Guernsey, 234
Fort Hill, 157
Fort Knocque, 40
Fort Lafayette, 172

Fort La Fleur d'Épée, 192
Fort Lee, 162
Fort Mathilde, 192
Fort Moultrie, 159, 174
Fort Rahmanieh, 206
Fort Royal, 192
Fort St. Philip, 121
Fort Washington, 161, 162
Fort William, 95, 96, 149
Fortescue, Captain, 117
Fortescue, Hon. J. W., *A History of the British Army*, 67, 73, 309
Forth, Captain Thomas, 97
Four Mile Bridge, 52
Fowler, Corporal John, killed, 170
Fowler, Captain William, 123, 133, 137
Fownes, Mr. William, 52
Fox, Captain John, 123, 133, 139, 140, 146
Foxhill, 20
Foy, General, 278
France and Great Britain, 120, 143; America, 169; Egypt, 204; Russia, 214; Napoleon, 276; Occupation by Allies, 290, 291
Frankfort-on-the-Main, 105, 129
Frankfurt, regiment of, 266
Fraser, Lieut. Alex, killed, 63
Fraser, Lieut.-General Mackenzie, 220, 221, 226, 231
Frazer, Ensign, 7
Frederick the Great, 128
Freehold, 168
French Huguenots, 13, 20
French troops in Ireland, 19, 28; in Low Countries, 35-50, 54-90; in War of Austrian succession, 105-18; in Seven Years' War, 128-43; in America, 183; at Ostend, 197; in Egypt, 205-6; in Martinique, 221-4; in Peninsula, 225-71; at Flushing, 232; in Waterloo campaign, 277-87
Freshwater Gate, 209
Fribertshausen, 134
Friedberg, 64
Fritzlar, 134, 135
Fryer, Lieut. Charles, 253, 271
Fuente Guinaldo, 244
Fuentes de Oñoro, 244
Fullerton, Lieut. James, killed, 85
Furnes, 35
Fusilier regiments, 59

Gage, Lieut.-General, 153-6
Gale, Lieut. William, 92
Galicia, 257
Gallegos, 245, 246
Galveston, 185
Galway, 20, 30, 31
Galway, Lord, 73
Garden, Lieut. A., death, 192
Garnons, Lieut. Wynne, 190; death, 192
Garonne River, 269, 270
Garwood, Colonel, 246
Gates, General, 168, 176
Gavre, 77
Gazetteer, The, 150
Geete Rivers, 69, 71, 72
Gembloux, 48

Genappe, 49
Genestet, Captain James, 37, 39
Gentleman's Magazine, 310
George II, 98, 99, 103, 105-8, 114, 115, 128; death, 138
George III, 144, 150, 151, 167, 188, 207, 209
George Island, 225
Georgia, 174, 175
Germaine, Lord George, 167
German Legion, King's, 211, 214, 215, 279
German troops at Copenhagen, 215; at Albuera, 239
Germantown, 166, 167
Germersheim, 68
Gesecke, 139
Ghent, 38-41, 48, 73-81, 85, 89, 105, 112, 277
Ghent-Bruges Canal, 48
Gibbins, 2nd Lieut. Robert, 123, 124
Gibbons, Captain, 171
Gibraltar, 100, 102, 103, 122, 144, 146, 203, 208, 210; Mess records, 307
Ginckle, Lieut.-General de. See ATHLONE, EARL OF
Gironde River, 271
Glasgow, 97, 119, 148, 187
Gledstanes, General A., 246
Gledstanes, Lieut., 255
Glengarry, 96
Glengarry Fencible Regiment, 197
Glen Moriston, 96
Gloucester, 51, 93
Gloucester (America), 182, 183
Gloucester, Duke of, 150
Gloucester Point, 168
Goat, first reference to, 157
Godalming, 113
Gold, Colonel, 286
Golegao, 236
Goodrich, Sir Henry, 37
Goor, Lieut.-General, 62
Gorcum, 56
Gorden, Lieut., 7
Gordon, Ensign, 256
Gordon, Lieut.-Colonel Sir Charles, 190
Gordon, Lieut. James, 85
Gore, Major-General, 99
Gorteen, 51
Gosport, 272, 275, 277
Göttingen, 138
Goubet, Captain, 37
Gould, 2nd Lieut. Edward, 97
Gould, Captain Paston, 137
Gowan's Road, 159
Grace, Colonel, 16
Graham, Sir Thomas, 257, 258, 264
Grammont, 48, 277
Gramont, Duc de, 106
Granby, Lord, 130, 134, 136, 138, 140, 142
Grand Bay, 192
Grande Lézarde River, 222
Grant, General, 160
Granville, 127
Gravesend, 39, 50, 93, 115
Gravesend Bay, 159
Green, Captain, 212
Greene, General, 179-81
Greenfield, 173

INDEX

Greenock, 186
Greenwich, 92, 105, 115, 146, 188
Greenwich (America), 152
Gregg, Lieut. Edward, 111, 117
Grenada redoubt, 264
Grenade, 270
Grenville, General Richard, 187, 276; career, 300
Grey, General Sir Charles, 192, 193, 196
Griffin, Major-General, 135
Griffith, Ensign, 7
Griffith, Lieut., 212
Griffiths, Lieut. J. E. A., 216, 255, 263
Griffiths, Lieut. W. A., 283
Grobenstein, 142
Groenewald, 78
Groomsport, 4
Gros Morne, 192
Grosvenor, General Thomas, 213, 214
Grove, General, 94, 97
Grove, Lieut. Grey, 133, 137, 160
Grove, Sir Thomas, 3
Guadeloupe, 192
Guadiana, 247
Guarena River, 250
Gudersberg, 138
Guernsey, 197, 198, 234, 246
Guildford, 113, 120, 188
Guildford (America), 179–81
Guyon, Lieut. Stephen, 172, 177; killed, 184

Haarlem Heights, 161
Hackney, 92
Hague, The, 56, 57, 60, 71, 76, 88
Hahlen, 132
Haie Sainte, La, 278, 279
Hailsham, 209
Haine, 76, 83
Hakensack River, 162
Hal, 49, 76, 110, 277, 278, 282
Halifax, 195
Halifax (Nova Scotia), 158, 159, 218, 221, 225, 233, 235
Halkeit, A., Lieut., 190; Captain, 193, 197
Halkett, Colonel, 286
Hall, Lieut., 239; killed, 241
Hall, Major J., 197
Haltrup, 141
Hamilton, Brigadier, 58
Hamilton, Lieut., 7
Hamilton, Colonel Frederick, 36
Hamilton, Lord George, 27, 43
Hamilton, Captain John, 37, 42
Hamm, 130, 139
Hampstead, 92, 149
Hampton, 143
Hampton Court, 144
Hanau, 105, 107
Hanem, 129
Hanger, Major, 177
Hanging Rock, 176
Hanover, 129, 130, 211
Hanover, Elector of (George I), 76
Hanson, Lieut. H. H., 197, 200
Harborough, 92
Hare, Captain R. G., 234
Harley, Secretary (Robert, Earl of Oxford), 63, 70

Harris, Lieut. Isaac, 239, 241, 255, 262, 269
Harrison, Captain, killed, 63
Harrison, J. C., Lieut., 241, 248; Captain, 261, 291
Hart, Quartermaster, 195
Hartingues, 267
Harton, Surgeon, 95
Hartrum, 128
Harvey, General, 240
Harwich, 35, 92, 93, 109, 112, 113, 143, 212, 214
Hasted, 212
Haswell, Lieut. John, 123
Haverford West, 246, 255
Hawes, Lieut. Nathaniel, 111
Hawkshawe, Colonel, 241
Hawthorne, Lieut. Arthur, 123, 124
Hawtyn, Captain Joseph, 248; killed, 283
Heathfield, Lord, 100
Heighington, Lieut. John, 171
Heir-Apparent Frederick (Danish prize), 216
Heister, General de, 160
Helchin, 80
Helder Expedition, 198–201
Helston, 151
Helvoetsluys, 56
Hemans, Mrs., 254
Hemming, Ensign Richard, 39
Hemmington, Lieut.-Colonel, 147, 148
Herbert, Colonel Charles, 3; wounds himself, 5; report on, 7; murdered at Aughrim, 27; career, 293–4
Herbert of Cherbury, Henry, 4th Baron, 2; career, 293
Herdeeren Heights, 116
Hereford, 91–94
Heron, General Peter, 217
Hertford, 112
Hesse, 130, 134, 138, 141
Hesse, Landgrave of, 48
Hesse-Cassel, 83
Hessians at Namur, 45; in Low Countries, 60; at Blenheim, 64, 65; in America, 159–68
Heurne, 77
Heusden, 56
Hewitt, Captain Peter, 95, 113, 117, 123
Hickman, Captain William, 95, 101, 111
Highgate, 149
Highlake (Hoylake), 4, 9
Highlanders, 140
Hill, Edward, Lieut., 197, 200–1 (wreck of *Valk*), 203; Captain, 244
Hill, Lieut.-Colonel J. Humphrey Edward, 272, 283
Hill, Lieut.-General Lord (Sir Rowland), his brigade, 227; in Peninsular War, 242, 257–69; in Waterloo campaign, 277–86; his high opinion of 23rd, 290
Hillsborough, 179
Hilsea, 144, 185
Hitchin, 97
Höchst, 105
Hochstadt, 64

Hodgson, 2nd Lieut. Owen, 123
Hoggard, Lieut., 200
Hoghton, General, 222, 240–3
Holland, 231
Holland, Stadtholder of, 198
Holly, Mount, 168
Holmes, 2nd Lieut., 248
Holmes, Major R. P., 281–3
Holstein, 214
Holstein-Ploen, Duke of, 40, 45
Holywell, 212
Hompesch, 87, 88
Honiton, 202, 266
Hookes, Captain Hugh, 6, 7, 29
Hope, General Sir John, 221, 226, 264, 265
Hornsey, 92
Horsfall, Captain, 148
Horsham, 202, 230, 231, 234
Hotham, Captain, 169
Houat, 202
Hougoumont, 278–82
Hounslow, 98
Houston, Major-General William, 235, 275
Houthem, 41
Howard, Major-General, in Seven Years' War, 134, 137, 140
Howard, Major-General (1814), 272
Howe, Admiral Viscount, 169–171
Howe, General Sir William, in American War, 155–67; mentioned, 187, 190; career, 299; his *Orderly Book*, 309
Howill, Ensign, 7
Hudson River, 158, 162, 172
Huerta, 250
Hull, 214
Hunt, 2nd Lieut. John, 123
Hurford, Captain, 211, 212, 241; Lieut.-Colonel, 272
Huske, General John, 107–38; death, 138; career, 298–9
Hutchinson, General, 205
Huy, 39, 61, 69
Hyde Park Corner, 92

Igel, 69
India, 227
Indies, East, 126
Ingoldsby, Brigadier, 110, 111
Ingoldsby, Major Henry, 64
Ingoldsby, Sir Henry, 8
Ingoldsby, Lieut.-General Richard, 36–68, 74; career, 296–7
Ingoldstadt, 64, 67
Ingram, Sergeant James, 248
Innes, 2nd Lieut., 172
Inverness, 95, 96, 119
Inversnaid, 146, 147
Ireland under James II, 1; unsettled, 191
Irish House of Commons, 190
Irueta, 260
Isaac, Lieut., killed, 111
Isis, H.M.S., 170
Isleworth, 98
Islington, 92, 98
Ivybridge, 272
Izard, William, Lieut., 111; Captain, 114, 117, 120

Jamaica, 191–3
James II, 1, 5, 6, 10–12, 22

INDEX

James's Island, 174
Jasaut (?), Lieut., 42
Jeffrey, Colonel, 104
Jeffreys, Major-General Charles, 144
Jemappes, 83
Jennings, 2nd Lieut., killed, 216
Jérémie, 194
Jersey, 99
Jervis, Admiral John, 193
Jevereau, Isaac, Lieut., 64; Captain, 85
Jocelyn, Lieut. the Hon. Thomas, 242, 255
Jodrell, Captain, 95
Johnshaven, 146
John's Island, 174
Johnson, Mr. Benjamin, 274
Johnson, Captain H. C., 283
Johnson, Ensign William, 43
Johnston, Lieut., 95
Johnston, Captain Alexander, 111; killed, 117
Johnston, Lieut.-General James, 185, 186
Johnston, Lieut. William, 243, 248
Joiner, 2nd Lieut., 239
Jolliffe, Captain Charles, 269; killed, 283
Jones, Captain, 43, 50
Jones, Ensign, 7
Jones, Lieut.-Colonel, 64
Jones, Major Edward, 202
Jones, Evan, Lieut., 190; Lieut.-Colonel, 214
Jones, Lieut. Griffith, 64, 67
Jones, Captain James, 7, 34, 37, 39
Jones, Captain John, 6, 7, 37
Jones, Adjutant W. H., 234
Joyeuse, 267
Joyeuse, Admiral Villaret, 224
Juliers, 62

Kaiserswörth, 57
Kane, Brigadier-General Richard, *Campaigns of William and the Duke of Marlborough*, 309
Katrick (? Carrick), Lieut., 64
Kay, Chaplain, 95
Keith, Admiral, 203
Keith, Lieut., 199; Captain, 244
Kempt, Major-General Sir J., 279, 291
Kendal, Mayor of, 114
Kennett Square, 165
Kenny, Surgeon Mate, 95
Kensington, 92, 112
Kent, Duke of (Prince Edward), 192, 208
Kentish Town, 112
Kessel, 64
Kew, 102, 105, 188
Kidderminster, 195
Kilcashel, 26
Kilcullen Bridge, 16
Kilkenny, 15, 17, 19
Killaloe, 17
Killarney, 51
Killishandra, 9
Kingsbridge, 266
Kingsbridge (America), 161
King's County, 19
Kingscourt, 190
Kingsley, Brigadier, 131
Kingston, 98, 143, 151

Kingweston, 18
Kinsale, 19, 20, 90
Kips Bay, 161
Kirch Dünckern, battle of, 140-1
Kirke, Major-General, 15, 19
Kjoge Bay, 215
Knot, Lieut., 7
Knox, Cornet Andrew, 52
Knyphausen, General, 162-8
Koesfeld, 128
Krofdorf, 134
Kruse, Colonel, 266

La Bassée, 86
La Bogarna (?) de Morilles, 253
Laggan, Loch, 96
La Hogue, Cape, 32, 33
Laignières, 83
Lalo, Colonel, 74
Lamb, Sergeant R., *Journal of Occurrences during American War*, 309
Lambert, General, 288
Lambert, Colonel John, 122
La Melonière, General, 15, 40, 41
Lancaster (America), 166, 184
Landau, 67
Landguard Fort, 109
Landrecies, 89
Lanesborough, 91
Languedoc, French navy, 169
Lanier, Major-General, 19
Lanz River, 262
Laton, 2nd Lieut., 95
Lauder, Colonel, 43
Lauffeld, battle of, 113, 116-7
Lauzun, General, 12, 20
Layhoule, 126
Leahy, Captain J. T., 212, 218, 248, 272
Lech River, 64
Ledbury, 93
Ledbury Wickware, 51
Lediard's *Life of Marlborough*, 86
Ledwith, Lieut., 241, 260; death from wounds, 263
Lee, 150
Lee, Captain, 37
Leebody, Lieut. William, killed, 287
Leeds, 187, 234
Leekey, Lieut. A., 207
Leesam, 212
Lefebvre, Marshal, 220
Leicester, 122-5
Leinster, Duke of (Count M. Schomberg), 33, 34
Leith, 101, 118, 146
Leith, General, 248
Leland, Major-General John, 189, 190
Lennox, General, 210
Lens, 87
Lenthall, Lieut. John, 156
Leominster, 93, 94
Leonard, Lieut., killed, 249
Lesaca, 263
Leslie, General, 178
Leslie, Lieut. Samuel, 118, 124
Lessines, 77, 112
Letterkenny, 54
Leuse, 110
Lewes, 102, 234

Lewisham, 150
Lexden Heath, 104
Lexington, 153-5
Liège, 58, 69
Ligonier, Colonel Sir John, 112, 117
Ligonier, Lord, 150
Lille, 79-81 (siege), 87, 112, 197, 198, 282
Limberg, 61
Limerick, 16, 17, 20-23, 30, 31, 51, 52
Lincoln, 97, 149
Lincoln, General, 174, 175
Lippe River, 129, 130
Lisajenhonjen, 212
Lisbon, 220, 235, 239, 242, 255
Lisburn, 8, 9
Lively, H.M.S., 156
Liverpool, 208, 217, 291
Llanwrst, 212
Llerena, 239, 242
Llewelyn, 2nd Lieut. B., 234, 244, 246; death from wounds, 248
Lloyd, Captain, 205
Lloyd, Lieut., 7, 95
Lloyd, Lieut. Charles, 197
Lloyd, Colonel Edward, 36
Lloyd, Lieut. Evan, 39, 43
Lloyd, Richard, Ensign, 113; Captain, 123
Lloyd, Lieut. Watkin, death, 192
Lloyd, Lieut. W. P., 288
Lloyd's Patriotic Fund, 215
Lobau, Comte de, 281
Logroño, 259
London, 32, 46, 112, 115, 185, 210, 231, 234
London Evening Post, 104, 150
London Gazette, 29, 43, 46, 91, 98, 107, 310
Londonderry, 1, 53-55
Longford, 20, 21
Long Island, 159, 161, 174, 177, 185
Loo, 39
Lorne, General the Marquis of, 148
Lorraine, 68
Lort, Lieut. Roger, 111
Lort, Major Roger, 111
Losack, Lieut.-Colonel James, 213
Lottum, Count, 83, 84
Loughborough, 123, 125
Loughbrickland, 5
Loughrea, 29, 30, 219
Louis XIV and James II, 20-22; and William III, 31, 55; threatens invasion of England, 32; constructs fortified lines from Namur to the sea, 40; makes peace with the Duke of Savoy, 47; accepts Spanish Crown for his grandson, 54; in consequent War, 61, 74-76; proposes peace, 82
Louis XV, 103, 117, 118
Louis XVIII proclaimed at Bordeaux, 269
Louis of Baden, Prince, as Ally of Marlborough, 62-69
Louvain, 38, 70, 73, 76
Lovelace, Lord, 3
Lowe, Lieut, 118
Lowell, Mr. Justice, 33
Lowen, Mr., 197
Löwendahl, Marshal, 116, 118

INDEX

Lowes, Lieut. William, 117
Lückner, Lieut.-General, 142
Ludlow, 3, 94, 98
Lugo, 225, 226, 229
Lurgan, 55
Luton, 97
Lutterworth, 92
Luttrell's *Historical Relation*, 8, 33, 34, 37
Lutzingen, 64, 66
Luxemburg, Marshal, 35, 38, 39; death, 39
Lynch's Creek, 176
Lys River, 38, 40, 41, 48, 82, 87, 109

Macartney, Brigadier, 72
McCowan's Ford, 178
Macdonald, Captain, 235, 241; death from wounds, 242
Macdonald, Colonel, 198, 199
Macdonald, Lieut., 253
McDonald, Hon. Godfrey, 198
McEvers, John, 2nd Lieut., 186; Captain, death, 192
Macfarlane, Brigadier-General, 215
Macgowan's Hill, 161
Mackay, General, 25, 27, 45
McKay, Major-General, 150
Mackenzie, Lieut., 145
Mackenzie, Major, 187, 202
McLaughlin, Lieut. Archibald, 117
McLaughlin, Private, 256
MacLean, Lieut. A., 196, 199, 200
McLellan, Lieut., 241, 262
McManus, Lieut. Roger, 92
Madra, 51
Madrid, 220, 254, 257
Macseyk, 58, 60
Maestricht, 60-62, 68, 105, 116-8
Magaw, Colonel, 162
Magherafelt, 217
Maidstone, 120
Main River, 105, 106
Mainwaring, Captain, 6, 7
Mainwaring, Colonel, 291
Mainwaring, Major R. Broughton, *Historical Record of the Royal Welch Fusiliers*, 164, 168, 245, 248, 309
Mair, Lieut. Charles, killed, 184
Maitland, General, 210, 223, 279, 280
Major, Ensign, 7
Malgré Tout, 221
Mallow, 16
Malpas, 218
Malplaquet, battle of, 83-85
Malta, 203, 207
Manchester, 94, 98, 99, 149, 185-7, 195, 209, 217, 218, 231
Mann, Ensign, 7
Mannheim, 62
Manningham, Brigadier-General, 228
Mar, Earl of, 91
Marburg, 134, 138
Margate, 56, 196
Maria Theresa, Empress, 103, 115, 128
Maricburg, 34
Mariekirk, 48
Marigot des Roseaux, 192
Marine Regiments, 103, 104
Market Street, 97

Marlay, Major Thomas, 120, 124, 137
Marlborough, 103, 104
Marlborough, John Churchill, Duke of, ordered to Ireland, 19; capture of Cork and Kinsale, 20; in Low Countries, 32, 38, 56; Captain-General, 57, 58; created Duke of Marlborough, 58; campaigns of 1703-11, 60-88; deprived of all offices, 89; campaign, 253; *Letters and Despatches*, 309
Marlborough, 2nd Duke of, 126-9; death, 129
Marmont, Marshal, 242-5, 249-52
Marmorice Bay, 204
Marque River, 80
Marsin, Marshal, 62, 66
Martinique, 191-3, 218; capture, 221-5
Mary, Queen, 29, 32, 34
Maryburgh, 119
Maryland, 184
Maryland Brigades, 176
Marylebone, 6
Masolary, Captain Henry, 101
Massachusetts, 153
Masséna, Marshal, 234-8
Maurice of Saxe, Prince, 108, 110, 116
Mauvillon, historian, 128
Maw, Captain, killed, 248
Maya, 259, 260
Mayence, 62, 105
Maynooth, 52
Mayorga, 220
Meade, Lieut. the Hon. Edward, killed, 205
Mecan, Thomas, Lieut., 137; Captain, 166, 171; Major, 176
Mediterranean, 121
Medows, Brigadier-General Sir William, 168, 169
Mehaigne River, 69, 70
Mehayne (Main) River, 35, 38
Meldert, 74
Melle, 112
Melsungen, 138
Melville Island, 225
Menin, 48, 108
Menotoring, 154
Menou, General, 205
Merbe Braine, 282
Mercer, Lieut., 239
Mercier, Lieut. Philip, 123, 137
Meredith, Brigadier, 68, 74
Merioneth, 210
Mess Records, Regimental, 301-8
Meuse River, 35, 40, 43, 58, 61, 62, 69, 73, 117
Middelburg, 233
Middlebrook, 164
Midhurst, Captain, 212
Milford, 246
Militia, 210, 211, 217, 231, 246, 266, 275
Mills, Captain, 8
Mills, Lieut. C., 211
Mina, General, 259
Minchinhampton, 51
Minden, battle of, 130-4
Minorca, 120, 121-2 (siege), 123, 125, 203, 204

Mitchell, Colonel H. H., in Waterloo campaign, 277-87
Mockler-Ferryman, Lieut.-Colonel A. F., *Life of a Regimental Officer*, 309
Mold, 212
Mole St. Nicholas, 191, 192
Molke, Lieut.-General, 112
Moloigne, Abbey of, 47
Monaghan, 190
Monckton, General Robert, 150
Moncrieffe, Major, 155
Monkstown, 190, 217
Monmouth, 98
Monmouth (America), 168
Monro, 2nd Lieut., 124
Mons, 49, 76, 83, 85, 110, 286
Monsieur River, 222
Montagu, Captain, 241
Montagu, Colonel Edward, 98
Montagu, Duke of, 115
Montargyer, Colonel, 34, 37, 50
Mont Blanc (village), 270
Monte Mero, 226
Montluc, regiment of, 70
Mont Rave, 270
Montrose, 146
Moor, Lieut. Henry, 43
Moore, General Sir John, at Aboukir Bay, 204; in Peninsular War, 219-27; death from wounds, 227
Mooreghem, 77
Mordaunt, Sir John, 120
Morgan, General, 178, 179
Morgan, George, Captain, 39; Major, 67
Morgan, Colonel Sir John, 33, 34; death, 36; career, 295-6
Morillo, General, 260
Morne Bruneau, 192, 222
Morne Fortuné, 192
Morris, 2nd Lieut. J., death, 192
Morrissey, Sergeant-Major, 287
Moselle River, 61, 62, 68, 69, 76
Mostyn, 136, 139
Motherbank anchorage, 208
Moucherron, Danish ship, 209
Moy, 9
Moyle, Major-General, 101
Mullingar, 21, 22, 52, 91
Mumford, Lieut., 7; Captain, 37
Munro, Assistant-Surgeon, 284
Münster, 128-30, 138
Murcella, 238
Murray, General Sir George, *Marlborough's Letters and Despatches*, 309
Muy, Chevalier de, 136
Myers, Colonel Sir W., 192, 235, 240; killed, 241
Mystic River, 156

Nairn, 95, 119
Namur, 35, 39-47 (siege), 49, 69-71, 87
Nanclares, 258
Napier, Captain, 120, 124
Napier, Captain, at Waterloo, 286
Napier, Colonel W. F. P., *History of the War in the Peninsula*, 220, 240-1, 251, 309

INDEX

Napoleon Bonaparte, Emperor of the French, makes overtures to Spanish Court, 202; aims in Egypt shattered, 206; makes demands on Denmark, 214; in Peninsula, 219, 220, 225; maritime rivalry, 231; Wellington to crush power, 259; forfeits throne, 271; escape from Elba, 276; at Waterloo, 278-80
Nassau, Count, 23, 38
Nassau, regiment of, 266
Nassau-Saarbruck, 45
Nava del Rey, 250
Navan, 52
Navarre, regiment of, 106
Navesink, 168
Nebel River, 64-66
Neckar River, 62
Neerhespen, 70
Nenagh, 52
Ness, Loch, 94
Nesselborn, 134
Netherlands, 31, 32
Neuilly-sur-Seine, 288, 291
Neustadt, 135
Nevill, Lieut., 262
New Brunswick, 168
Newburgh, 146
Newbury, 31, 103, 114, 115, 125
Newcastle, 97, 99, 102, 146, 187
Newcastle (America), 165
Newcastle, Duke of, 101, 129, 135
Newhaven (America), 173
Newington, 112
New Jersey, 164, 165
New London, 173, 182
Newmarket, 51
Newport, Isle of Wight, 291
New Rochelle, 162
Newry, 4-8, 53
New York, 151, 159-75, 182, 185
Ney, Marshal, in Peninsula, 225, 236-8; at Waterloo, 278-81
Nicholls, Ensign, 146
Nichols, Lieut. Ingram, 171
Nieuport, 34, 38
Nightingall, General, 238
Nimeguen, 57, 68
Ninety-six, Post, 178
Ninove, 49
Nive River, 265
Nivelle River, 263-5 (battle), 275
Nivelles, 48, 277, 278, 281, 282, 286
Noailles, Duc de, 105, 108
Nore, Buoy of the, 35
Norfolk, Duke of, 2
Norken, 78, 79
North British Fusiliers, 59
North Carolina, 177-81
North Foreland, 196
North Hants Militia, 210
North River, 162, 163
Norwalk, 173
Norwalk Bay, 163
Norway, 200
Norwich, 2, 196
Nottingham, 102
Nottingham, Earl of, 37, 58
Nottingham Fencible Regiment, 197
Nova Scotia, 167, 189, 218, 224, 225, 233, 235
Nuremberg, 64

Oakes, Lieut. Hildebrand, 117
Oberglau, 64-66
Ober-Morschen, 138
Oeyregave, 267
Offenbach, 108
Offley, Lieut. W., 196, 223, 235; Major, killed, 253
Offuz, 72
O'Flaherty, Lieut., 254, 260
Ogilvy, Lieut., 43; Captain, killed, 63
O'Hara, Brigadier-General, 180
Ohm, 138
Oisy, 87
Old Bridge, 10-14
O'Laughlin, Major-General, 263
Oleac, 269
Oleron, Gave d', 268
Olivença, 239
Omagh, 53, 55
Oman, Charles W. C., *A History of the Peninsular War*, 309
O'Neal, Sir Donald, 21
O'Neil, Sir Neil, 11, 15
Oost Kapelle, 232
Opdam, General, 60, 61
Orange, House of, 201
Orange, Prince of, 80, 84
Orchies, 83, 87
O'Regan, Teague, 9
Orkney, Lord, 63, 84, 88
Ormonde, Duke of, 15, 89
Ormy, Lieut., 7
Orpin, Lieut. George, 123, 124, 133, 137
Orr, Surgeon's Mate Hugh, 171
Orrery, Lord, 82
Orthes, battle of, 267-9, 275
Osborne, General Sir George, 188
Osnaburg, 134, 141
Ostend, 34-38, 49, 73, 75, 105, 112, 196-7 (battle), 277
Ostend-Bruges Canals, 49
Ostendon, 212
Oswestry, 98
Ottery, 266
Ottoman Empire, 207
Oudenarde, 39, 77-79, 85, 277
Oughton, General, 147, 148
Overkirk, Marshal, 56-80
Oxford, 3, 122

Pack, General, 245, 251, 270, 279
Paddington, 112
Paderborn, 134, 138, 139
Padstow, 144, 145
Paget, Ensign Justinian, killed, 43
Paget, General Lord, 211, 226-9, 232
Pakenham, General, 222, 234, 235, 244, 245, 251, 252
Palmer, 2nd Lieut., 239
Pampeluna, 258-60, 263, 264
Pancorbo, 257
Pancras, 92
Panella, 237
Parey, Ensign, 7
Paris, 225, 271, 283, 288
Parker, Lieut. Nevil, killed, 85
Parker, Captain Robert, *Memories of the Most Remarkable Military Transactions*, 310
Parliament, 1, 2, 31, 32, 50, 55, 75, 103

Parry, John, Lieut., 39; Captain, killed, 46
Parry, Lieut. Robert, 170
Parslow, Major-General, 146
Passage, 20
Paterson, Lieut. John, 67
Patten, Captain, 239
Patterson, Ensign John, 43
Patterson, Lieut. Joseph, 123, 124, 133
Pau, Gave de, 267, 268
Pauillac, 271, 272
Pearson, Captain, 205; Major T., 213, 223; Colonel, 245, 272
Peckham, 112, 113
Pedrogao, 244
Peek's Hill, 163
Peer, 58, 61
Peers, Colonel Newsham, wounded at Malplaquet, 85; mentioned, 95, 99, 101, 102; Colonel of the 23rd, 103-8; killed at Dettingen, 107; career, 298
Pemberton, Lieut. H. P., 288, 291
Pembroke, Earl of, 115
Peninsula, 202, 255, 275
Pennefather, Colonel Mathew, 85
Pennsylvania, 164, 184
Pennyfeather, Lieut. Mathew, 56
Penny London Post, 115
Penryn, 151
Penzance, 145, 151
Percy, Brigadier-General Earl, 152-4, 162
Percy, Captain the Hon. F. J., 234
Permanent Additional Forces Act, 210
Perth, 94, 148
Perth Amboy, 168
Peter, Captain Thomas, 171, 181, 184, 190, 304
Petersburg, 58
Petersburg (America), 181, 182
Petersfield, 31, 102
Petershead, 146
Petit Crève-Cœur, 287
Petten, 198
Pettener, Lieut. George, 143
Peymaun, General, 215, 216
Peyrehorade, 267
Philadelphia, 165-7, 183
Philip Duke of Anjou (Philip V of Spain), 54
Philipps, 2nd Lieut. Grismond, 234, 239
Philipsburg, 67
Picton, General Sir Thomas, 248, 251, 262, 279, 289
Pierse, Captain, 212
Pigeon Island, 224
Piggott, Lieut. Southwell, 64
Pigot, General, 156
Pitt, William (Earl of Chatham), 126-8
Pitt, William (the Younger), 210, 211
Planchenoit, 279, 281
Plunkett, Captain Christopher, 8
Plymouth, 115, 120, 145, 151, 202, 230, 271
Point-à-Pitre, 192
Point Pleasant, 225
Pole, Edward Sacheverel, Major, 102, 122; Lieut.-Colonel, 124, 133, 137, 142

INDEX

Polhill, Lieut. William, 190; death, 192
Polish Lancers, 240
Polk's Mill, 177
Pollos, 250
Pombal, 236
Ponsonby, General Sir W., 279
Pont d'Espierre, 38
Ponte de Murcella, 238
Poole, Captain, 120
Popham, Admiral Sir Home, 197
Porchester Castle, 144
Portadown, 55
Portalegre, 238
Port-au-Prince, 191-3
Porte St. Nicolas (Namur), 43
Porteous Riot, 100
Porter, Brigadier-General, 94
Porter, Lieut., 123
Portland, Lord, 27
Portsdown Hill, 33
Portsmouth, 31, 33, 99, 109, 185, 189, 209, 216-8, 230, 231, 234
Portsmouth (America), 182
Portsoy, 149
Portugal, 214, 220, 233-56
Portuguese troops, 237-67
Portumna, 30
Postenhagen, 141
Potter, W. M., Captain, 242; Brevet-Major, died of wounds, 247, 248
Powell, Lieut., 7
Powell, Captain John, 67, 85, 92, 95
Power, Major-General Sir M., 291
Power, Surgeon, 223
Poyntz Pass, 190
Preston, 98, 186, 195
Preston, H.M.S., 169
Pretender, the, 75, 91, 114
Prevost, General Sir George, 218, 221-5, 233
Price, Captain, 6, 7
Price, Lieut., 7
Price, Lieut. Edward, killed, 63
Price, Lieut. Edward, 164, 171
Price, Lieut. Richard, 107
Priel, 291
Prince Regent, 276, 291
Proby, Captain, 120
Proville, 287
Prussian troops in Low Countries, 60; at Waterloo, 279, 281
Pryce, Lieut. John, 101; killed, 111
Pryce, Lieut. John, 122
Public Record Office, 2, 37, 75, 148, 205
Puebla, La, 258
Puerto de Maya, 260
Pulteney, Lieut.-General Sir James, 202, 203
Purcell, Colonel Toby, 8, 21-33; career, 294-5
Purefoy, Captain Francis, 7, 37, 39, 43
Purfleet, 195
Putnam, Colonel, 155, 159
Putney, 151
Puzeaux, 287
Pyrenees, 259, 262, 275

Quakers, 113
Quatre Bras, 213, 278
Queen's County, 19
Queen's Rangers, 173
Quesnoy, 89
Quiberon Bay, 202
Quinta de Berbo, 243

Rain, 64
Rainey, Captain Patrick, 124, 137
Ramillies, battle of, 71-73
Ramsay, Major-General, 38-43, 48
Ramsgate, 198, 211
"Rapparees," 20, 21, 52
Rariton River, 168
Rathcondra, 22
Rathkeale, 51
Rathvillan (Rathfryland), 8
Rawdon, Lord, 175, 176, 181
Raynor, Captain John, 170, 171
Read, Major-General, 114
Reading, 2, 114, 115, 120, 125
Redbourn, 92, 97
Redinha, 237
Reedy Creek, 180
Reedy Fork, 179
Regiments :

ARTILLERY
1st Brigade in America, 156
Brigades in Peninsula in 1808, 228-9

CAVALRY
D'Auvergne's, 84
Bowle's Dragoons, 102
Conyngham's Dragoons, 27
Coy's Horse, 19
7th Hussars, 269
Inniskilling Dragoons, 4, 279
Inniskilling Horse, 4, 14
Irish Dragoons, 14
Irish Horse, 13, 27
21st Lancers, 227
Light Dragoons, 89, 215
7th Light Dragoons, 229
10th Light Dragoons, 229
15th Light Dragoons, 137, 229
17th Light Dragoons, 156, 196
19th Light Dragoons, 187
26th Light Dragoons, 208
O'Neal's Dragoons, 21
O'Neil's Dragoons, 11
Portland's Horse, 27
Rich's Dragoons, 115, 119
1st Royal Dragoons, 279
Scots Greys, 279
Vivian's, 269

FOOT GUARDS
1st Guards, 60, 63, 64, 71, 74, 89, 226, 228
3rd Guards, 112, 196, 228
Coldstream Guards, 196
Grenadiers, 160, 168, 199
Guards, 42, 139, 168, 178-80, 183, 250, 279-82
Irish Guards, 13

INFANTRY
1st Foot, 42, 63, 71, 74, 82, 112, 194 (note), 207, 213, 228
2nd Foot, 5, 11, 15, 27
4th Foot, 11, 120, 152, 153, 156, 163-5, 167, 214, 226
5th Foot, 40, 153, 165, 231
6th Foot, 151, 192

Regiments (*continued*) :
INFANTRY (*continued*)
7th Foot, 40, 42, 59, 121, 146, 150, 173, 177, 215, 218, 221, 222, 237, 240, 242, 243, 253, 261, 288, 290, 291
8th Foot, 71, 74, 76, 207, 208, 210, 215, 218
9th Foot, 5, 23, 150, 192, 227
10th Foot, 64, 152, 153, 167
11th Foot, 5, 135, 139, 140, 142, 196, 197, 242
12th Foot, 15, 27, 110, 112, 129, 131, 134, 187
13th Foot, 11, 110
14th Foot, 42, 219, 228, 276, 282, 287, 291
15th Foot, 150, 163
16th Foot, 42, 49, 55, 74, 80, 112
17th Foot, 45, 149, 189
18th Foot, 36, 40, 45, 49, 68, 76, 80, 153, 195
20th Foot, 27, 112, 128, 129, 131, 133, 143, 261, 263, 288
21st Foot, 59, 64, 74, 80, 112, 116
22nd Foot, 27, 189, 191, 193
23rd Foot. See WELCH FUSILIERS, ROYAL
24th Foot, 64, 80, 120
25th Foot, 43, 131, 207, 208
26th Foot, 228, 231
27th Foot, 76, 128, 163, 237, 242, 251, 261
28th Foot, 71, 167, 254
29th Foot, 138, 151
31st Foot, 190, 202
32nd Foot, 231
33rd Foot, 126, 135, 140, 142, 144, 159, 173, 175, 177, 180, 188
34th Foot, 120
35th Foot, 187, 191, 193
37th Foot, 120, 129, 131, 134
38th Foot, 152, 153, 164
39th Foot, 228
40th Foot, 204, 205, 237, 261, 288
41st Foot, 191, 193, 195, 196
42nd Foot, 110, 159, 160, 162, 167, 226
43rd Foot, 153, 219, 228, 229, 291
44th Foot, 156, 159, 163, 197
46th Foot, 155
47th Foot, 152, 153, 189
48th Foot, 253, 261
49th Foot, 164, 165, 167, 196, 197
50th Foot, 226
51st Foot, 131, 135, 139, 140, 142, 228, 276, 280, 282, 287, 291
52nd Foot, 153, 202, 280
53rd Foot, 146
54th Foot, 146
55th Foot, 198, 199
57th Foot, 159, 173, 243
59th Foot, 153, 156, 228
62nd Foot, 189
63rd Foot, 202
64th Foot, 159, 163
67th Foot, 263
68th Foot, 126, 127
70th Foot, 144
71st Foot, 160, 177, 181, 282
76th Foot, 228
81st Foot, 228

INDEX

Regiments (*continued*):

INFANTRY (*continued*)

88th Foot, 210
89th Foot, 195
90th Foot, 186
92nd Foot, 285
95th Foot, 202, 214, 228, 229
97th Foot, 237
13th Veteran Battalion, 257
1st West India Regiment, 221, 222

REGIMENTS MENTIONED UNDER COLONELS' NAMES

Bligh's, 109
Bridges's, 52
Brudenell's, 51
Buchan's, 45
Collingwood's, 40
Colyear's, 49
Dalrymple's, 71
Deloraine's, 99
Erle's, 11
Fielding's Invalids, 99
Ffoulk's, 27
Fleming's, 109
Gower's, 5, 7
Grove's, 92, 96, 97
Hamilton's, 27, 90
Handasyd's, 101, 105
Kingston's, 5
La Melonière's Huguenots, 40
Lauder's, 43
Ligonier's, 109
Mackay's, 45
Maxwell's, 136, 137, 140
Mitchelburne's, 52
Murray's, 114
Orkney's, 63
Orrery's, 82
Preston's, 90
Primrose's, 90
Pulteney's, 119
Sankey's, 7
Saunderson's, 43
Skelton's, 109
Stuart's, 5, 7, 28
Sybourgh's, 90
Wharton's, 5
Wolfe's Marines, 103, 109

FOREIGN REGIMENTS

Bradford's Portuguese, 251
7th Caçadores (Portuguese), 261
Campbell's Portuguese, 260
Danish Horse, 13, 14
Dutch Blue Guards, 13, 15
Eppinger's Dutch Dragoons, 27
Hardenberg's Hanoverians, 131
Hessian Regiment of Bose, 178
Pack's Portuguese, 245, 251, 270
Polish Lancers, 240
Regiment of Frankfurt, 266
Regiment of Nassau, 266
Regiment of Navarre, 106
Spry's Portuguese, 252
Stubb's Portuguese, 251

Regulus, H.M.S., 195
Reigate, 102
Renaix, 277
Renown, H.M.S., 169
Revell, Captain Tristram, 123

Revolution of 1688, 1
Reynell, Lieut. Charles, 123, 133
Reynier, General, 238
Reynolds, Colonel, 286
Rhada, Marquess de, 30
Rheinberg, 137
Rhine, 62, 67, 68, 76, 105, 133, 137, 139
Rhodes, 204
Rice, Colonel Samuel, 280, 309
Rich, Lieut., 117
Richard, Lieut. Charles, 53, 64
Richards, Major, 6, 7
Richardson, Captain James, 195
Richelieu, Duc de, 121
Richmond (America), 182
Richmond, Duke of, 115, 145
Ridgefield, 163
Ridley, Captain Robert, 123
Rifle Corps, formation of, 202. See REGIMENTS: 95TH FOOT
Rigaud, rebel, 193
Ritel, 69
Roach, Captain Simon, 96
Roberts, Lieut. Richard, 197
Roberts, Lieut. William, 111
Robertson, Surgeon W., 171
Robinson, 2nd Lieut., 95
Robinson, Major-General C. W., *Wellington's Campaigns*, 310
Robinson, Corporal Thomas, 242
Robinson, Lieut. William, killed, 181
Rochambeau, Count de, 183
Rochefort, 34
Rochester, 92, 93, 113, 146
Rodd, Lieut. Thomas, 111
Roman Camp, 205
Romsey, 102
Roncesvalles, 254, 259, 260
Rookby, Mr. Justice, 33
Roosbeck, 38
Roscommon, Earl of, 3
Roscrea, 16
Rose, Major, 263
Rosendahl, 57
Roskelly, Lieut., 223
Ross, Major, 190
Ross, Major-General Robert, 261, 266
Ross Castle, 51
Rosslyn, General Lord, 215
Rossnaree, 10, 11, 12
Rousselaer, 39, 40
Row, Brigadier, 64; mortally wounded at Blenheim, 65
Rowlands, 2nd Lieut. Reginald, killed, 67
Rowley, Captain William, 123, 124
Royal Military Asylum, 234
Royals. See REGIMENTS: 1ST FOOT
Roydon, Ensign, killed in duel, 33, 34
Rugby, 92
Rugeley's Mills, 175, 176
Rugen, 215
Ruremonde, 58, 60, 62, 68
Rush, 52, 53
Russell, Admiral, 32-34
Russia and France, 214
Russia, Emperor of, 290
Ruvigny, commander of Horse, 28, 29
Ryde, 208
Ryswick, Peace of, 50, 54, 55

Saar River, 69
Sabine, Ensign, 7; 2nd Lieut., 95
Sabine, Captain Joseph, 111
Sabine, General Joseph, 7, 37, 64-103; career, 297-8
Sabugal, 245, 249
Sackville, General Lord George, 125, 126, 129; behaviour at Minden, 132-3
Sackville Fort, 225
Sahagun, 220
St. Agnes, 145
St. Albans, 92, 119, 218
St. Andrew Gate (Lille), 80, 81
St. Barbe, 264, 265
St. Boës, 268, 269
St. Christopher, 225
St. Colomb, 145
St. Domingo, 191-4
St. Foix, 269
St. Germans, General, 135
St. Helens, 34, 126, 127
St. Ives, 109, 151
St. James's, 74, 107
St. John, Henry, Secretary of State, 69, 75
St. Luce, 223
St. Lucia, 192
St. Lys, 270
St. Magdalene Gate (Lille), 80, 81
St. Malo, 33, 34, 126, 127
St. Martin's Gate (Lille), 80
St. Neots, 109
St. Nicholas Island, 151
St. Pé, 266
St. Quentin Lennock, 49
St. Ruth, General, 22-29; killed at Aughrim, 28
St. Sever, 269
St. Sypière, 270
St. Venant, 87
St. Vincente (bastion), 248
Salamanca, 220, 230, 244, 245, 249-53 (battle), 257, 275
Salisbury, 3
Salisbury (America), 179
Salsine Abbey (Namur), 45
Sambre River, 40, 48
Sanchez, Julian (Spanish guerilla leader), 244
San Christobal, 249
Sanderson, Ensign William, 56
Sandy Hook, 158, 159, 168, 169, 174
San Felices de Chico, 246
San Sebastian, 259, 262-3 (siege)
Santa Margarita, 226
Santa Maria (bastion), 247, 248
Santa Marta, 250
Santarem, 234, 235, 238
Saragossa, 259
Sarre, 264
Sarsfield, General, 16, 17, 28, 29
Satchwell, 2nd Lieut. David, 264
Saumarez, Lieut.-General Sir Thomas, as Lieutenant, 169, 171; Captain, 180, 184
Saunderson, Colonel, 43
Savoy, Duke of, 48
Saxe, Marshal. See MAURICE OF SAXE
Saxon troops, 131
Saxony, 128
Scarpe River, 82, 88

I—21

INDEX

Scawen, Lieut. John, 85
Scheldt River, 38, 39, 41, 48, 77, 78, 80, 89, 108, 111, 231
Schellenberg, battle of the, 62-64
Schledehausen, 143
Schomberg, Count Meinhardt, 11-15
Schomberg, Duc de, 3-14; killed, 13
Schulemberg, General, 83, 84
Schultz, General, 72
Schuylkill River, 166
Scotland, 32, 75, 92
Scots, The Royal. See REGIMENTS: 1ST FOOT
Scots Magazine, 119
Scott, Ensign David, 242
Scott, Sir Edward, 20
Scott, Major-General George, 188
Secretary-at-War. See WAR OFFICE
Sedley (? Sidley), Lieut., 254
Seine, 127
Seligenstadt, 106
Selim III, Grand Signior, 207
Selwyn, Colonel, 43
Service, Surgeon's Mate William, death, 192
Seselingen, 67
Sevenoaks, 120
Seven Years' War, 123, 128-43
Seville, 244, 246, 249
Seward, Major-General T., 267
Shannon, 15-17, 23-25, 30
Shaw, Captain, 216
Sheerness, 92, 93
Sheffield, 118
Sherburn, 3
Shovell, Admiral Sir Cloudisley, 34
Shrewsbury, 98
Siborne, Major-General H. T., *Waterloo Letters*, 281, 310
Sidley, Lieut. Anthony G., 253, 254, 257, 283
Sierck, 69
Sierra Morena, 249
Silesia, 128
Skerritt, Colonel, 256
Skinner, P. K., 2nd Lieut., 186, 304; Captain, 193; Major, 197, 198
Skorreshard, 215
Skrine, F. H., *Fontenoy*, 310
Slane Bridge, 10, 11
Slangenberg, General, 61
Sleaford, 97
Slough, 188
Smith, Assistant-Surgeon, 255
Smith, Lieut.-Colonel Francis, 153
Smith, Major-General, 186
Smith, Sergeant, 287
Smyth, Lieut. Hugh, 56; death from wounds, 67
Smythe, Captain Lionel, 170, 171
Smythies, Captain, *History of the 40th Regiment*, 205
Sobral, 234
Soest, 139
Soignies, 44, 74, 76, 278
Solmes, Count, 4, 19, 21, 36
Sombref, 48
Somerset, General Lord Charles, 201, 231
Sorauren, 260, 262
Sordes, 267
Soubise, Marshal de, 139-42
Soult, Marshal, in Peninsular War, 220-71

Sourier, heights of, 222, 223
Sourville, Marquis de, 83
Southampton, 102, 103, 122, 146, 151, 198, 207
South Carolina, 174-8, 181
Southgate, 185
Southwark, 50, 115
Soutilla, 255, 256
Spain, 202, 219, 249
Spanish troops at Namur, 45; in Peninsular War, 220, 239, 240, 244, 258
Spencer, General Brent, 242
Spithead, 189, 195
Spörcken, General von, 130-2, 135, 136, 142
Springfield, 185
Spry, Brigadier-General, 252
Staines, 188
Stainforth, Captain, 241, 242, 248; killed, 262
Stainforth, 2nd Lieut. George, 271
Stainville, M. de, 142
Stair, Field-Marshal the Earl of, 104, 105, 108
Stanley, Brigadier, 58
Stannard, 2nd Lieut. Edward, 92, 95
Staten Island, 159, 164, 168
States-General, 1, 60, 61, 86
Stedman, C., *History of the American War*, 310
Stedman, Lieut., 7
Stedman, Captain David, 43, 56
Steele, 2nd Lieut. F., death, 192
Steenkirk, 35
Steinheim, 67
Stevens, Lieut.-General, 198
Stevenson, Thomas, receives commission, 113
Stevenswaert, 58
Stewart, Major-General William, 240, 243
Stirling, Colonel, 162
Stirling, General Lord, 159
Stockport, 212, 218, 231
Stoke, 2nd Lieut., 95
Stoke Newington, 92
Stonehaven, 146
Stony Point, 172
Story, Rev. George, *Impartial History of the Wars in Ireland*, 7, 21, 26, 310
Stourbridge, 207, 212
Strabane, 53
Stralsund, 214, 215
Strangeways, Captain, 255
Stroud, 51, 113
Stubb, Colonel, 251
Subijana de Alava, 258
Subijana de Moullos, 257
Suck River, 26
Sudbury, 201
Sullivan, General, 160, 166
Sullivan's Island, 174
Sumter, Colonel, 176
Sunderland, 97, 187
Sutherland, Lieut. James, 123
Sutton, Brigadier, 89
Sutton, Major C., 234; Lieut.-Colonel, 272
Swords, 15, 52, 53
Sydney (? Sidley), Lieut., 253
Sympler, Major, 286

Tagus River, 220, 233, 236, 245, 246
Taisnières, 83, 84
Talbot, Richard. See TYRCONNEL
Talbot, Lieut.-Colonel R., 197
Tallard, Marshal, 61-67
Talmash, General, 24, 28, 29, 34
Tanderagee, 55, 190
Tarbes, 269
Tarleask, 76
Tarleton, Colonel Banastre, 175, 176, 178, 179, 182; *History of the Campaign in the Southern Provinces of North America*, 310
Tarrant's Tavern, 179
Taube, Count, 132
Taviers, 71
Tayler, Captain, 6, 7
Taylor, Lieut., 95
Taylor, Captain Arthur, 111
Teale, Isaac, Apothecary General, 36
Teesdale, 2nd Lieut. William, 123
Tenby, 111
Terneuse, 231
Terra Nova (Namur), 45
Tetuan Bay, 203
Thames River, 128
Thetford, Captain Edward, 92
Thomar, 236
Thomas, Captain Robert, 7, 29
Thomières, General, 251
Thorp, Lieut. Samuel, 228, 239, 241
Thurgen, General, 67
Thurles, 22
Thwaites, Captain, 253
Tiburon, 192, 193
Tiffin, Brigadier, 52
Tilburg, 115
Tilbury, 92
Tilsit, Treaty of, 214
Tipperary, 19
Tirlemont, 38
Tiverton, 146
Tongres, 60, 71
Tonnant, French navy, 169
Topham, Quartermaster, 21
Torbay, 34
Tordesillas, 249, 250
Tormes River, 249-52, 257
Toro, 220, 249, 250, 257
Torre de Mouro, 242
Torrens, Colonel, 253
Tory, *Journal*, 131
Tottenham Court, 112
Toulon, 121
Toulouse, 228, 269, 270 (battle), 275
Tournay, 76, 82-83 (siege), 86, 88, 110
Tower of London, 98
Towers, Lieut., 291
Townshend, General, 140
Tralee, 51
Trant, Colonel, 238
Traves, 249
Treeve, Lieut., 241
Trenchard, Sir John, 33
Trèves, 68
Trim, 52
Tringham, Captain L. W. H., 227
Trotter, Lieut. R., 291
Truro, 151
Tryon, Major-General, 163, 173
Tucker, Lieut. T. E., 234

INDEX

Tuckey, Lieut., 248
Tuckey, Lieut. Timothy, 171
Tudela, 259
Turenne, Marshal, 3
Tybee, 174
Tynemouth, 75, 187
Tyrconnel, Earl of (Richard Talbot), 1, 5, 22, 23

Udell, General, 160
Ulm, 62, 67
Ulster, flight of southern Irish colonists to, 1
Ulster Journal of Archæology, 310
Ulster troops, 13
Upnor Castle, 92
Upton, 195
Urachree, 26
Ustaritz, 265, 267
Utrecht, Peace of, 89
Uxbridge, 195

Valenciennes, 286
Valentia, 51
Valk, Dutch frigate, 200–1
Valladolid, 220, 254, 257, 259
Valverde, 239
Vauban, Marshal, 40, 80, 82
Vaudemont, Prince de, 40, 41, 44, 48, 49
Vaughan, Captain Perkins, 56
Vaughan, Major-General, 164, 165, 172
Vauxhall (America), 152
Veale, Volunteer W. Richard, 164
Vedbeck, 215
Veere, 232
Vellinghausen, 140
Vendôme, Marshal, 68, 73–80
Venloo, 58
Venner, Colonel Samuel, 36
Vera, 264
Verden, 212
Verdon Roads, 271
Verplank's Neck, 172
Versailles, 80
Vienna, 61
Vigo, 94, 202, 203
Villaboa, 245
Villafranca, 220, 225, 229
Villalba, 260
Villanova, 235
Villars, Marshal, 82–89
Villa Velha, 247
Villefranque, 265, 266
Villeroi, Marshal, 39–50, 60–73
Villodas, 258
Vilvorde, 38
Vincent, Ensign Thomas, 56
Virginia, 176, 180–4; Militia, 176
Virginia, Co. Cavan, 52
Viscarret, 260
Vischer, Lieut. H., 197, 198, 200
Vitry, 86
Vittoria, 253, 254, 257–9 (battle), 275
Volunteers of Ireland, 173, 175

Wade, Marshal, 97, 99, 103, 108, 109
Waite, Captain, 95
Waite, Lieut.-Colonel John, 114, 118
Wakefield, 146

Walcheren Expedition, 228, 231–3, 235
Waldeck, Prince of, 32, 110, 116
Waldegrave, Major-General, 129, 131
Wales, Prince of, 115, 157, 188
Walker, Captain, killed, 262
Walker, Lieut. H., 244, 246, 248; Captain, 263
Wallis, Lieut. W. O., 171
Walpole, Sir Robert, 103, 104
Walton, Colonel Clifford, *History of the British Standing Army*, 310
Wambeln, 139
Wangenheim, 131
Wanneghem, 78
Wansbrough, Lieut., 95
Wansbrough, Major, 95, 97
Wantage, 31
Wappoo Cut, 174
Warburg, 136, 137
Ware, 112
Waring, Captain Timothy, 6, 7, 29
War Office, 2, 97, 102, 114, 144, 150, 156, 186, 205
Warrington, 94, 98, 99, 218
Washington, General George, 157–61, 182
Waterford, 16, 51, 90, 93, 189
Waterloo, 44; battle, 277–88
Wavre, 48
Weaver, Lieut. John, 95; killed, 111
Webb, Brigadier, 71, 72
Webber, Major R. T., 227
Webster, Lieut.-Colonel, 175–80; death from wounds, 181
Webster, Private, 101
Weekly Journal, 92
Welch nationality, 213, 216
Welch Fusiliers, Royal (23rd Foot):
  1st Battalion raised, 3; serve as marines, 33–37; precedence, 38, 90; warrant of January 2, 1696, 47; become Fusiliers, 59; Royal, 90; Prince of Wales's Own, 91; reviewed by Prince of Wales, 92; by General Sabine, 95; by George II, 98, 102, 105, 115
  2nd Battalion formed, 122–3; becomes 68th Regiment, 127; again formed, 210; records, 211–2, 213, 217–8, 219–21, 225–33, 234–5, 246, 255, 266–7, 275; disbanded, 276
  Battle honours: Namur 1695, 47; Blenheim, 85; Ramillies, 85; Oudenarde, 85; Malplaquet, 85; Dettingen, 108; Minden, 134; the Sphinx superscribed "Egypt," 207; Martinique, 224; Corunna, 228; Albuhera, 242; Badajoz, 248–9; Salamanca, 253; Vittoria, 259; Pyrenees, 262; Nivelle, 265; Orthes, 269; Toulouse, 270; Peninsula, 275; Waterloo, 285
  Foreign service: in Low Countries, 37–50, 56–90; in War of Austrian Succession, 105–12, 115–8; at Minorca, 120–2; attack on St. Malo, 126–7; in Seven Years' War, 128–43; in North America, 151–85; in West Indies, 191–5; attack on Ostend, 196–7; Helder Expedition, 198–201; against Spain, 202; against Napoleon in Egypt, 204–7; at Gibraltar, 208; in Hanover, 211–2; at Copenhagen, 215–6; in Nova Scotia, 218–33; in Martinique, 218–24; in Peninsular War, 233–72; in Waterloo campaign, 277–86; near Paris, 287–91
  Great Britain, 31–33, 50–51, 91–105, 112–5, 118–27, 143–51, 185–9, 195–8, 201–2, 208–14, 216–8, 272–6, 291; muster in December 1692, 35; Porteous riot at Edinburgh, 100–1; salvage of ships, 145
  Ireland, 4–31, 51–55, 90–91, 93, 189–90, 219; musters at Dundalk, 6, 7; pay in 1689, 8, 9; order from William III, 16; expenditure in Co. Down, 18, 19; on Irish Establishment, 21, 90; losses at Aughrim, 29; licence to brew beer, 31
  Regimental Goat, first reference, 157
  Regimental Mess Records, 301–8
  Succession of Colonels, 293–300
Weldon, Lieut. John, 92, 95
Wellington, Duke of, in Peninsular War, 233–71; in Waterloo campaign, 276–85; correspondence with Sir Lowry Cole, 288–90; mentioned, 290, 291
Wenlock, 98
Werle, 139
Wesel, 137
Weser River, 130, 131, 211
West Florida, 167
West Indies, 173, 190, 195, 221, 225
Westphalen's *Campaigns of Duke Ferdinand*, 139
Westphalia, 130, 136
Wetzell Mill, 180
Wexford, 15, 90, 189
Whaley, 2nd Lieut., 123
Whalley, Lieut., 239, 248
Whitaker, Commodore Edward, 56
Whitchurch, 98
Whitehall, 167
Whiteby, Ensign, 7
Whitemore, Lieut., 7
White Plains, 162
Whitley, Captain Roger, 34
Whittingham, Ensign Daniel, 39
Whitwood, Captain, 8
Whyte, General, 191, 193
Wickers, John, 234
Wicklow, 21, 90, 91, 189
Wigan, 212
Wight, Isle of, 126, 127, 144, 207, 209, 288, 291
Wilhelmstadt, 115, 143
Wilhelmstahl, 142
Wilkinson, Lieut. John, 169, 171
William III, authorises Lord Herbert of Cherbury to raise regiment, 2; "Letter of

INDEX

Service" to Duke of Norfolk, 2; joins Army in Ireland, 9-18; against Louis XIV, 31, 55; in Holland, 32; in Flanders, 35; at the Hague, 38; at Loo, 39; in command in Flanders, 40-50; in Holland, 56, 57; death, 57
Williamsburg, 182, 183
Williamson, General Sir Adam, 191
Williamson, Surgeon, 304
Willmot, Captain, 33, 34
Wills, Captain Thomas, 169
Wills, Lieut.-General, 92
Wilmington, 181
Wilson, Captain, 95
Wilson, Colonel R. T., *History of the British Expedition to Egypt*, 310
Wilton, 3
Wimbledon, 151
Winchester, 102, 103, 122, 125, 143, 185, 275
Winchester (America), 184
Windsor, 143, 144, 188
Wingate, 2nd Lieut., 248, 255
Wingfield, Captain, 6
Winn, Captain Walter, 6
Winnsborough, 177
Winslow, 2nd Lieut., 186

Wissemburg, 68
Witherow, Rev. Thomas, *The Boyne and Aghrim*, 310
Witney, 31
Withers, General, 58, 60, 76
Wogan, Captain, 6
Wokingham (?), 146
Wolseley, Colonel, 9, 14
Wolseley, Lord, *Life of Marlborough*, 38
Wolverhampton, 92, 99
Wolverine, H.M.S., 196
Wood, Lieut., 141
Woodbridge, 212
Woolwich, 115
Worcester, 97, 155, 195, 207-9, 272-4, 284
Worcester, General, 163, 164
Worcum, 56
Works consulted, list of, 309-10
Wreden, 138
Wrexham, 98, 208-13, 227, 291
Würtemburg, Duke of, in Ireland, 9, 20-24; in Flanders, 40, 41; crosses the Danube, 64
Wutginau, General, 140
Wyatt, Lieut.-Colonel W. E., 217, 219, 228, 230
Wyk-aan-Zee, 199

Wynendael, 49
Wynne, Captain Henry, 234, 269
Wynne, Lieut. Watkin, 235; death, 244
Wynyard, Major-General, 187

Yadkin River, 179
Yansi, 263
Yarmouth, 200, 201, 216
Yeovil, 209
York, 97, 102, 103, 217, 276
York, Duke of, 188, 199, 200, 206, 210, 290
York Redoubt, 225
York River, 182, 183
Yorktown, siege of, 182-4
Young, Lieut. Benjamin, 123
Young, Lieut. Robert, 123
Young, R. M., *Old Belfast*, 310
Ypres, 40, 108

Zadora River, 258
Zadossa River, 253
Zafra, 239
Zamora, 257
Ziegenhain, 138
Zubiri, 260, 262
Zuyder Zee, 199
Zype position, 200

Printed for
Forster Groom & Co., Ltd.,
by
Hazell, Watson & Viney, Ld., London and Aylesbury